THE SPIRIT C

BY

William Law

The Spirit of Prayer

Part One

Chapter I: Treating of some Matters preparatory to the Spirit of Prayer

[Pryr-1.1-1] THE greatest Part of Mankind, nay of Christians, may be said to be asleep; and that particular Way of Life, which takes up each Man's Mind, Thoughts, and Actions, may be very well called his particular Dream. This Degree of Vanity is equally visible in every Form and Order of Life. The Learned and the Ignorant, the Rich and the Poor, are all in the same State of Slumber, only passing away a short Life in a different kind of Dream. But why so? It is because Man has an Eternity within him, is born into this World, not for the Sake of living here, not for any Thing this World can give him, but only to have Time and Place, to become either an eternal Partaker of a Divine Life with God, or to have an hellish Eternity among fallen Angels: And therefore, every Man who has not his Eye, his Heart, and his Hands, continually governed by this twofold Eternity, may justly be said to be fast asleep, to have no awakened Sensibility of Himself. And a Life devoted to the Interests and Enjoyments of this World, spent and wasted in the Slavery of earthly Desires, may be truly called a Dream; as having all the Shortness, Vanity, and Delusion of a Dream; only with this great Difference, that when a Dream is over, nothing is lost but Fictions and Fancies; but when the Dream of Life is ended only by Death, all that Eternity is lost for which we were brought into Being. Now there is no Misery in this World, nothing that makes either the Life or Death of Man to be full of Calamity, but this Blindness and Insensibility of his State, into which he so willingly, nay obstinately plunges himself. Every Thing that has the Nature of Evil and Distress in it takes its rise from hence. Do but suppose a Man to know himself, that he comes into this World on no other Errand, but to rise out of the Vanity of Time into the Riches of Eternity; do but suppose him to govern his inward Thoughts and outward Actions by this View of himself, and then to him every Day has lost all its Evil; Prosperity and Adversity have no Difference, because he receives and uses them both in the same Spirit; Life and Death are equally welcome, because equally Parts of his Way to Eternity. For poor and miserable as this Life is, we have all of us free Access to all that is Great, and Good, and Happy, and carry within ourselves a Key to all the Treasures that Heaven has to bestow upon us.— We starve in the midst of Plenty, groan under Infirmities, with the Remedy in our own Hand; live and die without knowing and feeling any Thing of the One, only Good, whilst we have it in our Power to know and enjoy it in as great a Reality, as we know and feel the Power of this World over us: For Heaven is as near to our Souls, as this World is to our Bodies; and we are created, we are redeemed, to have our Conversation in it. God, the only Good of all intelligent Natures, is not an absent or distant God, but is more present in and to our Souls, than our own Bodies; and we are Strangers to Heaven, and without God in the World, for this only Reason, because we are void of that Spirit of Prayer, which alone can, and never fails to unite us with the One, only Good, and to open Heaven and the Kingdom of God within us. A Root set in the finest Soil, in the best Climate, and blessed with all that Sun, and Air, and Rain can do for it, is not in so sure a Way of its Growth to Perfection, as every Man may be, whose

Spirit aspires after all that, which God is ready and infinitely desirous to give him. For the Sun meets not the springing Bud that stretches towards him with half that Certainty, as God, the Source of all Good, communicates himself to the Soul that longs to partake of Him.

[Pryr-1.1-2] We are all of us, by Birth, the Offspring of God, more nearly related to him than we are to one another; for in him we live, and move, and have our Being. The first Man that was brought forth from God had the Breath and Spirit of Father, Son, and Holy Ghost, breathed into him, and so he became a living Soul. Thus was our first Father born of God, descended from Him, and stood in Paradise in the Image and Likeness of God. He was the Image and Likeness of God, not with any Regard to his outward Shape or Form, for no Shape has any Likeness to God; but he was in the Image and Likeness of God, because the Holy Trinity had breathed their own Nature and Spirit into him. And as the Deity, Father, Son, and Holy Spirit, are always in Heaven, and make Heaven to be everywhere, so this Spirit, breathed by them into Man, brought Heaven into Man along with it; and so Man was in Heaven, as well as on Earth, that is, in Paradise, which signifies an heavenly State, or Birth of Life.

[Pryr-1.1-3] Adam had all that Divine Nature, both as to an heavenly Spirit, and heavenly Body, which the Angels have. But as he was brought forth to be a Lord and Ruler of a new World, created out of the Chaos or Ruins of the Kingdom of fallen Angels; so it was necessary that he should also have the Nature of this new created World in himself, both as to its Spirit and Materiality. Hence it was, that he had a Body taken from this new created Earth, not such dead Earth as we now make Bricks of, but the blessed Earth of Paradise, that had the Powers of Heaven in it, out of which the Tree of Life itself could grow. Into the Nostrils of this outward Body, was the Breath or Spirit of this World breathed; and in this Spirit and Body of this World, did the inward celestial Spirit and Body of Adam dwell: it was the Medium or Means through which he was to have Commerce with this World, become visible to its Creatures, and rule over it and them. Thus stood our first Father; an Angel both as to Body and Spirit (as he will be again after the Resurrection) yet dwelling in a Body and Spirit taken from this new created World, which however was as inferior to him, as subject to him, as the Earth and all its Creatures were. It was no more alive in him, no more brought forth its Nature within him, than Satan and the Serpent were alive in him at his first Creation. And herein lay the Ground of Adam's Ignorance of Good and Evil; it was because his outward Body, and the outward World (in which alone was Good and Evil) could not discover their own Nature, or open their own Life within him, but were kept inactive by the Power and Life of the celestial Man within it. And this was Man's first and great Trial; a Trial not imposed upon him by the mere Will of God, or by Way of Experiment; but a Trial necessarily implied in the Nature of his State: He was created an Angel, both as to Body and Spirit; and this Angel stood in an outward Body, of the Nature of the outward World; and therefore, by the Nature of his State, he had his Trial, or Power of choosing, whether he would live as an Angel, using only his outward Body as a Means of opening the Wonders of the outward World to the Glory of his Creator; or whether he would turn his Desire to the opening of the bestial Life of the outward World in himself, for the Sake of knowing the Good and Evil that was in it. The Fact is certain, that he lusted after the Knowledge of this Good and Evil, and made use of the Means to obtain it. No sooner had he got this Knowledge, by the opening of the bestial Life and Sensibility within him, but in that Day, nay, in that Instant, he died; that is his heavenly Spirit with its heavenly Body were both extinguished in him; but his Soul, an immortal Fire that could not die, became a poor Slave in Prison of bestial Flesh and Blood. See here the Nature and Necessity of our Redemption; it is to redeem the first Angelic Nature that departed from Adam; it is to make that heavenly Spirit and Body which Adam lost, to be alive again in all the human

Nature; and this is called Regeneration. See also the true Reason why only the Son, or eternal Word of God, could be our Redeemer; it is because he alone, by whom all Things were at first made, could be able to bring to Life again that celestial Spirit and Body which had departed from Adam. See also why our blessed Redeemer said, "Except a Man be born again of Water and the Spirit, he cannot enter into the Kingdom of Heaven." He must be born again of the Spirit, because Adam's first heavenly Spirit was lost: he must be born again of Water, because that heavenly Body which Adam lost, was formed out of the heavenly Materiality, which is called Water. Thus in the Revelation of St. John, the heavenly Materiality, out of which the Bodies of Angels and also of Adam were formed, is called a glassy Sea, as being the nearest and truest Representation of it that can be made to our Minds. The Necessity of our regaining our first heavenly Body, is the Necessity of our eating the Body and Blood of Christ. The Necessity of having again our first heavenly Spirit, is declared by the Necessity of our being Baptized by the Holy Ghost. Our Fall is nothing else, but the Falling of our Soul from this celestial Body and Spirit into a bestial Body and Spirit of this World. Our rising out of our fallen State, or Redemption, is nothing else but the regaining our first angelic Spirit and Body, which in Scripture is called our inward, or new Man, created again in Christ Jesus. See here, lastly, the true Ground of all the Mortifications of Flesh and Blood, required in the Gospel; it is because this bestial Life of this outward World should not have been opened in Man; it is his Separation from God, and Death to the Kingdom of Heaven; and therefore, all its Workings, Appetites, and Desires, are to be restrained and kept under, that the first heavenly Life, to which Adam died, may have Room to rise up in us.

[Pryr-1.1-4] But to return. That Adam was thus an Angel at his first Creation, dwelling in an outward Body and outward World, incapable of receiving any Impressions from them, and able to rule them at his Pleasure; that all outward Nature was a State of Life below him, in Subjection to him; that neither Sun, nor Stars, nor Fire, nor Water, nor Earth, nor Stones, could act upon him, or hurt him, is undeniably plain from hence; because his first and great Sin, which cost him his angelic Life, and took from him his Crown of Glory, consisted in this, that he lusted to know, and took the Means of knowing, what Good and Evil are in the bestial Life of this World: For this plainly demonstrates, that before his Sin, whilst he stood in the first State of his Creation, that he was an Angel in Nature and Power, that neither his own outward Body, nor any Part of outward Nature, had any Power in him or upon him; for had his own outward Body, or any Element of outward Nature, had any Power to act upon him, to make any Impressions, or raise any Sensations in him, he could not have been ignorant of Good and Evil in this World. Therefore, seeing that his eating of the forbidden Tree, was that alone which opened this Knowledge in him, it is a Demonstration, that in his first State he was in this World as an Angel, that was put into the Possession of it only to rule as a superior Being over it; that he was to have no Share of its Life and Nature, no Feeling of Good or Evil from it, but to act in it as a heavenly Artist, that had Power and Skill to open the Wonders of God in every Power of outward Nature. An Angel, we read, used at a certain Time to come down into a Pool at Jerusalem; the Water stirred by the Angel gave forth its Virtues, but the Angel felt no Impressions of Weight, or Cold from the Water. This is an Image of Adam's first Freedom from, and Power over all outward Nature. He could wherever he went, do as this Angel did, make every Element, and elementary Thing, discover all the Riches of God that were hidden in it, without feeling any Impressions of any kind from it. This was to have been the Work both of Adam and his Offspring, to make all the Creation show forth the Glory of God, to spread Paradise over all the Earth, till the Time came, that all the Good in this World was to be called back to its first State, and all the Evil in every Part left to be possessed by the Devil and his Angels. But since He fell from this first State into an Animal of this World, his Work is changed, and he must now labour with Sweat to till the cursed Earth, both for Himself and the Beasts upon it.

[Pryr-1.1-5] Let us now consider some plain and important Truths, that follow from what has been said above.

[Pryr-1.1-6] First, it is plain that the Sin and Fall of Adam did not consist in this, viz., that he had only committed a single Act of Disobedience, and so might have been just as He was before, if God had pleased to overlook this single Act of Disobedience, and not to have brought a Curse upon him and his Posterity for it.— Nothing of this is the Truth of the Matter, either on the Part of God, or on the Part of Man.

[Pryr-1.1-7] Secondly, it is plain also, that the Command of God, not to lust after, and eat of the forbidden Tree, was not an arbitrary Command of God, given at Pleasure, or as a mere Trial of Man's Obedience; but was a most kind and loving Information given by the God of Love to his new-born Offspring, concerning the State He was in, with Regard to the outward World: Warning him to withdraw all Desire of entering into a Sensibility of its Good and Evil; because such Sensibility could not be had, without his immediate dying to that Divine and heavenly Life which he then enjoyed. "Eat not," says the God of Love, "of the Tree of Knowledge of Good and Evil, for in the Day thou eatest thereof you will surely die."

[Pryr-1.1-8] As if it had been said, "I have brought Thee into this Paradise, with such a Nature as the Angels have in Heaven. By the Order and Dignity of thy Creation, every Thing that lives and moves in this World is made subject to Thee, as to their Ruler. I have made Thee in thy outward Body of this World, to be for a Time a little lower than the Angels, till Thou hast brought forth a numerous Offspring, fit for that Kingdom which They have lost. The World around Thee, and the Life which is newly awakened in it, is much lower than Thou art; of a Nature quite inferior to thine. It is a gross, corruptible State of Things, that cannot stand long before me; but must for a while bear the Marks of those Creatures, which first made Evil to be known in the Creation. The Angels, that first inhabited this Region, where Thou art to bring forth a new Order of Beings, were great and powerful Spirits, highly endowed with the Riches and Powers of their Creator. Whilst they stood (as the Order of Creation requires) in Meekness and Resignation, under their Creator, nothing was impossible to them; there was no End of their glorious Powers throughout their whole Kingdom. Perpetual Scenes of Light, and Glory, and Beauty, were rising and changing through all the Height and Depth of their glassy Sea, merely at their Will and Pleasure. But finding what Wonders of Light and Glory they could perpetually bring forth; how all the Powers of Eternity, treasured up in their glassy Sea, unfolded themselves, and broke forth in ravishing Forms of Wonder and Delight, merely in Obedience to their Call; they began to admire and even adore themselves, and to fancy that there was some Infinity of Power hidden in themselves, which they supposed was kept under, and suppressed, by that Meekness, and Subjection to God, under which they acted. Fired and intoxicated with this proud Imagination, they boldly resolved, with all their eternal Energy and Strength, to take their Kingdom, with all its Glories, to themselves, by eternally abjuring all Meekness and Submission to God. No sooner did their eternal potent Desires fly in this Direction of a Revolt from God, but in the Swiftness of a Thought Heaven was lost; and they found themselves dark Spirits, stripped of all their Light and Glory. Instead of Rising up above God (as they hoped) by breaking off from Him, there was no End of their eternal Sinking into new Depths of Slavery, under their own self- tormenting Natures. As a Wheel going down a Mountain, that has no bottom, must continually keep on its Turning, so are they whirled down by the Impetuosity of their own wrong turned Wills, in a continual Descent from the Fountain of all Glory, into the bottomless Depths of their own dark, fiery, working Powers. In no Hell, but what their own natural Strength had awakened; bound in no Chains, but their own unbending, hardened Spirits; made such, by their renouncing, with all their eternal Strength, all Meekness, and Subjection to God. In that Moment, the beautiful Materiality of their Kingdom, their glassy Sea in which they dwelt, was by the wrathful rebellious Workings of these apostate Spirits broken all into Pieces, and became a black Lake, a horrible Chaos of Fire and Wrath, Thickness and Darkness, a Height and Depth of the confused, divided, fighting Properties of Nature. My creating Fiat stopped the Workings of these rebellious Spirits, by dividing the Ruins of their wasted Kingdom, into an Earth, a Sun, Stars, and separated Elements. Had not this Revolt of Angels brought forth that disordered Chaos, no such Materiality as this outward World is made of had ever been known. Gross compacted Earth, Stones, Rocks, wrathful Fire here, dead Water there, fighting Elements, with all their gross Vegetables and Animals, are Things not known in Eternity, and will be only seen in Time, till the great Designs are finished, for which Thou are brought forth in Paradise. And then, as a Fire awakened by the rebel Creature, began all the Disorders of Nature, and turned that glassy Sea into a Chaos, so a last Fire, kindled at my Word, shall thoroughly purge the Floor of this World. In those purifying Flames, the Sun, the Stars, the Air, the Earth and Water, shall part with all their Dross, Deadness, and Division, and all become again that first, heavenly Materiality, a glassy Sea of everlasting Light and Glory, in which Thou and thy Offspring shall sing Hallelujahs to all Eternity. Look not therefore, thou Child of Paradise, look not with a longing Eye after any Thing in this outward World. There are the Remains of the fallen Angels in it; Thou hast nothing to do in it, but as a Ruler over it. It stands before Thee, as a Mystery big with Wonders; and Thou, whilst an Angel in Paradise, hast Power to open and display them all. It stands not in thy Sphere of Existence; it is, as it were, but a Picture, and transitory Figure of Things; for all that is not Eternal, is but as an Image in a Glass, that seems to have a Reality, which it has not. The Life which springs up in this Figure of a World, in such an infinite Variety of Kinds and Degrees, is but as a Shadow; it is a Life of such Days and Years, as in Eternity have no Distinction from a Moment. It is a life of such Animals and Insects, as are without any Divine Sense, Capacity, or Feeling. Their Natures have nothing in them, but what I commanded this new modelled Chaos, this Order of Stars and fighting Elements, to bring forth.

[Pryr-1.1-9] "Now Adam, observe, I will open to Thee a great Mystery. The heavenly Materiality of the Angels' Kingdom before their Revolt was a glassy Sea, a Mirror of beauteous Forms, Figures, Virtues, Powers, Colours, and Sounds, which were perpetually springing up, appearing and changing in an infinite Variety, to the Manifestation of the Wonders of the Divine Nature, and to the Joy of all the Angelical Kingdom. This heavenly Materiality had its Fruits and Vegetables, much more real than any that grow in Time, but as different from the Grossness of the Fruits of this World, as the heavenly Body of an Angel is different from the Body of the grossest Beast upon Earth. In this angelical Kingdom, the one Element (which is now in four Parts) was then a fruitful Mother of Wonders, continually bringing forth new Forms and Figures of Life; not Animals, Beasts, or Insects, but beautiful Figures, and ideal Forms of the endless Divisibility, and Degrees of Life, which only broke forth as delightful Wonders of the Depth of the Riches of the Divine Nature, and to tune the Voices of Angels with Songs of Praise to the infinite Source of Life. And hence, O Adam, is that endless infinite Variety both of the Animal and Vegetable Life in this perishable World. For no Fruits or Vegetables could have sprung up in the divided Elements, but because they are the divided Parts of that one heavenly Materiality, or glassy Sea, in which angelical Fruits had formerly grown forth. No animal Life could have arose from Stars, Air, and Water, but because they are all of them the gross Remains of that one Element, in which the Figures and Images of Life had once risen up in such an infinite Variety of Degrees and Kinds. Hence it was, that when my creating Fiat spoke to these new ranged Stars, and Elements, and bid Life awake in them all according to its Kind, they all obeyed my Word, and every Property of Nature strove to bring forth, after the Kind and Manner as it had done in the Region of Eternity. This, my Son, is the Source and Original of all that infinite Variety, and Degrees of Life, both of Animals and Vegetables, in this World. It is because all outward Nature, being fallen from Heaven, must yet, as well as it can, do and work as it had done in Heaven.

[Pryr-1.1-10] "In Heaven, all Births and Growths, all Figures and spiritual Forms of Life, though infinite in Variety, are yet all of a heavenly Kind, and only so many Manifestations of the Goodness, Wisdom, Beauty, and Riches of the Divine Nature. But in this new modelled Chaos, where the Disorders that were raised by Lucifer are not wholly removed, but Evil and Good must stand in Strife, till the last purifying Fire, here every Kind and Degree of Life, like the World from whence it springs, is a Mixture of Good and Evil in its Birth.

[Pryr-1.1-11] "Therefore, my Son, be content with thy angelical Nature, be content, as an Angel in Paradise, to eat Angels' Food, and to rule over this mixed, imperfect, and perishing World, without partaking of its corruptible, impure, and perishing Nature. Lust not to know how the Animals feel the Evil and Good which this Life affords them; for if Thou couldst feel what they feel, Thou must be as they are; Thou canst not have their Sensibility, unless Thou hast their Nature: thou canst not at once be an Angel and an earthly Animal. If the bestial Life is raised up in Thee, the same Instant the heavenly Birth of thy Nature must die in Thee. Therefore turn away thy Lust and Imagination from a Tree, that can only help Thee to the Knowledge of such Good and Evil, as belongs only to the Animals of this outward World; for nothing but the bestial Nature can receive Good or Evil from the Stars and Elements; they have no Power, but over that Life which proceeds from them. Eat therefore only the Food of Paradise; be content with Angels' Bread; for if Thou eatest of this Tree, it will unavoidably awaken and open the bestial Life within Thee; and in that Moment, all that is heavenly must die, and cease to have any Power in thee. And Thou must fall into a Slavery for Life, under the divided fighting Powers of Stars and Elements. Stripped of thy angelical Garment, that hid thy outward Body under its Glory, Thou wilt become more naked than any Beast upon Earth, be forced to seek from Beasts a Covering, to hide thee from the Sight of thine own Eyes. A shameful, fearful, sickly, wanting, suffering, and distressed Heir of the same speedy Death in the Dust of the Earth, as the poor Beasts, whom Thou wilt thus have made to be thy Brethren."

[Pryr-1.1-12] This Paraphrase I leave to the Reflection of the Reader, and proceed to show,

[Pryr-1.1-13] Thirdly, that the Misery, Distress, and woeful Condition, which Adam by his Transgression brought upon Himself, and all his Posterity, was not the Effect of any severe vindictive Wrath in God, calling for Justice to his offended Sovereignty, and inflicting Pains and Punishments suitable to the Greatness of his just Indignation, and Anger at the disobedient Creature.

[Pryr-1.1-14] If Adam, contrary to the Will of God, and for the Sake of some new-fancied Knowledge, had broken both his own Legs, and put out both his Eyes, could it with any Show of Truth and Reason have been said, that God, in the Severity of his Wrath at so heinous an Offense, had punished Adam with Lameness and Blindness? And if it be further supposed, that God seeing Adam lying in this lame and blind Condition, came and spoke kindly to him, informing him of a Secret of Love, which He had in Heaven, which He promised to send him immediately by his highest Messenger of Love; assuring him, that by the Use of this heavenly

Secret or Divine Power, his Legs and Eyes should, in some Course of Time, be infallibly restored to him, even in a better State than they were in at the first; must it not be still more unreasonable and absurd, to charge anything of this Lameness and Blindness upon a Wrath in God kindled against Adam? Nay, is it not clear, in the Highest Degree, that in all this Matter Adam had nothing from God, but the Overflowings of mere Love and Goodness, and that he had no Lameness and Blindness, but from his own voluntary Acts upon himself?

[Pryr-1.1-15] This is a simple, but clear Representation of the Case, how Matters stood betwixt God and our first Father, when by his own Act and Deed he extinguished that Divine Life, in which God had created him. Adam had no more Hurt, no more Evil done to Him, at his Fall, than the very Nature of his own Action brought along with it upon himself. He lusted to have the Sensibility of that Good and Evil, which the Beasts of this World have. He was told, that it could not be had without the Loss of his heavenly Life; because such Loss was as necessarily implied in the Nature of the Thing itself, as Blindness is implied in the Extinction of the Eyes. However, he ventured to make the Trial, and chose to eat of That, which could and did open this Sensibility of earthly Good and Evil in him. No sooner was this Sensibility opened in him, but he found it to be a Subjection and Slavery to all outward Nature, to Heat and Cold, to Pains and Sickness, Horror of Mind, disturbed Passions, Misery, and Fears of Death. Which is in other Words only saying, that he found it to be an Extinction of that Divine, angelical Nature, which till then had kept him insensible and incapable of any hurtful Impressions, from any or all the Powers of this World. Therefore, to charge his miserable State, as a Punishment inflicted upon him by the severe Wrath of an incensed God, is the same Absurdity as in the former supposed Lameness and Blindness. Because the whole Nature of all that miserable Change, both as to Body and Soul, which then came upon him, was neither more, nor less, than what was necessarily implied in that which he chose to do to himself. And therefore it had nothing of the Nature of a Punishment inflicted from without, but was only that which his own Action had done in and to himself: Just as the Man that puts out his own Eyes, has only that Darkness and Blindness, which his own Action has brought forth in himself.

[Pryr-1.1-16] From this short, yet plain and true Account of this Matter, we are at once delivered from a Load of Difficulties that have been raised about the Fall of Man, and Original Sin. It has been a great Question, How the Goodness of God could punish so small and single an Act of Disobedience in Adam, with so great a Punishment? Here the Sovereignty of God has been appealed to, and has set the Matter right; and from this Sovereignty, thus asserted, came forth the Systems of absolute Election, and absolute Reprobation. But for our Comfort it appears, that the Question here put concerns neither God nor Man, that it relates not at all to the Matter, and has no Existence, but in the Brains of those that formed it. For the Action in which Adam's Sin consisted, was such an Act, as in itself implied all that miserable Change that came upon him, and so was not a small, or single Act of Disobedience, nor had the least Punishment, of any kind, inflicted by God upon it. All that God did on this Transgression was mere Love, Compassion, and Relief administered to it. All the Sovereignty that God here showed, was a Sovereignty of Love to the fallen Creature. So that all the Volumes on this Question may be laid aside, as quite beside the Point. Another, and the greatest Question of all, and which Divines of all Sorts have been ever solving, and yet never have solved, is this: How it can consist with the Goodness of God, to impute the Sin of Adam to all his Posterity? But here, to our Comfort again, it may be said, that this Question is equally a vain Fiction with the other, and has nothing to do with the Procedure of God towards Mankind. For there is no Imputation of the Sin of Adam to his Posterity, and so no Foundation for a Dispute upon it. How absurd would it be to say, that God imputes the Nature, or the Body and Soul of Adam to his Posterity? for have they not the Nature of Adam by a natural Birth from him, and not by Imputation from God? Now this is all the Sin that Adam's Posterity have from him, they have only their Flesh and Blood, their Body and Soul from him, by a Birth from him, and not imputed to them from God. Instead therefore of the former Question, which is quite beside the Matter, it should have been asked thus, How it was consistent with the Goodness of God, that Adam could not generate Children of a Nature and Kind quite superior to himself? This is the only Question that can be asked with relation to God; and yet it is a Question whose Absurdity confutes itself. For the only Reason why Sin is found in all the Sons of Adam, is this, it is because Adam of earthly Flesh and Blood, cannot bring forth a holy Angel out of himself, but must beget children of the same Nature and Condition with himself. And therefore here again it may be truly said, that all the laborious Volumes on God's imputing Adam's Sin to his Posterity, ought to be considered as waste Paper.{See Appeal to all that Doubt, &c., page 198. Letter to the Bishop of London, page 70.}

[Pryr-1.1-17] But further, as it is thus evident from the Nature of Adam's Transgression, that all his Misery came from the Nature of his own Action, and that nothing was inflicted upon him, from a Wrath or Anger in God at him, so is it still much more so, from a Consideration of the Divine Nature. For it is a glorious and joyful Truth, (however suppressed in various Systems of Divinity) that from Eternity to Eternity, no Spark of Wrath ever was, or ever will be in the holy Triune God. If a Wrath of God was anywhere, it must be everywhere, if it burned once, it must burn to all Eternity. For everything that is in God himself is boundless, incapable of any Increase or Diminution, without Beginning, and without End. It is as good Sense, as consistent with the Divine Nature, to say that God, moved by a Wrath in and from Himself, began the Creation, as that a Wrath in God ever punished any Part of it. Nature and Creature is the only Source from whence, and the Seat in which, Wrath, Pain, and Vexation can dwell. Nor can they ever break forth either in Nature or Creature, but so far as either this, or that, has lost its State in God. This is as certain, as that Storms and Tempests, Thunder and Lightnings, have no Existence in Heaven. God, considered in Himself, is as infinitely separate from all Possibility of doing Hurt, or willing Pain to any Creature, as He is from a Possibility of suffering Pain or Hurt from the Hand of a Man. And this, for this plain Reason, because He is in himself, in his holy Trinity, nothing else but the boundless Abyss of all that is Good, and Sweet, and Amiable, and therefore stands in the utmost Contrariety to every Thing that is not a Blessing, in an eternal Impossibility of willing and intending a Moment's Pain or Hurt to any Creature. For from this unbounded Source of Goodness and Perfection, nothing but infinite Streams of Blessing are perpetually flowing forth upon all Nature and Creature, in a more incessant Plenty, than Rays of light Stream from the Sun. And as the Sun has but one Nature, and can give forth nothing but the Blessings of Light, so the holy Triune God has but one Nature and Intent towards all the Creation, which is, to pour forth the Riches and Sweetness of his Divine Perfections, upon every Thing that is capable of them, and according to its Capacity to receive them.

[Pryr-1.1-18] The Goodness of God breaking forth into a Desire to communicate Good, was the Cause and the Beginning of the Creation. Hence it follows, that to all Eternity, God can have no Thought, or Intent towards the Creature, but to communicate Good; because he made the Creature for this sole End, to receive Good. The first Motive towards the Creature is unchangeable; it takes its Rise from God's Desire to communicate Good; and it is an eternal Impossibility, that anything can ever come from God, as his Will and Purpose towards the Creature, but that same Love and Goodness which first created it: he must always will that to it, which he willed at the Creation of it. This is the amiable Nature of God, he is the Good, the unchangeable, overflowing Fountain of Good, that sends forth nothing but Good to all Eternity. He is the Love itself, the unmixed, unmeasurable Love, doing nothing but from Love, giving nothing but Gifts of Love, to every Thing that He has made; requiring nothing of all his Creatures, but the Spirit and Fruits of that Love, which brought them into Being. Oh, how sweet is this Contemplation of the Height and Depth of the Riches of Divine Love! With what Attraction must it draw every thoughtful Man, to return Love for Love to this overflowing Fountain of boundless Goodness? What Charms has that Religion, which discovers to us our Existence in, Relation to, and Dependence upon this Ocean of Divine Love! View every Part of our Redemption, from Adam's first Sin, to the Resurrection of the Dead, and you will find nothing but successive Mysteries of that first Love, which created Angels and Men. All the Mysteries of the Gospel are only so many Marks and Proofs of God's desiring to make his Love triumph, in the Removal of Sin and Disorder from all Nature and Creature.

[Pryr-1.1-19] But to return, and consider further the Nature of Adam's Fall, We have seen that it consisted of no arbitrary Punishment inflicted on him by a Wrath raised in God, but was only such a State of Misery, as his own Action necessarily brought upon him. Let us now see what happened to his Soul, a little more distinctly, and how it differed from what it was before his Fall, in its heavenly State.

[Pryr-1.1-20] The Angels that kept their State, and those that fell from it, were at first of one and the same Nature; the Angels that fell, did not lose all their Nature, for then they must have fallen into nothing; they only lost the heavenly and Divine Part of it, and therefore there is something still remaining in them, that is also in the holy Angels, and which is common to both of them. Now this which they did not lose, because it cannot be lost, is a certain Root of Life, or Ground of their Existence, which when once in Being, cannot be broken, and in which the unceasing Eternity, or Immortality of their Nature consists, a Root or first Ground of Life, equally capable of a Heavenly Birth, or of a Birth and Growth into Hell. Now that there is this Root of Life in Angels, and that it is something quite distinct from their heavenly Nature, is very plain from hence, that the Devils have lost their heavenly, and yet have kept their eternal and immortal Nature; therefore that in which their Eternity and Immortality consists, must be something entirely distinct from their heavenly Nature, and must be also the same with that, in which the Eternity and Immortality of the holy Angels consists. For the fallen Angels have no other eternal Root in them, but that which they had before their Fall, and which they brought from Heaven; and therefore that which is, and must be eternal and undying in their Nature, is the same eternal Root of Life, which is in the Angels that kept their State. And consequently, the only Difference betwixt an Angel and a Devil, is this, that in the Angel its eternal Root of Life generates a Birth of the Light and holy Spirit of God in it; and in a Devil, this eternal Root of Life has lost this Birth, and the Power of bringing it forth again. Now here is to be truly seen the real Difference betwixt the Soul of Adam before, and after his Fall. Before his Fall, it had the Nature of an Angel of God, in which the Divine Birth of the Light and holy Spirit of God sprung up, but when contrary to the Will, and Command of God, a bestial Life was awakened in him, the heavenly Life was necessarily extinguished. The Soul therefore having lost that heavenly Birth which made it like an Angel of God, had nothing remaining in it, but that eternal and immortal Root of Life, which is the very Essence of a fallen Angel. But here we must observe a great and happy Difference, betwixt the Soul of Adam, though dead to all that was heavenly, and the Soul of a Devil. The Angels that extinguished the Birth of Heaven in themselves, fell directly into the horrible Depths of their own strong self-tormenting Nature, or their own Hell, and that for these two Reasons.

[Pryr-1.1-21] First, because there was nowhere else for them to fall into, but into this tormenting Sensibility of their own fiery, wrathful, darkened Nature.

[Pryr-1.1-22] Secondly, because their Revolt from God was an Attempt, and Intent to be higher and greater by awakening, and trusting to their own natural Powers, than they had hitherto been by Submission to God. They would have a Greatness that sprung only from themselves, and therefore they found That which they sought, they found themselves left to all the Greatness that was in themselves, and that was their Hell, viz., a fiery Strength of a self-tormenting Nature, because separate from the one Source of Light and Love, of Peace and Joy.

[Pryr-1.1-23] But Adam, though his Soul was as entirely dead to Heaven, as the Souls of the Devils were, yet fell not into their Hell, for these two Reasons.

[Pryr-1.1-24] First, because his Angelical Man dwelt in a Body taken from this outward World, which Body did not die at his Transgression, therefore his Soul that had lost its Heavenly Light, did not fall directly into the Devil's Hell, but it fell into a Body of Earthly Flesh and Blood, which being capable of the Enjoyments and Satisfactions of this Life, could, whilst it lasted, keep the Soul insensible of its own fallen State, and hellish Condition.

[Pryr-1.1-25] Secondly, because Adam not aspiring to be above, or without God by his own proud Strength, but only lusting to enter in a Sensibility of the Good and Evil of the bestial Life of this World, he found only That which he sought, and fell into no other State or Misery, than that bestial Life, which his own Actions and Desires had opened in him. And therefore this outward World stood him in great Stead, it prevented his immediate Falling into the State of Fallen Angels.

[Pryr-1.1-26] But then, as there was nothing that kept him out of the Hell of Fallen Angels, but his Body of Earthly Flesh and Blood, and as this was now as mortal in him, as it was in the Beasts, and lay at the Mercy of a thousand Accidents, that could every Moment take it from him, so he was in his fallen State, standing as it were on the Brinks of Hell, liable every Moment to be pushed into it.

[Pryr-1.1-27] See here the deep Ground and absolute Necessity of that new Birth, of Word, Son, and Spirit of God, which the Scripture speaks so much of. It is because our Soul, as fallen, is quite dead to, and separate from the Kingdom of Heaven, by having lost the Light and Spirit of God in itself; and therefore it is, and must be incapable of entering into Heaven, till by this new Birth, the Soul gets again its first Heavenly Nature.

[Pryr-1.1-28] If thou hast nothing of this Birth when thy Body dies, then thou hast only that Root of Life in Thee, which the Devils have, thou art as far from Heaven, and as incapable of it, as they are; thy Nature is their Nature, and therefore their Habitation must be thine. For nothing can possibly hinder thy Union with Fallen Angels, when thou diest, but a Birth of That in thy Soul, which the Fallen Angels have lost.

[Pryr-1.1-29] How pitiable, therefore, or rather how hurtful is that Learning, which uses all its Art of Words, to avoid and lose the true Sense of our Saviour's Doctrine concerning the new Birth, which is necessary to fallen Man, by holding, that the Passages asserting the new Birth, are only a figurative, strong Form of Words concerning something, that is not really a Birth, or Growth of a new Nature, but may, according to the best Rules of Criticism, signify, either our Entrance into the Society of Christians, by the Rite of Baptism, or such a new Relation, as a Scholar may have with his Master, who by a Conformity to the Terms of Union, or by copying his Ways and Manners, may, by a Figure of Speech, be said to be born again of him.

[Pryr-1.1-30] Now let it here be observed, that no Passage of Scripture is to be called, or esteemed as a figurative Expression, but where the literal Meaning cannot be allowed, as implying something that is either bad in itself, or impossible, or inconsistent with some plain and undeniable Doctrines of Scripture. Now that this is not the Case here, is very evident. For who will presume to say, that for the Soul of fallen Man to be born again of the Son, or Light, and Holy Spirit of God, is in the literal Sense of the Words, a Thing bad in itself, or impossible, or inconsistent with any plain and undeniable Doctrines of Scripture? The Critics therefore, who, in this Matter, leave the literal Meaning of the Words, and have Recourse to a figurative Sense, are without Excuse, and have nothing they can urge as a Reason for so doing, but their own Skill in Words. But it may be further added as a just Charge against these Critics, that their fixing these Passages to a figurative Meaning, is not only without any Ground, or Reason for so doing, but is also a bad Meaning, impossible to be true, and utterly inconsistent with the most plain, and fundamental Doctrines of Scripture. Now that this is the Case here, may in Part be seen by the following Instance.

[Pryr-1.1-31] Let it be supposed, that a human Body had lost the Light, and Air of this World, and was in a State of Death, because both these were quite extinguished in it. Must it not be said, that this human Body cannot see, or enter again into the Life of this World, unless the Light and Air of this World get again a new Birth in it: Is there here any Occasion, or any Room to form a Doubt, how these Words are to be understood, or any Possibility to mistake the Meaning of them? What a Philosopher would he be, who for fear of being called an Enthusiast, should here deny the literal Meaning of a new Birth of Light and Air, and think himself sufficiently justified in flying from it, because in his great Reading, he had seen the Words, Birth, Light and Air, sometimes, and upon some Occasions, used only in a figurative Sense?

[Pryr-1.1-32] Now this is exactly, and to a Tittle the Case of the Soul, as fallen, and lying in the same State of Death to the Kingdom of God, till a new Birth of the Light and Spirit of God be again brought forth in it. And therefore the Necessity of understanding these Words in their literal Meaning, the Absurdity of flying to a figurative Sense of the new Birth, and the Impossibility of that being the true one, is equally plain, and certain in both these Cases.

[Pryr-1.1-33] Now that the Soul, as fallen, is in this real State of Death, is a Doctrine not only plain from the whole Tenor of Scripture, but affirmed in all Systems of Divinity. For all hold, and teach, that Man unredeemed, must at the Death of his Body have fallen into a State of Misery, like that of the fallen Angels. But how can this be true, unless it be true, that the Life of Heaven was extinguished in the Soul, and that Man had really lost that Light, and Spirit of God, which alone can make any Being capable of living in Heaven? All therefore that I have here, and elsewhere said, concerning the Death of the Soul by its Fall, and its wanting a real new Birth of the Son, and Holy Spirit of God in it, in order to its Salvation, cannot be denied, but by giving up this great, fundamental Doctrine, namely, "That Man in his fallen State, and unredeemed, must have been eternally lost." For it cannot be true, that the Fall of Man unredeemed, would have kept him forever out of Heaven, but because his Fall had absolutely put an End to the Life of Heaven in his Soul.

[Pryr-1.1-34] On the other Hand, it cannot be true that Jesus Christ is his Redeemer, and does deliver him from his fallen State, unless it be true, that Jesus Christ helps him to a new Birth of that Light and Spirit of God, which was extinguished by his Fall. For nothing could possibly be the Redemption, or Recovery of Man, but Regeneration alone. His Misery was his having lost the Life and Light of Heaven from his Soul, and therefore nothing in all the Universe of Nature, but a new Birth of that which he had lost, could be his Deliverance from his fallen State.

[Pryr-1.1-35] And therefore if Angels after Angels had come down from Heaven to assure him, that God had no Anger at him, he would still have been in the same helpless State; nay, had they told him, that God had Pity and Compassion towards him, he had yet been unhelped; because in the Nature of the Thing, nothing could make so much as a Beginning of his Deliverance, but that which made a Beginning of a new Birth in him, and nothing could fully effect his Recovery, but which perfectly finished the new Birth of all that heavenly Life which he had lost.

[Pryr-1.1-36] The Gospel tells us of a certain Man who fell among Thieves, who stripped him, and wounded him, and left him half dead; that first a Priest, then a Levite coming that Way, both of them avoided the poor Man, by passing on the other Side.

[Pryr-1.1-37] Here it is plain that this Priest and Levite left the poor Man in the same helpless State in which they found him. Let it now be supposed, that instead of going on the other Side of the Road, they had come up to him, and poured Oil and Wine into his Wounds, only in a figurative Sense of the Words, that is, that they had spoken such Words to him, Words so soft, so oily, and reviving, that in a just Figure of Speech, they might be called a pouring of Wine and Oil into his Wounds. Now had they done this, must it not still be said, that the poor Man's Wounds and Nakedness were still left in their first helpless State? And all for this plain Reason, because the poor Man was naked, and wounded, not in a figurative Sense of the Words, but really and truly, and therefore could have no Help or Benefit, but from real Oil and Wine really poured into his Wounds. And for the same plain Reason, the fallen Soul, really dead to the Kingdom of Heaven, can have no Help but by a new Birth of the Light and Spirit of Heaven, really brought forth again in it. When Adam lay in his Death Wounds to the Kingdom of God, had the highest Order of Archangels, or Seraphims come by that Way, they could only have done as the Priest and Levite did, go on the other Side; or if they had come up to him, and done all they could for him, it could only have been such a Good or Relief to him, as by a Figure of Speech might be so called.

[Pryr-1.1-38] For as Adam had extinguished the Light and Spirit of God in himself, so no one could be the good Samaritan to him, or pour that Wine and Oil into his Wounds, which they wanted, but He who was the Author and Source of Light and Life to every Being that lives in Heaven.

[Pryr-1.1-39] One would wonder how any Persons, that believe the great Mystery of our Redemption, who adore the Depths of the Divine Goodness, in that the Son of God, the second Person in the Trinity, became a Man himself, in order to make it possible for Man by a Birth from him to enter again into the Kingdom of God, should yet seek to, and contend for, not a real, but a figurative Sense of a new Birth in Jesus Christ. Is there any Thing more inconsistent than this? Or can any Thing strike more directly at the Heart of the whole Nature of our Redemption? God became Man, took upon him a Birth from the fallen Nature. But why was this done? Or wherein lies the adorable Depth of this Mystery? How does all this manifest the Infinity of the Divine Love towards Man? It is because nothing less than this mysterious Incarnation (which astonishes Angels) could open a Way, or begin a Possibility, for fallen Man to be born again from above, and made again a Partaker of the Divine Nature. It was because Man was become so Dead to the Kingdom of Heaven, that there was no Help for him through all Nature. No Powers, no Abilities of the highest Order of Creatures, could kindle the least Spark of Life in him, or help him to the least Glimpse of that heavenly Light which he had lost. Now when all Nature and Creature stood round about Adam as unable to help him, as he was to help himself, and all of them unable to help him, for this Reason, because that which he had lost, was the Life and Light of Heaven, how glorious, how adorable is that Mystery, which enables us to say, that when Man laid thus incapable of any Relief from all the Powers and Possibilities of Nature, that then the Son, the Word of God, entered by a Birth into this fallen Nature, that by this mysterious

Incarnation all the fallen Nature might be born again of him according to the Spirit, in the same Reality, as they were born of Adam according to the Flesh? Look at this Mystery in this true Light, in this plain Sense of Scripture, and then you must be forced to fall down before it, in Adoration of it. For all that is great and astonishing in the Goodness of God, all that is glorious and happy with regard to Man, is manifestly contained in it.

[Pryr-1.1-40] But tell me, I pray, what becomes of all this, what is there left in any Part of this Mystery, if this new Birth, for the Sake of which God became Man, is not really a new Birth in the Thing itself, is not, as the Scripture affirms, a real Birth of the Son and the Spirit of God in the Soul, but something or other, this or that, which the Critics say, may be called a new Birth, by a certain Figure of Speech? Is not this to give up all our Redemption at once, and a turning all the Mysteries of our Salvation into mere empty, unmeaning Terms of Speech? He that should deny the Reality of the Resurrection, upon Pretence, that by the Rules of Criticism, it needs not signify a real coming out of a State of Natural Death, might have more to say for himself both from Reason and Scripture, than he that denies the Reality of the new Birth in Jesus Christ. For this new Birth is not a Part, but the Whole of our Salvation. Every Thing in Religion, from the Beginning to the end of Time, is only for the Sake of it. Nothing does us any Good, but either as it helps forward our Regeneration, or as it is a true Fruit or Effect of it.

[Pryr-1.1-41] All the glad Tidings of the Gospel, all the Benefits of our Saviour, however variously expressed in Scripture, all center in this one Point, that he is become our Light, our Life, our Resurrection, our Holiness and Salvation; that we are in Him new Creatures, created again unto Righteousness, born again of Him, from above, of the Spirit of God. Every Thing in the Gospel is for the Sake of this new Creature, this new Man in Christ Jesus, and nothing is regarded without it. What Excuse therefore can be made for that Learning, which, robbing us of the true Fruits of the Tree of Life, leaves us nothing to feed upon, but the dry Dust of Words?

[Pryr-1.1-42] "I am the Vine, ye are the Branches." Here Christ, our second Adam, uses this Similitude to teach us, that the new Birth that we are to have from Him is real, in the most strict and literal Sense of the Words, and that there is the same Nearness of Relation, betwixt Him and his true Disciples, that there is betwixt the Vine and its Branches, that He does all that in us, and for us, which the Vine does to its Branches. Now the Life of the Vine must be really derived into the Branches, they cannot be Branches, till the Birth of the Vine is brought forth in them. And therefore as sure as the Birth of the Vine must be brought forth in the Branches, so sure is it, that we must be born again of our second Adam. And that unless the Life of the holy Jesus be in us by a Birth from Him, we are as dead to Him, and the Kingdom of God, as the Branch is dead to the Vine, from which it is broken off.

[Pryr-1.1-43] Again our blessed Saviour says, "Without me, ye can do Nothing." The Question is, when, or how a Man may be said to be without Christ? Consider again the Vine and its Branches: A Branch can then only be said to be without its Vine, when the Vegetable Life of the Vine is no longer in it. This is the only Sense, in which he can be said to be without Christ; when He is no longer in us, as a Principle of a heavenly Life, we are then without Him, and so can do nothing, that is, Nothing that is good or holy. A Christ not in us, is the same Thing as a Christ not ours. If we are only so far with Christ, as to own and receive the History of his Birth, Person, and Character, if this is all that we have of Him, we are as much without him, as much left to ourselves, as little helped by Him, as those evil Spirits which cried out, "We know Thee, who thou art, the Holy One of God." For those evil Spirits, and all the fallen Angels, are totally without Christ, have no Benefit from Him, for this one and only Reason, because Christ is not in Them; Nothing of the Son of God is generated, or born in them. Therefore every Son of Adam, that has not something of the Son of God generated, or born within Him, is as much without Christ, as destitute of all Help from Him, as those evil Spirits who could only make an outward Confession of Him.

[Pryr-1.1-44] It is the Language of Scripture, that Christ in us is our Hope of Glory; that Christ formed in us, living, growing, and raising his own Life and Spirit in us, is our only Salvation. And indeed all this is plain from the Nature of the Thing; for since the Serpent, Sin, Death and Hell, are all essentially within us, the very Growth of our Nature, must not our Redemption be equally inward, an inward essential Death to this State of our Souls, and an inward Growth of a contrary Life within us? If Adam was only an outward Person, if his whole Nature was not our Nature, born in us, and derived from Him into us, it would be Nonsense to say, that his Fall is our Fall. So in like manner, if Christ, our second Adam, was only an outward Person, if He entered not as deeply into our Nature as the first Adam does, if we have not as really from Him a new inward, spiritual Man, as we have outward Flesh and Blood from Adam, What Ground could there be to say, that our Righteousness is from Him, as our Sin is from Adam?

[Pryr-1.1-45] Let no one here think to charge me with Disregard to the Holy Jesus, who was born of the Virgin Mary, or with setting up an inward Saviour in Opposition to the outward Christ, whose History is recorded in the Gospel. No: It is with the utmost Fullness of Faith and Assurance, that I ascribe all our Redemption to that blessed and mysterious Person, that was then born of the Virgin Mary, and will assert no inward Redemption but what wholly proceeds from, and is effected by that Life-giving Redeemer, who died on the Cross for our Redemption.

[Pryr-1.1-46] Was I to say, that a Plant or Vegetable must have the Sun within it, must have the Life, Light, and Virtues of the Sun incorporated in it, that it has no Benefit from the Sun, till the Sun is thus inwardly forming, generating, quickening, and raising up a Life of the Sun's Virtues in it, would this be setting up an inward Sun, in Opposition to the outward one? Could any Thing be more ridiculous than such a Charge? For is not all that is here said of an inward Sun in the Vegetable, so much said of a Power and Virtue derived from the Sun in the Firmament? So in like manner, all that is said of an inward Christ, inwardly formed, and generated in the Root of the Soul, is only so much said of an inward Life, brought forth by the Power and Efficacy of that Blessed Christ, that was born of the Virgin Mary.

Chapter II: Discovering the true Way of turning to God, and of finding the Kingdom of Heaven, the Riches of Eternity, in our Souls

[Pryr-1.2-1] THOU hast seen, dear Reader, the Nature and Necessity of Regeneration, be persuaded therefore fully to believe, and firmly to settle in thy Mind this most certain Truth, that all our Salvation consists in the Manifestation of the Nature, Life, and Spirit of Jesus Christ, in our inward new Man. This alone is Christian Redemption, this alone delivers from the Guilt and Power of Sin, this alone redeems, renews, and regains the first Life of God in the Soul of Man. Every Thing besides this, is Self, is Fiction, is Propriety, is own Will, and however coloured, is only thy old Man, with all his Deeds. Enter therefore with all thy Heart into this Truth, let thy Eye be always upon it, do every Thing in View of it, try every Thing by the Truth of it, love Nothing but for the Sake of it. Wherever thou goest, whatever thou dost, at Home, or Abroad, in the Field, or at Church, do all in a Desire of Union with Christ, in Imitation of his Tempers and Inclinations, and look upon all as Nothing, but that which exercises, and increases the Spirit and

Life of Christ in thy Soul. From Morning to Night keep Jesus in thy Heart, long for Nothing, desire Nothing, hope for Nothing, but to have all this within Thee changed into the Spirit and Temper of the Holy Jesus. Let this be thy Christianity, thy Church, and thy Religion. For this new Birth in Christ thus firmly believed, and continually desired, will do every Thing that thou wantest to have done in Thee, it will dry up all the Springs of Vice, stop all the Workings of Evil in thy Nature, it will bring all that is Good into Thee, it will open all the Gospel within Thee, and thou wilt know what it is to be taught of God. This longing Desire of thy Heart to be one with Christ will soon put a stop to all the Vanity of thy Life, and nothing will be admitted to enter into thy Heart, or proceed from it, but what comes from God and returns to God: thou wilt soon be, as it were, tied and bound in the Chains of all holy Affections and Desires, thy Mouth will have a Watch set upon it, thy Ears would willingly hear nothing that does not tend to God, nor thy Eyes be open, but to see, and find Occasions of doing Good. In a Word, when this Faith has got both thy Head and thy Heart, it will then be with thee, as it was with the Merchant who found a Pearl of great Price, it will make thee gladly to sell all that thou hast, and buy it. For all that had seized and possessed the Heart of any Man, whatever the Merchant of this World had got together, whether of Riches, Power, Honour, Learning, or Reputation, loses all its Value, is counted but as Dung, and willingly parted with, as soon as this glorious Pearl, the new Birth in Christ Jesus, is discovered and found by him. This therefore may serve as a Touchstone, whereby every one may try the Truth of his State; if the old Man is still a Merchant within thee, trading in all sorts of worldly Honour, Power, or Learning, if the Wisdom of this World is not Foolishness to thee, if earthly Interests, and sensual Pleasures, are still the Desire of thy Heart, and only covered under a Form of Godliness, a Cloak of Creeds, Observances, and Institutions of Religion, thou mayest be assured, that the Pearl of great Price is not yet found by thee. For where Christ is born, or his Spirit rises up in the Soul, there all Self is denied, and obliged to turn out; there all carnal Wisdom, Arts of Advancement, with every Pride and Glory of this Life, are as so many heathen Idols all willingly renounced, and the Man is not only content, but rejoices to say, that his Kingdom is not of this World.

[Pryr-1.2-2] But thou wilt perhaps say, How shall this great Work, the Birth of Christ, be effected in me? It might rather be said, since Christ has an infinite Power, and also an infinite Desire to save Mankind, how can anyone miss of this Salvation, but through his own unwillingness to be saved by Him? Consider, how was it, that the Lame and Blind, the Lunatic and Leper, the Publican and Sinner, found Christ to be their Saviour, and to do all That for them, which they wanted to be done to them? It was because they had a real Desire of having That which they asked for, and therefore in true Faith and Prayer applied to Christ, that his Spirit and Power might enter into them, and heal That which they wanted, and desired to be healed in them. Everyone of these said in Faith and Desire, "Lord, if thou wilt, thou canst make me whole." And the Answer was always this, "According to thy Faith, so be it done unto Thee." This is Christ's Answer now, and thus it is done to every one of us at this Day, as our Faith is, so is it done unto us. And here lies the whole Reason of our falling short of the Salvation of Christ, it is because we have No Will to it.

[Pryr-1.2-3] But you will say, Do not all Christians desire to have Christ to be their Saviour? Yes. But here is the Deceit; all would have Christ to be their Saviour in the next World, and to help them into Heaven when they die, by his Power, and Merits with God. But this is not willing Christ to be thy Saviour; for his Salvation, if it is had, must be had in this World; if He saves Thee, it must be done in this Life, by changing and altering all that is within Thee, by helping thee to a new Heart, as He helped the Blind to see, the Lame to walk, and the Dumb to speak.

For to have Salvation from Christ, is nothing else but to be made like unto Him; it is to have his Humility and Meekness, his Mortification and Self-denial, his Renunciation of the Spirit, Wisdom, and Honours of this World, his Love of God, his Desire of doing God's Will, and seeking only his Honour. To have these Tempers formed and begotten in thy Heart, is to have Salvation from Christ. But if thou willest not to have these Tempers brought forth in thee, if thy Faith and Desire does not seek, and cry to Christ for them in the same Reality, as the Lame asked to walk, and the Blind to see, then thou must be said to be unwilling to have Christ to be thy Saviour.

[Pryr-1.2-4] Again, Consider, How was it, that the carnal Jew, the deep-read Scribe, the learned Rabbi, the Religious Pharisee, not only did not receive, but crucified their Saviour? It was because they willed, and desired no such Saviour as He was, no such inward Salvation as He offered to them. They desired no Change of their own Nature, no inward Destruction of their own natural Tempers, no Deliverance from the Love of themselves, and the Enjoyments of their Passions; they liked their State, the Gratifications of their Old Man, their long Robes, their broad Phylacteries, and Greetings in the Markets. They wanted not to have their Pride and Self-love dethroned, their Covetousness and Sensuality to be subdued by a new Nature from Heaven derived into them. Their only Desire was the Success of Judaism, to have an outward Saviour, a temporal Prince, that should establish their Law and Ceremonies over all the Earth. And therefore they crucified their Dear Redeemer, and would have none of his Salvation, because it all consisted in a Change of their Nature, in a new Birth from above, and a Kingdom of Heaven to be opened within them by the Spirit of God.

[Pryr-1.2-5] Oh Christendom, look not only at the old Jews, but see thyself in this Glass. For at this Day (Oh sad Truth to be told!) at this Day, a Christ within us, an inward Saviour raising a Birth of his own Nature, Life and Spirit within us, is rejected as gross Enthusiasm, the learned Rabbi's take Counsel against it. The Propagation of Popery, the Propagation of Protestantism, the Success of some particular Church, is the Salvation which Priests and People are chiefly concerned about.

[Pryr-1.2-6] But to return. It is manifest, that no one can fail of the Benefit of Christ's Salvation, but through an unwillingness to have it, and from the same Spirit and Tempers which made the Jews unwilling to receive it. But if thou wouldst still further know, how this great Work, the Birth of Christ, is to be effected in thee, then let this joyful Truth be told thee, that this great Work is already begun in every one of us. For this Holy Jesus, that is to be formed in thee, that is to be the Saviour and new Life of thy Soul, that is to raise thee out of the Darkness of Death into the Light of Life, and give thee Power to become a Son of God, is already within thee, living, stirring, calling, knocking at the Door of thy Heart, and wanting nothing but thy own Faith and good Will, to have as real a Birth and Form in thee, as He had in the Virgin Mary. For the eternal Word, or Son of God, did not then first begin to be the Saviour of the World, when He was Born in Bethlehem of Judea; but that Word which became Man in the Virgin Mary, did, from the Beginning of the World, enter as a Word of Life, a Seed of Salvation, into the first Father of Mankind, was inspoken into him, as an ingrafted Word, under the Name and Character of a Bruiser of the Serpent's Head. Hence it is, that Christ said to his Disciples, "the Kingdom of God is within you"; that is, the Divine Nature is within you, given unto your first Father, into the Light of his Life, and from him, rising up in the Life of every Son of Adam. Hence also the holy Jesus is said to be the "Light, which lighteth every Man that cometh into the World." Not as He was born at Bethlehem, not as He had an human Form upon Earth; in these Respects he could not be said to have been the Light of every Man that cometh into the World; but as He was that eternal Word, by which all Things were created, which was the Life and Light of all Things, and which had as a second Creator entered again into fallen Man, as a Bruiser of the Serpent; in this Respect it was truly said of our Lord, when on Earth, that "He was that Light which lighteth every Man, that cometh into the World." For he was really and truly all this, as He was the Immanuel, the God with us, given unto Adam, and in him to all his Offspring. See here the Beginning and glorious Extent of the Catholic Church of Christ, it takes in all the World. It is God's unlimited, universal Mercy to all Mankind; and every human Creature, as sure as he is born of Adam, has a Birth of the Bruiser of the Serpent within him, and so is infallibly in Covenant with God through Jesus Christ. Hence also it is, that the Holy Jesus is appointed to be Judge of all the World, it is because all Mankind, all Nations and Languages have in him, and through him been put into Covenant with God, and made capable of resisting the Evil of their fallen Nature.

[Pryr-1.2-7] When our blessed Lord conversed with the Woman at Jacob's Well, he said unto her, "If thou knewest the Gift of God, and who it is that talketh with thee, thou wouldest have asked of Him, and He would have given Thee living Water." How happy (may anyone well say) was this Woman of Samaria, to stand so near this Gift of God, from whom she might have had living Water, had she but vouchsafed to have asked for it! But, dear Christian, this Happiness is thine; for this Holy Jesus, the Gift of God, first given into Adam, and in him to all that are descended from him, is the Gift of God to Thee, as sure as thou art born of Adam; nay, hast thou never yet owned him, art thou wandered from him, as far as the Prodigal Son from his Father's House, yet is he still with Thee, he is the Gift of God to Thee, and if thou wilt turn to Him, and ask of Him, he has living Water for Thee.

[Pryr-1.2-8] Poor Sinner! consider the Treasure thou hast within Thee, the Saviour of the World, the eternal Word of God lies hid in Thee, as a Spark of the Divine Nature, which is to overcome Sin and Death, and Hell within Thee, and generate the Life of Heaven again in thy Soul. Turn to thy Heart, and thy Heart will find its Saviour, its God within itself. Thou seest, hearest, and feelest nothing of God, because thou seekest for Him abroad with thy outward Eyes, thou seekest for Him in Books, in Controversies, in the Church, and outward Exercises, but there thou wilt not find him, till thou hast first found Him in thy Heart. Seek for Him in thy Heart, and thou wilt never seek in vain, for there He dwelleth, there is the Seat of his Light and Holy Spirit.

[Pryr-1.2-9] For this turning to the Light and Spirit of God within Thee, is thy only true turning unto God, there is no other Way of finding Him, but in that Place where he dwelleth in Thee. For though God be everywhere present, yet He is only present to Thee in the deepest, and most central Part of thy Soul. Thy natural Senses cannot possess God, or unite Thee to Him, nay thy inward Faculties of Understanding, Will, and Memory, can only reach after God, but cannot be the Place of his Habitation in Thee. But there is a Root, or Depth in Thee, from whence all these Faculties come forth, as Lines from a Centre, or as Branches from the Body of the Tree. This Depth is called the Centre, the Fund or Bottom of the Soul. This Depth is the Unity, the Eternity, I had almost said, the Infinity of thy Soul; for it is so infinite, that nothing can satisfy it, or give it any Rest, but the infinity of God. In this Depth of the Soul, the Holy Trinity brought forth its own living Image in the first created Man, bearing in Himself a living Representation of Father, Son, and Holy Ghost, and this was his Dwelling in God and God in him. This was the Kingdom of God within Him, and made Paradise without Him. But the Day that Adam did eat of the forbidden earthly Tree, in that Day he absolutely died to this Kingdom of God within Him. This Depth or Centre of his Soul having lost its God, was shut up in Death and Darkness, and became a Prisoner in an earthly Animal, that only excelled its Brethren, the Beasts, in an upright Form, and serpentine Subtlety. Thus ended the Fall of Man. But from that Moment that the God of Mercy inspoke into Adam the Bruiser of the Serpent, from that Moment all the Riches and Treasures of the Divine Nature came again into Man, as a Seed of Salvation sown into the Centre of the Soul, and only lies hidden there in every Man, till he desires to rise from his fallen State, and to be born again from above.

[Pryr-1.2-10] Awake then, thou that Sleepest, and Christ, who from all Eternity has been espoused to thy Soul, shall give Thee Light. Begin to search and dig in thine own Field for this Pearl of Eternity, that lieth hidden in it; it cannot cost Thee too much, nor canst thou buy it too dear, for it is All, and when thou has found it, thou wilt know, that all which thou hast sold or given away for it, is as mere a Nothing, as a Bubble upon the Water.

[Pryr-1.2-11] But if thou turnest from this heavenly Pearl, or tramplest it under thy Feet, for the sake of being Rich, or Great, either in Church or State, if Death finds Thee in this Success, thou canst not then say, that though the Pearl is lost, yet something has been gained instead of it. For in that parting Moment, the Things, and the Sounds of this World, will be exactly alike; to have had an Estate, or only to have heard of it, to have lived at Lambeth twenty Years, or only have twenty Times passed by the Palace, will be the same Good, or the same Nothing to Thee.

[Pryr-1.2-12] But I will now show a little more distinctly, what this Pearl of Eternity is. First, it is the Light and Spirit of God within Thee, which has hitherto done Thee but little Good, because all the Desire of thy Heart has been after the Light and Spirit of this World. Thy Reason, and Senses, thy Heart and Passions, have turned all their Attention to the poor Concerns of this Life, and therefore thou art a Stranger to this Principle of Heaven, this Riches of Eternity within Thee. For as God is not, cannot be truly found by any Worshippers, but those who worship Him in Spirit and in Truth, so this Light and Spirit, though always within us, is not, cannot be found, felt, or enjoyed, but by those whose whole Spirit is turned to it.

[Pryr-1.2-13] When Man first came into Being, and stood before God as his own Image and Likeness, this Light and Spirit of God was as natural to him, as truly the Light of his Nature, as the Light and Air of this World is natural to the Creatures that have their Birth in it. But when Man, not content with the Food of Eternity, did eat of the earthly Tree, this Light and Spirit of Heaven was no more natural to him, no more rose up as a Birth of his Nature, but instead thereof, he was left solely to the Light and Spirit of this World. And this is that Death, which God told Adam, he should surely die, in the Day that he should eat of the forbidden Tree.

[Pryr-1.2-14] But the Goodness of God would not leave Man in this Condition. A Redemption from it was immediately granted, and the Bruiser of the Serpent brought the Light and Spirit of Heaven once more into the human Nature, not as it was in its first State, when Man was in Paradise, but as a Treasure hidden in the Centre of our Souls, which should discover, and open itself by Degrees, in such Proportion, as the Faith and Desires of our Hearts were turned to it. This Light and Spirit of God thus freely restored again to the Soul, and lying in it as a secret Source of Heaven, is called Grace, Free Grace, or the Supernatural Gift, or Power of God in the Soul, because it was something that the Natural Powers of the Soul could no more obtain. Hence it is, that in the greatest Truth, and highest Reality, every stirring of the Soul, every Tendency of the Heart towards God and Goodness, is justly and necessarily ascribed to the Holy Spirit, or the Grace of God. It is because this first Seed of Life, which is sown into the Soul, as the Gift or Grace of God to fallen Man, is itself the Light and Spirit of God, and therefore every Stirring, or Opening of this Seed of Life, every awakened Thought or Desire that arises from it, must be called the Moving, or the Quickening of the Spirit of God; and therefore that new Man which arises from it, must of all Necessity be said to be solely the Work and Operation of God. Hence also we have an easy and plain Declaration of the true Meaning, solid Sense, and certain Truth, of all those Scriptures, which speak of the Inspiration of God, the Operation of the Holy Spirit, the Power of the Divine Light, as the sole and necessary Agents in the Renewal and Sanctification of our Souls, and also as being Things common to all Men. It is because this Seed of Life, or Bruiser of the Serpent, is common to all Men, and has in all Men a Degree of Life, which is in itself so much of the Inspiration, or Life of God, the Spirit of God, the Light of God, which is in every Soul, and is its Power of becoming born again of God. Hence also it is, that all Men are exhorted not to quench, or resist, or grieve the Spirit, that is, this Seed of the Spirit and Light of God that is in all Men, as the only Source of Good. Again, the Flesh lusteth against the Spirit, and the Spirit against the Flesh. By the Flesh and its Lustings, are meant the mere human Nature, or the natural Man, as He is by the Fall; by the Spirit is meant the Bruiser of the Serpent, that Seed of the Light and Spirit of God, which lieth as a Treasure hid in the Soul, in order to bring forth the Life that was lost in Adam. Now as the Flesh has its Life, its Lustings, whence all sorts of Evil are truly said to be inspired, quickened, and stirred up in us, so the Spirit being a Living principle within us, has its Inspiration, its Breathing, its Moving, its Quickening, from which alone the Divine Life, or the Angel that died in Adam, can be born in us.

[Pryr-1.2-15] When this Seed of the Spirit, common to all Men, is not resisted, grieved, and quenched, but its Inspirations and Motions suffered to grow and increase in us, to unite with God, and get Power over all the Lusts of the Flesh, then we are born again, the Nature, Spirit, and Tempers of Jesus Christ are opened in our Souls, the Kingdom of God is come, and is found within us. On the other Hand, when the Flesh, or the Natural Man has resisted and quenched this Spirit or Seed of Life within us, then the works of the Flesh, Adultery, Fornication, Murders, Lying, Hatred, Envy, Wrath, Pride, Foolishness, worldly Wisdom, carnal Prudence, false Religion, hypocritical Holiness, and serpentine Subtlety, have set up their Kingdom within us.

[Pryr-1.2-16] See here in short, the State of Man as redeemed. He has a Spark of the Light and Spirit of God, as a Supernatural Gift of God given into the Birth of his Soul, to bring forth by Degrees a New Birth of that Life which was Lost in Paradise. This Holy Spark of the Divine Nature within Him, has a natural, strong and almost infinite Tendency, or Reaching after that eternal Light and Spirit of God, from whence it came forth. It came forth from God, it came out of God, it partaketh of the Divine Nature, and therefore it is always in a State of Tendency and Return to God. And all this is called the Breathing, the Moving, the Quickening of the Holy Spirit within us, which are so many Operations of this Spark of Life tending towards God. On the other Hand, The Deity as considered in itself, and without the Soul of Man, has an infinite, unchangeable Tendency of Love, and Desire towards the Soul of Man, to unite and communicate its own Riches and Glories to it, just as the Spirit of the Air without Man, unites and communicates its Riches and Virtues to the Spirit of the Air that is within Man. This Love, or Desire of God towards the Soul of Man, is so great, that He gave his only begotten Son, the Brightness of his Glory, to take the human Nature upon him, in its fallen State, that by this mysterious Union of God and Man, all the Enemies of the Soul of Man might be overcome, and every human Creature might have a Power of being born again according to that Image of God, in which he was first created. The Gospel is the History of this Love of God to Man. Inwardly he has a Seed of the Divine Life given into the Birth of his Soul, a Seed that has all the Riches of Eternity in it, and is always wanting to come to the Birth in him, and be alive in God. Outwardly he has Jesus Christ, who as a Sun of Righteousness, is always casting forth his enlivening Beams on this inward Seed, to kindle and call it forth to the Birth, doing that to this Seed of Heaven in Man, which the Sun in the Firmament is always doing to the vegetable Seeds in the Earth.

[Pryr-1.2-17] Consider this Matter in the following Similitude. A Grain of Wheat has the Air and Light of this World enclosed, or incorporated in it: This is the Mystery of its Life, this is its Power of Growing, by this it has a strong continual Tendency of uniting again with that Ocean of Light and Air, from whence it came forth, and so it helps to kindle its own Vegetable Life.

[Pryr-1.2-18] On the other Hand, That great Ocean of Light and Air, having its own Offspring hidden in the Heart of the Grain, has a perpetual strong Tendency to unite, and communicate with it again. From this Desire of Union on both Sides, the Vegetable Life arises, and all the Virtues and Powers contained in it.

[Pryr-1.2-19] But here let it be well observed, that this Desire on both Sides cannot have its Effect, till the Husk and gross Part of the Grain falls into a State of Corruption and Death, till this begins, the Mystery of Life hidden in it, cannot come forth. The Application here may be left to the Reader. I shall only observe, that we may here see the true Ground, and absolute Necessity, of that dying to ourselves, and to the World, to which our Blessed Lord so constantly calls all his Followers. An universal Self-Denial, a perpetual Mortification of the Lust of the Flesh, the Lust of the Eyes, and the Pride of Life, is not a Thing imposed upon us by the mere Will of God, is not required as a Punishment, is not an Invention of dull and monkish Spirits, but has its Ground and Reason in the Nature of the Thing, and is absolutely necessary to make Way for the New Birth, as the Death of the Husk and gross Part of the Grain, is necessary to make Way for its vegetable Life.

[Pryr-1.2-20] But Secondly, this Pearl of Eternity is the Wisdom and Love of God within Thee. In this Pearl of thy Serpent Bruiser, all the Holy Nature, Spirit, Tempers, and Inclinations of Christ, lie as in a Seed in the Centre of thy Soul, and Divine Wisdom and heavenly Love will grow up in Thee, if thou givest but true Attention to God present in thy Soul. On the other Hand, There is hidden also in the Depth of thy Nature the Root, or Possibility of all the hellish Nature, Spirit, and Tempers of the fallen Angels. For Heaven and Hell have each of them their Foundation within us, they come not into us from without, but spring up in us, according as our Will and Heart is turned either to the Light of God, or the Kingdom of Darkness. But when this Life, which is in the midst of these two Eternities, is at an End, either an Angel, or a Devil will be found to have a Birth in us.

[Pryr-1.2-21] Thou needest not therefore run here, or there, saying, Where is Christ? Thou needest not say, Who shall ascend into Heaven, that is, to bring down Christ from above? Or who shall descend into the Deep, to bring Christ from the Dead? For behold the Word, which is the Wisdom of God, is in thy Heart, it is there as a Bruiser of thy Serpent, as a Light unto thy Feet and Lanthorn unto thy Paths. It is there as an Holy Oil, to soften and overcome the wrathful fiery Properties of thy Nature, and change them into the humble Meekness of Light and Love. It is there as a speaking Word of God in thy Soul; and as soon as thou art ready to hear, this eternal speaking Word will speak Wisdom and Love in thy inward Parts, and bring forth the Birth of Christ, with all his Holy Nature, Spirit, and Tempers, within Thee. Hence it was (that is, from this Principle of Heaven, or Christ in the Soul) hence I say it was, that so many eminent Spirits, Partakers of a Divine Life, have appeared in so many Parts of the heathen World; glorious Names, Sons of Wisdom, that shone, as Lights hung out by God, in the midst of idolatrous Darkness. These were the Apostles of a Christ within, that were awakened and commissioned by the inward Bruiser of the Serpent, to call Mankind from the blind Pursuits of Flesh and Blood, to know themselves, the Dignity of their Nature, the Immortality of their Souls, and the Necessity of Virtue to avoid eternal Shame and Misery. These Apostles, though they had not the Law, or written Gospel to urge upon their Hearers, yet having turned to God, they found, and preached the Gospel, that was written in their Hearts. Hence one of them could say this divine Truth, viz., That such only are Priests and Prophets, who have God in themselves. Hence also it is, that in the Christian Church, there have been in all Ages, amongst the most illiterate, both Men and Women, who have attained to a deep Understanding of the Mysteries of the Wisdom and Love of God in Christ Jesus. And what wonder? Since it is not Art or Science, or Skill in Grammar or Logic, but the Opening of Divine Life in the Soul, that can give true Understanding of the Things of God. This Life of God in the Soul, which for its Smallness at first, and Capacity for great Growth, is by our Lord compared to a Grain of Mustard Seed, may be, and too generally is suppressed and kept under, either by worldly Cares, or Pleasures, by vain Learning, Sensuality, or Ambition. And all this while, whatever Church, or Profession any Man is of, he is a mere Natural Man, unregenerate, unenlightened by the Spirit of God, because this Seed of Heaven is choked, and not suffered to grow up in him. And therefore his Religion is no more from Heaven than his fine Breeding; his Cares have no more Goodness in them than his Pleasures; his Love is worth no more than his Hatred; his Zeal for this, or against that Form of Religion, has only the Nature of any other worldly Contention in it. And thus it is, and must be with every mere natural Man, whatever Appearances he may put on, he may, if he pleases, know himself to be the Slave, and Machine of his own corrupt Tempers and Inclinations, to be enlightened, inspired, quickened and animated by Self-love, Self-esteem, and Self-seeking, which is the only Life, and Spirit of the mere natural Man, whether he be Heathen, Jew, or Christian.

[Pryr-1.2-22] On the other Hand, wherever this Seed of Heaven is suffered to take Root, to get Life and Breath in the Soul, whether it be in Man, or Woman, young or old, there this new born inward Man is justly said to be inspired, enlightened, and moved by the Spirit of God, because his whole Birth and Life is a Birth from above, of the Light and Spirit of God; and therefore all that is in him, has the Nature, Spirit, and Tempers of Heaven in it. As this regenerate Life grows up in any Man, so there grows up a true and real Knowledge of the whole Mystery of Godliness in himself. All that the Gospel teaches of Sin and Grace, of Life and Death, of Heaven and Hell, of the New and Old Man, of the Light and Spirit of God, are Things not got by Hearsay, but inwardly known, felt and experienced in the Growth of his own new born Life. He has then an Unction from above which teaches him all Things, a Spirit that knoweth what it ought to pray for, a Spirit that prays without ceasing, that is risen with Christ from the Dead, and has all its Conversation in Heaven, a Spirit that hath Groans and Sighs that cannot be uttered, that travaileth and groaneth with the whole Creation, to be delivered from Vanity, and have its glorious Liberty in that God, from whom it came forth.

[Pryr-1.2-23] Again, Thirdly, this Pearl of Eternity is the Church, or Temple of God within Thee, the consecrated Place of Divine Worship, where alone thou canst worship God in Spirit, and in Truth. In Spirit, because thy Spirit is that alone in Thee, which can unite, and cleave unto God, and receive the Workings of his Divine Spirit upon Thee. In Truth, because this Adoration in Spirit, is that Truth and Reality, of which all outward Forms and Rites, though instituted by God, are only the Figure for a Time, but this Worship is Eternal. Accustom thyself to the Holy Service of this inward Temple. In the midst of it is the Fountain of Living Water, of which thou mayest drink, and live forever. There the Mysteries of thy Redemption are celebrated, or rather opened in Life and Power. There the Supper of the Lamb is kept; the Bread that came down from Heaven, that giveth Life to the World, is thy true Nourishment: all is done, and known in real Experience, in a living Sensibility of the Work of God on the Soul. There the Birth, the Life, the Sufferings, the Death, the Resurrection and Ascension of Christ, are not merely remembered, but inwardly found, and enjoyed as the real States of thy Soul, which has followed Christ in the

Regeneration. When once thou art well grounded in this inward Worship, thou wilt have learnt to live unto God above Time, and Place. For every Day will be Sunday to thee, and wherever thou goest, thou wilt have a Priest, a Church, and an Altar along with Thee. For when God has all that He should have of thy Heart, when renouncing the Will, Judgment, Tempers and Inclinations of thy old Man, thou art wholly given up to the Obedience of the Light and Spirit of God within Thee, to Will only his Will, to Love only in his Love, to be Wise only in his Wisdom, then it is, that every Thing thou doest is as a song of Praise, and the common Business of thy Life is a conforming to God's Will on Earth, as Angels do in Heaven.

[Pryr-1.2-24] Fourthly, and Lastly, this Pearl of Eternity is the Peace and Joy of God within Thee, but can only be found by the Manifestation of the Life and Power of Jesus Christ in thy Soul. But Christ cannot be thy Power and thy Life, till in Obedience to his Call, thou deniest thyself, takest up thy daily Cross, and followest Him, in the Regeneration. This is peremptory, it admits of no Reserve or Evasion, it is the one Way to Christ and Eternal Life. But be where thou wilt, either here, or at Rome, or Geneva, if Self is undenied, if thou livest to thine own Will, to the Pleasures of thy natural Lust and Appetites, Senses and Passions, and in Conformity to the vain Customs, and Spirit of this World, thou art dead whilst thou livest, the Seed of the Woman is crucified within Thee, Christ can profit thee Nothing, thou art a Stranger to all that is holy and heavenly within Thee, and utterly incapable of finding the Peace and Joy of God in thy Soul. And thus thou art Poor, and Blind, and Naked, and Empty, and livest a miserable Life in the Vanity of Time; whilst all the Riches of Eternity, the Light and Spirit, the Wisdom and Love, the Peace and Joy of God are within Thee. And thus it will always be with Thee, there is no Remedy, go where thou wilt, do what thou wilt, all is shut up, there is no open Door of Salvation, no Awakening out of the Sleep of Sin, no Deliverance from the Power of thy corrupt Nature, no Overcoming of the World, no Revelation of Jesus Christ, no Joy of the New Birth from above, till dying to thy Self and the World, thou turnest to the Light, and Spirit, and Power of God in thy Soul. All is fruitless, and insignificant, all the Means of thy Redemption are at a Stand, all outward Forms are but a dead Formality, till this Fountain of living Water is found within Thee.

[Pryr-1.2-25] But thou wilt perhaps say, How shall I discover this Riches of Eternity, this Light, and Spirit, and Wisdom, and Peace of God, treasured up within me? Thy first Thought of Repentance, or Desire of turning to God, is thy first Discovery of this Light and Spirit of God within Thee. It is the Voice and Language of the Word of God within Thee, though thou knowest it not. It is the Bruiser of thy Serpent's Head, thy Dear Immanuel, who is beginning to preach within Thee, that same which He first preached in public, saying, "Repent, for the Kingdom of Heaven is at Hand." When therefore but the smallest Instinct or Desire of thy Heart calleth Thee towards God, and a newness of Life, give it Time and Leave to speak; and take care thou refuse not Him that speaketh. For it is not an Angel from Heaven that speaketh to Thee, but it is the eternal speaking Word of God in thy Heart, that Word which at first created Thee, is thus beginning to create Thee a second Time unto Righteousness, that a new Man may be formed again in Thee in the Image and Likeness of God. But above all Things, beware of taking this Desire of Repentance to be the Effect of thy own Natural Sense and Reason, for in so doing thou losest the Key of all the Heavenly Treasure that is in Thee, thou shuttest the Door against God, turnest away from Him, and thy Repentance (if thou hast any) will be only a vain, unprofitable Work of thy own Hands, that will do Thee no more Good, than a Well that is without Water. But if thou takest this awakened Desire of turning to God, to be, as in Truth it is, the coming of Christ in thy Soul, the Working, Redeeming Power of the Light and Spirit of the holy Jesus within Thee, if thou dost reverence and adhere to it, as such, this Faith will save Thee, will make

Thee whole; and by thus believing in Christ, though thou wert dead, yet shalt thou live.

[Pryr-1.2-26] Now all dependeth on thy right Submission and Obedience to this speaking of God in thy Soul. Stop therefore all Self-activity, listen not to the Suggestions of thy own Reason, run not on in thy own Will, but be retired, silent, passive, and humbly attentive to this new risen Light within Thee. Open thy Heart, thy Eyes, and Ears, to all its Impressions. Let it enlighten, teach, frighten, torment, judge, and condemn Thee, as it pleaseth, turn not away from it, hear all it says, seek for no Relief out of it, consult not with Flesh and Blood, but with a Heart full of Faith and Resignation to God, pray only this Prayer, that God's Kingdom may come, and his Will be done in thy Soul. Stand faithfully in this State of Preparation, thus given up to the Spirit of God, and then the Work of thy Repentance will be Wrought in God, and thou wilt soon find, that He that is in Thee, is much greater than all that are against Thee.

[Pryr-1.2-27] But that thou mayest do all this the better, and be more firmly assured, that this Resignation to, and Dependence upon the working of God's Spirit within Thee, is right and sound, I shall lay before Thee two great, and infallible, and fundamental Truths, which will be as a Rock for thy Faith to stand upon.

[Pryr-1.2-28] First, That through all the whole Nature of Things, nothing can do, or be a real Good to thy Soul, but the Operation of God upon it. Secondly, that all the Dispensations of God to Mankind, from the Fall of Adam, to the preaching of the Gospel, were only for this one End, to fit, prepare, and dispose the Soul for the Operation of the Spirit of God upon it. These two great Truths well and deeply apprehended, put the Soul in its right State, in a continual Dependence upon God, in a Readiness to receive all Good from Him, and will be a continual Source of Light in thy Mind. They will keep Thee safe from all Errors, and false Zeal in Things, and Forms of Religion, from a Sectarian Spirit, from Bigotry, and Superstition; they will teach Thee the true Difference between the Means and End of Religion; and the Regard thou showest to the Shell, will be only so far, as the Kernel is to be found in it.

[Pryr-1.2-29] Man, by his Fall, had broken off from his true Centre, his proper Place in God, and therefore the Life and Operation of God was no more in Him. He was fallen from a Life in God into a Life of Self, into an animal Life of Self-love, Self-esteem, and Self-seeking in the poor perishing Enjoyments of this World. This was the Natural State of Man by the Fall. He was an Apostate from God, and his natural Life was all Idolatry, where Self was the great Idol that was worshipped instead of God. See here the whole Truth in short. All Sin, Death, Damnation, and Hell is nothing else but this Kingdom of Self, or the various Operations of Self-love, Self-esteem, and Self-seeking, which separate the Soul from God, and end in eternal Death and Hell.

[Pryr-1.2-30] On the other Hand, all that is Grace, Redemption, Salvation, Sanctification, Spiritual Life, and the New Birth, is nothing else but so much of the Life and Operation of God found again in the Soul. It is Man come back again into his Centre or Place in God, from whence he had broken off. The Beginning again of the Life of God in the Soul, was then first made, when the Mercy of God inspoke into Adam a Seed of the Divine Life, which should bruise the Head of the Serpent, which had wrought itself into the human Nature. Here the Kingdom of God was again within us, though only as a Seed, yet small as it was, it was yet a Degree of the Divine Life, which if rightly cultivated, would overcome all the Evil that was in us, and make of every fallen Man a new born Son of God.

[Pryr-1.2-31] All the Sacrifices and Institutions of the ancient Patriarchs, the Law of Moses, with all its Types, and Rites, and Ceremonies, had this only End; they were the Methods of Divine Wisdom for a Time, to keep the Hearts of Men from the Wanderings of Idolatry, in a State of Holy Expectation upon God, they were to keep the first Seed of Life in a State of Growth, and make Way for the further Operation of God upon the Soul; or, as the Apostle speaks, to be as a Schoolmaster unto Christ, that is, till the Birth, the Death, the Resurrection and Ascension of Christ, should conquer Death and Hell, open a new Dispensation of God, and baptize Mankind afresh with the Holy Ghost, and Fire of Heaven. Then, that is, on the Day of Pentecost, a new Dispensation of God came forth; which on God's Part, was the Operation of the Holy Spirit in Gifts and Graces upon the whole Church; and on Man's Part, it was the Adoration of God in Spirit and in Truth. Thus all that was done by God, from the Bruiser of the Serpent given to Adam, to Christ's sitting down on the right Hand of God, was all for this End, to remove all that stood between God and Man, and to make Way for the immediate and continual Operation of God upon the Soul; and that Man, baptized with the Holy Spirit, and born again from Above, should absolutely renounce Self, and wholly give up his Soul to the Operation of God's Spirit, to know, to love, to will, to pray, to worship, to preach, to exhort, to use all the Faculties of his Mind, and all the outward Things of this World, as enlightened, inspired, moved and guided by the Holy Ghost, who by this last Dispensation of God, was given to be a Comforter, a Teacher, and Guide to the Church, who should abide with it forever.

[Pryr-1.2-32] This is Christianity, a spiritual Society, not because it has no worldly Concerns, but because all its Members, as such, are born of the Spirit, kept alive, animated and governed by the Spirit of God. It is constantly called by our Lord the Kingdom of God, or Heaven, because all its Ministry and Service, all that is done in it, is done in Obedience and Subjection to that Spirit, by which Angels live, and are governed in Heaven. Hence our blessed Lord taught his Disciples to pray, that this Kingdom might come, that so God's Will might be done on Earth, as it is in Heaven; which could not be, but by that same Spirit, by which it is done in Heaven. The short is this: The Kingdom of Self is the Fall of Man, or the great Apostasy from the Life of God in the Soul; and everyone wherever he be, that liveth unto Self, is still under the Fall and great Apostasy from God. The Kingdom of Christ is the Spirit and Power of God dwelling and manifesting itself in the Birth of a new inward Man; and no one is a Member of this Kingdom, but so far as a true Birth of the Spirit is brought forth in him. These two Kingdoms take in all Mankind, he that is not of one, is certainly in the other; Dying to one is Living to the other.

[Pryr-1.2-33] Hence we may gather these following Truths: First, Here is shown the true Ground and Reason of what was said above, namely, That when the Call of God to Repentance first ariseth in thy Soul, thou art to be retired, silent, passive, and humbly attentive to this new risen Light within thee, by wholly stopping, or disregarding the Workings of thy own Will, Reason, and Judgment. It is because all these are false Counselors, the sworn Servants, bribed Slaves of thy fallen Nature, they are all Born and Bred in thy Kingdom of Self; and therefore if a new Kingdom is to be set up in thee, if the Operation of God is to have its Effect in thee, all these natural Powers of Self are to be silenced and suppressed, till they have learned Obedience and Subjection to the Spirit of God. Now this is not requiring thee to become a Fool, or to give up thy Claim to Sense and Reason, but is the shortest Way to have thy Sense and Reason delivered from Folly, and thy whole rational Nature strengthened, enlightened, and guided by that Light, which is Wisdom itself.

[Pryr-1.2-34] A child that obediently denies his own Will, and own Reason, to be guided by the Will and Reason of a truly wise and understanding Tutor, cannot be said to make himself a Fool, and give up the Benefit of his rational Nature, but to have taken the shortest Way to have his own Will and Reason made truly a Blessing to him.

[Pryr-1.2-35] Secondly, Hence is to be seen the true Ground and Necessity of that universal Mortification and Self-denial with regard to all our Senses, Appetites, Tempers, Passions and

Judgments. It is because all our whole Nature, as fallen from the Life of God, is in a State of Contrariety to the Order and End of our Creation, a continual Source of disorderly Appetites, corrupt Tempers, and false Judgments. And therefore every Motion of it is to be mortified, changed and purified from its natural State, before we can enter into the Kingdom of God. Thus when our Lord saith, "Except a Man hateth his Father and Mother, yea, and his own Life, he cannot be my Disciple"; it is because our best Tempers are yet carnal, and full of the Imperfections of our fallen Nature. The Doctrine is just and good; not as if Father and Mother were to be hated; but that Love, which an unregenerate Person, or natural Man, hath towards them, is to be hated, as being a blind Self- love, full of all the Weakness and Partiality, with which fallen Man loves, honours, esteems, and cleaves to himself. This Love, born from corrupt Flesh and Blood, and polluted with Self, is to be hated and parted with, that we may love them with a Love born of God, with such a Love, and on such a Motive, as Christ has loved us. And then the Disciple of Christ far exceeds all others in the Love of Parents. Again, Our own Life is to be hated; and the Reason is plain, it is because there is nothing lovely in it. It is a Legion of Evil, a monstrous Birth of the Serpent, the World, and the Flesh; it is an Apostasy from the Life and Power of God in the Soul, a Life that is Death to Heaven, that is pure unmixed Idolatry, that lives wholly to Self, and not to God; and therefore all this own Life is to be absolutely hated, all this Self is to be denied and mortified, if the Nature, Spirit, Tempers and Inclinations of Christ are to be brought to Life in us. For it is as impossible to live to both these Lives at once, as for a Body to move two contrary Ways at the same Time. And therefore all these Mortifications and Self-denials have an absolute Necessity in the Nature of the Thing itself.

[Pryr-1.2-36] Thus when our Lord further saith, unless a Man forsake all that he hath, he cannot be my Disciple; the Reason is plain, and the Necessity absolute. It is because all that the natural Man hath, is in the Possession of Self-love, and therefore this Possession is to be absolutely forsaken, and parted with. All that he hath, is to be put into other Hands, to be given to Divine Love, or this natural Man cannot be changed into a Disciple of Christ. For Self-love in all that it hath, is earthly, sensual, and devilish, and therefore must have all taken away from it; and then to the natural Man all is lost, he hath nothing left, all is laid down at the Feet of Jesus. And then all Things are common, as soon as Self-love has lost the Possession of them. And then the Disciple of Christ, though having nothing, yet possesseth all Things, all that the natural Man has forsaken, is restored to the Disciple of Christ an hundred-fold. For Self-love, the greatest of all Thieves, being now cast out, and all that he had stolen and hidden thus taken from him, and put into the Hands of Divine Love, every Mite becomes a large Treasure, and Mammon opens the Door into everlasting Habitations. This was the Spirit of the first Draught of a Christian Church at Jerusalem, a Church made truly after the Pattern of Heaven, where the Love that reigns in Heaven reigned in it, where Divine Love broke down all the selfish Fences, the Locks and Bolts of me, mine, my own, &c., and laid all Things common to the Members of this new Kingdom of God on Earth.

[Pryr-1.2-37] Now though many Years did not pass after the Age of the Apostles, before Satan and Self got footing in the Church, and set up Merchandise in the House of God, yet this one Heart, and one Spirit, which then first appeared in the Jerusalem Church, is that one Heart and Spirit of Divine Love, to which all are called, that would be true Disciples of Christ. And though the Practice of it is lost as to the Church in general, yet it ought not to have been lost; and therefore every Christian ought to make it his great Care and Prayer, to have it restored in himself. And then, though born in the Dregs of Time, or living in Babylon, he will be as truly a Member of the first heavenly Church at Jerusalem, as if he had lived in it, in the Days of the

Apostles. This Spirit of Love, born of that celestial Fire, with which Christ baptizes his true Disciples, is alone that Spirit, which can enter into Heaven, and therefore is that Spirit which is to be born in us, whilst we are on Earth. For no one can enter in Heaven, till he is made heavenly, till the Spirit of Heaven is entered into him. And therefore all that our Lord hath said of denying and dying to Self, and of his parting with all that he has, are Practices absolutely necessary from the Nature of the Thing.

[Pryr-1.2-38] Because all turning to Self is so far turning from God, and so much as we have of Self-love, so much we have of a hellish, earthly Weight, that must be taken off, or there can be no Ascension into Heaven. But thou wilt perhaps say, If all Self-love is to be renounced, then all Love of our Neighbour is renounced along with it, because the Commandment is, only to love our Neighbour as ourselves. The Answer here is easy, and yet no Quarter given to Self-love. There is but one only Love in Heaven, and yet the Angels of God love one another in the same manner, as they love themselves. The Matter is thus: The one supreme, unchangeable Rule of Love, which is a Law to all intelligent Beings of all Worlds, and will be a Law to all Eternity, is this, viz., That God alone is to be loved for himself, and all other Beings only in Him, and for Him. Whatever intelligent Creature lives not under this Rule of Love, is so far fallen from the Order of his Creation, and is, till He returns to this eternal Law of Love, an Apostate from God, and incapable of the Kingdom of Heaven.

[Pryr-1.2-39] Now if God alone is to be loved for Himself, then no Creature is to be loved for itself; and so all Self-love in every Creature is absolutely condemned.

[Pryr-1.2-40] And if all created Beings are only to be loved in and for God, then my Neighbour is to be loved, as I love myself, and I am only to love myself, as I love my Neighbour, or any other created Being, that is only in and for God. And thus the Command of loving our Neighbour as ourselves, stands firm, and yet all Self-love is plucked up by the Roots. But what is loving any Creature, only in, and for God? It is when we love it only as it is God's Work, Image, and Delight, when we love it merely as it is God's, and belongs to him, this is loving it in God, and when all that we wish, intend, or do to it, is done from a Love of God, for the Honour of God, and in Conformity to the Will of God, this is loving it for God. This is the one Love that is, and must be the Spirit of all Creatures that live united to God. Now this is no speculative Refinement, or fine-spun Fiction of the Brain, but the simple Truth, and a first Law of Nature, and a necessary Band of Union between God and the Creature. The Creature is not in God, is a Stranger to Him, has lost the Life of God in itself, whenever its Love does not thus begin and end in God.

[Pryr-1.2-41] The Loss of this Love, was the Fall of Man, as it opened in him a Kingdom of Self, in which Satan, the World, and the Flesh, could all of them bring forth their own Works. If therefore Man is to rise from his Fall, and return to his Life in God, there is an absolute necessity that Self, with all his Brood of gross Affections, be deposed, that his first Love in and for which he was created, may be born again in him. Christ came into the World to save Sinners, to destroy the Works of the Devil. Now Self is not only the Seat and Habitation, but the very Life of Sin. The Works of the Devil are all wrought in Self, it is his peculiar Workhouse, and therefore Christ is not come as a Saviour from Sin, as a Destroyer of the Works of the Devil in any of us, but so far as Self is beaten down, and overcome in us. If it is literally true, what our Lord said, That his Kingdom was not of this World, then it is a Truth of the same Certainty, that no one is a Member of this Kingdom, but he that in the literal Sense of the Words renounces the Spirit of this World. Christians might as well part with half the Articles of their Creed, or but half believe them, as really to refuse, or but by halves enter into these Self-denials.

[Pryr-1.2-42] For all that is in the Creed, is only to bring forth this Dying and Death to all and every Part of the old Man, that the Life and Spirit of Christ may be formed in us.

[Pryr-1.2-43] Our Redemption is this new Birth; if this is not done, or doing in us, we are still unredeemed. And though the Saviour of the World is come, He is not come in us, He is not received by us, is a Stranger to us, is not ours, if his Life is not within us. His life is not, cannot be within us, but so far as the Spirit of the World, Self-love, Self-esteem, and Self-seeking, are renounced, and driven out of us.

[Pryr-1.2-44] Thirdly, Hence we may also learn the true Nature and Worth of all Self-denials and Mortifications. As to their Nature, considered in themselves, they have nothing of Goodness or Holiness, nor are any real Parts of our Sanctification, they are not the true Food or Nourishment of Divine Life in our Souls, they have no Quickening, Sanctifying Power in them; their only Worth consists in this, that they remove the Impediments of Holiness, break down that which stands between God and us, and make Way for the Quickening, Sanctifying Spirit of God to operate on our Souls. Which Operation of God is the one only Thing that can raise the Divine Life in the Soul, or help it to the smallest Degree of real Holiness, or Spiritual Life. As in our Creation, we had only that Degree of a Divine Life, which the Power of God derived into us; as then all that we had, and were, was the sole Operation of God in the Creation of us; so in our Redemption, or regaining that first Perfection, which we have lost, all must be again the Operation of God; every Degree of the Divine Life restored in us, be it ever so small, must and can be nothing else but so much of the Life and Operation of God found again in the Soul. All the Activity of Man in the Works of Self-denial has no Good in itself, but is only to open an Entrance for the one only Good, the Light of God, to operate upon us.

[Pryr-1.2-45] Hence also we may learn the Reason, why many People not only lose the Benefit, but are even worse for all their Mortifications. It is because they mistake the whole Nature and Worth of them. They practice them for their own Sakes, as Things good in themselves, they think them to be real Parts of Holiness, and so rest in them, and look no further, but grow full of Self-esteem, and Self-admiration, for their own Progress in them. This makes them Self-sufficient, morose, severe Judges of all those that fall short of their Mortifications.

[Pryr-1.2-46] And thus their Self-denials do only that for them, which Indulgences do for other People, they withstand and hinder the Operation of God upon their Souls, and instead of being really Self-denials, they strengthen and keep up the Kingdom of Self.

[Pryr-1.2-47] There is no avoiding this fatal Error, but by deeply entering into this great Truth, that all our own Activity and Working has no Good in it, can do no Good to us, but as it leads and turns us in the best Manner to the Light and Spirit of God, which alone brings Life and Salvation into the Soul. Stretch forth thy Hand, said our Lord to the Man that had a withered Hand; he did so, and it was immediately made whole as the other.

[Pryr-1.2-48] Now had this Man any Ground for Pride, or a high Opinion of himself, for the Share he had in the Restoring of his Hand? Yet just such is our Share in the Raising up of the Spiritual Life within us. All that we can do by our own Activity, is only like this Man's stretching out his Hand; the rest is the Work of Christ, the only Giver of Life to the withered Hand, or the dead Soul. We can only then do living Works, when we are so far born again, as to be able to say with the Apostle, "Yet not I, but Christ that liveth in me." But to return, and further show, how the Soul that feels the Call of God to Repentance is to behave under it, that this stirring of the Divine Power in the soul may have its full Effect, and bring forth the Birth of the new Man in Christ Jesus. We are to consider it (as in Truth it is) as the Seed of the Divine Nature within us, that can only grow by its own Strength and Union with God. It is a Divine Life, and therefore can grow from nothing but Divine Power. When the Virgin Mary conceived the Birth of the holy Jesus, all that she did towards it herself, was only this single Act of Faith and Resignation to God; "Behold the Handmaid of the Lord, be it unto me according to thy Word." This is all that we can do towards the Conception of that new Man that is to be born in ourselves. Now this Truth is easily consented to, and a Man thinks he believes it, because he consents to it, or rather, does not deny it. But this is not enough, it is to be apprehended in a deep, full, and practical Assurance, in such a Manner as a Man knows and believes that he did not create the Stars, or cause Life to rise up in himself. And then it is a Belief, that puts the Soul into a right State, that makes room for the Operation of God upon it. His Light then enters with full Power into the Soul, and his holy Spirit moves and directs all that is done in it, and so Man lives again in God as a new Creature. For this Truth thus firmly believed, will have these two most excellent Effects: First, It will keep the Soul fixed, and continually turned towards God, in Faith, Prayer, Desire, Confidence, and Resignation to Him, for all that it wants to have done in it, and to it; which will be a continual Source of all Divine Virtues and Graces. The Soul thus turned to God must be always receiving from Him. It stands at the true Door of all Divine Communications, and the Light of God as freely enters into it, as the Light of the Sun enters into the Air. Secondly, It will fix and ground the Soul in a true and lasting Self-denial. For by thus knowing and owning our own Nothingness and Inability, that we have no other Capacity for Good, but that of receiving it from God alone, Self is wholly denied, its Kingdom is destroyed; no room is left for spiritual Pride and Self-esteem; we are saved from a Pharisaical Holiness, from wrong Opinions of our own Works and good Deeds, and from a Multitude of Errors, the most dangerous to our Souls, all which arise from the Something that we take ourselves to be either in Nature or Grace. But when we once apprehend but in some good Degree, the All of God, and the Nothingness of ourselves, we have got a Truth, whose Usefulness and Benefit no Words can express. It brings a Kind of Infallibility into the Soul in which it dwells; all that is vain, and false, and deceitful, is forced to vanish and fly before it. When our Religion is founded on this Rock, it has the Firmness of a Rock, and its Height reaches unto Heaven. The World, the Flesh, and the Devil, can do no hurt to it; all Enemies are known, and all disarmed by this great Truth dwelling in our Souls. It is the Knowledge of the All of God, that makes Cherubims and Seraphims to be Flames of Divine Love. For where this All of God is truly known, and felt in any Creature, there its whole Breath and Spirit is a Fire of Love, nothing but a pure disinterested Love can arise up in it, or come from it, a Love that begins and ends in God. And where this Love is born in any Creature, there a Seraphic Life is born along with it. For this pure Love introduces the Creature into the All of God; all that is in God is opened in the Creature, it is united with God, and has the Life of God manifested in it.

[Pryr-1.2-49] There is but one Salvation for all Mankind, and that is the Life of God in the Soul. God has but one Design or Intent towards all Mankind, and that is to introduce or generate his own Life, Light, and Spirit in them, that all may be as so many Images, Temples, and Habitations of the Holy Trinity. This is God's good Will to all Christians, Jews, and Heathens. They are all equally the Desire of his Heart, his Light continually waits for an Entrance into all of them, his Wisdom crieth, she putteth forth her Voice, not here, or there, but everywhere, in all the Streets of all the Parts of the World.

[Pryr-1.2-50] Now there is but one possible Way for Man to attain this Salvation, or Life of God in the Soul. There is not one for the Jew, another for a Christian, and a Third for the Heathen. No; God is one, human Nature is one, Salvation is one, and the Way to it is one; and that is, the Desire of the Soul turned to God. When this Desire is alive and breaks forth in any Creature under Heaven, then the lost Sheep is found, and the Shepherd has it upon his Shoulders. Through this Desire the Poor prodigal Son leaves his Husks and Swine, and hasteth to his Father: it is because of this Desire, that the Father sees the Son, while yet afar off, that he runs out to meet him, falleth on his Neck, and kisseth him. See here how plainly we are taught, that no sooner is this Desire arisen, and in Motion towards God, but the Operation of God's Spirit answers to it, cherishes and welcomes its first Beginnings, signified by the Father's seeing, and having Compassion on his Son, whilst yet afar off, that is, in the first Beginnings of his Desire. Thus does this Desire do all, it brings the Soul to God, and God into the Soul, it unites with God, it co-operates with God, and is one Life with God. Suppose this Desire not to be alive, not in Motion either in a Jew, or a Christian, and then all the Sacrifices, the Service, the Worship either of the Law, or the Gospel, are but dead Works, that bring no Life into the Soul, nor beget any Union between God and it. Suppose this Desire to be awakened, and fixed upon God, though in Souls that never heard either of the Law or the Gospel, and then the Divine Life, or Operation of God, enters into them, and the new Birth in Christ is formed in those who never heard of his Name. And these are they "that shall come from the East, and from the West and sit down with Abraham, and Isaac, in the Kingdom of God."

[Pryr-1.2-51] Oh my God, just and good, how great is thy Love and Mercy to Mankind, that Heaven is thus everywhere open, and Christ thus the common Saviour to all that turn the Desire of their Hearts to thee! Oh sweet Power of the Bruiser of the Serpent, born in every Son of Man, that stirs and works in every Man, and gives every Man a Power, and Desire, to find his Happiness in God! O holy Jesus, heavenly Light, that lightest every Man that cometh into the World, that redeemeth every Soul that follows thy Light, which is always within Him! O Holy Trinity, immense Ocean of divine Love in which all Mankind live, and move, and have their Being! None are separated from thee, none live out of thy Love, but all are embraced in the Arms of thy Mercy, all are Partakers of thy Divine Life, the Operation of thy holy Spirit, as soon as their Heart is turned to Thee! Oh plain, and easy, and simple Way of Salvation, wanting no Subtleties of Art or Science, no borrowed Learning, no Refinements of Reason, but all done by the simple natural Motion of every Heart, that truly longs after God. For no sooner is the finite Desire of the Creature in motion towards God, but the infinite Desire of God is united with it, co-operates with it. And in this united Desire of God and the Creature, is the Salvation and Life of the Soul brought forth. For the Soul is shut out of God, and imprisoned in its own dark Workings of Flesh and Blood, merely and solely, because it desires to live to the Vanity of this World. This Desire is its Darkness, its Death, its Imprisonment, and Separation from God.

[Pryr-1.2-52] When therefore the first Spark of a Desire after God arises in thy Soul, cherish it with all thy Care, give all thy Heart into it, it is nothing less than a Touch of the Divine Loadstone, that is to draw Thee out of the Vanity of Time into the Riches of Eternity. Get up therefore and follow it as gladly, as the Wise Men of the East followed the Star from Heaven that appeared to them. It will do for Thee, as the Star did for them, it will lead Thee to the Birth of Jesus, not in a Stable at Bethlehem in Judea, but to the Birth of Jesus in the dark Centre of thy own fallen Soul.

[Pryr-1.2-53] I shall conclude this first Part, with the Words of the heavenly Illuminated, and blessed Jacob Behmen.

[Pryr-1.2-54] "It is much to be lamented, that we are so blindly led, and the Truth withheld from us through imaginary Conceptions; for if the Divine Power in the inward Ground of the Soul was manifest, and working with its Lustre in us, then is the whole Triune God present in the Life and Will of the Soul, and the Heaven, wherein God dwells, is opened in the Soul, and There, in the

Soul, is the Place where the Father begets his Son, and where the Holy Ghost proceeds from the Father and the Son.

[Pryr-1.2-55] "Christ saith, I am the Light of the World, he that followeth me, walketh not in Darkness. He directs us only to himself, He is the Morning Star, and is generated and riseth in us, and shineth in the Darkness of our Nature. O how great a Triumph is there in the Soul, when he ariseth in it! then a Man knows, as he never knew before, that he is a Stranger in a foreign Land."

A PRAYER

[Pryr-1.2-56] Oh heavenly Father, infinite, fathomless Depth of never- ceasing Love, save me from myself, from the disorderly Workings of my fallen, long corrupted Nature, and let mine Eyes see, my Heart and Spirit feel and find, thy Salvation in Christ Jesus.

[Pryr-1.2-57] O God, who madest me for thyself, to show forth thy Goodness in me, manifest, I humbly beseech Thee, the Life-giving Power of thy holy Nature within me; help me to such a true and living Faith in Thee, such Strength of Hunger and Thirst after the Birth, Life, and Spirit of thy Holy Jesus in my Soul, that all that is within me, may be turned from every inward Thought, or outward Work, that is not Thee, thy holy Jesus, and heavenly working in my Soul. Amen.

Part Two

The First Dialogue Between Academicus, Rustics and Theophilus at which Humanus was present

[Pryr-2.1-1] ACAD.   Well met, honest Rusticus. I can now tell you with much Pleasure, that we shall soon see a Second Part of The Spirit of Prayer. And as soon as I get it, I will come and read it to you.

[Pryr-2.1-2] Rust. I have often told you, Academicus, that I wondered at your Eagerness and Impatience to see more of this Matter. As to my Part, I have no such Thirst within me, and should make no Complaint, if it never came out.

[Pryr-2.1-3] Acad. My Friend Rusticus, you cannot read; and that is the Reason, that you are not in my State of Impatience, to see another Book.

[Pryr-2.1-4] Rust. Indeed, Academicus, you quite mistake the Matter. The First Part of the Spirit of Prayer you read to me more than three or four times, and that is the Reason, why I am in no State of Eagerness after a Second Part. I have found in the First Part, all that I need to know of God, of Christ, of myself, of Heaven, of Hell, of Sin, of Grace, of Death, and of Salvation: That all these Things have their Being, their Life, and their Working, in my own Heart: That God is always in me, that Christ is always within me; that he is the inward Light and Life of my Soul, a Bread from Heaven, of which I may always eat; a Water of eternal Life springing up in my Soul, of which I may always drink. O my Friend, these Truths have opened a new Life in my Soul: I am brought home to myself; the Veil is taken off from my Heart; I have found my God; I know that his Dwelling-place, his Kingdom, is within me. What need we then call out for Books written only with Pen and Ink, when such a Book as this, so full of Wonders, is once opened in our own Hearts? My Eyes, my Ears, my Thoughts, are all turned inwards, because all that God, and Christ, and Grace, are doing for me, all that the Devil, the World, and the Flesh, are working against me, are only to be known, and found there. What need then of so much News from abroad, since all that concerns either Life or Death, are all transacting, and all at work, within me?

[Pryr-2.1-5] How could I be said to have felt these great Truths, to be sensible of these Riches of Eternity treasured up in my Soul, to know what a great Good the Divine Nature is in me, and to me, if, instead of turning all the Desire and Delight of my Heart towards them, I only felt a Longing and Desire to read more concerning the Spirit of Prayer? No, Academicus, another, and a better Fire is kindled within me; my Heart is in motion, and all that is within me tends towards God; and I find that nothing concerns me more, than to keep my Heart from wandering after anything else. I now know to what it is that I am daily to die, and to what it is that I am daily to live; and therefore look upon every Day as lost, that does not help forwards both this Death, and this Life, in me. I have not yet done half, what the First Part of the Spirit of Prayer directs me to do; and therefore have but little Occasion to call out for a Second.

[Pryr-2.1-6] Theoph. Indeed, Academicus, I must own, that honest Rusticus, as you called him, has spoken well. Your Education has so accustomed you to the Pleasure of reading Variety of Books, that you hardly propose any other End in reading, than the Entertainment of your Mind: Thus the Spirit of Prayer has only awakened in you a Desire to see another Part upon the same Subject. This Fault is very common to others, as well as Scholars, and even to those who only delight in reading good Books.

[Pryr-2.1-7] Philo for this twenty Years has been collecting and reading all the spiritual Books he can hear of. He reads them, as the Critics read Commentators and Lexicons, to be nice and exact in telling you the Style, Spirit, and Intent of this or that spiritual Writer, how one is more accurate in this, and the other in that. Philo will ride you forty Miles in Winter to have a Conversation about spiritual Books, or to see a Collection larger than his own. Philo is amazed at the Deadness and Insensibility of the Christian World, that they are such Strangers to the inward Life and spiritual Nature of the Christian Salvation; he wonders how they can be so zealous for the outward Letter and Form of Ordinances, and so averse to that spiritual Life, that they all point at, as the one thing needful. But Philo never thinks how wonderful it is, that a Man who knows Regeneration to be the Whole, should yet content himself with the Love of Books upon the new Birth, instead of being born again himself. For all that is changed in Philo, is his Taste for Books. He is no more dead to the World, no more delivered from himself, is as fearful of Adversity, as fond of Prosperity, as easily provoked, and pleased with Trifles, as much governed by his own Will, Tempers, and Passions, as unwilling to deny his Appetites, or enter into War with himself, as he was twenty Years ago. Yet all is well with Philo; he has no Suspicion of himself; he dates the Newness of his Life, and the Fullness of his Light, from the time that he discovered the Pearl of Eternity in spiritual Authors.

[Pryr-2.1-8] All this, Academicus, is said on your Account, that you may not lose the Benefit of this Spark of the Divine Life that is kindled in your Soul, but may conform yourself suitably to so great a Gift of God.

[Pryr-2.1-9] It demands at present an Eagerness of another Kind, than that of much reading, even upon the most spiritual Matters.

[Pryr-2.1-10] Acad. I thank you, Theophilus, for your good Will towards me; but did not imagine my Eagerness after such Books to be so great and dangerous a Mistake. And if I do not yet entirely give in to what you say, it is because a Friend of yours has told us (and as I thought by way of Direction) that he has been a diligent Reader of all the spiritual Authors, from the apostolical Dionysius down to the illuminated Guion, and celebrated Fenelon of Cambray. And therefore it would never have come into my Head, to suspect it to be a Fault, or dangerous, to follow his Example.

[Pryr-2.1-11] Theoph. I have said nothing, my Friend, with a Design of hindering your Acquaintance with all the truly spiritual Writers. I would rather in a right Way help you to a true Intimacy with them: For they are Friends of God, entrusted with his Secrets, and Partakers of the Divine Nature: And he that converses rightly with them, has a Happiness, that can hardly be over-valued.

[Pryr-2.1-12] My Intention is only to abate, for a time, a Spirit of Eagerness after much reading, which in your State has more of Nature than Grace in it; which seeks Delight in a Variety of new Notions, and rather gratifies Curiosity, than reforms the Heart.

[Pryr-2.1-13] Suppose you had seen an Angel from Heaven, who had discovered to you a Glimpse of its own internal Brightness, and of that glorious Union in which it lived with God, opening more of itself to the inward Sight of your Mind, than you could either forget or relate. Suppose it had told you with a piercing Word, and living Impression, that all its own angelic and heavenly Brightness was hid in yourself, concealed from you under a bestial Covering of Flesh and Blood; that this Flesh and Blood was become the Master of it, would not suffer it to breathe, or stir, or come to Life in you. Suppose it had told you, that all your Life had been spent in helping this Flesh and Blood to more and more Power over you, to hinder you from knowing and feeling this Divine Life within you. Suppose it had told you, that to this Day you had lived in the grossest Self-idolatry, loving, serving, honouring, and adoring yourself instead of loving, serving, and adoring God with all your Heart, and Soul, and Spirit: That all your Intentions, Projects, Cares, Pleasures, and Indulgences, had been only so much Labour to bring you to the Grave in a total Ignorance of that great Work, for which alone you were born into the World.

[Pryr-2.1-14] Suppose it had told you, that all this Blindness and Insensibility of your State, was obstinately and willfully brought upon yourself, because you had boldly slighted and resisted all the daily inward and outward Calls of God to your Soul, all the Teachings, Doings, and Sufferings, of a Son of God to redeem you. Suppose it left you with this Farewell, "O Man awake; thy Work is great, thy Time is short, I am thy last Trumpet; the Grave calls for thy Flesh and Blood, thy Soul must enter into a new Lodging. To be born again, is to be an Angel: Not to be born again is to become a Devil."

[Pryr-2.1-15] Tell me now, Academicus, what would you expect from a Man who had been thus awakened, and pierced by the Voice of an Angel? Could you think he had any Sense left, if he was not cast into the deepest Depth of Humility, Self-dejection, and Self-abhorrence? Casting himself, with a broken Heart, at the Feet of the Divine Mercy, desiring nothing but that, from that Time, every Moment of his Life might be given unto God, in the most perfect Denial of every Temper, Will, and Inclination, that nourished the Corruption of his Nature: Wishing and praying from the Bottom of his Heart, that God would lead him into and through every thing inwardly and outwardly, that might destroy the evil Workings of his Nature, and awaken all that was holy and heavenly within him; that the Seed of Eternity, the Spark of Life, that he had so long quenched and smothered under earthly Rubbish, might breathe, and come to Life, in him.

[Pryr-2.1-16] Or would you think he was enough affected with this angelic Visit, if all that it had awakened in him, was only a Longing and eager Desire to hear the same, or another Angel talk again?

[Pryr-2.1-17] Acad. O Theophilus, you have said enough: For all that is within me consents to the Truth and Justness of what you have said. I now feel in the strongest Manner, that I have been rather amused, than edified, by what I have read.

[Pryr-2.1-18] Theoph. A spiritual Book, Academicus, is a Call to as real and total a Death to the

Life of corrupt Nature, as that which Adam died in Paradise, was to the Life of Heaven. He indeed died at once totally to the Divine Life in which he was created: But as our Body of Earth is to last to the End of our Lives; so to the End of our earthly Life, every Step we take, every Inch of our Road, is to be made up of Denial, and dying to ourselves; because all our Redemption consists in our regaining that first Life of Heaven in the Soul, to which Adam died in Paradise. And therefore the one single Work of Redemption, is the one single Work of Regeneration, or the raising up of a Life, and Spirit, and Tempers, and Inclinations, contrary to that Life and Spirit which we derive from our earthly fallen Parents. To think therefore of anything, but the continual, total Denial of our earthly Nature, is to overlook the very one thing on which all depends. And to hope for anything, to trust or pray for anything, but the Life of God, or a Birth of Heaven, in our Souls, is as useless to us, as placing our Hope and Trust in a graven Image. Thus saith the Christ of God the one Pattern, and Author of our Salvation: "If any Man will be my Disciple, let him deny himself, hate his own Life, take up his daily Cross, and follow me." And again: "Unless a Man be born again from above, of Water and the Spirit, he cannot see, or enter into, the Kingdom of God."

[Pryr-2.1-19] Now is your time, Academicus, to enter deeply into this great Truth. You are just come out of the Slumber of Life, and begin to see with new Eyes the Nature of your Salvation. You are charmed with the Discovery of a Kingdom of Heaven hidden within you, and long to be entertained more and more with the Nature, Progress, and Perfection of the new Birth, or the Opening of the Kingdom of God in your Soul.

[Pryr-2.1-20] But my Friend, stop a little. It is indeed great Joy, that the Pearl of great Price is found; but take notice, that it is not yours, you can have no Possession of it, till as the Merchant did, you sell all that you have, and buy it. Now Self is all that you have, it is your sole Possession; you have no Goods of your own, nothing is yours but this Self. The Riches of Self are your own Riches; but all this Self is to be parted with before the Pearl is yours. Think of a lower Price, or be unwilling to give thus much for it, plead in your Excuse, that you keep the Commandments, and then you are that very rich young Man in the Gospel, who went away sorrowful from our Lord, when he had said, "If thou wilt be perfect," that is, if thou wilt obtain the Pearl, "sell all that thou hast, and give to the Poor"; that is, die to all thy Possession of Self, and then thou hast given all that thou hast to the Poor: all that thou hast is devoted and used for the Love of God and thy Neighbour. This selling all, Academicus, is the Measure of your dying to Self; all of it is to be given up; it is an apostate Nature, a stolen Life, brought forth in Rebellion against God: it is a continual Departure from him. It corrupts everything it touches; it defiles everything it receives; it turns all the Gifts and Blessings of God into Covetousness, Partiality, Pride, Hatred, and Envy. All these Tempers are born, and bred, and nourished, in Self; they have no other Place to live in, no Possibility of Existence, but in that Creature which is fallen from a Life in God, into a Life in Self.

[Pryr-2.1-21] Acad. Pray, Sir, tell me more plainly, what this Self is, since so much depends upon it.

[Pryr-2.1-22] Theoph. It is Hell, it is the Devil, it is Darkness, Pain, and Disquiet. It is the one only Enemy of Christ, the great Antichrist. It is the Scarlet Whore, the fiery Dragon, the old Serpent, the devouring Beast, that is mentioned in the Revelation of St. John.

[Pryr-2.1-23] Acad. You rather terrify than instruct me, by this Description.

[Pryr-2.1-24] Theoph. It is indeed a very frightful Matter; it contains everything that Man has to dread and hate, to resist and avoid. Yet be assured, my Friend, that, careless and merry as the World is, every Man that is born into it, has all these Enemies to overcome within himself. And

every Man, till he is in the Way of Regeneration, is more or less governed by them. No Hell in any remote Place, no Devil that is separate from you, no Darkness or Pain that is not within you, no Antichrist either at Rome or England, no furious Beast, no fiery Dragon, without, or apart from you, can do you any Hurt. It is your own Hell, your own Devil, your own Beast, your own Antichrist, your own Dragon, that lives in your own Heart's Blood, that alone can hurt you. [Pryr-2.1-25] Die to this Self, to this inward Nature; and then all outward Enemies are overcome. Live to this Self, and then, when this Life is out, all that is within you, and all that is without you, will be nothing else but a mere seeing and feeling this Hell, Serpent, Beast, and fiery Dragon. [Pryr-2.1-26] See here, Academicus, the twofold Nature of every Man. He has within him a redeeming Power, the Meekness of the heavenly Life, called the Lamb of God. This seed is surrounded, or encompassed, with the Beast of fleshly Lusts, the Serpent of Guile and Subtlety, and the Dragon of fiery Wrath. This is the great Trial, or strife of human Life, whether a Man will live to the Lusts of the Beast, the Guile of the Serpent, the Pride and Wrath of the fiery Dragon, or give himself up to the Meekness, Patience, the Sweetness, the Simplicity, the Humility, of the Lamb of God.
[Pryr-2.1-27] This is the Whole of the Matter between God and the Creature. On one Side, Fire and Wrath, awakened first by the rebellious Angels; and on the other Side, the Meekness of the Lamb of God, the Patience of Divine Love coming down from Heaven, to stop and overcome the Fire and Wrath that is broken out in Nature and Creature. Your Father Adam has introduced you into the Fire and Wrath of the fallen Angels, into a World from whence Paradise is departed. Your Flesh and Blood is kindled in that Sin, which first brought forth a murdering Cain. But, dear Soul, be of good Comfort, for the Meekness, the Love, the Heart, the Lamb of God, is become Man, has set himself in the Birth of thy own Life, that in him, and with him, and by a Birth from him, Heaven and Paradise may be again opened both within thee, and without thee, not for a Time, but to all Eternity.
[Pryr-2.1-28] Once more, Academicus. Every Man in this World stands essentially in Heaven, and in Hell, both as to that which is within him and that which is without him: For Man and the World are both in the same fallen state. The Curse in the Earth is that same thing in outward Nature, that the Loss of the Divine Life was to the Soul of Adam. The whole World, in all its Nature, is nothing else but a real Mixture of Heaven and Hell. The Sun and Water of this World, is that which keeps under and overcomes the Darkness, Wrath, and Fire of Hell, and carries on the vegetable and animal Life that is in it. The Light of the Sun blesses all the Workings of the Elements, and the cool softening Essence of the Water, keeps under the Fire and Wrath of Nature. In all animal Creatures, the Birth of Light in their own Life, and the Water of their own Blood, both produced by the Light of the Sun, and the Water of outward Nature, bring forth an Order of earthly Creatures, that can enjoy the Good that is in this World in Spite of the Wrath of Hell, and the Malice of Devils.
[Pryr-2.1-29] But Man has more than all this; for being at first created an Angel, and intended by the Mercy of God to be an Angel again, he has the Light of Heaven, and the Water of eternal Life, both given to Adam in that Seed of the Woman, which was to bruise the Head of the Serpent that is, to overcome the Curse, the Fire, and Wrath, or Hell, that was awakened in the fallen Soul. So that Man has not only, in common with the other Animals, the Light and Water of outward Nature, to quench the Wrath of his own Life in this mixed World, but he has the Meekness, the Light, the Love, the Humility of the Holy Jesus, as a Seed of Life born in his Soul, to bring forth that first Image of God, in which Adam was created. This, my Friend, is the true Ground of all true Religion: It means nothing, it intends nothing, but to overcome that earthly

Life, which overcame Adam in the Fall, that made him a Prisoner of Hell, and a Slave to the corrupt Workings of earthly Flesh and Blood. And therefore you may see, and know with a mathematical Certainty, that the one thing necessary for every fallen Soul, is to die to all the Life that we have from this World, that the Life of Heaven may be born again in him. The Life of this World is the Life of the Beast, the Scarlet Whore, the old Serpent and the fiery Dragon.

[Pryr-2.1-30] Hence it is that Sin rides in triumph over Church and State, and from the Court to the Cottage all is over-run with Sensuality, Guile, Falseness, Pride, Wrath, Envy, Selfishness, and every form of Corruption. Every one swims away in this Torrent, but he who hears and attends to the Voice of the Son of God within him, calling him to die to this Life, to take up his Cross, and follow him. Much learned Pains has been often taken to prove Rome, or Constantinople, to be the Seat of the Beast, the Antichrist, the Scarlet Whore, &c. But, alas! they are not at such a Distance from us, they are the Properties of fallen human Nature, and are all of them alive in our own Selves, till we are dead or dying to all the Spirit and Tempers of this World. They are everywhere, in every Soul, where the heavenly Nature, and Spirit of the Holy Jesus is not. But when the human Soul turns from itself, and turns to God, dies to itself, and lives to God in the Spirit, Tempers, and Inclinations of the Holy Jesus, loving, pitying, suffering, and praying for all its Enemies, and overcoming all Evil with Good, as this Christ of God did; then, but not till then, are these Monsters separate from it. For Covetousness and Sensuality of all kinds, are the very devouring Beast; Religion governed by a worldly, trading Spirit, and gratifying the partial Interest of Flesh and Blood, is nothing else but the Scarlet Whore; Guile, and Craft, and Cunning, are the very Essence of the old Serpent; Self-Interest and Self-Exaltation are the whole Nature of Antichrist. Pride, Persecution, Wrath, Hatred and Envy, are the very Essence of the fiery Dragon.

[Pryr-2.1-31] This, Academicus, is the fallen human Nature, and this is the old Man, which is alive in every one, though in various Manners, till he is born again from above. To think therefore of anything in Religion, or to pretend to real Holiness, without totally dying to this old Man, is building Castles in the Air, and can bring forth nothing, but Satan in the form of an Angel of Light. Would you know, Academicus, whence it is, that so many false Spirits have appeared in the World, who have deceived themselves and others with false Fire, and false Light, laying Claim to Inspirations, Illuminations, and Openings of the Divine Life, pretending to do Wonders under extraordinary Calls from God? It is this; they have turned to God without turning from themselves; would be alive in God, before they were dead to their own Nature; a thing as impossible in itself, as for a Grain of Wheat to be alive before it dies.

[Pryr-2.1-32] Now Religion in the Hands of Self, or corrupt Nature, serves only to discover Vices of a worse kind, than in Nature left to itself. Hence are all the disorderly Passions of religious Men, which burn in a worse Flame than Passions only employed about worldly Matters: Pride, Self-Exaltation, Hatred and Persecution, under a Cloak of religious Zeal, will sanctify Actions, which Nature, left to itself, would be ashamed to own.

[Pryr-2.1-33] You may now see, Academicus, with what great Reason I have called you, at your first setting out, to this great Point, the total dying to Self, as the only Foundation of a solid Piety. All the fine Things you hear or read of an inward and spiritual Life in God, all your Expectations of the Light and Holy Spirit of God, will become a false Food to your Soul, till you only seek for them through Death to Self.

[Pryr-2.1-34] Observe, Sir, the Difference which Clothes make in those, who have it in their Power to dress as they please: Some are all for Show, Colours, and Glitter; others are quite fantastical and affected in their Dress; Some have a grave and solemn Habit; others are quite simple and plain in the whole manner. Now all this Difference of Dress, is only an outward Difference, that covers the same poor Carcase, and leaves it full of all its own Infirmities. Now all the Truths of the Gospel, when only embraced and possessed by the old Man, make only such superficial Difference, as is made by Clothes. Some put on a solemn, formal, prudent, outside Carriage; others appear in all the Glitter and Show of religious Colouring, and spiritual Attainments; but under all this outside Difference, there lies the poor fallen Soul, imprisoned, unhelped, in its own fallen State. And thus it must be, it is not possible to be otherwise, till the spiritual Life begins at the true Root, grows out of Death, and is born in a broken Heart, a Heart broken off from all its own natural Life. Then Self-hatred, Self-contempt, and Self-denial, are as suitable to this new-born Spirit, as Self-love, Self-esteem, and Self-seeking, are to the unregenerate Man. Let me, therefore, my Friend, conjure you, not to look forward, or cast about for spiritual Advancement, till you have rightly taken this first Step in the spiritual Life. All your future Progress depends upon it: For this Depth of Religion goes no deeper than the Depth of your Malady: For Sin has its Root in the Bottom of your Soul, it comes to Life with your Flesh and Blood, and breathes in the Breath of your natural Life; and therefore, till you die to Nature, you live to Sin; and whilst this Root of Sin is alive in you, all the Virtues you put on, are only like fine painted Fruit hung upon a bad Tree.

[Pryr-2.1-35] Acad. Indeed, Theophilus, you have made the Difference between true and false Religion as plain to me, as the Difference between Light and Darkness. But all that you have said, at the same time, is as new to me, as if I had lived in a Land, where Religion had never been named. But pray, Sir, tell me how I am to take this first Step, which you so much insist upon.

[Pryr-2.1-36] Theoph. You are to turn wholly from yourself, and to give up yourself wholly unto God, in this or the like twofold Form of Words or Thoughts:

[Pryr-2.1-37] "Oh my God, with all the Strength of my Soul, assisted by thy Grace, I desire and resolve to resist and deny all my own Will, earthly Tempers, selfish Views, and Inclinations; every thing that the Spirit of this World, and the Vanity of fallen Nature, prompts me to. I give myself up wholly and solely unto Thee, to be all thine, to have, and do, and be, inwardly and outwardly, according to thy good Pleasure. I desire to live for no other Ends, with no other Designs, but to accomplish the Work which thou requirest of me, an humble, obedient, faithful, thankful Instrument in thy Hands to be used as thou pleasest."

[Pryr-2.1-38] You are not to content yourself, my Friend, with now and then, or even many times, making this Oblation of yourself to God. It must be the daily, the hourly Exercise of your Mind; till it is wrought into your very Nature, and becomes an essential State and Habit of your Mind, till you feel yourself as habitually turned from all your own Will, selfish Ends, and earthly Desires, as you are from Stealing and Murder; till the whole Turn and bent of your Spirit points as constantly to God, as the Needle touched with the Loadstone does to the North. This, Sir, is your first and necessary Step in the spiritual Life; this is the Key to all the Treasures of Heaven; this unlocks the sealed Book of your Soul, and makes room for the Light and Spirit of God to arise up in it. Without this, the spiritual Life is but spiritual Talk, and only assists Nature to be pleased with an Holiness that it has not.

[Pryr-2.1-39] The Necessity of this first Step, and the Folly of pretending to succeed without it, is thus represented by our blessed Lord: What man intending to build a House,—

[Pryr-2.1-40] All our Ability and Preparation to succeed in this great Affair, lie in this first Step. You may perhaps think this an hard Saying. But do not go away sorrowful, like the young Man in the Gospel, because he had great Possessions. For, my Friend, you little think what a Deliverance you will have from all Hardships, and what a Flow of Happiness is found even in this Life, as soon as the Soul is thus dead to Self, freed from its own Passions, and wholly given up to God; of which I shall speak to you by and by. I have told you the Price of the new Birth. I shall now leave you to consider, whether you will be so wise a Merchant, as to give up all the Wealth of the old Man for this heavenly Pearl. I do not expect your Answer now, but will stay for it till To-morrow.

[Pryr-2.1-41] But pray, Gentlemen, who is this Humanus? I do not remember to have seen him before; He seems not willing to speak, yet is often biting his Lips at what is said.

[Pryr-2.1-42] Rust. This Humanus, Sir, is my Neighbour; but so ignorant of the Nature of the Gospel, that he is often trying to persuade me into a Disbelief of it. I say ignorant (though he is a learned Man) because I am well assured, that no Man ever did, or can oppose the Gospel, but through a total Ignorance of what it is in itself; For the Gospel, when rightly understood, is irresistible; it brings more good News to the human Nature, than Sight to the Blind, Limbs to the Lame, Health to the Sick, or Liberty to the condemned Slave. But this Neighbour of mine has never yet been in Sight of the Truth, as it is in the Gospel; he knows nothing of the Grounds and Reason of it, but what he has picked up out of Books, that have been written against it, and for it. He often makes use of one Maxim of the Gospel, to overthrow it, and wonders that so plain and honest a Man as I am, will not submit to it. He says, if it be a Truth, as the Gospel saith, That the Tree must be known by its Fruit, and that a good Tree cannot bring forth corrupt Fruit, we need only look at the Lives of Christians, the Craft of Priests, the Wars, Contentions, Hatreds, Sects, Parties, Heresies, Divisions, Outrages, and Persecutions, which Christianity has brought forth, we need only look at this, to have all our Senses and Reason assure us, that the Gospel must be a bad Tree.

[Pryr-2.1-43] But this is enough concerning the Man. He comes with me at his own earnest Desire, which has lately seized him, and upon his own strict Promise, not to interrupt our Conversation; but to be a silent Hearer, till it is all over. And therefore, if you please, Sir, I beg our Conversation may for a while turn upon the chief Points asserted in The Spirit of Prayer, for two Reasons; first, that Academicus may see what Reasons I had for saying, that Book had given me a sufficient Instruction; and also that Humanus, hearing these great Points, may hear the whole Ground and Nature, the Necessity and Blessedness of the Christian Redemption, set forth in such a Degree of Light, and Truth, and Amiableness, as he had no Notion of before.

[Pryr-2.1-44] Theoph. Your Neighbour is welcome, and I pray God to give him an Heart attentive to those Truths, which have made so good an Impression upon you. The first Point that you desire us to speak to, is concerning the Original of this temporal World. How God was moved to create it, upon the Fall of a whole Host, or Kingdom of Angels, who, by their Revolt from God, lost the Divine Light, and awakened in themselves, and the Region in which they dwelt, the dark, wrathful Fire of Hell: For Hell is nothing else, but Nature departed, or excluded, from the Beams of Divine Light. The Materiality of their Kingdom was spiritual, and the Light that glanced through it, that filled its Transparency with an Infinity of glorious Wonders, was the Son of God, the brightness of the Father's Glory. The Spirit that animated the inward Life of those glorious Angels, and that moved with its sweet Breath, through all this glassy Sea, opening and changing new Scenes in the Mirror of Divine Wisdom, was the Holy Spirit of God, that eternally proceeds from the Father and the Son. Thus did these celestial Spirits live, move, and have their Being, in God. All was Heaven, and they all were so many created Gods, eternally sinking down, and rising up, into new Heights and Depths of the Riches of the Divine Nature. With this Degree of Glory and Happiness was the whole Extent of the Place of this World filled, before the Angels fell: and to this Degree of Happiness, and heavenly Glory, will the whole

Place of this World be again raised, when the Love of God shall have finished the great Work of the Redemption of Mankind. Heaven again, and Angels again, raised out of the Misery of Time, to sing eternal Praises to the Holy Trinity, and to the Lamb that has overcome Sin, and Death, and Hell, and turned all the Wrath, and Misery and Darkness of this World, into an Heaven never more to be changed. Oh Rusticus, what Sentiments do these Things raise in you?

[Pryr-2.1-45] Rust. Indeed, Sir, they almost make me to forget, that I am in the Body. You have set me upon a Mountain, from which, whether I look backwards, or forwards, or downwards, all is equally surprising: backwards, a Breach made in Heaven, the first Opening of Hell and Darkness, and a new Creation out of the Ruins of the fallen Angels; forwards, Time and all temporal Nature rising again into its first Eternity; downwards, a Globe of Earth, the Seat of War between Heaven and Hell, where Men are born to partake of the dreadful Strife, and have only the little Span of Life, either to overcome with God, or be overcome by the Devil. Oh, Sir, what great things are these? I wish that all the World, as well as my Neighbour Humanus, were forced to be silent Hearers of them. But pray, Sir, go on.

[Pryr-2.1-46] Theoph. When God saw the Darkness that was upon the Face of the Deep, and the whole angelic Habitation become a Chaos of Confusion, the Spirit of God moved upon the Face of the Waters; that is, the Spirit of God began to operate again in this outward Darkness, that covered this once transparent glassy Sea; for from a glassy Sea it was become a Deep covered with Darkness, which was soon to take another Nature; to have its Fire and Wrath converted into Sun and Stars; its Dross and Darkness into a Globe of Earth; its Mobility and Moisture into Air and Water; when the Spirit of God began to move and operate in it. But before this Chaos had entered into this new Order, God said, "Let there be Light"; and there was Light. This Light, my Friend, was not the present Light of this World, which now governs the Night and the Day; for the Sun, the Moon, and Stars, were not created till the fourth Day. But the Light which God then spoke forth, was a Degree of Heaven, that was commanded to glance into the darkened Deep, which penetrated through all the Depth of the Chaos, and intermixed itself through every Part; not turning the Whole into a Region of Light, but only by its quickening Virtue fitting, disposing, and preparing every Part to take that Change, which every following Day of the Creation was to bring forth, in and out of this darkened Deep: For Darkness is Death, and Light is Life. This was the Nature and Work of that first Light, which God called forth on the first Day: It was God's baptizing the dead Chaos with the Spirit of Life, that it might be capable of a Resurrection into a new Creation.

[Pryr-2.1-47] See here the Uniformity of the divine Procedure, with regard both to fallen Nature and Creature. When the Creature (Man) was fallen, his Redemption was begun by God's speaking a Seed of Light, called the Seed of the Woman, into the Birth of his Life. This alone could qualify him for the new Creation in Christ Jesus. When Nature was fallen, its Restoration was begun in the same Manner: Light was commanded to enter into it, or rather to rise up in it: this was its Power or Possibility of coming out of its fallen State.

[Pryr-2.1-48] Marvel not, Rusticus, that I call this first Light of the first Day, a Degree of Heaven: For Light is natural, essential, and inseparable from Heaven; it belongs only to Heaven; and wherever else it is, it is only there as a Gift from Heaven. And therefore so much as there is of Light in this World, so much there is of Heaven in it. Darkness is natural, essential, and inseparable from Hell; and can be nowhere else, but where Hell can in some Degree open and discover itself. And wherever, and in what Degree, Darkness can show itself; there, and in the same Degree, is the Nature of Hell known and felt. This World is made up of Light and Darkness, not only as it consists of Day and Night, but because every earthly thing is itself a

Mixture of Light and Darkness. The Darkness is the Evil, and the Light is the Good, that is in every thing. If the Darkness was predominant in Vegetables, they would all be rank Poison; if in Animals, they would be all as so many wrathful venomous Serpents of Hell. If the Light did quite suppress the Darkness in Vegetables, they would be like the Fruits which were to have been Man's Food in Paradise.

[Pryr-2.1-49] Rust. These Things, Theophilus, strike a most amazing Light into all the Mysteries both of Nature and Grace. But they do not more enlighten, than they edify the Mind. They are all reforming Truths; they have the Nature of Alternatives, they purge the Heart of all its Dross; they force it to drop all its Pretensions to earthly things, as the poor deceitful Baits of fallen Nature; and to long for nothing, but to have That first Heaven and Life in God, for which Angels and Men were at first created. But I want to show to my friend Humanus, as it were in one View, that Chain of Truths, which follows from what you have said: Though I had rather you would do it.

[Pryr-2.1-50] Theoph. Agreed: And I will set them in order thus. First, That the Place of this World is the very Place, or Region, which belonged to Lucifer, and his Angels. 2dly, That everything that we see in this World, all its Elements, the Stars, the Firmament, &c., are nothing else but the invisible Things of the fallen World, made visible in a new and lower State of Existence. 3dly, that before the Rebellion of the Angels there was nothing but God, and Heaven, and heavenly Beings. Light, and Love, and Joy, and Glory, with all the Wonders thereof, were the only things seen and felt by the Angels. Darkness and Fire, with every Quality thereof, were absolutely unknown to the Angels; they had no more Suspicion of them, than of the possibility of Sickness, Pains, Heat, and Cold. All they aimed at, was at being higher in the Glories, and Powers, and Light, of that Heaven in which they lived. But their turning to their own Strength to effect this, was their whole turning from God, and a falling into Nature without God, which was the first Discovery of Darkness, Wrath, and Fire, and Pain, and Torment. 4thly, hence it appears, that Darkness is the Ground of the Substance, or Materiality of Nature; Fire is its Life; and Light is its glorious Transmutation into the Kingdom of Heaven; and Spirit is the Opener of all its Wonders. All that can be conceived, is either God, or Nature, or Creature; God is the Holy Trinity without, or before Nature; but Nature is the Manifestation of the Holy Trinity in a triune Life of Fire, Light, and Spirit.

[Pryr-2.1-51] 5thly. Here we see the plain and true Original of all Evil, without any Perplexity, or Imputation upon God: That Evil is nothing else but the Wrath, and Fire, and Darkness of Nature broken off from God: That the Punishment, the Pain, or the Hell of Sin, is no designedly prepared, or arbitrary Penalty inflicted by God, but the Natural and necessary State of the Creature, that leaves, or turns from God. 6thly, That the Will of the Creature is the only Opener of all Evil or Good in the Creature; the Will stands between God and Nature, and must in all its Workings unite either with God, or Nature: the Will totally resigned, and given up to God, is one Spirit with God, and God dwelleth in it; the Will turned from God, is taken Prisoner in the Wrath, Fire, and Darkness of Nature.

[Pryr-2.1-52] 7thly. Here we see, how and why a Creature can lose, and die to all its Happiness and Perfection, and, from a beauteous Angel become a deformed Devil. It is because Nature has no Beauty, Happiness, or Perfection, but solely from the Manifestation or Birth of the Holy Trinity in it. God manifested in Nature, is the only Blessing, Happiness, and Perfection of Nature. Therefore the Creature, that in the Working of its Will is turned from God, must have as great a Change brought forth in it, as that of Heaven into Hell, forced to live, but to have no other Life, but that of its own gnawing Worm left to itself.

[Pryr-2.1-53] 8thly. Hence we see the deep Ground, and absolute Necessity, of the Christian

Redemption, by a Birth from above, of the Light and Spirit of God, demonstrated in the most absolute Degree of Certainty. It is because all Nature is in itself nothing, but an hungry wrathful Fire of Life, a tormenting Darkness, unless the Light and Spirit of God kindle it into a Kingdom of Heaven. And therefore the fallen Soul can have no possible Relief, or Redemption, it must be, to all Eternity, an hungry, dark, fiery, tormenting Spirit of Life, unless the Light, or Son, and Spirit of God, be born again in it.

[Pryr-2.1-54] Hence also it follows, that in all the Possibility of Things, there is and can be but one Happiness, and one Misery. The one Misery, is Nature and Creature left to itself; the one Happiness, is the Life, the Light, and Spirit of God, manifested in Nature and Creature. This is the true Meaning of those Words of our Lord, "There is but one that is good, and that is God."

[Pryr-2.1-55] 9thly. Hence it is also seen, that there is and can be but one true Religion for the fallen Soul, and that is, the Dying to Self, to Nature and Creature; and a turning with all the Will, the Desire, and Delight of the Soul to God. Sacrifices, Oblations, Prayers, Praises, Rites, and Ceremonies, without this are but as sounding Brass, and tinkling Cymbals. Nay, Zeal, and Constancy, and Warmth, and Fervour, in the Performance of these religious Practices, is not the Matter; for Nature and Self-love can do all this. But these religious Practices are then only Parts of true Religion, when they mean nothing, seek nothing, but to keep up a continual Dying to Self, and all worldly things, and turn all the Will, Desire, and Delight of the Soul to God alone. Lastly, There is and can be only one Salvation for the fallen Soul, and that is Heaven opened again in the Soul, by the Birth of such a Life, Light, and Spirit, as is born in Angels. For Adam was created to possess that Heaven from which the Angels fell; but nothing can enter into Heaven, but the angelic Life, which is born of Heaven. The Loss of this angelic Life was the Fall of Adam, or that Death which he died, on the Day he did eat of the earthly Fruit; therefore the Regeneration, or new Birth of his first angelic Life, is the one only Salvation of the fallen Soul. Ask not therefore, whether we are saved by Faith, or by Works? for we are saved by neither of them. Faith and Works are at first only preparatory to the new Birth; afterwards they are the true genuine Fruits and Effects of it. But the new Birth, a Life from Heaven, the new Creature, called Christ in us, is the one only Salvation of the fallen Soul. Nothing can enter into Heaven, but this Life which is born of, and comes from Heaven.

[Pryr-2.1-56] Rust. I thank you, Theophilus, for setting these awakening Truths in so strong a Light. And I think it is not possible for my friend Humanus to be unaffected with them.

[Pryr-2.1-57] They must needs open in him a new Way of thinking about Religion, and show him the deep and solid Ground of the absolute Necessity of the Christian Redemption, and incline him to be a willing Hearer of that which follows.

[Pryr-2.1-58] Theoph. I hope it will be so, Rusticus; and what I would here, and through every Point we speak of, observe to your Friend Humanus, is this: That the Christian Religion is the one only true Religion of Nature, deeply and necessarily founded in the Nature of Things; that its Doctrines are not founded in an arbitrary Appointment of God, but have their natural and necessary Reason, why they cannot be otherwise, as has here been shown in the one great Point of Regeneration, which is the Whole of Man's Salvation, and the one only thing intended by all Revelation, from the Fall of Man to the End of the World. Now the true Ground of the one true Religion of Nature cannot be known, or seen into, but by going back to the Beginning of Things, and showing how they came into their present State. We must find out, why and how Religion came to be necessary, and on what its Necessity is founded. Now this cannot be done, unless we find out, what Sin, and Evil, and Death, and Darkness, are in themselves; and how they came into Nature and Creature. For this alone can show us, what Religion is true, is natural, is necessary, and alone sufficient to remove all Evil, Sin, and Disorder, out of the Creation. For this Reason, we began with the Grounds and Reasons of the Creation of this World, showing how it came to be as it is. But this could not be done, but by going so far back as the Fall of Angels. For it was their Revolting from God, that brought Wrath, and Fire, and Thickness, and Darkness, and Death, into Nature and Creature; and so gave occasion to this new Creation, and to its being in such a State, and of such a Nature, as it is.

[Pryr-2.1-59] For who does not see, that this first Deadness, Thickness, Wrath, Fire, and Darkness, caused by the Angels' Sin, are the very Materials out of which this World is made? For are not the Fire, the Air, the Water, the Earth, the Rocks and Stones of this World, the Rage of Heat and Cold, the Succession of Day and Night, the Wrath of Storms and Tempests, an undeniable and daily Proof of all this? Now when we thus see what Sin, and Evil, and Death, and Darkness, are in Nature, and how they came into it, then we see also, how and what they are, and how they came into the Creature; because the Creature has its Form, its Being, in and out of Nature. They came into Nature, or rose up in it, by Nature's being broken off from God, and so losing the Light and Spirit of God, which made it to be a Kingdom of Heaven; we see also, that when this disordered Nature was to be taken out of its fallen State by a new Creation, that, to do this, the Spirit of God moved, or entered again into the Darkness of the Waters, and the Light of God was called into it. A plain Proof, that the Malady of Nature, was nothing else but its Loss of the Light and Spirit of God working in it. This shows us also, that the fallen Creature is to be restored, or put into a Way of Recovery, in one and the same Way as fallen Nature; viz., by the Spirit, and Light of God entering into it again, and bringing forth a new Birth, or Creation in Christ Jesus. Just as the Spirit and Light entering into the Chaos, created or turned the Angels' ruined Kingdom into a Paradise on Earth. God help him, who can see no Light or Truth here! Your Friend Humanus lays claim to a Religion of Nature and Reason: I join with him, with all my Heart. No other Religion can be right, but that which has its Foundation in Nature. For the God of Nature can require nothing of his Creatures, but what the State of their Nature calls them to. Nature is his great Law, that speaks his whole Will both in Heaven and on Earth; and to obey Nature, is to obey the God of Nature, to please him, and live to him, in the highest Perfection. God indeed has many After-laws; but it is after his Creatures have fallen from Nature, and lost its Perfection. But all these After-laws have no other End or Intention, but to repair Nature, and bring Men back to their first natural State of Perfection. What say you now, Academicus, to all these Matters?

[Pryr-2.1-60] Acad. You, Sir, and Rusticus, both of you know, how these Matters have affected me, ever since I read the book called The Appeal to all that Doubt, &c. From that Time, I have stood upon new Ground; I have seen things in such a Newness of Light and Reality, as makes me take my former Knowledge for a Dream. A Dream I may justly say, since all my Labour was taken up in searching into a Seventeen hundred Years' History of Doctrines, Disputes, Decrees, Heresies, Schisms, and Sects, wherever to be found, in Europe, Asia, and Africa. From this goodly Heap of Stuff crowded into my Mind, I have been settling Matters betwixt all the present Christian Divisions both at home and abroad, according to the best Rules of Criticism; having little or no other Idea of a religious Man, than that of a stiff Maintainer of certain Points against all those that oppose them. And in this respect, I believe I may say, that I only swam away in the common Torrent.

[Pryr-2.1-61] And in this labourious Dream I had in all Likelihood ended my Days, had not that Book, and some others of the like kind, shown me, that Religion lay nearer home, was not to be dug out of Disputes, but lay hid in myself, like a Seed, which, for want of its proper

Nourishment, could not come to the Birth. But however, though Matters stand thus with myself, and I seem to be entered into a Region of Light, yet I must not forget to tell you, what some of my learned Friends object to all this. They say, that in those Books, there are many Things asserted, which have not the plain Letter of Scripture to support them; and therefore Men of sober Learning, are cautious of giving into Opinions, not strictly grounded on the plain Letter of Scripture, however fine and plausible they may seem to be.

[Pryr-2.1-62] Theoph. Is there not some Reason, Academicus, to take this Objection of your learned Friends to be a mere Pretence? For what is more fully grounded upon the plain Letter of Scripture, than the Doctrine of a real Regeneration, a new Birth of the Word, the Son, and Holy Spirit of God, really brought forth in the Soul? And yet this plain Letter of Scripture, upon the most important of all Points, the very Life, and Essence, and whole Nature of our Redemption, is not only overlooked, but openly opposed, by the Generality of Men of sober Learning. But this Point, has not only the plain Letter of Scripture for it, but what the Letter asserts, is absolutely required by the whole Spirit and Tenor of the New Testament. All the Epistles of the Apostles proceed upon the supposed Certainty of this one great Point.

[Pryr-2.1-63] A Son of God, united with, and born in our Nature, that his Nature may have a Birth in us; an Holy Spirit, breathing in the Birth and Life of our Souls, quickening the dead Life of fallen Adam, is the Letter and Spirit of the Apostles' Writings; grounded upon the plain Letter of our Lord's own Words, that unless we are born again from above, of the Son, Word, Water, and Spirit of God, we cannot enter or see the Kingdom of Heaven.

[Pryr-2.1-64] Again: Is it not the plain Letter of Scripture, that Adam died the Day that he did eat of the earthly Tree? Have we not the most solemn Asseveration of God for the Truth of this? Was not the Change which Adam found in himself a Demonstration of the Truth of this Fact? Instead of the Image and Likeness of God in which he was created, the Beauty of Paradise, he was stripped of all his Glory, confounded at the shameful Deformity of his own Body, afraid of being seen, and unable to see himself uncovered; delivered up a Slave to the Rage of all the Stars and Elements of this World, not knowing which Way to look, or what to do in a World, where he was dead to all that he formerly felt, and alive only to a new and dreadful Feeling of Heat and Cold, Shame and Fear, and horrible Remorse of Mind, at his sad Entrance in a World, whence Paradise, and God, and his own Glory, were departed. Death enough surely!

[Pryr-2.1-65] Death in its highest Reality, much greater in its Change, than when an Animal of earthly Flesh and Blood is only changed into a cold lifeless Carcase.

[Pryr-2.1-66] A Death, that In all Nature has none like it, none equal to it, none of the same Nature with it, but that which the Angels died, when, from Angels of God, they became living Devils, serpentine, hideous Forms, and Slaves to Darkness. Say that the Angels lost no Life, that they did not die a real Death, because they are yet alive in the Horrors of Darkness, and then you may say, with the same Truth, that Adam did not die, when he lost God, and Paradise, and the first Glory of his Creation, because he afterwards lived and breathed in a World which was outwardly, in all its Parts, full of the same Curse that was within himself. But further, not only the plain Letter of the Text, and the Change of State, which Adam found in himself, demonstrated a real Death to his former State; but the whole Tenor of Scripture absolutely requires it; all the System of our Redemption proceeds upon it. For tell me, I pray, What need of a Redemption, if Adam had not lost his first State of Life? What Need of the Deity to enter again into the human Nature, not only as acting, but taking a Birth in it, and from it? What need of all this mysterious Method, to bring the Life from above again into Man, if the Life from above had not been lost? Say that Adam did not die, and then tell me, what Sense or Reason there is in saying, that the Son of God became Man, and died on the Cross to restore to him the Life that he had lost? It is true indeed, that Adam, in his Death to the Divine Life, was left in the Possession of an earthly Life. And the Reason is plain why he was so: For his great Sin consisted in his Desire and Longing to enter into the Life of this world, to know its good and evil, as the Animals of this World do; it was his choosing to have a Life of this World after this new Manner, and his entering upon the Means of attaining it, that was his Death to the Divine Life. And therefore it is no Wonder, that after his Death to Heaven and Paradise, he found himself still alive as an earthly Animal. For the Desire of this earthly Life was his great Sin, and the Possession of this earthly Life was the proper Punishment and Misery that belonged to his Sin; and therefore it is no wonder that that Life, which was the proper Punishment, and real Discovery of the Fruits of his Sin, should subsist, after his Sin had put an End to the Life of Paradise and God in him. But wonderful it is to a great Degree, that any Man should imagine, that Adam did not die on the Day of his Sin, because he had as good a Life left in him, as the Beasts of the Field have.

[Pryr-2.1-67] For is this the Life or is the Death that such Animals die, the Life and Death with which our Redemption is concerned? Are not all the Scriptures full of a Life and Death of a much higher Kind and Nature? And do not the Scriptures make Man the perpetual Subject to whom this higher Life and Death belong? What Ground or Reason therefore can there be to think of the Death of an Animal of this World, when we read of the Death, that Adam was assuredly to die the Day of his Sin? For does not all that befel him on the Day of his Sin, show that he lost a much greater Life, suffered a more dreadful Change, than that of giving up the Breath of this World? For in the Day of his Sin, this Angel of Paradise, this Lord of the new Creation, fell from the Throne of his Glory (like Lucifer from Heaven) into the State of a poor, darkened, naked, distressed Animal of gross Flesh and Blood, unable to bear the odious Sight of that which his new-opened Eyes forced him to see; inwardly and outwardly feeling the Curse awakened in himself, and all the Creation, and reduced to have only the Faith of the Devils, to believe and tremble. Proof enough, surely, that Adam was dead to the Life, and Light, and Spirit of God; and that, with this Death, all that was Divine and heavenly in his Soul, his Body, his Eyes, his Mind, and Thoughts, was quite at an End. Now this Life to which Adam then died, is that Life which all his Posterity are in want of, and cannot come out of that State of that Death into which he fell, but by having this first Life of Heaven born again in them. Now is there any Reason to say, that Mankind, in their Natural State, are not dead to that first Life in which Adam was created, because they are alive to this World? Yet this is as well as to say, that Adam did not die a real Death, because he had afterwards an earthly Life in him. How comes our Lord to say, that unless ye eat the Flesh, and drink the Blood, of the Son of Man, ye have no Life in you? Did he mean, ye have no earthly Life in you? How comes the Apostle to say, He that hath the Son of God hath Life, but he that hath not the Son of God hath not Life? Does he mean the Life of this World? No. But both Christ and his Apostle assert this great Truth, that all Mankind are in the State of Adam's first Death, till they are made alive again, by a Birth of the Son, and the Holy Spirit of God brought forth in them. So plain is it, both from the express Letter, and Spirit of Scripture, that Adam died a real Death to the Kingdom of God in the Day of his Sin. Take away this Death, and all the Scheme of our Redemption has no Ground left to stand upon.

[Pryr-2.1-68] Judge now, Academicus, Who leaves the Letter of Scripture, your learned Friends, or the Author of the Appeal? They leave it, they oppose it, in that which is the very Life of Christianity.

[Pryr-2.1-69] For without the Reality of a new Birth, founded on the Certainty of a real Death in the Fall of Adam, the Christian Scheme is but a skeleton of empty Words, a Detail of strange

Mysteries between God and Man, that do nothing, and have nothing to do.

[Pryr-2.1-70] On the other hand, look now at the things set forth in the Appeal, concerning the Fall of Angels, the Nature and Effects of their Revolt, and the Creation of this World as deduced therefrom. They neither leave, nor oppose any Letter, or Doctrine of Scripture. They add nothing to Religion, but the full Proof of all its Articles; they intend nothing but to open the original Ground, and true Reason, of the Christian Redemption, and the absolute Necessity of its being such, as the Gospel declares. Now the Letter of Scripture does not do this in open Words; it sets not forth the why, and how things are, either in Nature or Grace; it teaches not the Ground or Philosophy of the Christian Faith; it contents itself with bare Facts and Doctrines, and calls for simple Faith and Obedience. No Wonder therefore, that when the natural and necessary Ground of the Christian Redemption is opened, that the Letter of Scripture is not Step by Step appealed to, for everything that is said. And yet many things may be sufficiently grounded on Scripture, that are not so expressed in the Letter. The Sadducees denied, that there was any Resurrection at all; and this they did, because they could not find it in the express Letter of the Five Books of Moses. And yet it seems, that the Resurrection was plainly and strongly taught there: For thus saith our Lord,—That the Dead shall rise again, Moses showed at the Bush, when he said, "The Lord is the God of Abraham, Isaac, &c. For he is not the God of the Dead, but of the Living."{Luke xx.37.38} This shows us that a thing may be fully and sufficiently proved from Scripture, which is not plainly expressed in the Letter. And thus stands the Matter with regard to those great, and edifying Truths set forth in the Appeal. They are truly scriptural, they have their Ground and Authority from Scripture, though not so open and express in the Letter, as Matters of Faith and necessary Doctrine are. For is not the Fall of Angels a Scripture-Truth? Is not the Desolation which their Fall brought into Nature, and the very Place of this World a Scripture-Truth? What else can be meant by Darkness upon the Face of the Deep? What Darkness, or what Deep, but in the Place of this World? What Darkness, or State of the Deep, but that, which God was about to raise out of its disordered State? And does not the Letter of Scripture show, that out of this Darkness and Waters, and State of the Deep, the Spirit and Light of God entering into them, brought forth the Earth, the Stars, the Sun, and all the Elements, into a Form of a new World?

[Pryr-2.1-71] To ask for a particular Text of Scripture, saying in so many express Words, that the Place of this World is the very Place and extent of the Kingdom of the fallen Angels, is quite ridiculous, and without the least Ground in Reason, as is enough shown in the Appeal. For does not our Lord expressly call the Devil, a Prince of this World? But how could this Name belong to him, but because he is here in his own first Region and Territories, and has still some Power, till all the Evil that he has raised in it, shall be entirely separated from it? For was not this World raised out of the Materials of the fallen Angels' Kingdom, and was not the Wrath, and Fire, and Darkness of their Fall, still in some Degree remaining in every Part of this World, they could have no more Power in it, than they have in Heaven; they must be as entirely incapable of seeing or entering into it, as they are of seeing or entering into the Kingdom of Heaven: For they have nothing but Evil in their Nature; they can touch nothing, move nothing, see nothing, feel nothing, taste nothing, act in nothing, but that very Evil, Darkness, Fire, and Wrath, and Disorder, which they first awakened and kindled both in themselves, and their Kingdom. And therefore it is a Truth of the utmost Certainty, that they can be nowhere, but where there is something of that Evil still subsisting which they brought forth. And this may pass for Demonstration (if there be any such thing) that the Scriptures themselves demonstrate the Place of this World, to be the very Place and Region in which the Angels fell. And they still are here, because their Kingdom is not wholly delivered from all the Evil they had raised in it, but is to stand for a Time, only in a State of Recovery, where they themselves must see, in spite of all the Rage and Malice of their fiery Darts, that the Mystery of a Lamb of God, born upon Earth, will raise Creatures of Flesh and Blood, amidst the Ruins of their spoiled Kingdom, to be an Host of Angels in Heaven restored, and themselves plunged into an Hell, that is cut off from every thing, but their own Wrath, Fire, and Darkness. And all this, Academicus, to make it known through all the Regions of Eternity, that Pride can degrade the highest Angels into Devils, and Humility raise fallen Flesh and Blood to the Thrones of Angels. This, this is the great End of God's raising a new Creation, out of a fallen Kingdom of Angels; for this End it stands in its State of War, a War betwixt the Fire and Pride of fallen Angels, and the Meekness and Humility of the Lamb of God: It stands its Thousands of Years in this Strife, that the last Trumpet may sound this great Truth, through all the Heights and Depths of Eternity, "That Evil can have no Beginning, but from Pride; nor any End, but from Humility."

[Pryr-2.1-72] Oh Academicus, what a Blindness there is in the World! What a Stir is there amongst Mankind about Religion, and yet almost all seem to be afraid of That, in which alone is Salvation!

[Pryr-2.1-73] Poor Mortals! What is the one Wish and Desire of your Hearts? What is it that you call Happiness, and matter of Rejoicing? Is it not when every thing about you helps you to stand upon higher Ground, gives full Nourishment to Self-esteem, and gratifies every Pride of Life? And yet Life itself is the Loss of every thing, unless Pride be overcome. Oh stop a while in Contemplation of this great Truth. It is a Truth as unchangeable as God; it is written and spoken through all Nature; Heaven and Earth, fallen Angels, and redeemed Men, all bear Witness to it. The Truth is: Pride must die in you, or nothing of Heaven can live in you. Under the Banner of this Truth, give up yourselves to the meek and humble Spirit of the Holy Jesus, the Overcomer of all Fire, and Pride, and Wrath. This is the one Way, the one Truth, and the one Life. There is no other open Door into the Sheepfold of God. Everything else is the Working of the Devil in the fallen Nature of Man. Humility must sow the Seed, or there can be no Reaping in Heaven. Look not at Pride only as an unbecoming Temper; not at Humility only as a decent Virtue; for the one is Death, and the other is Life; the one is all Hell, and the other is all Heaven.

[Pryr-2.1-74] So much as you have of Pride, so much you have of the fallen Angel alive in you; so much you have of true Humility; so much you have of the Lamb of God within you. Could you see with your Eyes what every Stirring of Pride does to your Soul, you would beg of everything you meet, to tear the Viper from you, though with the Loss of an Hand, or an Eye. Could you see what a sweet, Divine, transforming Power there is in Humility, what an heavenly Water of Life it gives to the fiery Breath of your Soul, how it expels the Poison of your fallen Nature, and makes Room for the Spirit of God to live in you, you would rather wish to be the Footstool of all the World, than to want the smallest Degree of it. Excuse, Academicus, this little Digression, if it be such, for the Subject we were upon, forced me into it.

[Pryr-2.1-75] Acad. Indeed, Sir, the Lesson you have here given, is the same that the whole Nature of the Fall of Angels, and the whole Nature of the Redemption of Man, daily reads to every Creature; and he, who alone can redeem the World, has plainly shown us, wherein the Life and Spirit of our Redemption must consist, when he saith, Learn of me, for I am meek and lowly of Heart. Now if this Lesson is unlearnt, we must be said to have left our Master, as those Disciples did, who went back, and walked no more with him.{John vi.} But if you please, Theophilus, we will now break off till the Afternoon.

[Pryr-2.1-76] Theoph. Give me Leave first, Academicus, but just to mention one Point more, to show you still further, how unreasonably your Friends object to the Appeal the Want of the plain Letter of Scripture. Now let it be supposed, that the Account of the Fall of Angels, the Creation, &c., given in the Appeal, has not Scripture enough; — Take then the contrary Opinion, which is that of your Friends; viz., That all Worlds, and all Things, are created out of nothing.

[Pryr-2.1-77] Show me now, Academicus, I do not say a Text, but the least Hint of Scripture, that by all the Art of commenting, can so much as be drawn to look that way. It is a Fiction, big with the grossest Absurdities, and contrary to every thing that we know, either from Nature or Scripture, concerning the Rise and Birth, and Nature of Things, that have begun to be. Adam was not created out of nothing; for the Letter of Moses tells us in the plainest Words, out of what he was created or formed, both as to his inward, and his outward Nature. He tells us also as expressly out of what, Eve, the next Creature, was created. But from the Time of Adam and Eve, the Creation of every human Creature is a birth out of its Parents' Body and Soul, or whole Nature. And to show us how all things, or Worlds, as well as all living Creatures, are not created out of nothing, St. Paul appeals to this very Account, that Moses gives of the Woman's being formed out of the Man; but "all things" (says he) "are out of God."{1 Cor. ix.12} Here this Fiction of a Creation out of nothing, is by the plain and open Letter of Scripture, absolutely removed from the whole System of created things, or things which begin to be; for St. Paul's Doctrine is, that all things come into Being, out of God, in the same Reality, as the Woman was formed or created out of Man. So again, "There is to us but one God, out of whom are all things" {1 Cor. viii.6} ; for so you know the Greek should be translated, not "of," but "out of" God: not "of," but "out of" the man. The Fiction therefore, which I speak of, is not only without but expressly contrary to, the plain Letter of Scripture. For every thing that we see, every Creature that has Life, is by the Scripture-account a Birth from something else. And here, Sir, you are to take Notice of a Maxim that is not deniable, that the Reason why any thing proceeds from a Birth, is the Reason why every thing must do so. For a Birth would not be in Nature, but because Birth is the only Procedure of Nature. Nature itself is a Birth from God, the first Manifestation of the hidden, inconceivable God, and is so far from being out of nothing, that it is the Manifestation of all that in God, which was before unmanifest. As Nature is the first Birth, or Manifestation of God, or Discovery of the Divine Powers, so all Creatures are the Manifestation of the Powers of Nature, brought into a Variety of Births, by the Will of God, out of Nature. The first Creatures that are the nearest to the Deity, are out of the highest Powers of Nature, by the Will of God, willing that Nature should be manifested in the Rise and Birth of Creatures out of it. Nature, directed and governed by the Wisdom of God, goes on in the Birth of one thing, out of another. The spiritual Materiality of Heaven brings forth the Bodies, or heavenly Flesh and Blood of Angels, as the Materiality of this World brings forth the Birth of gross Flesh and Blood. The spiritual Materiality of Heaven, so far as the extent of the Kingdom of fallen Angels reached, has by various Changes occasioned by their Fall, gone through a Variety of Births, or Creations, till some of it came down to the Thickness of Air and Water, and the Hardness of Earth and Stones. But when things have stood in this State their appointed Time, the last purifying Fire, kindled by God, will take away all Thickness, Hardness, and Darkness, and bring all the divided Things and Elements of this World back again, to be that first glassy Sea, or heavenly Materiality, in which the Throne of God is set, as was seen by St. John, in the Revelation made to him.

[Pryr-2.1-78] But the Fiction of the Creation out of nothing, is not only contrary to the Letter and Spirit of the Scripture-account of the Rise and Birth of Things, but is in itself full of the grossest Absurdities, and horrid Consequences. It separates every thing from God, it leaves no Relation between God and the Creature, nor any Possibility for any Power, Virtue, Quality, or Perfection of God, to be in the Creature: for if it is created out of nothing, it cannot have something of God in it. But I here stop: For, as you know, we have agreed, if God permit, to have hereafter one Day's entire Conversation on the Nature and End of the Writings of Jacob Behmen, and the right Use and Manner of reading them; and all that, as preparatory to a more correct English Edition of his Works, so this and some other Points shall be adjourned to that Time. In the Afternoon, we will proceed only on such Matters, as may further set the Christian Redemption in its true and proper Light before your Friend Humanus.

[Pryr-2.1-79] Acad. I am very glad, Theophilus, that I have mentioned these Objections to you, though they were of no Weight with me, since you have thereby had an Occasion of giving so full an Answer to them. The Matter stands now in this plain and easy Point of Light.

[Pryr-2.1-80] In the Appeal we have a System of uniform Truths, concerning the Fall of Angels, their spoiled and darkened Kingdom, and the creation of this World as raised out of it. We have the Creation and Fall of Man, his Regeneration, and the Manner of it, all opened and explained according to the Letter and Tenor of Scripture, from their deepest Ground, in such a manner, as to give Light and Clearness into all the Articles of the Christian Faith; to expel all Difficulties and Absurdities that had crept into it; and the whole Scheme of our Redemption proved to be absolutely necessary, both from Scripture, and all that is seen and known in Nature and Creature.

[Pryr-2.1-81] On the other hand, the Opinion which is, and must be received, if the Account in the Appeal is rejected, appears to be a Fiction, that has no Sense, no Reason, no Fact, no Appearance in Nature, nor one single Letter of Scripture, to support it, but stands in the utmost Contrariety to all that the Scripture saith of the Creation of every thing, and is in itself full of the grossest Absurdities, raising Darkness and Difficulties in all Parts of Religion, that can never be removed from it. For a Creation that has nothing of God in it, can explain nothing that relates to God: For a Creation out of nothing, has no better Sense in it, than a Creation into nothing. My Friends, for this time, Adieu.

The Second Dialogue

[Pryr-2.2-1] THEOPH. Let us now speak of Adam in his first Perfection, created by God to be a Lord and Ruler of this new-created World, to people it with an Host of angelic Men, till Time had finished its Course, and all things fitted to be restored to that State, from which they were fallen by the Revolt of Angels.

[Pryr-2.2-2] For the Restoration of all things to their first glorious State, by making the Good to overcome the Evil, was the End which God proposed by the State and Manner of this new Creation.

[Pryr-2.2-3] Adam was the chosen Instrument of God, to conduct this whole Affair, to keep up this new-made World in the State in which God had created it, not to till the Earth, which we now plough, but to keep That, which is now called the Curse in the Earth, covered, hid, and overcome, by that Paradise in which he was created. For this End, he was created in a twofold Nature, of the Powers of Heaven, and the Powers of this World. Inwardly, he had the celestial Body and Soul of an Angel, and he had this angelic Nature united to a Life and Body taken from the Stars and Elements of this outward World. As Paradise overcame, and concealed all the Wrath of the Stars and Elements, and kept that Evil, which is called the Curse, from being known or felt, so Adam's angelic, heavenly Nature, which was the Paradise of God within him, kept him quite ignorant of the Properties of that earthly Nature that was under it. He knew, and saw, and felt nothing in himself, but a Birth of Paradise, that is, a Life, Light, and Spirit of Heaven: for he had no difference from an Angel in Heaven, but that this World was joined to him, and put under his Feet. And this was done, because he was created by God to be the restoring Angel, to do all that in this outward World, which God would have to be done in it, before it could be restored to its first State. And therefore he must have the Nature of all this World in him, because he was to act in it, and upon it, as its restoring Angel; and yet with such Distinction from it, with such Power upon it, and over it, as the Light has upon and over Darkness. Does not now the whole Spirit of the Scriptures consent to this account of Adam's first Perfection? Do not all the chief Points of our Redemption demand this Perfection in Adam unfallen? How else could his Fall bring on the Necessity of the Gospel-Redemption of a new Birth from above, of the Word and Holy Spirit of God? For had he not had this Perfection of Nature at first, his Redemption could not have consisted in the Revival of this Birth and Perfection in him. For had it been something less than the Loss of an angelic and heavenly Life, that had happened to him by his Fall, had it been only some Evil, that related to a Life of this World, nothing else but some Remedy from this World, could have been his Redemption. But since it is the Corner-stone of the Gospel, that nothing less than the eternal Word, which was Man's Creator, could be his Redeemer, and that by a new Birth from above, it is a Demonstration, that he was at first created an Angel, born from above, and such a Partaker of the Divine Life, as the Angels are; and that his Fall was a real Death or Extinction of his angelic Life.

[Pryr-2.2-4] Now the Letter of Moses is express for this first Perfection of Adam. God said, "Let us make Man in our own Image, after our Likeness." How different is this from the Creation of the Animals of this World? What can you think or say higher of an Angel? Or what Perfection can an Angel have, but that of being in the Image and after the Likeness of God? But now what an Absurdity would it be, to hold that Adam was created in the Image and Likeness of God, and yet had not in him so much as the Image and Likeness of an Angel? Again, was not Paradise lost, was not Evil and the Curse awakened in all the Elements, as soon as Adam fell? And does not this prove, beyond all Contradiction, that Adam was created by God, as I said above, to be the restoring Angel; to have Power over all the outward World; to keep all its Evil from being known or felt; till the Fall of Angels from Heaven had been repaired by a Race of angelic Men born on Earth? But how could he do, and be all this, for which he was created by God, how could he keep up the Life of Heaven and Paradise in himself, and this new World, unless the Life of Heaven had been his own Life? Or how could he be the Father of an Offspring that were to have no Evil, nor so much as the Knowledge of what was Good and Evil in this World? Could anything but an heavenly Man bring forth an heavenly Offspring? Or could he be said to have the Life of this World opened in him in his Creation, who was to bring forth a Race of Beings, insensible of the Good and Evil in this World? For every thing that has the Life of this World opened in it, is under an absolute necessity of knowing and feeling its Good and Evil.

[Pryr-2.2-5] Secondly, that Adam, when he first entered into the World, had the Nature and Perfection of an Angel, is further plain from Moses, who tells us, that he was made at first both Male and Female in one Person; and that Eve, or the Female Part of him, was afterwards taken out of him. Now this Union of the Male and Female in him, was the Purity, or Virgin Perfection of his Life, and is the very Perfection of the angelic Nature. This we are assured of from our Lord himself, who, in Answer to the Question of the Sadducees, said unto them, "Ye do err, not knowing the Scriptures, and the Power of God; for in the Resurrection they neither marry, nor are given in Marriage, but are as the Angels in Heaven."{Matt. xxii. 29,30} Or, as in St. Luke, "for they are equal to the Angels of God." Here we have a twofold Proof of the angelic

Perfection of Adam: (1) Because we are told, that that State in which he was created, neither Male nor Female, but with both Natures in his one Person, is the very Nature and Perfection of the Angels of God in Heaven. (2) Because everyone who shall have a Part in this Resurrection, shall then have this angelic Perfection again; to be no more Male or Female, or a Part of the Humanity, but such perfect, complete, undivided Creatures, as the Angels of God are. But now this Perfection could not belong to the Humanity after the Resurrection, but because it belonged to the first Man before his Fall: For nothing will be restored, but that which was first lost; nothing rise again, but that which should not have died; nor any thing be united, but that which should not have been parted. The short is this: Man is at last to have a Nature equal to that of the Angels. This Equality consists in this, that as they have, so the Humanity will have, both Male and Female Nature in one Person.

[Pryr-2.2-6] But the Humanity was thus created at first, Male and Female in one Person, therefore the Humanity had at first a Nature and Perfection equal to that of the Angels. Thus is the Letter of Moses much more plain for the angelic Perfection of Adam in his Creation, than it is for the Resurrection of the Dead; and yet we have our Lord's Word for it, that Moses sufficiently proved the Resurrection of the Dead. What say you, Academicus, to this Matter?

[Pryr-2.2-7] Acad. I will here just mention what my good old Tutor says: The Author of the Appeal, says he, founds all his Scheme of Regeneration or Redemption on a supposed threefold Life, in which Adam was created. His sole Proof of this threefold Life is taken from this text of Moses: "God breathed into Man the Breath of Lives, and Man became a living Soul." From this Phrase, The Breath of Lives, the Appeal, without any Authority from the Text, observes thus; "Here the highest, and most Divine Original is not darkly, but openly, absolutely, and in the strongest Form of Expression, ascribed to the Soul," &c. A vain Assertion, says my Tutor; for the Breath of Life or Lives is used by Moses only as a Phrase for animal Life. This is plainly seen, Gen. vii. ver. 21. "And all flesh died, — all in whose Nostrils was the Breath of Lives."

[Pryr-2.2-8] Behold, says he, the very Phrase, which the Appeal takes to be so full a Proof of the high Dignity, and threefold Life of God in the Soul, here made use of to denote the Life of every kind of Animal. And therefore, says he, if this Phrase proves the Soul of Adam to be a Mirror of the Holy Trinity, it proves the same of every Breath in the Nostrils of every Creature.

[Pryr-2.2-9] Theoph. To make short work, Academicus, with your Tutor's Confutation, as he thinks, of the capital Doctrine of the Appeal, I shall only quote the whole Period, as it stands in the Appeal.

"God breathed into him the Breath of Lives (spiraculum vitarum) and Man became a living Soul. Here," says the Appeal, "the Notion of a Soul, created out of nothing, is in the plainest, strongest Manner, rejected by the first written Word of God; and no Jew or Christian can have the least Excuse for falling into such an Error: Here the highest and most Divine Original is not darkly, but openly, absolutely ascribed to the Soul. It came forth as a Breath of Life, or Lives, out of, and from the Mouth of God; and therefore did not come out of the Womb of nothing, but is what it is, and has what it has in itself, from, and out of, the first and highest of all Beings."

Here, Academicus, behold the Falseness and Weakness of your Tutor's Observation. — The Appeal, you plainly see, proves only from the Text of Moses, the high Original of the Soul; and only for this Reason, because it is the Breath of God, breathed into Man. The Appeal makes no Use of the Expression, Breath of Lives, takes no Notice of it, deduces nothing from it, but solely considers the Act of God, as breathing the Spirit of the Soul from himself; and from this Act of God, the high Birth and Dignity of the Soul is most justly affirmed. And the Appeal makes this Observation solely to prove, that the Soul is not created out of nothing. This is the one, sole, open, and declared Intent of the Appeal, in all this Paragraph. But your Tutor, overlooking all this, though nothing else is there, makes the Author of the Appeal to affirm the threefold Life of God in the Soul, merely from the phrase of the Breath of Lives, when there is not one single Word about it. For the Appeal not only has not the least Hint in this Place of any such Matter, to be proved from the Breath of Lives, but through the whole Book there is not the smallest Regard paid to this Expression, nor any Argument ever deduced from it. How strange is all this in your good old Tutor!

[Pryr-2.2-10] The Matter is plainly this; the Author of the Appeal looks wholly to the Action of God, breathing his own Spirit into Adam; and from this Breathing, he justly affirms the Divine Nature of the Soul; all his Argument is deduced from thence. Now if your Tutor, or anyone else, could show, that God breathed his own Spirit into every Animal, and with this Intent, that it might come forth in his own Image and likeness, then the Distinction and high Birth of the Soul, pleaded for by the Appeal, would indeed be lost. But till then, the Appeal must, and therefore will for ever, stand unconfuted in its Assertion of the Dignity and Divine Birth of the Soul.

[Pryr-2.2-11] Again; behold, Academicus, a still further Weakness chargeable upon your Tutor. You have seen, that his Reasoning upon the Breath of Lives, is meddling with something that the Appeal meddles not with, makes no Account of: But your Tutor has conjured it up for his own Use; and yet see what a poor Use he makes of it. He affirms that Moses uses only the Breath of Lives, as a Phrase for animal Life. How does he prove this? Why, truly from this Reason, because Moses uses the same Phrase when he speaks of the Lives of all Animals.

[Pryr-2.2-12] Now does not every Englishman know, that we make use of the same four Letters of the Alphabet, when we say the Life of a Man, the Life of a Beast, and the Life of a Plant? That we use the same five Letters, when we say the Death of a Man, the Death of a Beast, and the Death of a Plant? But will it thence follow, that the Life and Death of Men, and Beasts, and Plants, are of the same Nature and Degree, and have the same Good and Evil in them? Yet this is full as well, as to conclude, that the Breath of Life in Man, and the Breath of Life in Animals, is of the same Nature and Degree, has the same Goodness and Excellency in it, because the same Words, made up of the same Letters, express them both. Your Tutor therefore, Academicus, and not the Author of the Appeal, is the Person that reasons weakly from the Phrase of the Breath of Lives: For that Author never so much as offers to argue from it. His Proof of the threefold Life of God in the Soul, so far as it is deduced from the text of Moses, lies wholly in this; that it is the Breath and Spirit of the triune God, breathed forth from this triune Deity into Man. This, sure, is no small Proof of its having the triune Nature of God in it. And this threefold Life of the Soul, thus plainly deducible from the Letter of Moses, is shown to be absolutely certain, from every chief Doctrine and Institution, nay, from the whole Nature of our Redemption: and all the Gospel is shown to set its Seal to this great Truth, the threefold Life of God in the Soul. Nay, every thing in Nature, Fire, and Light, and Air; every thing that we know of Angels, of Devils, of the animal Life of this World; are all in the plainest and strongest Manner, from the Beginning to the End of the Appeal, made so many Proofs of the threefold Life of the triune God in the Soul. Thus says the Appeal; No Omnipotence can make you a Partaker of the Life of this outward World, without having the Life of this outward World born in your own creaturely Being; the Fire, and Light, and Air of this World, must have their Birth in your own creaturely Being, or you cannot possibly live in, or have a Life from outward Nature. And therefore no Omnipotence can make you a Partaker of the beatific Life, or Presence of the Holy Trinity, unless that Life stands in the same triune State within you, as it does without you. Again: Search to Eternity, says the Appeal, why no Devil or Beast can possibly enter into Heaven, and there can only this one Reason be assigned for it, because neither of them have the triune holy Life of God in them. But enough of this Mistake of your good old Tutor. Rusticus will I am afraid chide you for being the Occasion of this long Digression from the Point we were speaking to.

[Pryr-2.2-13] Rust. Truly, Sir, I do not know what to make of these great Scholars; they seem to have more Love for the Shadow of an Objection, than for the most substantial Truths. I think I here see a great Reason, why our Saviour chose poor and illiterate Fishermen to be his Apostles. St. Paul was the only Man that had some Learning, and he was a Persecutor of Christ, till such time as God made as it were Scales to fall from his Eyes;—And then he became a powerful Apostle. But let us return to your Account of the first created Perfection of Man, and the Degree of his falling from it. It is one of the best Doctrines that I ever heard in my Life. It not only stirs up every thing that is good, and makes me hate every thing that is evil, in me; but it gives so good a Sense, so sound a Meaning to every Mystery of the Gospel, that it makes every thing our Saviour has done for us, and every thing he requires of us, to be equally necessary and beneficial to us. But suppose now our Fall not to be a Change of Nature, not a Death to our first Life, but only a single Sin or Mistake in the first Man; What a Difficulty is there in supposing so great a Scheme of Redemption to set right a single Mistake in one single Creature? Again, What could Man have to do with Angels and Heaven, if he had not, at his Creation, had the Nature of Heaven and Angels in him? But pray, Sir, begin again just where you left off.

[Pryr-2.2-14] Theoph. I was indeed, Rusticus, at that Time just going to say, that Adam had lost much of his first Perfection before his Eve was taken out of him; which was done to prevent worse Effects of his Fall, and to prepare a means for his Recovery, when his Fall should become total, as it afterwards was, upon the eating of the earthly Tree of Good and Evil.

[Pryr-2.2-15] "It is not good that Man should be alone," saith the Scripture: This shows, that Adam had altered his first State, had brought some Beginning of Evil into it, and had made that not to be good, which God saw to be good, when he created him. And therefore as a less Evil, and to prevent a greater, God divided the first perfect human Nature into two Parts, into a Male and a Female Creature; and this, as you shall see by and by, was a wonderful Instance of the Love and Care of God towards this new Humanity. It was at first, the total Humanity in one Creature, who should in that State of Perfection, have brought forth his own Likeness out of himself, in such Purity of Love, and such Divine Power, as he himself was brought forth by God: The Manner of his own Birth from God, was the Manner that his own Offspring should have had a Birth from him; all done by the pure Power of a Divine Love. Man stood no longer in the Perfection of his first State, as a Birth of Divine Love, than whilst he loved himself only as God loved him, as in the Image, and after the Likeness of God. This Purity of Love, and Delight in the Image of God, would have carried on the Birth of the Humanity, in the same Manner, and by the same Divine Power, as the first Man was brought forth: For it was only a Continuation of the same generating Love that gave Birth to the first Man. But Adam turned away his Love from the Divine Image, which he should only have loved, and desired to propagate out of himself. He gazed upon this outward World, and let in an adulterate Love into his Heart, which desired to know the Life that was in this World. This impure Desire brought the Nature of this World into him. His first Love and Divine Power, had no Strength left in it; it was no longer a Power of bringing forth a Divine Birth from himself. His first Virginity was lost by an adulterate Love, which had turned its Desire into this World. This State of Inability, is that which is called his falling into a deep Sleep: And in this Sleep, God divided this overcome Humanity into a Male and Female.

[Pryr-2.2-16] The first Step therefore towards the Redemption or Recovery of Man, beginning to fall, was the taking his Eve out of him, that so he might have a second Trial in Paradise; in which if he failed, another effectual Redeemer might arise out of the Seed of the Woman. Oh my Friends, what a wonderful Procedure is there to be seen in the Divine Providence, turning all Evil, as soon as it appears, into a further Display and Opening of new Wonders of the Wisdom and Love of God! Look back to the first Evil, which the Fall of Angels brought forth. The Darkness, Wrath, and Fire, of fallen Nature, were immediately taken from them, and turned into a new Creation, where those apostate Angels were to see all the Evil that they had raised in their Kingdom, turned against them, and made the Ground of a new Race of Beings, which were to possess those Thrones which they had lost. Look now at Adam brought into the World in such an angelic Nature, as he, and all his redeemed Sons, will have after the Resurrection; an Angel at first, and an Angel at last; with Time, and Misery, and Sin, and Death, and Hell, all of them felt, and all overcome betwixt the two glorious Extremes. When this first human Angel, through a false, impure Love, lost the Divine Power of generating his own Likeness out of himself, God took Part of his Nature from him, that so the Eye of his Desire, which was turned to the Life of this World, might be directed to that Part of his Nature which was taken from him. And this is the Reason of my saying before, that this was chosen as a less Evil, and to avoid a greater; for it was a less Degree of falling from his first Perfection, to love the Female Part of his own divided Nature, than to turn his Love towards that, which was so much lower than his own Nature. And thus, at that Time, Eve was an Help, that was truly and properly meet for him, since he had lost his first Power of being himself the Parent of an angelic Offspring, and stood with a longing Eye, looking towards the Life of this World.

[Pryr-2.2-17] But the most glorious Effect of this Division into Male and Female is yet to come. For when Adam and Eve had joined in the eating of the Tree of Good and Evil, and so were totally fallen from God and Paradise, into the Misery and Slavery of the bestial Life of this World; when this greatest of all Evils had thus happened to these two divided Parts of the Humanity; when all the Angel was lost, and nothing but a shameful, frightened Animal of this World, was to be seen in this divided Male and Female; then in, and by, and through this Division, did God open and establish the glorious Scheme of an universal Redemption to these fallen Creatures, and all their Offspring, by the mysterious Seed of the Woman.

[Pryr-2.2-18] Had Adam stood in his first State of Perfection, as a Birth of Divine Love, and loving only the Divine Image and Likeness in himself, this Love would have been itself the fruitful Parent of an holy Offspring; no Eve had been taken out of him, nor any Male or Female ever known in human Nature: All his Posterity had been in him secured, and the earthly Tree of Good and Evil had never been seen in Paradise. But though he lost this first generating Power of Divine Love, and stood as a barren Tree, yet seeing God's Purpose of raising an Offspring from Adam, to possess the Thrones of fallen Angels must go on and succeed, therefore that, Adam might yet have an Offspring, God took from him that, which is called the Female Part of his Nature, that by this means, both a Posterity, and a Saviour, might proceed from him: For through this Division of Man, God would, in a wonderful Manner, do that which Adam should have done, before he was divided.

[Pryr-2.2-19] For out of this Female Part, and after the Fall, God would raise, without the Help of Adam, that same glorious angelic Man, which Adam should have brought forth before and without his Eve; which glorious Man is therefore called the Second Adam: 1. As having in his Humanity that very Perfection, which the First Adam had in his Creation. 2. Because he was to do all that for Mankind, by a Birth of Redemption from him, which they should have had by a Birth of Nature from Adam, had he kept his first State of Perfection. What say you, Academicus, to all this?

[Pryr-2.2-20] Acad. Truly, Sir, there seems to be so much Light, and Truth, and Scripture, for all this Account that you have given of these Matters, as must even force one to consent to it. But then all our Systems of Divinity, to which learned Men are chained, are quite silent of these Matters. I never before heard of this gradual Fall of Adam, nor this angelic State of his first Creation, and Power of bringing forth his own Offspring, and therefore can hardly believe it so strongly as I would, and as the Truth seems to demand of me.

[Pryr-2.2-21] Rust. Pray, Sir, let me speak to Academicus: He seems to be so hampered with Learning, that I can hardly be sorry, that I am not a great Scholar.

[Pryr-2.2-22] Can anything be more punctually related in Scripture than the gradual Fall of Adam? Do not you see, that he was created first with both Natures in him? Is it not expressly told you, that Eve was not taken out of him, till such Time as it was not good for him to be as he then was, and yet God saw that it was good when he created him? Is it not plain therefore, that he had fallen from the Goodness of his first Creation, and therefore his Fall was not at once, nor total, till his eating of the earthly Tree? Again, as to his being an Angel at his first Creation, because of both Natures in him, is it not sufficiently plain from his being declared to be an Angel of the same Nature at last, in the Resurrection? For this is an Axiom that cannot be shaken, that Nothing can rise higher, than its first created Nature; and therefore an Angel at last, must have been an Angel at first. Do you think it possible for an Ox in Tract of Time to be changed into a rational Philosopher? Yet this is as possible, as for a Man that has only by his Creation the Life of this World in him, to be changed into an Angel of Heaven. The Life of this World can reach no further than this World; no Omnipotence of God can carry it further; and therefore, if Man is to be an Angel at the last, and have the Life of Heaven in him, he must of all Necessity, in his Creation, have been created an Angel, and had his Life kindled from Heaven; because no Creature can possibly have any other Life, or higher Degree of Life, than that which his Creation brought forth in him.

[Pryr-2.2-23] Theoph. Marvel not, Academicus, at that which has been said of the first Power of Adam, to generate in a Divine Manner an holy Offspring, by the Power of that Divine Love which gave Birth to himself; for he was born of that Love for no other End, than to multiply Births of it; and whilst his Love continued to be one with that Love, which brought him into Being, nothing was impossible to it. For Love is the great Creating Fiat that brought forth every Thing, that is distinct from God, and is the only working Principle that stirs, and effects every Thing that is done in Nature and Creature. Love is the Principle of Generation from the highest to the lowest of Creatures; it is the first Beginning of every Seed of Life; every Thing has its Form from it; every Thing that is born is born in the Likeness, and with the Fruitfulness, of that same Love that generateth and beareth it; and this is its own Seed of Love within itself, and is its Power of fructifying in its Kind.

[Pryr-2.2-24] Love is the holy, heavenly, magic Power of the Deity, the first Fiat of God; and all Angels, and eternal Beings, are the first Births of it. The Deity delights in beholding the ideal Images, which rise up and appear in the Mirror of his own eternal Wisdom. This Delight becomes a loving Desire to have living Creatures in the Form of these Ideas; and this loving Desire is the generating heavenly Parent, out of which Angels, and all eternal Beings are born. Every Birth in Nature is a Consequence of this first prolific Love of the Deity, and generates from that which began the first Birth. Hence it is, that through all the Scale of Beings, from the Top to the Bottom of Nature, Love is the one Principle of Generation of every Life; and every Thing generates from the same Principle, and by the same Power, by which itself was generated.

Marvel not therefore, my Friend, that Adam, standing in the Power of his first Birth, should have a Divine Power of bringing forth his own Likeness. But I must now tell you, that the greatest Proof of this glorious Truth is yet to come: for I will show you that all the Gospel bears Witness to that heavenly Birth, which we should have had from Adam alone.— This Birth from Adam is still the one Purpose of God, and must be the one Way of all those, that are to rise with Christ to an Equality with the Angels of God. All must be Children of Adam; for all that are born of Man and Woman, must lay aside this polluted Birth, and be born again of a second Adam, in that same Perfection of an holy angelic Nature, which they should have had from the first Adam, before his Eve was separated from him. For it is an undeniable Truth of the Gospel, that we are called to a new Birth, different in its whole Nature, from that which we have from Man and Woman, or there is no Salvation; and therefore it is certain from the Gospel, that the Birth which we have from Adam, divided into Male and Female, is not the Birth that we should have had, because it is the one Reason, why we are under a Necessity of being born again of a Birth from a second Adam, who is to generate us again in that Purity and Divine Power, in and by which we should have been born of the first angelic Adam.

[Pryr-2.2-25] A Divine Love in the first pure and holy Adam, united with the Love of God, willing him to be the Father of an holy Offspring, was to have given Birth to a Race of Creatures from him. But Adam fulfilled not this Purpose of God; he awakened in himself a false Love, and so all his Offspring were forced to be born of Man and Woman, and thereby to have such impure Flesh and Blood as cannot enter into the Kingdom of Heaven. Is not this Proof enough, that this Birth from Adam and Eve is not the first Birth that we should have had? Will anyone say, How could Adam have such a Power to bring forth a Birth in such a Spiritual Way, and so contrary to the present State of Nature? The whole Nature of the Gospel is a full Answer to this Question. For are we not all to be born again in the same Spiritual Way, and are we not, merely by a Spiritual Power, to have a Birth of heavenly Flesh and Blood? The Strangeness of such a Power in the first Adam, is only just so strange, and hard to be believed, as the same Power in the second Adam; and who is called the second Adam for no other Reason, but because he stands in the Place of the first, and is to do That, which the first should have done. And therefore our having from him a new heavenly Flesh and Blood raised in us by a Spiritual Power, superior to the common Way of Birth in this World, is the strongest of Proofs, that we should have been born of Adam in the same Spiritual Power, and so contrary to the Birth of Animals into this World. For all that we have from the second Adam, is a Proof that we should have had the same from Adam the first:—A Divine Love in Adam the first, was to have brought forth an holy Offspring. A Divine Faith now takes its Place, in the second Birth, and is to generate a new Birth from the second Adam, is to eat his Flesh, and Drink his Blood, by the same Divine Power, by which we should have had a Birth of the angelic Flesh and Blood of our first Parent. Thus, Academicus, is this Birth from Adam alone no Whimsy, or Fiction, or fine-spun Notion, but the very Birth that the Gospel absolutely requires, as the Substance of our Redemption. There is no Room to deny it, without denying the whole Nature of our Redemption. On the other hand, the Birth that we have from Adam divided into Male and Female, is through all Scripture declared to be the Birth of Misery, of Shame, of Pollution, of sinful Flesh and Blood; and is only a Ground and Reason, why we must be born again of other Flesh and Blood, before we can enter into the Kingdom of Heaven. This Truth therefore, that we were to have had an heavenly Birth from Adam, depends not upon this, or that particular Text of Scripture, but is affirmed by the whole Nature of our Redemption, and the whole Spirit of Scripture, representing our Birth from this World as shameful, as that of the wild Ass's Colt, and calling for a new Birth from above, as absolutely necessary, if Man is to have a Place amongst the Angels of God. And therefore it may be affirmed, that so sure as it is from Scripture, that Christ is become our second Adam, to help us to such a Birth, so sure is it from Scripture, that we should have had the same Birth from our first Parent, who, if not fallen, could have wanted no Redeemer of his Offspring, and therefore must have brought forth that same Birth, which we have from Christ, but could not have from the Birth of Man and Woman. I must now only just mention to you a Passage much to the Matter in Hand, taken from the second Epistle of St. Clemens, a Bishop of Rome, who lived in the very Time of the Apostles. He relates, that Christ being asked, when his Kingdom should come, gave this Answer: "When two Things shall become one, and that which is outward be as that which is inward, the Male with the Female, and neither Man nor Woman." There wants no comment here: I shall only observe, that the Meaning of the Words, "When that which is outward shall be as that which is inward," seems plainly to be this, when the outward Life or Birth is come to be as the inward angelic Life is, then the Birth will be one, the Male and Female in one, and then the Kingdom of God is come. These Words were in the next Century quoted by Clemens of Alexandria, though with some Alteration. The same Author also relates another Answer given by our Lord, to much the same Question, put by Salome, where our Lord's answer was thus: "When ye shall have put off, or away, the Garment of Shame and Ignominy, and when two shall become one, the Male and the Female united, and neither Man nor Woman." The Garment of Shame and Ignominy, is plainly that Clothing of Flesh and Blood, at the Sight of which both Adam and Eve were ashamed.

[Pryr-2.2-26] Acad. I am fully satisfied, Theophilus, with the Account you have given of the first Perfection, and Divine State of our first Parent. And I think nothing can be plainer, than that we were to have been born of him to the same heavenly Birth, which we now are to receive from Christ, our second Adam. But I must still say, that I am afraid, your critical Adversaries will here find some Pretense, to charge you with a Tendency, at least, to that Heresy, which held Marriage to be unlawful, since you here hold that it came in by Adam's falling from his first Perfection.

[Pryr-2.2-27] Theoph. I own, my Friend, that there is no knowing when one is safe from Men of that Stamp. But as for me my Eye is only upon Truth; and wherever that leads, there I follow; they, if they please, may persecute it with Objections. Here is not the least Pretense for the Charge you speak of: for here is no more Condemnation of Marriage, as unlawful, than there is a Condemnation of God, for keeping up the State, and Life of this World. The Continuation of the World, though fallen, is a glorious Proof and Instance of the Goodness of God, that so a Race of new-born Angels may be brought forth in it. Happy therefore is it, that we have such a World as this to be born into, since we are only born, to be born again to the Life of Heaven. Now Marriage has the Nature of this fallen World; but it is God's appointed Means of raising the Seed of Adam to its full Number. Honourable therefore is Marriage in our fallen State, and happy is it for Man to derive his Life from it, as it helps him to a Power of being eternally a Son of God.

[Pryr-2.2-28] Nor does this Original of Marriage cast the smallest Reflection upon the Sex, as if they brought all, or any Impurity into the human Nature. No, by no means. The Impurity lies in the division, and that which caused it, and not in either of the divided Parts. And the female Part has this Distinction, though not to boast of, yet to take Comfort in, that the Saviour of the World is called the Seed of the Woman, and had his Birth only from the female Part of our divided Nature. But Rusticus, I see, wants to speak.

[Pryr-2.2-29] Rust. Indeed, sir, I do. But it is only to observe to you, what a System of solid, harmonious, and great Truths are here opened to our View, by this Consideration of the first angelic State of Adam, and his falling from it into an earthly animal Life of this World; created at first an human Angel, with an host of Angels in his Loins, and then falling from this State, with this particular Circumstance, that he had not only undone himself, but had also involved an innocent, and almost numberless Posterity in the same Misery, who now must all be born of him in his fallen Condition. Thus looking at this Creation of so noble and high a Creature, and his Fall, as introducing so extensive a Train of Misery, how worthy of God, how becoming a Love and Wisdom that are infinite, does all the stupendous Mystery of our Redemption appear! It was to restore an Angel, big with an angelic Offspring, an Angel that God had created to carry on the great Work of his new Creation, to bring Time with all its Conquests back into Eternity, an Angel in whom, and with whom, were fallen an innocent, numberless Posterity, that had not yet begun to breathe.

[Pryr-2.2-30] What a Sense and Reasonableness does this State of Things give to all those Passages of Scripture, which bring a God incarnate from Heaven, to remedy this sad Scene of Misery, that was opened on Earth! What less than God, could awaken again the dead angelic Life! What less than God's entering into the human Birth itself, and becoming one of it, and with it, could generate again the Life of God in every human Birth? The Scripture saith, "God so loved the World";—"God spared not his only Son";—"Christ laid down his Life for us"; &c. How glorious a Sense is there in all these Sayings, when it is considered, that all this was done for so high and Divine a Creature, created by God for such great Ends, and full of a Posterity, that was to have filled an Heaven restored? In this Light, every Part of our Redemption gives a Glory, a Wisdom, and Goodness to God, which far surpasses every other View we can possibly take of them: Whereas if you lessen this angelic Dignity of the first Man, if you suppose his Fall to be less than that of falling, with all his Posterity, from an angelic Life, into the earthly, animal Life of this World, Slaves to Sin and Misery, all the Fabric of our Redemption is full of such Wonders, as can only be wondered at. Thus, if you consider this World, and Man its highest Inhabitant made out of nothing, and with only the Breath of this earthly Life breathed into his Nostrils, what is there to call for this great Redemption from Heaven?

[Pryr-2.2-31] Again, if you consider the Fall of Man, only as a single Act of Disobedience to a positive, arbitrary Command of God, this is to make all the Consequences of his Fall unexplicable. For had the first Sin been only a single Act of Disobedience, it had been more worthy of Pardon, than any other Sin, merely because it was the first, and by a Creature that had as yet no Experience. But to make the first single Act of Disobedience, not only unpardonable, but the Cause of such a Curse and Variety of Misery entailed upon all his Posterity, from the Beginning to the End of Time; and to suppose, that so much Wrath was raised in God at this single Act of Disobedience, that nothing could make an Atonement for it, but the stupendous Mystery of the Birth, Sufferings, and Death, of the Son of God; is yet further impossible to be accounted for. In this Case, the supposed Wrath, and Goodness of God, are equally inexplicable. And from hence alone, have sprung up the detestable Doctrines, about the Guilt and Imputation of the first Sin, and the several Sorts of partial, absolute Elections, and Reprobations, of some to eternal Happiness, and others to be Firebrands of Hell to all Eternity. Detestable may they well be called, since if Lucifer could truly say, that God from all Eternity determined, and created him to be that wicked hellish Creature that he is, he might then add, Not unto him, but unto his Creator, must all his Wickedness be ascribed. How innocent, how tolerable is the Error of Transubstantiation, when compared with this absolute Election and Reprobation! It indeed cannot be reconciled to our Senses and Reason, but then it leaves God, and Heaven, possessed of all that is holy and good; but this Reprobation-Doctrine, not only overlooks all Sense and Reason, but confounds Heaven and Hell, takes all Goodness from the Deity, and leaves us nothing to detest in the Sinner, but God's eternal irresistible Contrivance to make him to be such. [Pryr-2.2-32] But now, when we take this Matter of the Creation, and Fall of Man, as Truth, and Fact, and Scripture, plainly represent it, every Thing that can awaken in ourselves a Love, and Desire to be like unto God, is to be found in it. Whilst Man stood in his first Perfection, unturned from God, this World was under his Feet; Paradise was the Element in which he lived; the Spirit of God was his Life; the Son of God was his Light; he was in the World, as much above it, and with as full Distinction from it, as incapable of being hurt by it, as an Angel, that only comes with a Divine Commission into it. The whole World was a Gift, put into his Hands; the Standing, or Fall of it was left to him; as his Will and Mind should work so should either Paradise, or a cursed Earth overcome. God, by this new Creation, had so altered the wrathful State of Lucifer's fallen Kingdom, that the Evil that had been raised in it, was hid and overcome by the Good. It was thus created, and put into this new State, for this sole End, that a human Angel might keep Paradise alive, and bring forth a paradisiacal Host of Angels, in the very Place, where the fallen Angels had brought forth their Evil. But all these great Things, depended upon Adam's conforming to the Designs of God, and living in this World in such a State, as God had created him in. He could not conform to the Designs of God any other Way, than by the rectitude of his Will, willing that which God willed, both in the Creation of him, and the World.

[Pryr-2.2-33] Whilst his Will stood thus inclined, the new Creation was preserved, himself was an Angel, and the World a Paradise. No Evil would have been known either in Plant, or Fruit, or Animal, nor could have been known, but by the declining Will, and Desire of Man calling it forth. His first longing Look towards the Knowledge of the Life of this World, was the first loosening of the Reins of Evil.— It began to have Life, and a Power of stirring, as soon as his Desire began to be earthly; hence the Curse, or Evil, hid in the Earth, could begin to show itself, and got a Power of giving forth an evil Tree, whose Fruit was the Key to the Knowledge of Good and Evil; a Tree which could not have grown, had he willed nothing, but that which God willed in the Creation of him.

[Pryr-2.2-34] He was not the Creator of this bad Tree, no more than he was the Creator of the good Trees, that grew in Paradise. But as the heavenly Rectitude of his Will kept up the heavenly Powers of Paradise in the Earth, so when his Will began to be earthly, it opened a Passage for the natural Evil; that was hid in the Earth, to bring forth a Tree in its own Likeness. The Earth as now, had then a natural Power of bringing forth a Tree of its own Nature, viz., Good and Evil, but Paradise was that heavenly Power, which hindered it from bringing forth such Productions: but when the Keeper of Paradise turned a Wish from God, and Paradise, after a bad Knowledge, then Paradise lost some of its Power, and the Curse, or Evil, hid in the Earth, could give forth a bad Tree. But see now the Goodness, and Compassion of God towards this mistaken Creature; for no sooner had Adam, by the abuse of his Power and Freedom, given occasion to the Birth of this evil Tree, but the God of Love informs him of the dreadful Nature of it, commands him not to eat of it, assuring him, that Death was hid in it, that Death to his angelic Life, would be found in the Day that he should eat of it. A plain Proof, if anything can be plain, that this Tree came not from God, was not according to his own Will and Purpose towards Adam, but from such a natural Power in the Earth, as could not show itself, till the strong Will and Desire of Adam, beginning to be earthly, worked with That, which was the Evil hid in the Earth. But pray, Theophilus, do you now speak again.

[Pryr-2.2-35] Theoph. The short of the Matter then, my Friend, is this: neither Adam, nor any other Creature, has at its Creation, or Entrance into Life, any arbitrary Trial imposed upon it by God. The natural State of every intelligent Creature is its one only Trial; and it cannot sin, but by departing from that Nature, or falling from that State in which it was created. Adam was created an human Angel in Paradise, and he had no other Trial but this, whether he would live in Paradise, as an Angel of God, insensible of the Life, or the Good and Evil, of this earthly World. This was the Tree of Life, and the Tree of Death, that must stand before him; and the Necessity of his choosing either the one, or the other, was a Necessity founded in his own happy Nature.

[Pryr-2.2-36] The true Account therefore of the Fall of Adam, is a gradual Declension, or Tendency of his will, from the Life of Paradise into the Life of this World, till he was at last wholly fallen into it, and swallowed up by it. The first Beginning of his Lust towards this World, was the first Beginning of his Fall, or Departure from the Life of Heaven and Paradise; and his eating of the earthly Tree, was his last and finishing Step of his Entrance into, and under the full Power of this World. This was the true Nature of his Fall. On the other hand, all that we see on the part of God, is a gradual Help, administered by God to this falling Creature, suitable to every Degree of his falling, till at last, in the Fullness of his Fall, an universal Redeemer of him, and his Posterity, was given by a Second Adam, to regenerate again the whole Seed of Adam the First.

[Pryr-2.2-37] Thus, the first Degree of his Lust towards this World had some Stop put to it, by the taking his Eve out of him; that so his Desire into the Life of this World, might be in some measure lessened. When his Lust into this World still went on, and gave Occasion to the Birth of the evil Tree, a suitable Remedy was here given by God; for God laid a Prohibition upon it, and declared the Death that must be received from it. When he was further so overcome by his lusting Desire, as to eat of the Tree that had the Nature of this World in it, and so lost his first Life, and angelic Clothing, then God, even then all Goodness and Mercy to him, only told him of the Curse and Misery that was opened in Nature; that himself and Posterity must be sweating, labouring Animals, in a fallen World, till their sickly, shameful, naked, new-gotten Bodies mixed and mouldered in the Corruption of that Earth, whose Fruits they had chosen to know, instead of those of Paradise.

[Pryr-2.2-38] Now all this is Nothing of a Penalty wrathfully inflicted by God, but was the natural State of Adam, as soon as his own Lust had led him out of an heavenly Paradise, into the earthly Life of this World. God brings no Misery upon him, but only shows the Misery that he had opened in himself, by not keeping to the State in which he was created. And no sooner had God informed this miserable Pair of the State they had brought upon themselves, but, in that Moment, his eternal Love begins a Covenant of Redemption, that was to begin in them, and in and through them extend itself to all their Posterity. A Beginning of a new Birth, called the Seed of the Woman, was, like the first Breath of Life, breathed or inspoken again into the Light of their Life, which, as an Immanuel, or God with them, should be born in all their Posterity, and be their Power of becoming again such Sons of God, as should fulfill the first Designs of the Creation of Adam, and fill Heaven again with that Host of Angels which it had lost. Thus from the Creation of Adam, through all the Degrees of his Fall to the Mystery of his Redemption, everything tells you, that God is Love. Nay the very Possibility of his having so great a Fall, gives great Glory to the Goodness and Love of God towards him. He was created an Angel, and therefore had the highest Perfection of an Angel, which is a Freedom of Willing. Secondly. He was created to be the restoring Angel of this new Creation. Now these two Things, which were his highest Glory, and greatest Marks of the divine Favour, were the only Possibility of his falling. Had he not had an angelic Freedom of Will, he could not have had a false Will; had he not had all Power given unto him over this World, he could not have fallen into it? It was this Divine and high Power over it, that opened a Way for his Entrance, or falling into it.—Thus,

Academicus, from this View of Man, we come to the utmost Certainty of a threefold Nature or Life in him. 1. He is the Son of a fallen Angel. 2. He is the Son of a Male and Female of this bestial World. 3. He is a Son of the Lamb of God, and has a Birth of Heaven again in his Soul. Hence we see also, that all that we have to fear, to hate, and renounce; all that we have to love, to desire, and pray for; is all within ourselves. No Man can be miserable, but by falling a Sacrifice to his own inward Passions and Tempers; nor anyone happy, but by overcoming himself. How ridiculous would a Man seem to you, who should torment himself, because the Land in America was not well tilled? Now everything that is not within you, that has not its Birth and Growth in your own Life, is at the same Distance from you, is as foreign to your own Happiness or Misery, as an American Story. Your Life is all that you have; and nothing is a Part of it, or makes any Alteration in it, but the Good or Evil that is in the Workings of your own Life. Hence you may see why our Saviour, who, though he had all Wisdom, and came to be the Light of the World, is yet so short in his Instructions, and gives so small a Number of Doctrines to Mankind, whilst every Moral Teacher, writes Volumes upon every single Virtue. It is because he knew what they knew not, that our whole Malady lies in this, that the Will of our Mind, the Lust of our Life, is turned into this World; and that nothing can relieve us, or set us right, but the turning the Will of our Mind, and the Desire of our Hearts to God, and that Heaven which we had lost. And hence it is, that he calls us to nothing, but a total Denial of ourselves, and the Life of this World, and to a Faith in him, as the Worker of a new Birth and Life in us. Did we but receive his short Instructions with true Faith, and Simplicity of Heart, as the Truth of God, we should not want anyone to comment or enlarge upon them. A Traveller that has taken a wrong Road, does not want an Orator to discourse to him on the Nature of Roads, but to be told, in short, which is his right Way. Now this is our Case; it was not a Number of things that brought about our fall; Adam only took up a wrong Will; that Will brought him, and us into our present State, or Road of Life; and therefore our Saviour uses not a Number of Instructions to set us right; he only tells us to renounce the false Will, which brought Adam into the Life of this World, and to take up that Will, which should have kept him in Paradise. Observe now, my Friend, the great Benefit that we have from the foregoing Account of Man's original Perfection, and the Nature of his Fall. It opens the true Ground of our Religion, and the absolute Necessity of it; it forces us to know, that our whole natural Life is a mistaken Road, and that Christ is alone our true Guide out of it. It teaches us every Reason for renouncing ourselves, and loving the whole Nature of our Redemption, as the greatest Joy and Desire of our Hearts. We are not only compelled, as it were, to hunger after it, to run with Eagerness into its Arms, but are also delivered from all Mistakes about it, from all the Difficulties and Perplexities, which divided Sects and Churches have brought into it. For, from this View of things, we see, not uncertainly, but with the fullest Assurance, that our Will, and our Heart is all, that nothing else either finds or loses God; and that all our Religion is only the Religion of the Heart. We see with open Eyes, that as a Spirit of Longing after the Life of this World, made Adam and us to be the poor Pilgrims on Earth that we are, so the Spirit of Prayer, or the longing Desire of the Heart after Christ, and God, and Heaven, breaks all our Bonds asunder, casts all our Cords from us, and raises us out of the Miseries of Time, into the Riches of Eternity. Thus seeing and knowing our first and our present State, everything calls us to Prayer; and the Desire of our Heart becomes the Spirit of Prayer. And when the Spirit of Prayer is born in us, then Prayer is no longer considered, as only the Business of this or that Hour, but is the continual Panting or Breathing of the Heart after God. Its Petitions are not picked out of Manuals of Devotion; it loves its own Language, it speaks most when it says least. If you ask what its Words are, they are Spirit, they are Life, they are Love, that unite with God.

[Pryr-2.2-39] Acad. I apprehend, Sir, that what you here say of the Spirit of Prayer, will be taken by some People for a Censure upon Hours and Forms of Prayer; though I know you have no such Meaning.

[Pryr-2.2-40] Rust. Pray let me speak again to Academicus: His Learning seems to be always upon the Watch, to find out some Excuse for not receiving the whole Truth. Does not Theophilus here speak of the Spirit of Prayer, as a State of the Heart, which is become the governing Principle of the Soul's Life? And if it is a living State of the Heart, must it not have its Life in itself, independent of every outward Time and Occasion? And yet must it not, at the same Time, be that alone which disposes and fits the Heart to rejoice and delight in Hours, and Times, and Occasions of Prayer? Suppose he had said, that Honesty is an inward living Principle of the Heart, a Rectitude of the Mind, that has all its Life and Strength within itself: Could this be thought to Censure all Times and Occasions of performing outward Acts of Honesty? Now the Spirit of Prayer differs from all outward Acts and Forms of Prayer, just as the Honesty of the Heart, or a living Rectitude of Mind, differs from outward and occasional Acts of Honesty. And yet should a Man overlook, or disregard Times and Occasions of outward acts of Honesty, on Pretence that true Honesty was an inward living Principle of the Heart, who would not see that such a one had as little of the inward Spirit, as of the outward Acts of Honesty? St. John saith, "If any man hath this World's Goods, and seeth his Brother hath need, and shutteth up his Bowels of Compassion to him, how dwelleth the Love of God in him?" Just so, and with the same Truth, it may be said, if a Man overlooketh, neglecteth, or refuseth, Times and Hours of Prayer, how dwelleth the Spirit of Prayer in him? And yet, its own Life and Spirit is vastly superior to, independent of, and stays for no particular Hours, or Forms of Words. And in this Sense it is truly said, that it has its own Language, that it wants not to pick Words out of Manuals of Devotion, but is always speaking forth Spirit and Life, and Love towards God. But pray, Theophilus, do you go on, as you intended.

[Pryr-2.2-41] Theoph. I shall only add, before we pass on to another Point, that, from what has been said of the first State and Fall of Man, it plainly follows, that the Sin of all Sins, or the Heresy of all Heresies, is a worldly Spirit. We are apt to consider this Temper only as an Infirmity, or pardonable Failure; but it is indeed the great Apostasy from God and the Divine Life. It is not a single Sin, but the whole Nature of all Sin, that leaves no Possibility of coming out of our fallen State, till it be totally renounced with all the Strength of our Hearts. Every Sin, be it of what kind it will, is only a Branch of the worldly Spirit that lives in us. There is but one that is good, saith our Lord, and that is God. In the same Strictness of Expression it must be said, there is but one Life that is good, and that is the Life of God and Heaven. Depart in the least Degree from the Goodness of God, and you depart into Evil; because nothing is good but his Goodness.

[Pryr-2.2-42] Choose any Life, but the Life of God and Heaven, and you choose Death; for Death is nothing else but the Loss of the Life of God. The Creatures of this World have but one Life, and that is the Life of this World: this is their one Life, and one Good. Eternal Beings have but one Life, and one Good, and that is the Life of God. The Spirit of the Soul is in itself nothing else but a Spirit breathed forth from the Life of God, and for this only End, that the Life of God, the Nature of God, the Working of God, the Tempers of God, might be manifested in it. God could not create Man to have a Will of his own, and a Life of his own, different from the Life and Will that is in himself; this is more impossible than for a good Tree to bring forth corrupt Fruit. God can only delight in his own Life, his own Goodness, and his own Perfections; and therefore cannot love or delight, or dwell, in any Creatures, but where his own Goodness and Perfections are to be found. Like can only unite with Like, Heaven with Heaven, and Hell with Hell; and therefore the Life of God must be the Life of the Soul, if the Soul is to unite with God. Hence it is, that all the Religion of fallen Man, all the Methods of our Redemption, have only this one End, to take from us that strange and earthly Life we have gotten by the Fall, and to kindle again the life of God and Heaven in our Souls; Not to deliver us from that gross and sordid Vice called Covetousness, which Heathens can condemn, but to take the whole Spirit of this World entirely from us, and that for this necessary Reason, because All that is in the World, the Lust of the Flesh, the Lust of the Eyes, and the Pride of Life, is not of the Father, that is, is not that Life, or Spirit of Life, which we had from God by our Creation, but is of this World, {1 John 2:16} is brought into us by our Fall from God into the Life of this World. And therefore a worldly Spirit is not to be considered, as a single Sin, or as something that may consist with some real Degrees of Christian Goodness, but as a State of real Death to the Kingdom and Life of God in our Souls. Management, Prudence, or an artful Trimming betwixt God and Mammon, are here all in vain; it is not only the Grossness of an outward, visible, worldly Behaviour, but the Spirit, the Prudence, the Subtlety, the Wisdom of this World, that is our Separation from the Life of God.

[Pryr-2.2-43] Hold this therefore, Academicus, as a certain Truth, that the Heresy of all Heresies is a worldly Spirit. It is the whole Nature and Misery of our Fall; it keeps up the Death of our Souls, and, so long as it lasts, makes it impossible for us to be born again from above. It is the greatest Blindness and Darkness of our Nature, and keeps us in the grossest Ignorance both of Heaven and Hell. For though they are both of them within us, yet we feel neither the one, nor the other, so long as the Spirit of this World reigns in us. Light and Truth, and the Gospel, so far as they concern Eternity, are all empty Sounds to the worldly Spirit. His own Good, and his own Evil, govern all his Hopes and Fears; and therefore he can have no Religion, or be further concerned in it, than so far as it can be made serviceable to the Life of this World. Publicans and Harlots are all born of the Spirit of this World; but its highest Birth, are the Scribes, and Pharisees, and Hypocrites, who turn Godliness into Gain, and serve God for the Sake of Mammon; these live, and move, and have their Being, in and from the Spirit of this World.— Of all Things therefore, my Friend, detest the Spirit of this World, or there is no Help; you must live and die an utter Stranger to all that is divine and heavenly. You will go out of the World in the same Poverty and Death to the Divine Life, in which you entered it. For a worldly, earthly Spirit can know nothing of God; it can know nothing, feel nothing, taste nothing, delight in nothing, but with earthly Senses, and after an earthly Manner. The natural Man, saith the Apostle, receiveth not the Things of the Spirit of God, they are Foolishness unto him. He cannot know them, because they are spiritually discerned; that is, they can only be discerned by that Spirit, which he hath not. Now the true Ground and Reason of this, and the absolute Impossibility for the natural Man to receive and know them, how polite, and learned, and acute soever he be, is this; it is because all real Knowledge is Life, or a living Sensibility of the Thing that is known. There is no Light in the Mind, but what is the Light of Life; so far as our Life reaches, so far we understand, and feel, and know, and no further. All after this, is only the Play of our Imagination, amusing itself with the dead Pictures of its own Ideas. Now this is all that the natural Man, who hath not the Life of God in him, can possibly do with the Things of God. He can only contemplate them, as Things foreign to himself, as so many dead Ideas, that he receives from Books, or Hearsay; and so can learnedly dispute and quarrel about them, and laugh at those as Enthusiasts, who have a living Sensibility of them. He is only the worse for his hearsay, dead

Ideas of Divine Truths; they become a bad Nourishment of all his natural Tempers: He is proud of his Ability to discourse about them, and loses all Humility, all Love of God and Man, through a vain and haughty Contention for them. His Zeal for Religion is Envy and Wrath; his Orthodoxy is Pride and Obstinacy; his Love of the Truth is Hatred and Ill-will to those who dare to dissent from him. This is the constant Effect of the Religion of the natural Man, who is under the Dominion of the Spirit of this World. He cannot know more of Religion, nor make a better Use of his Knowledge, than this comes to; and all for this plain Reason, because he stands at the same Distance from a living Sensibility of the Truth, as the Man that is born blind, does from a living Sensibility of Light. Light must first be the Birth of his own Life, before he can enter into a real Knowledge of it. Yet so ignorant is the natural Man with all his learned Acuteness, that he does not so much as know, that there is, and must be, this great Difference between real Knowledge, and dead Ideas of Things; and that a Man cannot know anything, any further than as his own Life opens the Knowledge of it in himself.

[Pryr-2.2-44] The Measure of our Life is the Measure of our Knowledge; and as the Spirit of our Life worketh, so the Spirit of our Understanding conceiveth. If our Will worketh with God, though our natural Capacity be ever so mean and narrow, we get a real Knowledge of God, and heavenly Truths; for every thing must feel that in which it lives.

[Pryr-2.2-45] But if our Will works with Satan, and the Spirit of this World, let our Parts be ever so bright, our Imaginations ever so soaring, yet all our living Knowledge, or real Sensibility, can go no higher or deeper, than the Mysteries of Iniquity, and the Lusts of Flesh and Blood. For where our Life is, there, and there only, is our Understanding; and that for this plain Reason, because as Life is the Beginning of all Sensibility, so it is and must be the Bounds of it; and no Sensibility can go any further than the Life goes, or have any other Manner of Knowledge, than as the Manner of its Life is. If you ask what Life is, or what is to be understood by it? It is in itself nothing else but a working Will; and no Life could be either good or evil, but for this Reason, because it is a working Will: Every Life, from the highest Angel to the lowest Animal, consists in a working Will; and therefore as the Will worketh, as that is with which it uniteth, so has every Creature its Degree, and Kind, and Manner of Life; and consequently as the Will of its Life worketh, so it has its Degree, and Kind, and Manner of Conceiving and Understanding, of Liking and Disliking. For nothing feels, or tastes, or understands, or likes, or dislikes, but the Life that is in us. The Spirit that leads our Life, is the Spirit that forms our Understanding. The Mind is our Eye, and all the Faculties of the Mind see every thing according to the State the Mind is in. If selfish Pride is the Spirit of our Life, every thing is only seen, and felt, and known, through this Glass. Every thing is dark, senseless, and absurd to the proud Man, but that which brings Food to this Spirit. He understands nothing, he feels nothing, he tastes nothing, but as his Pride is made sensible of it, or capable of being affected with it. His working Will, which is the Life of his Soul, liveth and worketh only in the Element of Pride; and therefore what suits his Pride, is his only Good; and what contradicts his Pride, is all the Evil that he can feel or know. His Wit, his Parts, his Learning, his Advancement, his Friends, his Admirers, his Successes, his Conquests, all these are the only God and Heaven, that he has any living Sensibility of. He indeed can talk of a Scripture-God, a Scripture-Christ, and Heaven; but these are only the ornamental Furniture of his Brain, whilst Pride is the God of his Heart. We are told, that God resisteth the Proud, and giveth Grace to the Humble. This is not to be understood, as if God, by an arbitrary Will, only chose to deal thus with the proud and humble Man. Oh no. The true Ground is this, The Resistance is on the Part of Man. Pride resisteth God, it rejecteth him, it turneth from him, and chooseth to worship and adore something else instead of him; whereas

Humility leaveth all for God, falls down before him, and opens all the Doors of the Heart for his Entrance into it. This is the only Sense, in which God resisteth the Proud, and giveth Grace to Humble. And thus it is in the true Ground and Reason of every Good and Evil that rises up in us; we have neither Good nor Evil, but as it is the natural Effect of the Workings of our own Will, either with, or against God; and God only interposes with his Threatenings and Instructions, to direct us to the right Use of our Wills, that we may not blindly work ourselves into Death, instead of Life. But take now another Instance like that already mentioned. Look at a Man whose working Will is under the Power of Wrath. He sees, and hears, and feels, and understands, and talks wholly from the Light and Sense of Wrath. All his Faculties are only so many Faculties of Wrath; and he knows of no Sense or Reason, but that which his enlightened Wrath discovers to him. I have appealed, Academicus, to these Instances, only to illustrate and confirm that great Truth, which I before asserted, namely, that the working of our Will, or the State of our Life, governs the State of our Mind, and Forms the Degree and Manner of our Understanding and Knowledge; and that as the Fire of our Life burns, so is the Light of our Life kindled: and all this only to show you the utter Impossibility of knowing God, and Divine Truths, till your Life is Divine, and wholly Dead to the Life and Spirit of this World; since our Light and Knowledge can be no better, or higher, than the State of our Life and Heart is. Tell me now, do you feel the Truth of all this? I say feel, because no Truth is possessed, till you have a Feeling and living Sensibility of it.

[Pryr-2.2-46] Acad. Oh! Sir, you have touched every String of my Heart; and I now wish, with the Psalmist, that I had the Wings of a Dove, that I might flee away, and be at Rest; flee away from the Spirit of this World, to be at Rest in the sweet Tranquillity of a Life born again of God. You know, Sir, that in the Morning you told me of a certain first Step, that of all Necessity must be the Beginning of a spiritual Life; you gave me till To-morrow to speak my Mind and Resolution about it. But you have now extorted my Answer from me, I cannot stay a Moment longer: With all the Strength that I have, I turn from every Thing that is not God, and his holy Will; with all the Desire, Delight, and Longing of my Heart, I give up myself wholly to the Life, Light, and Holy Spirit of God; pleased with nothing in this World, but as it gives Time, and Place, and Occasions, of doing and being that, which my heavenly Father would have me to do, and be; seeking for no Happiness from this earthly fallen Life, but that of overcoming all its Spirit and Tempers. But I believe, Theophilus, that you had something further to say.

[Pryr-2.2-47] Theoph. Indeed, Academicus, there is hardly any knowing, when one has said enough of the evil Effects of a worldly Spirit. It is the Canker that eateth up all the Fruits of our other good Tempers; it leaves no Degree of Goodness in them, but transforms all that we are, or do, into its own earthly Nature. The Philosophers of old, began all their Virtue in a total Renunciation of the Spirit of this World. They saw with the Eyes of Heaven, that Darkness was not more contrary to Light, than the Wisdom of this World was contrary to the Spirit of Virtue; therefore they allowed of no Progress in Virtue, but so far as a Man had overcome himself, and the Spirit of this World.

[Pryr-2.2-48] This gave a Divine Solidity to all their Instructions, and proved them to be Masters of true Wisdom. But the Doctrine of the Cross of Christ, the last, the highest, the most finishing Stroke given to the Spirit of this World, that speaks more in one Word than all the Philosophy of voluminous Writers, is yet professed by those, who are in more Friendship with the World, than was allowed to the Disciples of Pythagoras, Socrates, Plato, or Epictetus.

[Pryr-2.2-49] Nay, if those ancient Sages were to start up amongst us with their Divine Wisdom, they would bid fair to be treated by the Sons of the Gospel, if not by some Fathers of the Church, as dreaming Enthusiasts.

[Pryr-2.2-50] But, Academicus, this is a standing Truth, The World can only love its own, and Wisdom can only be justified of her Children. The Heaven-born Epictetus told one of his Scholars, that then he might first look upon himself, as having made some true Proficiency in Virtue, when the World took him for a Fool; an Oracle like that, which said, The Wisdom of this World is Foolishness with God.

[Pryr-2.2-51] If you were to ask me, What is the Apostasy of these last Times, or whence is all the Degeneracy of the present Christian Church? I should place it all in a worldly Spirit. If here you see open Wickedness, there only Forms of Godliness; if here superficial Holiness, political Piety, crafty Prudence, there haughty Sanctity, partial Zeal, envious Orthodoxy; if almost everywhere you see a Jewish Blindness, and Hardness of Heart, and the Church trading with the Gospel, as visibly, as the old Jews bought and sold Beasts in their Temple; all these are only so many Forms and proper Fruits of the worldly Spirit. This is the great Net, with which the Devil becomes a Fisher of Men; and be assured of this, my Friend, that every Son of Man is in this Net, till through and by the Spirit of Christ, he breaks out of it.

[Pryr-2.2-52] I say the Spirit of Christ, for nothing else can deliver him from it. Trust now to any Kind, or Form of religious Observances, to any Number of the most plausible Virtues, to any Kinds of Learning, or Efforts of human Prudence, and then I will tell you what your Case will be; you will overcome one Temper of the World, only and merely by cleaving to another. For nothing leaves the World, nothing renounces it, nothing can possibly overcome it, but singly and solely the Spirit of Christ. Hence it is, that many learned Men, with all the rich Furniture of their Brain, live and die Slaves to the Spirit of this World; and can only differ from gross Worldlings, as the Scribes and Pharisees differ from Publicans and Sinners: It is because the Spirit of Christ, is not the one only thing that is the Desire of their Hearts; and therefore their Learning only Works in, and with the Spirit of this World, and becomes itself, no small Part of the Vanity of Vanities. Would you further know, Academicus, the evil Nature and Effects of a worldly Spirit, you need only look at the blessed Power and Effects of the Spirit of Prayer; for the one goes downwards with the same Strength, as the other goes upwards; the one betroths and weds you to an earthly Nature, with the same Certainty, as the other espouses, and unites you to Christ, and God, and Heaven. The Spirit of Prayer, is a pressing forth of the Soul out of this earthly Life; it is a stretching with all its Desire after the Life of God; it is a leaving, as far as it can, all its own Spirit, to receive a Spirit from above, to be one Life, one Love, one Spirit with Christ in God. This Prayer, which is an emptying itself of all its own Lusts, and natural Tempers, and an opening itself for the Light and Love of God to enter into it, is the Prayer in the Name of Christ, to which nothing is denied. For the Love which God bears to the Soul, his eternal, never-ceasing Desire to enter into it, to dwell in it, and open the Birth of his Holy Word, and Spirit in it, stays no longer, than till the Door of the Heart opens for him. For nothing does, or can keep God out of the Soul, or hinder his holy Union with it, but the Desire of the Heart turned from him. And the Reason of it is this; it is because the Life of the Soul is in itself nothing else but a working Will; and therefore wherever the Will worketh or goeth, there, and there only, the Soul liveth, whether it be in God, or in the Creature.

[Pryr-2.2-53] Whatever it desireth, that is the Fuel of its Fire; and as its Fuel is, so is the Flame of its Life. A Will, given up to earthly Goods, is as Grass with Nebuchadnezzar, and has one Life with the Beasts of the Field: For earthly Desires keep up the same Life in a Man and an Ox. For the one only Reason, why the Animals of this World have no Sense or Knowledge of God, is this; it is because they cannot form any other than earthly Desires, and so can only have an earthly Life. When therefore a Man wholly turneth his working Will to earthly Desires, he dies to the Excellency of his natural State, and may be said only to live, and move, and have his Being, in the Life of this World, as the Beasts have.— Earthly Food, &c., only desired and used for the Support of the earthly Body, is suitable to Man's present Condition, and the Order of Nature: But when the Desire, the Delight, and longing of the Soul is set upon earthly Things, then the Humanity is degraded, is fallen from God; and the Life of the Soul is made as earthly and bestial, as the Life of the Body: For the Creature can be neither higher nor lower, neither better nor worse, than as the Will worketh: For you are to observe, that the Will hath a Divine and magic Power; what it desireth, that it taketh, and of that it eateth and liveth. Wherever, and in whatever, the working Will chooseth to dwell and delight, that becomes the Soul's Food, its Condition, its Body, its Clothing, and Habitation: For all these are the true and certain Effects and Powers of the working Will.

[Pryr-2.2-54] Nothing doth, or can go with a Man into Heaven, nothing followeth into Hell, but that in which the Will dwelt, with which it was fed, nourished, and clothed, in this Life. And this is to be noted well, that Death can make no Alteration of this State of the Will; it only takes off the outward, worldly Covering of Flesh and Blood, and forces the Soul to see, and feel, and know, what a Life, what a state, Food, Body, and Habitation, its own working Will has brought forth for it. Oh Academicus, stop a while, and let your Hearing be turned into Feeling. Tell me, is there any thing in Life that deserves a Thought, but how to keep this Working of our Will in a right State, and to get that Purity of Heart, which alone can see, and know, and find, and possess God? Is there any thing so frightful as this worldly Spirit, which turns the Soul from God, makes it an House of Darkness, and feeds it with the Food of Time, at the Expense of all the Riches of Eternity?

[Pryr-2.2-55] On the other hand, what can be so desirable a Good as the Spirit of Prayer, which empties the Soul of all its own Evil, separates Death and Darkness from it, leaves Self, Time, and the World, and becomes one Life, one Light, one Love, one Spirit with Christ, and God, and Heaven?

[Pryr-2.2-56] Think, my Friends, of these Things, with something more than Thoughts; let your hungry Souls eat of the Nourishment of them as a Bread of Heaven; and desire only to live, that with all the Working of your Wills, and the whole Spirit of your Minds, you may live and die united to God: and thus let this Conversation end, till God gives us another Meeting.

The Third Dialogue

[Pryr-2.3-1] RUST.   I have brought again with me, Gentlemen, my silent Friend, Humanus, and upon the same Condition of being silent still. But though his Silence is the same, yet he is quite altered. For this twenty Years I have known him to be of an even cheerful Temper, full of Good-nature, and even quite calm and dispassionate in his Attacks upon Christianity, never provoked by what was said either against his Infidelity, or in Defence of the Gospel. He used to boast of his being free from those four Passions and Resentments, which, he said, were so easy to be seen, in many or most Defenders of the Gospel-Meekness. But now he is morose, peevish, and full of Chagrin, and seems to be as uneasy with himself, as with every Body else: whatever he says, is rash, satirical, and wrathful. I tell him, but he won't own it, that his Case is this: the Truth has touched him; but it is only so far, as to be his Tormentor. It is only as welcome to him, as a Thief that has taken from him all his Riches, Goods, and Armour, wherein he trusted. The Christianity he used to oppose is vanished; and therefore all the Weapons he had against it, are dropped out of his Hands. It now appears to stand upon another Ground, to have a deeper Bottom, and better Nature, than what he imagined; and therefore he, and his Scheme of Infidelity, are quite disconcerted. But though his Arguments have thus lost all their Strength, yet his Heart is left in the State it was; it stands in the same Opposition to Christianity as it did before, and yet without any Ideas of his Brain to support it. And this is the true Ground of his present, uneasy, peevish State of Mind. He has nothing now to subsist upon, but the resolute Hardness of his Heart, his Pride, and Obstinacy. These he cannot give up by the force of his Reason; his Heart cannot bear the Thoughts of such a Sacrifice; and yet he feels and knows, that he has no Strength left, but in a settled Hardness, Pride and Obstinacy, to continue as he is.— These, I own, are severe and hard Words: But, hard as they are, I am sure Humanus knows, that they proceed from the Softness and Affection of my Heart towards him, from a compassionate Zeal to show him where his Malady lies, and the Necessity of overcoming himself, before he can have the Blessing of Light, and Truth, and Peace. Though it is with some Reluctance, yet I have chosen thus to make my Neighbour known both to himself, and to you, that you may speak of such Matters as may give the best Relief to the State he is in.

[Pryr-2.3-2] Theoph. Indeed, Rusticus, I much approve of the Spirit you have here shown, with regard to your Friend, and hope he will take in good Part all that you have said. As for me, I embrace him with the utmost Tenderness of Affection. I feel and compassionate the trying State of his Heart, and have only this one Wish, that I could pour the heavenly Water of Meekness, and the Oil of Divine Love, into it. Let us force him to know, that we are the Messengers of Divine Love to him; that we seek not ourselves, nor our own Victory, but to make him victorious over his own Evil, and become possessed of a new Life in God. His Trial is the greatest and hardest that belongs to human Nature: And yet it is absolutely necessary to be undergone.

[Pryr-2.3-3] Nature must become a Torment and Burden to itself, before it can willingly give itself up to that Death, through which alone it can pass into Life. There is no true and real Conversion, whether it be from Infidelity, or any other Life of Sin, till a Man comes to know, and feel, that nothing less than his whole Nature is to be parted with, and yet finds in himself no Possibility of doing it. This is the Inability that can bring us at last to say, with the Apostle, When I am weak, then am I strong. This is the Distress that stands near to the Gate of Life; this is the Despair by which we lose all our own Life, to find a new one in God. For here, in this Place it is, that Faith, and Hope, and true Seeking to God and Christ, are born. —But till all is Despair in ourselves, till all is lost that we had any Trust in as our own; till then, Faith and Hope, and turning to God in Prayer, are only things learnt and practiced by Rule and Method; but they are not born in us, are not living Qualities of a new Birth, till we have done feeling any Trust or Confidence in ourselves. Happy therefore is it for your Friend Humanus, that he is come thus far, that everything is taken from him on which he trusted, and found Content in himself. In this State, one Sigh or Look, or the least Turning of his Heart to God for Help, would be the Beginning of his Salvation. Let us therefore try to improve this happy Moment to him, not so much by Arguments of Reason, as by the Arrows of that Divine Love which overflows all Nature and Creature.

[Pryr-2.3-4] For Humanus, though hitherto without Christ, is still within the Reach of Divine Love: He belongs to God; God created him for himself, to be an Habitation of his own Life, Light, and Holy Spirit; and God has brought him and us together, that the lost Sheep may be found, and brought back to its heavenly Shepherd.

[Pryr-2.3-5] Oh Humanus, Love is my Bait; you must be caught by it; it will put its Hook into your Heart, and force you to know, that of all strong Things, nothing is so strong, so irresistible, as Divine Love.

[Pryr-2.3-6] It brought forth all the Creation; it kindles all the Life of Heaven; it is the Song of all the Angels of God. It has redeemed all the World; it seeks for every Sinner upon Earth; it embraces all the Enemies of God; and from the Beginning to the End of Time, the one Work of Providence, is the one Work of Love.

[Pryr-2.3-7] Moses and the Prophets, Christ and his Apostles, were all of them Messengers of Divine Love. They came to kindle a Fire on Earth, and that Fire was the Love which burns in Heaven. Ask what God is? His name is Love; he is the Good, the Perfection, the Peace, the Joy, the Glory, and Blessing, of every Life. Ask what Christ is? He is the universal Remedy of all Evil broken forth in Nature and Creature. He is the Destruction of Misery, Sin, Darkness, Death, and Hell. He is the Resurrection and Life of all fallen Nature. He is the unwearied Compassion, the long-suffering Pity, the never-ceasing Mercifulness of God to every Want and Infirmity of human Nature.

[Pryr-2.3-8] He is the Breathing forth of the Heart, Life, and Spirit of God, into all the dead Race of Adam. He is the Seeker, the Finder, the Restorer, of all that was lost and dead to the Life of God. He is the Love, that, from Cain to the End of Time, prays for all its Murderers; the Love that willingly suffers and dies among Thieves, that Thieves may have a Life with him in Paradise; the Love that visits Publicans, Harlots, and Sinners, that wants and seeks to forgive, where most is to be forgiven.

[Pryr-2.3-9] Oh, my Friends, let us surround and encompass Humanus with these Flames of Love, till he cannot make his Escape from them, but must become a willing Victim to their Power. For the universal God is universal Love; all is Love, but that which is hellish and earthly. All Religion is the Spirit of Love; all its Gifts and Graces are the Gifts and Graces of Love; it has no Breath, no Life, but the Life of Love. Nothing exalts, nothing purifies, but the Fire of Love; nothing changes Death into Life, Earth into Heaven, Men into Angels, but Love alone. Love breathes the Spirit of God; its Words and Works are the Inspiration of God. It speaketh not of itself, but the Word, the eternal Word of God speaketh in it; for all that Love speaketh, that God speaketh, because Love is God. Love is Heaven revealed in the Soul; it is Light, and Truth; it is infallible; it has no Errors, for all Errors are the Want of Love. Love has no more of Pride, than Light has of Darkness; it stands and bears all its Fruits from a Depth, and Root of Humility. Love is of no Sect or Party; it neither makes, nor admits of any Bounds; you may as easily enclose the Light, or shut up the Air of the World into one Place, as confine Love to a Sect or Party. It lives in the Liberty, the Universality, the Impartiality of Heaven. It believes in one, holy, catholic God, the God of all Spirits; it unites and joins with the catholic Spirit of the one God, who unites with all that is good, and is meek, patient, well-wishing, and long-suffering over all the Evil that is in Nature and Creature. Love, like the Spirit of God, rideth upon the Wings of the Wind; and is in Union and Communion with all the Saints that are in Heaven and on Earth. Love is quite pure; it has no By-ends; it seeks not its own; it has but one Will, and that is, to give itself into everything, and overcomes all Evil with Good. Lastly, Love is the Christ of God; it cometh down from Heaven; it regenerateth the Soul from above; it blotteth out all Transgressions; it taketh from Death its Sting, from the Devil his Power, and from the Serpent his Poison. It healeth all the Infirmities of our earthly Birth; it gives Eyes to the Blind, Ears to the Deaf, and makes the Dumb to speak; it cleanses the Lepers, and casts out Devils, and puts Man in Paradise before he dies. It liveth wholly to the Will of him, of whom it is born; its Meat and Drink is, to do the Will of God. It is the Resurrection and Life of every Divine Virtue, a fruitful Mother of true Humility, boundless Benevolence, unwearied Patience, and Bowels of Compassion. This, Rusticus, is the

Christ, the Salvation, the Religion of Divine Love, the true Church of God, where the Life of God is found, and lived, and to which your Friend Humanus is called by us. We direct him to nothing but the inward Life of Christ, to the Working of the Holy Spirit of God, which alone can deliver him from the Evil that is in his own Nature, and give him a Power to become a Son of God.

[Pryr-2.3-10] Rust. My Neighbour has infinite Reason to thank you, for this lovely Draught you have given of the Spirit of Religion; he cannot avoid being affected with it. But pray let us now hear how we are to enter into this Religion of Divine Love, or rather what God has done to introduce us into it, and make us Partakers again of his Divine Nature.

[Pryr-2.3-11] Theoph. The first Work, or Beginning of this redeeming Love of God, is in that Immanuel, or God with us, given to the first Adam, as the Seed of the Woman, which in him, and all his Posterity, should bruise the Head, and overcome the Life of the Serpent in our fallen Nature. This is Love indeed, because it is universal, and reaches every Branch of the human Tree, from the first to the last Man, that grows from it. Miserably as Mankind are divided, and all at War with one another, everyone appropriating God to themselves, yet they all have but one God, who is the Spirit of all, the Life of all, and the Lover of all. Men may divide themselves, to have God to themselves; they may hate and persecute one another for God's sake; but this is a blessed Truth, that neither the Hater, nor the Hated, can be divided from the one, holy, catholic God, who with an unalterable Meekness, Sweetness, Patience, and Good-will towards all, waits for all, calls them all, redeems them all, and comprehends all in the outstretched Arms of his catholic Love. Ask not therefore how we shall enter into this Religion of Love and Salvation; for it is itself entered into us, it has taken Possession of us from the Beginning. It is Immanuel in every human Soul; it lies as a Treasure of Heaven, and Eternity in us; it cannot be divided from us by the Power of Man; we cannot lose it ourselves; it will never leave us nor forsake us, till with our last Breath we die in the Refusal of it. This is the open Gate of our Redemption; we have not far to go to find it. It is every Man's own Treasure; it is a Root of Heaven, a Seed of God, sown into our Souls by the Word of God; and, like a small Grain of Mustard-seed, has a Power of growing to be a Tree of Life. Here, my Friend, you should, once for all, mark and observe, where and what the true Nature of Religion is; for here it is plainly shown you, that its Place is within; its Work and Effect is within; its Glory, its Life, its Perfection, is all within; it is merely and solely the raising of a new Life, new Love, and a new Birth, in the inward Spirit of our Hearts. Religion (which is solely to restore Man to his first and right State in God) had its Beginning, and first Power, from the Seed of the Woman, the Treader on the Serpent's Head; and therefore all its Progress, from its Beginning to its last finished Work, is, and can be nothing else, but the growing Power and Victory of the Seed of the Woman, over all the Evil brought by the Serpent into human Nature. For the Seed of the Woman is the Spirit, and Power, and Life of God, given or breathed again into Man, to be the Raiser and Redeemer of that first Life, which he had lost. This was the spiritual Nature of Religion in its first Beginning, and this alone is its whole Nature to the End of Time; it is nothing else, but the Power, and Life, and Spirit of God, as Father, Son, and Holy Spirit, working, creating, and reviving Life in the fallen Soul, and driving all its Evil out of it. This is the true Rock, on which the Church of Christ is built; this is the one Church out of which there is no Salvation, and against which the Gates of Hell can never prevail.

[Pryr-2.3-12] Here therefore we are come to this firm Conclusion, that let Religion have ever so many Shapes, Forms, or Reformations, it is no true Divine Service, no proper Worship of God, has no Good in it, can do no Good to Man, can remove no Evil out of him, raise no Divine Life in him, but so far as it serves, worships, conforms, and gives itself up to this Operation of the holy, triune God, as living and dwelling in the Soul. Keep close to this Idea of Religion, as an inward, spiritual Life in the Soul; observe all its Works within you, the Death and Life that are found there; seek for no Good, no Comfort, but in the inward Awakening of all that is holy and heavenly in your Heart; and then, so much as you have of this inward Religion, so much you have of a real Salvation. For Salvation is only a Victory over Nature; so far as you resist and renounce your own vain, selfish, and earthly Nature, so far as you overcome all your own natural Tempers of the old Man, so far God enters into you, lives, and operates in you, he is in you the Light, the Life, and the Spirit, of your Soul; and you are in him that new Creature, that worships him in Spirit, and in Truth. For Divine Worship or Service is, and can be only performed by being like-minded with Christ; nothing worships God, but the Spirit of Christ his beloved Son, in whom he is well pleased. This is as true, as that no Man hath known the Father, but the Son, and he to whom the Son revealeth him. Look now at any thing as Religion, or Divine Service, but a strict, unerring Conformity to the Life and Spirit of Christ, and then, though every Day was full of Burnt-offerings, and Sacrifices, yet you would be only like those Religionists, who drew near to God with their Lips, but their Hearts were far from him.

[Pryr-2.3-13] For the Heart is always far from God, unless the Spirit of Christ be alive in it. But no one has the living Spirit of Christ, but he who in all his Conversation walketh, as he walked. Consider these Words of the Apostle, My little Children, of whom I travail in Birth, till Christ be formed in you. This is the Sum total of all, and, if this is wanting, all is wanting. Again, says he, He is not a Jew, which is one outwardly.— Circumcision is nothing, and Uncircumcision is nothing, but the new Creature is all. Nay, see how much further he carries this Point, in the following Words: Though I speak with the Tongues of Men and Angels, though I have the Gift of Prophecy, though I have all Faith, so that I could remove Mountains, &c. and have not Charity (that is, have not the Spirit of Christ) it profiteth me nothing. For by Charity here, the Apostle means neither more nor less, but strictly that same Thing, which, in other Places, he calls the new Creature, Christ formed in us, and our being led by the Spirit of Christ. According to the Apostle, nothing availeth but the new Creature, nothing availeth but the Spirit of Charity here described; therefore this Charity, and the new Creature, are only two different Expressions of one and the same Thing, viz., the Birth, and Formation of Christ in us. Thus saith he, If any Man have not the Spirit of Christ, he is none of his; nay, though he could say of himself (as our Lord says many will) Have I not prophesied in the Name of Christ, cast out Devils, and done many wonderful Works? yet such a one not being led by the Spirit of Christ, is that very man, whose high State the Apostle makes to be a mere Nothing, because he hath not that Spirit of Charity, which is the Spirit of Christ. Again, There is no Condemnation to those, who are in Christ Jesus; therefore to be in Christ Jesus, is to have that Spirit of Charity, which is the Spirit, and Life, and Goodness of all Virtues. Now here you are to observe, that the Apostle no more rejects all outward Religion, when he says Circumcision is nothing, than he rejects Prophesying, and Faith, and Alms-giving, when he says they profit nothing; he only teaches this solid Truth, that the Kingdom of God is within us, and that it all consists in the State of our Heart; and that therefore all outward Observances, all the most specious Virtues, profit nothing, are of no Value, unless the hidden Man of the Heart, the new Creature, led by the Spirit of Christ, be the Doer of them.

[Pryr-2.3-14] Thus, says he, They who are led by the Spirit of God, are the Sons of God. And therefore none else, be they who, or where, or what they will, Clergy, or Laity, none are, or can be, Sons of God, but they who give up themselves entirely to the Leading and Guidance of, the Spirit of God, desiring to be moved, inspired, and governed solely by it.

[Pryr-2.3-15] Again, We are of the Circumcision, who worship God in Spirit; and to show, that this is not a vain Pretence, he says in another Place, The Manifestation of the Spirit is given to every Man to profit withal. Therefore no Profit from anything else; all Preaching and Hearing is vain, and all Preachers and Hearers stand chargeable with the Vanity of their religious Performances, who think of Preaching, or Hearing profitably, any other Way, or by any other Power, than in and by the Holy Spirit of God dwelling and working in them. Thus again, If the Spirit of him, who raised Jesus from the Dead, dwell in you, he also shall quicken your mortal Bodies by his Spirit, which dwelleth in you. In vain therefore is Life expected, either for Body or Soul, but by the Holy Spirit dwelling in them. Again, Through him we both have Access by one Spirit to the Father; therefore this one Spirit is the one only Way to God, and Salvation. Thus does all Scripture bring us to this Conclusion, that all Religion is but a dead Work, unless it be the Work of the Spirit of God; and that Sacraments, Prayers, Singing, Preaching, Hearing, are only so many Ways of being fervent in the Spirit, and of giving up ourselves more and more to the inward working, enlightening, quickening, sanctifying Spirit of God within us; and all for this End, that the Curse of the Fall may be taken from us, that Death may be swallowed up in Victory, and a true, real, Christlike Nature formed in us, by the same Spirit, by which it was formed in the Holy Virgin Mary. Now for the true Ground, and absolute Necessity, of this turning wholly and solely to the Spirit of God, you need only know this plain Truth; namely, that the Spirit of God, the Spirit of Satan, or the Spirit of this World, are, and must be, the one or the other of them, the continual Leader, Guide, and Inspirer, of everything that lives in Nature. There is no going out from some one of these; the Moment you cease to be moved, quickened, and inspired by God, you are infallibly moved and directed by the Spirit of Satan, or the World, or by both of them. And the Reason is, because the Soul of Man is a Spirit, and a Life, that in its whole Being is nothing else but a Birth both of God and Nature; and therefore, every Moment of its Life, it must live in some Union and Conjunction, either with the Spirit of God governing Nature, or with the Spirit of Nature fallen from God, and working in itself. As Creatures therefore, we are under an absolute Necessity of being under the Motion, Guidance, and Inspiration of some Spirit, that is more and greater than our own. All that is put in our own Power, is only the Choice of our Leader; but led and moved we must be, and by that Spirit, to which we give up ourselves, whether it be to the Spirit of God, or the Spirit of fallen Nature. To seek therefore to be always under the Inspiration and Guidance of God's Holy Spirit, and to act by an immediate Power from it, is not proud Enthusiasm, but as sober and humble a Thought, as suitable to our State, as to think of renouncing the World, and the Devil: For they never are, or can be, renounced by us, but so far as the Spirit of God is living, breathing, and moving in us: And that for this plain Reason, because nothing is contrary to the Spirit of Satan, and the World, nothing works, or can work, contrary to it, but the Spirit of Heaven.

[Pryr-2.3-16] Hence our Lord said, He that is not with me, is against me; and he that gathereth not with me, scattereth; plainly declaring, that not to be with him, and led by his Spirit is to be led by the Spirit of Satan, and the World. Ask now, what Hell is? It is Nature destitute of the Light and Spirit of God, and full only of its own Darkness; nothing else can make it to be Hell. Ask what Heaven is? It is Nature quickened, enlightened, blessed, and glorified, by the Light and Spirit of God dwelling in it. What Possibility therefore can there be, of our dividing from Hell, or parting with all that is hellish in us, but by having the Life, Light, and Spirit of God living and working in us? And here again, my friends, you may see in the greatest Clearness, why nothing is available, nothing is Salvation, but the new Birth of a Christ-like Nature; it is because every thing else but this Birth, and Life of the Spirit, is only the Spirit of Satan, or the Spirit of this

World. Have you anything to object to these Things?

[Pryr-2.3-17] Acad. Truly, Sir, all Objections are over with me; you have taken from me every Difficulty or Perplexity that I had, either about Religion, or the Providence of God. I can now look back into the first Origin of Things with Satisfaction: I have seen how the World and Man began to be, in a Way highly worthy of the Divine Wisdom, and how they both came into their present Condition, and how they both are to rise out of it, and return back to their first State in a glorious Eternity. It now appears to me with the utmost Clearness, that to look for Salvation in any thing else, but the Light of God within us, the Spirit of God working in us, the Birth of Christ really brought forth in us, is to be as carnally minded, as ignorant of God, and Man, and Salvation, as the Jews were, when their Hearts were wholly set upon the Glory of their Temple-service, and a temporal Saviour to defend it, by a temporal Power. For every thing but the Light and Spirit of God bringing forth a Birth of Christ in the Soul, every thing else, be it what it will, has and can have no more of Salvation in it, than a temporal fighting Saviour. For what is said of the Impossibility of the Blood of Bulls, and of Goats, to take away Sins, must with the same Truth be said of all other outward creaturely Things; they are all at the same Distance from being the Salvation of the Soul, and in the same Degree of Inability to take away Sins, as the Blood of Bulls and Goats.

[Pryr-2.3-18] And all this for this plain Reason, because the Soul is a Spirit breathed forth from God himself, which therefore cannot be blessed but by having the Life of God in it; and nothing can bring the Life of God into it, but only the Light and Spirit of God. Upon this ground I stand in the utmost Certainty, looking wholly to the Light and Spirit of God for an inward Redemption from all the inward Evil that is in my fallen Nature. All that I now want to know is this, what I am to do, to procure this continual Operation of the Spirit of God within me. For I seem to myself, not to know this enough; and I am also afraid of certain Delusions, which I have heard many have fallen into, under Pretences of being led by the Spirit of God. Pray therefore, Theophilus, give me some Instructions on this Head.

[Pryr-2.3-19] Rust. Pray, Gentlemen, let an unlearned Man speak a Word here. Suppose, Academicus, you had a longing earnest Desire, to be governed by a Spirit of Plainness and Sincerity in your whole Conversation. Would this put you upon asking for Art, and Rules, and Methods, or consulting some learned Man, or Book, to direct you, and keep you from Delusion? Would you not know and feel in yourself, that your own earnest Desire, and Love of Sincerity and Plainness, and your own inward Aversion to everything that was contrary to it, must be the one and only possible Way of attaining it, and that you must have it in that Degree, as you loved and liked to act by it? Now there is no more of Art, or any Secret required to bring and keep you under the Direction of the Spirit of God, than under the Spirit of Plainness and Sincerity. The longing earnest Desire of the Heart, brings you into the safe Possession of the one, as it does of the other. For it has been enough proved, that the Spirit of Prayer forms the Spirit of our Lives, and every Man lives as the Spirit of Prayer leads him. Nay every Prayer for the Holy Spirit, is the Spirit itself praying in you. For nothing can turn to God, desire to be united to him, and governed by him, but the Spirit of God. The Impossibility of praying for the Spirit of God in vain, is thus shown by our blessed Lord: If ye, being evil, know how to give good gifts unto your children, how much more shall your heavenly Father give the Holy Spirit to those that ask for it? But here I stop.

[Pryr-2.3-20] Acad. I do not know how to understand what Rusticus has said. For do not all good Christians daily pray for the Spirit of God? yet how few are led by it? Pray, Theophilus, do you speak here.

[Pryr-2.3-21] Theoph. People may be daily at the Service of the Church, and read long Prayers at home, in which are many Petitions for the Holy Spirit, and yet live and die, led and governed by the Spirit of the World; because all these Prayers, whether we hear them read by others, or read them ourselves, may be done in Compliance only to Duties, Rules, and Forms of Religion, as Things we are taught not to neglect; but, being only done thus, they are not the true, real Working of the Spirit of the Heart, nor make any real Alteration in it. But you are to observe, that Rusticus spoke of the Spirit of Prayer, which is the Heart's own Prayer, and which has all the Strength of the Heart in it. And this is the Prayer that must be affirmed to be always effectual; it never returns empty; it eats and drinks that, after which it hungereth and thirsteth; and nothing can possibly hinder it from having that, which it prays for. This we are assured of from these Words of Truth itself; Blessed are they that hunger and thirst after righteousness, for they shall be filled. But this Blessedness could not belong to Hungering, if the truly Hungry and Thirsty, could ever be sent empty away. Every Spirit necessarily reaps that which it soweth, it cannot possibly be otherwise, it is the unalterable Procedure of Nature. Spirit is the first Power of Nature, every thing proceeds from it, is born of it, yields to it, and is governed by it. If the Spirit soweth to the Flesh, it reapeth that Corruption which belongs to the Flesh; if it soweth to the Spirit, it reapeth the Fruits of the Spirit, which are eternal Life. The Spirit of Prayer therefore is the Opener of all that is good within us, and the Receiver of all that is good without us; it unites with God, is one Power with him; it works with him, and drives all that is not God, out of the Soul. The Soul is no longer a Slave to its natural Impurity and Corruption, no longer imprisoned in its own Death and Darkness, but till the Fire from Heaven, the Spirit of Prayer is kindled in it.
[Pryr-2.3-22] Then begins the Resurrection, and the Life; and all that which died in Adam comes to Life in Christ. Ask not therefore, Academicus, what you are to do to obtain the Spirit of God, to live in it, and be led by it; for your Power of having it, and your Measure of receiving it, are just according to that Faith and Earnestness with which you desire to be led by it. For the hungry Spirit of Prayer is that Faith, to which all Things are possible, to which all Nature, though as high as Mountains, and as stiff as Oaks, must yield and obey. It heals all Diseases, breaks the Bands of Death, and calls the Dead out of their Graves. Look at the small Seeds of Plants, shut up in their own dead Husks, and covered with thick Earth, and see how they grow. What do they do? They hunger and thirst after the Light and Air of this World. Their Hunger eats that which they hunger after, and this is their Vegetation. If the Plant ceases to hunger, it withers and dies, though surrounded with the Air and Light of this World.
[Pryr-2.3-23] This is the true Nature of the spiritual Life; it is as truly a Growth or Vegetation, as that of Plants; and nothing but its own Hunger can help it to the true Food of its Life. If this hunger of the Soul ceases, it withers and dies, though in the midst of Divine Plenty. Our Lord, to show us that the new Birth is really a State of spiritual Vegetation, compares it to a small Grain of Mustard-seed, from whence a great Plant arises. Now every Seed has a Life in itself, or else it could not grow. What is this Life? It is nothing else but an Hunger in the Seed, after the Air and Light of this World; which Hunger, being met and fed by the Light and Air of Nature, changes the Seed into a living Plant. Thus it is with the Seed of Heaven in the Soul. It has a Life in itself, or else no Life could arise from it. What is this Life? It is nothing else but Faith, or an Hunger after God and Heaven; which no sooner stirs, or is suffered to stir, but it is met, embraced, and quickened, by the Light and Spirit of God and Heaven; and so a new Man in Christ, is formed from the Seed of Heaven, as a new Plant from a Seed in the Earth. Let us suppose now, that the Seed of a Plant had Sense and Reason, and that, instead of continually hungering after, and drawing in the Virtue of the Light and Air of our outward Nature, it should amuse, and content

its Hunger with reasoning about the Nature of Hunger, and the different Powers and Virtues of Light and Air; must not such a Seed of all Necessity wither away, without ever becoming a living Plant? Now this is no false Similitude of the Seed of Life in Man: Man has a Power of Drawing all the Virtue of Heaven into himself, because the Seed of Heaven is the Gift of God in his Soul, which wants the Light and Spirit of God to bring it to the Birth, just as the Seed of the Plant wants the Light and Air of this World; it cannot possibly grow up in God, but by taking in Light, Life, and Spirit from Heaven, as the Creatures of Time take in the Light, and Life, and Spirit of this World. If therefore the Soul, instead of hungering after Heaven, instead of eating the Flesh and Blood of the Christ of God, contents and amuses this Seed of Life with Ideas, and Notions, and Sounds, must not such a Soul of necessity wither, and die, without ever becoming a living Creature of Heaven? Wonder not therefore, Academicus, that all the Work of our Salvation and Regeneration is, by the Scripture, wholly confined to the Operation of the Light and Spirit of God, living and working in us. It is for the same Reason, and on the same Necessity, that the Life and Growth of the Creatures of this World, must be wholly ascribed to the Powers of this World, living and working in them. Nor does all this, in the least Degree, make a Man a Machine, or without any Power with regard to his Salvation. He must grow in God, as the Plants grow in this World, from a Power that is not his own, as they grow from the Powers of outward Nature. But he differs entirely from the Plants in this, that an uncontrollable Will, which is his own, must be the Leader and Beginner of his Growth either in God, or Nature. It is strictly true, that all Man's Salvation dependeth upon himself; and it is as strictly true, that all the Work of his Salvation, is solely the Work of God in his Soul. All his Salvation depends upon himself, because his Will-Spirit has its Power of Motion in itself. As a Will, it can only receive that which it willeth; every thing else is absolutely shut out of it. For it is the unalterable Nature of the Will, that it cannot possibly receive any thing into it, but that which it willeth; its Willing is its only Power of receiving; and therefore there can be no possible Entrance for God or Heaven into the Soul, till the Will-Spirit of the Soul desireth it; and thus all Man's Salvation dependeth upon himself. On the other hand, nothing can create, effect, or bring forth, a Birth or Growth of the Divine Life in the Soul, but that Light and Spirit of God, which brings forth the Divine Life in Heaven, and all heavenly Beings. And thus the Work of our Salvation is wholly and solely the Work of the Light and Spirit of God, dwelling and operating in us. Thus, Academicus, you see that God is all; that nothing but his Life and working Power in us, can be our Salvation; and yet that nothing but the Spirit of Prayer can make it possible for us to have it, or be capable of it. And therefore neither you, nor any other human Soul, can be without the Operation of the Light and Spirit of God in it, but because its Will-Spirit, or its Spirit of Prayer, is turned towards something else; for we are always in Union with that, with which our Will is united. Again: Look, Academicus, at the Light and Air of this World, you see with what a Freedom of Communication they overflow, enrich, and enliven every Thing; they enter every-where, if not hindered by something that withstands their Entrance. This may represent to you the ever-overflowing free Communication of the Light and Spirit of God, to every human Soul. They are everywhere; we are encompassed with them; our Souls are as near to them, as our Bodies are to the Light and Air of this World; nothing shuts them out of us, but the Will and Desire of our Souls, turned from them, and praying for something else. I say, praying for something else; for you are to notice this, as a certain Truth, that every Man's Life is a continual State of Prayer; he is no Moment free from it, nor can possibly be so. For all our natural Tempers, be they what they will, Ambition, Covetousness, Selfishness, Worldly-mindedness, Pride, Envy, Hatred, Malice, or any other Lust whatever, are all of them in reality, only so many different Kinds, and Forms of a Spirit of Prayer, which is as inseparable from the Heart, as Weight is from the Body. For every natural Temper is nothing else, but a Manifestation of the Desire and Prayer of the Heart, and shows us, how it works and wills. And as the Heart worketh, and willeth, such, and no other, is its Prayer. All else is only Form, and Fiction, and empty beating of the Air. If therefore the working Desire of the Heart is not habitually turned towards God, if this is not our Spirit of Prayer, we are necessarily in a State of Prayer towards something else, that carries us from God, and brings all kind of Evil into us. For this is the Necessity of our Nature; pray we must, as sure as our Heart is alive; and therefore when the State of our Heart is not a Spirit of Prayer to God, we pray without ceasing to some, or other Part of the Creation. The Man whose Heart habitually tends towards the Riches, Honours, Powers, or Pleasures of this Life, is in a continual State of Prayer towards all these Things. His Spirit stands always bent towards them; they have his Hope, his Love, his Faith, and are the many Gods that he worships: And though when he is upon his Knees, and uses Forms of Prayer, he directs them to the God of Heaven; yet these are in Reality the God of his Heart, and, in a sad Sense of the Words, he really worships them in Spirit, and in Truth. Hence you may see, Academicus, how it comes to pass, that there is so much Praying, and yet so little of true Piety amongst us. The Bells are daily calling us to Church, our Closets abound with Manuals of Devotion, yet how little Fruit! It is all for this Reason, because our Prayers are not our own; they are not the Abundance of our own Heart; are not found and felt within us, as we feel our own Hunger and Thirst; but are only so many borrowed Forms of Speech, which we use at certain Times and Occasions. And therefore it is no Wonder that little Good comes of it. What Benefit could it have been to the Pharisee, if, with an Heart inwardly full of its own Pride and Self-exaltation, he had outwardly hung down his Head, smote upon his Breast, and borrowed the Publican's Words, God be merciful to me a sinner? What greater Good can be expected from our Praying in the Words of David, or Singing his Psalms seven times a Say, if our Heart hath no more the Spirit of David in it, than the Heart of the Pharisee had of the Spirit of the humble Publican?

[Pryr-2.3-24] Acad. O Theophilus, Truth and Reason force me to consent to what you say; and yet I am afraid of following you: For you here seem to condemn Forms of Prayer in public, and Manuals of Devotion in private. What will become of Religion, if these are set aside or disregarded?

[Pryr-2.3-25] Theoph. Dear Academicus, abate your Fright. Can you think, that I am against your praying in the Words of David, or breathing his Spirit in your Prayers, or that I would censure your singing his Psalms seven times a Day? Remember how very lately I put into your Hands the Book called, A Serious Call to a Devout Life &c., and then think how unlikely it is, that I should be against Times and Methods of Devotion. At three several Times, we are told, our Lord prayed, repeating the same Form of Words; and therefore a set Form of Words are not only consistent with, but may be highly suitable to, the most Divine Spirit of Prayer. If your own Heart, for Days and Weeks, was unable to alter, or break off from inwardly thinking and saying, Hallowed be thy Name, thy Kingdom come, thy Will be done; if at other times, for Weeks and Months, it stood always inwardly in another Form of Prayer, unable to vary, or depart from saying, "Come, Lord Jesus, come quickly, with all thy holy Nature, Spirit, and Tempers, into my Soul, that I may be born again of Thee, a new Creature"; I should be so far from censuring such a Formality of Prayer, that I should say, Blessed and happy are they, whose Hearts are tied to such a Form of Words. It is not therefore, Sir, a set Form of Words that is spoken against, but an heartless Form, a Form that has no Relation to, or Correspondence with, the State of the Heart that uses it. All that I have said is only to teach you the true Nature of Prayer, that it is only the

Work of the Heart, and that the Heart only prays in Reality (whatever its Words are) for that which it habitually wills, likes, loves, and longs to have. It is not therefore the using the Words of David, or any other Saint, in your Prayers, that is censured, but the using them without that State of Heart, which first spoke them forth, and the trusting to them, because they are a good Form, though in our Hearts we have nothing that is like them. It would be good to say incessantly with holy David, My Heart is athirst for God.— As the Hart desireth the Waterbrooks, so longeth my Soul after Thee, O God. But there is no Goodness in saying daily these Words, if no such Thirst is felt, or desired in the Heart. And, my Friend, you may easily know, that dead Forms of Religion, and Numbers of repeated Prayers, keep Men content with their State of Devotion, because they make use of such holy Prayers; though their Hearts, from Morning to Night, are in a State quite contrary to them, and join no further in them, than in liking to use them at certain times.

[Pryr-2.3-26] Acad. I acquiesce, Theophilus, in the Truth of what you have said, and plainly see the Necessity of condemning what you have condemned; which is not the Form, but the heartless Form. But still I have a Scruple upon me: I shall be almost afraid of going to Church, where there are so many good Prayers offered up to God, as suspecting they may not be the Prayers or Language of my own Heart, and so become only a Lip-labour, or, what is worse, an Hypocrisy before God.

[Pryr-2.3-27] Theoph. I do not, Academicus, dislike your Scruple at all; for you do well to be afraid of saying any thing of yourself, or to God, in your Prayers, which your Heart does not truly say. It is also good for you to think, that many of the Prayers of the Church may go faster, and higher, than your Heart can in Truth go along with them. For this will put you upon a right Care over yourself, and so to live, that, as a true Son of your Mother the Church, your Heart may be able to speak her Language, conform to her Service, and find the Delight of your Soul in the Spirit of her Prayers. But this will only then come to pass, when the Spirit of Prayer is the Spirit of your Heart; then every good Word, whether in a Form, or out of a Form, whether heard, or read, or thought, will be as suitable to your Heart, as gratifying to it, as Food is to the hungry, and Drink to the thirsty Soul. But till the Spirit of the Heart is thus renewed, till it is emptied of all earthly Desires, and stands in an habitual Hunger and Thirst after God (which is the true Spirit of Prayer) till then, all our Forms of Prayer will be, more or less, but too much like Lessons that are given to Scholars; and we shall mostly say them, only because we dare not neglect them. But be not discouraged, Academicus; take the following Advice, and then you may go to Church without any Danger of a mere Lip-labour or Hypocrisy, although there should be an Hymn, or a Psalm, or a Prayer, whose Language is higher than that of your own Heart. Do this: Go to the Church, as the Publican went into the Temple; stand inwardly in the Spirit of your Mind, in that Form which he outwardly expressed, when he cast down his Eyes, smote upon his Breast, and could only say, God be merciful to me a sinner! Stand unchangeably (at least in your Desire) in this Form and State of Heart; it will sanctify every Petition that comes out of your Mouth; and when any thing is read, or sung, or prayed, that is more exalted and fervent than your Heart is, if you make this an Occasion of a further sinking down in the Spirit of the Publican, you will then be helped, and highly blessed, by those Prayers and Praises, which seem only to fit, and belong to, a better Heart than yours.

[Pryr-2.3-28] This, my Friend, is a Secret of Secrets; it will help you to reap where you have not sown, and be a continual Source of Grace in your Soul. This will not only help you to receive Good from those Prayers, which seem too good for the State of your Heart, but will help you to find Good from every thing else: for every thing that inwardly stirs in you, or outwardly happens to you, becomes a real Good to you, if it either finds or excites in you this humble Form of Mind: For nothing is in vain, or without Profit, to the humble Soul; like the Bee, it takes its Honey even from bitter Herbs; it stands always in a State of Divine Growth; and every thing that falls upon it, is like a Dew of Heaven to it. Shut up yourself therefore in this Form of Humility, all Good is enclosed in it; it is a Water of Heaven, that turns the Fire of the fallen Soul, into the Meekness of the Divine Life, and creates that Oil, out of which the Love to God and Man gets its Flame. Be inclosed therefore always in it; let it be as a garment wherewith you are always covered, and the Girdle with which you are girt; breathe nothing but in and from its Spirit; see nothing but with its Eyes; hear nothing but with its Ears; And then, whether you are in the Church, or out of the Church; hearing the Praises of God, or receiving Wrongs from Men, and the World, all will be Edification, and every Thing will help forward your Growth in the Life of God.

[Pryr-2.3-29] Acad. Indeed, Theophilus, this Answer to my Scruple is quite Good: I not only like, but I love it much: it gives as well an Unction to my Heart, as a Light to my Mind. All my Desire now is, to live no longer to the World, to myself, my own natural Tempers and Passions, but wholly to the Will of the blessed and adorable God, moved and guided by his Holy Spirit.

[Pryr-2.3-30] Theoph. This Resolution, Academicus, only shows that you are just come to yourself; for everything short of this earnest Desire to live wholly unto God, may be called a most dreadful Infatuation or Madness, an Insensibility that cannot be described. For what else is our Life, but a Trial for the greatest Evil, or Good, that an Eternity can give us? What can be so dreadful, as to die possessed of a wicked immortal Nature, or to go out of this World with Tempers, that must keep us for ever burning in our own Fire, and Brimstone? What has God not done to prevent this? His redeeming Love began with our Fall, and kindles itself as a Spark of Heaven in every fallen Soul. It calls every Man to Salvation, and every Man is forced to hear, though he will not obey his Voice. God has so loved the World, that his only Son hung and expired, bleeding on the Cross, not to atone his own Wrath against us, but to extinguish our own Hell within us, to pour his heavenly Love into us, to show us that Meekness, Suffering, and Dying to our own Fallen Nature, is the one, only possible Way, for fallen Man to be alive again in God. Are we yet Sons of Pride, and led away with Vanity? Do the Powers of Darkness rule over us? Do impure evil Spirits possess and drive on our Lives? Has Sin lost all its Power of frightening us? Is Remorse of Conscience no longer felt? Are Falsehood, Guile, Debauchery, Profaneness, Perjury, Bribery, Corruption, and Adultery, no longer seeking to hide themselves in Corners, but openly entering all our high Places, giving Battle to every Virtue, and laying Claim to the Government of the World? Are we thus near being swallowed up by a Deluge of Vice and Impiety? All this is not come upon us, because God has left us too much without Help from Heaven, or too much exposed us to the Powers of Hell; but it is because we have rejected and despised the whole Mystery of our Salvation, and trampled under Foot the precious Blood of Christ, which alone has that Omnipotence, that can either bring Heaven into us, or drive Hell out of us. O Britain, Britain, think that the Son of God saith unto thee, as he said, "O Jerusalem, Jerusalem, how often would I have gathered thy Children, as a Hen gathereth her Chickens under her Wings, and ye would not! Behold, your House is left unto you desolate." And now let me say, What aileth thee, O British Earth, that thou quakest, and the Foundations of thy Churches that they totter? Just that same aileth thee, as ailed Judah's Earth, when the Divine Saviour of the World, dying on the Cross, was reviled, scorned, and mocked, by the inhabitants of Jerusalem; then the Earth quaked, the Rocks rent, and the Sun refused to give its light. Nature again declares for God; the Earth, and the Elements can no longer bear our Sins: Jerusalem's Doom for Jerusalem's Sin, may well be feared by us. Oh ye miserable Pens dipped in Satan's Ink, that dare to publish the Folly of believing in Jesus Christ, where will you hide your guilty Heads, when Nature dissolved, shall show you the Rainbow, on which the crucified Saviour shall sit in Judgment, and every Work receive its Reward? O tremble! ye apostate Sons that come out of the Schools of Christ, to fight Lucifer's Battles, and do that for him, which neither he, nor his Legions can do for themselves. Their inward Pride, Spite, Wrath, Malice and Rage against God, and Christ, and human Nature, have no Pens but yours, no Apostles but you. They must be forced to work in the Dark, to steal privately into impure Hearts, could they not beguile you into a fond Belief, that you are Lovers of Truth, Friends of Reason, Detectors of Fraud, great Geniuses, and Moral Philosophers, merely and solely, because ye blaspheme Christ, and the Gospel of God. Poor deluded Souls, rescued from Hell by the Blood of Christ, called by God to possess the Thrones of fallen Angels, permitted to live only by the Mercy of God, that ye may be born again from above! my Heart bleeds for you. Think, I beseech you, in time, what Mercies ye are trampling under your Feet. Say not that Reason, and your intellectual Faculties, stand in your Way; that these are the best Gifts, that God has given you, and that these suffer you not to come to Christ. For all this is as vain a Pretense, and as gross a Mistake, as if ye were to say, that you had nothing but your Feet to carry you to Heaven. For your Heart is the best and greatest Gift of God to you; it is the highest, greatest, strongest, and noblest Power of your Nature; it forms your whole Life, be it what it will; all Evil, and all Good, comes from it; your Heart alone has the Key of Life and Death; it does all that it will; Reason is but its Plaything, and whether in Time or Eternity, can only be a mere Beholder of the Wonders of Happiness, or Forms of misery, which the right, or wrong Working of the Heart is entered into.

[Pryr-2.3-31] I will here give you an infallible Touch-stone, that will try all to the Truth. It is this: Retire from the World, and all Conversations, only for one Month; neither write, nor read, nor debate any thing in private with yourself; stop all the former Workings of your Heart and Mind; and, with all the Strength of your Heart, stand all this Month as continually as you can, in this following Form of Prayer to God. Offer it frequently on your Knees; but, whether sitting, standing, or walking, be always inwardly longing, and earnestly praying this one Prayer to God: "That, of his great Goodness, he would make known to you and take from your Heart, every Kind, and Form, and Degree of Pride, whether it be from evil Spirits, or your own corrupt Nature; and that he would awaken in you the deepest Depth and Truth of all that Humility, which can make you capable of his Light, and Holy Spirit."

Reject every Thought, but that of wishing, and praying in this Manner from the Bottom of your Heart, with such Truth and Earnestness, as People in Torment, wish and pray to be delivered from it. Now if you dare not, if your Hearts will not, cannot give themselves up in this manner to the Spirit of this Prayer, then the Touch-stone has done its Work, and you may be as fully assured, both what your Infidelity is, and from what it proceeds, as you can be of the plainest Truth in Nature. This will show you, how vainly you appeal to your Reason, and Speculation, as the Cause of your Infidelity; that it is full as false and absurd, as if Thieves and Adulterers should say, that their Theft and Adultery was entirely owing to their bodily Eyes, which showed them external Objects, and not to anything that was wrong or bad in their Hearts. On the other Hand, if you can, and will give yourselves up in Truth and Sincerity to this Spirit of Prayer, I will venture to affirm, that if ye had twice as many evil Spirits in you, as Mary Magdalen had, they will all be cast out of you, and ye will be forced with her, to weep with Tears of Love, at the Feet of the holy Jesus.

[Pryr-2.3-32] But here, my Friends, I stop, that we may return to the Matter we had in hand.

[Pryr-2.3-33] Rust. You have made no Digression, Theophilus, from our main Point, which was to recommend Christianity to poor Humanus. He must, I am sure, have felt the Death-blows, that you have here given to the Infidel Scheme. Their Idol of Reason, which is the vain God, that they worship in vain, is here like Dagon fallen to the Ground, never to rise up again. Humanus is caught by your Bait of Love, and I daresay he wants only to have this Conversation ended, that he may try himself to the Truth, by this divine Touch-stone, which you have put into his Hands.

[Pryr-2.3-34] Acad. Give me leave, Gentlemen, to add one Word to this Matter. Theophilus has here fairly pulled Reason out of its usurped Throne, and shown it to be a powerless, idle Toy, when compared to the royal Strength of the Heart, which is the kingly Power, that has all the Government of Life in its Hands. But if Humanus, or anyone else, would see Reason fully maintained in all its just Rights, and yet entirely disarmed of all its Pretenses to a Religion of its own, and the Truth of the Gospel fully proved to every Man, learned, or unlearned, from the known State of his own Heart; if he would see all this set forth in the strongest, clearest Light, he need only read about an hundred Pages of a Book {A Demonstration of the Gross and Fundamental Errors of a Late Book called A Plain Account of the Sacrament of the Lord's Supper} published about twelve Years ago, to which no Answer has, nor, it may be, ever will be given by any Patron of Reason, and Infidelity. And if Part of that Book (as I have often wished) beginning at page 70 to 117, was printed by itself, and known and read in every Part of the Kingdom, all Christians, though no Scholars, would have learning enough both to see the deep, true, and comfortable Foundation of their Gospel Faith, and the miserable Folly, and Ignorance of those, who would set up a Religion of human Reason instead of it. But now, Theophilus, I beg we may return to that very Point concerning Prayer, where we left off. I think my Heart is entirely devoted to God, and that I desire nothing but to live in such a State of Prayer, as may best keep me under the Guidance and Direction of the Holy Spirit. Assist me therefore, my dear Friend, in this important Matter; give me the fullest Directions that you can; and if you have any Manual of Devotion, that you prefer, or any Method that you would put me in, pray let me know it.

[Pryr-2.3-35] Rust. I beg leave to speak a Word to Academicus. I am glad, Sir, to see this Fire of Heaven, thus far kindled in your Soul; but wonder that you should want to know, how you are to keep up its Flame, which is like wanting to know, how you are to love and desire that, which you do love and desire. Does a blind, or sick, or lame Man want to know, how he shall wish and desire Sight, Health, and Limbs? or would he be at a Loss, till some Form of Words taught him how to long for them? Now you can have no Desire or Prayer for any Grace, or Help from God, till you in some Degree as surely feel the Want of them, and desire the Good of them, as the sick Man feels the Want, and desires the Good of Health. But when this is your Case, you want no more to be told how to pray, than the thirsty Man wants to be told what he shall ask for. Have you not fully consented to this Truth, that the Heart only can pray, and that it prays for nothing but that, which it loves, wills, and wishes to have? But can Love or Desire want Art, or Method, to teach it to be, that which it is? If from the Bottom of your Heart you have a sincere, warm Love for your most valuable Friend, would you want to buy a Book, to tell you, what Sentiments you feel in your Heart towards this Friend, what Comfort, what Joy, what Gratitude, what Trust, what Honour, what Confidence, what Faith, are all alive, and stirring in your Heart towards him? Ask not therefore, Academicus, for a Book of Prayers; but ask your Heart what is within it, what it feels, how it stirs, what it wants, what it would have altered, what it desires? and then, instead of calling upon Theophilus for Assistance, stand in the same Form of Petition to God.

[Pryr-2.3-36] For this turning to God according to the inward Feeling, Want, and Motion of your own Heart, in Love, in Trust, in Faith of having from him all that you want, and wish to have, this turning thus unto God, whether it be with, or without Words, is the best Form of Prayer in the World.— Now no Man can be ignorant of the State of his own Heart, or a Stranger to those Tempers, that are alive and stirring in him, and therefore no Man can want a Form of Prayer; for what should be the Form of his Prayer, but that which the Condition and State of his Heart demands? If you know of no Trouble, feel no Burden, want nothing to be altered, or removed, nothing to be increased or strengthened in you, how can you pray for any thing of this Kind? But if your Heart knows its own Plague, feels its inward Evil, knows what it wants to have removed, will you not let your Distress form the Manner of your Prayer? or will you pray in a Form of Words, that have no more Agreement with your State, than if a Man walking above-ground, should beg every Man he met, to pull him out of a deep Pit. For Prayers not formed according to the real State of your Heart, are but like a Prayer to be pulled out of a deep Well, when you are not in it. Hence you may see, how unreasonable it is to make a Mystery of Prayer, or an Art, that needs so much Instruction; since every Man is, and only can be, directed by his own inward State and Condition, when, and how, and what he is to pray for, as every man's outward State shows him what he outwardly wants. And yet it should seem, as if a Prayer-Book was highly necessary, and ought to be the Performance of great Learning and Abilities, since only our learned Men and Scholars make our Prayer-Books.

[Pryr-2.3-37] Acad. I did not imagine, Rusticus, that you would have so openly declared against Manuals of Devotion, since you cannot but know, that not only the most learned, but the most pious Doctors of the Church, consider them as necessary Helps to Devotion.

[Pryr-2.3-38] Rust. If you, Academicus, were obliged to go a long journey on Foot, and yet through a Weakness in your Legs could not set one Foot before another, you would do well to get the best travelling Crutches that you could.

[Pryr-2.3-39] But if, with sound and good Legs, you would not stir one Step, till you had got Crutches to hop with, surely a Man might show you the Folly of not walking with your own Legs, without being thought a declared Enemy to Crutches, or the Makers of them. Now a Manual is not so good an Help, as Crutches, and yet you see Crutches are only proper, when our Legs cannot do their Office. It is, I say, not so good an Help as Crutches, because that which you do with Crutches, is that very same Thing, that you should have done with your Legs; you really travel; but when the Heart cannot take one Step in Prayer, and you therefore read your Manual, you do not do that very same Thing, which your Heart should have done, that is, really pray. A fine Manual therefore is not to be considered as a Means of praying, or as something that puts you in a State of Prayer, as Crutches help you to travel; but its chief Use, as a Book of Prayers to a dead and hardened Heart that has no Prayer of its own, is to show it, what a State and Spirit of Prayer it wants, and at what a sad Distance it is from feeling all that Variety of humble, penitent, grateful, fervent, resigned, loving Sentiments, which are described in the Manual, that so, being touched with a View of its own miserable State, it may begin its own Prayer to God for Help. But I have done. Theophilus may now answer your earnest Request.

[Pryr-2.3-40] Theoph. Your earnest Desire, Academicus, to live in the Spirit of Prayer, and be truly governed by it, is a most excellent Desire; for to be a Man of Prayer is that which the Apostle means by living in the Spirit, and having our Conversation in Heaven. It is to have done, not only with the confessed Vices, but with the allowed Follies and Vanities of this World. To tell such a Soul of the Innocency of Levity, that it needs not run away from idle Discourse, vain Gaiety, and trifling Mirth, as being, the harmless Relief of our heavy Natures, is like telling the Flame, that it needs not always be ascending upwards. But here you are to observe, that this Spirit of Prayer is not to be taught you by a Book, or brought into you by an Art from without, but must be an inward Birth, that must arise from your own Fire and Light within you, as the Air arises from the Fire and Light of this World. For the Spirit of every Being, be it what or where it will, or be its Spirit of what Kind it will, is only the Breath or Spirit that proceeds from its own Fire and Light. In vegetative, sensitive, and intellectual Creatures, it is all in the same Manner; Spirit is the third Form of its Life, and is the Birth that proceeds from the other two; and is the Manifestation of their Nature and Qualities. For such as the Fire and Light are, such and no other, neither higher nor lower, neither better nor worse, is the Spirit that proceeds from them. Now the Reason why all, and every Life does, and must stand in this Form, is wholly and solely from hence, because the Deity, the one Source and Fountain of all Life, is a triune God, whose third Form is, and is called, the Spirit of God, proceeding from the Father, and the Son.

[Pryr-2.3-41] The painful Sense and Feeling of what you are, kindled into a working State of Sensibility by the Light of God within you, is the Fire and Light from whence your Spirit of Prayer proceeds. In its first kindling nothing is found or felt, but Pain, Wrath, and Darkness, as is to be seen in the first kindling of every Heat or Fire. And therefore its first Prayer is nothing else but a Sense of Penitence, Self-condemnation, Confession, and Humility. It feels nothing but its own Misery, and so is all Humility. This Prayer of Humility is met by the Divine Love, the Mercifulness of God embraces it; and then its Prayer is changed into Hymns, and Songs, and Thanksgivings. When this State of Fervor has done its Work, has melted away all earthly Passions and Affections, and left no Inclination in the Soul, but to Delight in God alone, then its Prayer changes again. It is now come so near to God, has found such Union with him, that it does not so much pray as live in God. Its Prayer is not any particular Action, is not the Work of any particular Faculty, not confined to Times, or Words, or Place, but is the Work of his whole Being, which continually stands in Fullness of Faith, in Purity of Love, in absolute Resignation, to do and be, what and how his Beloved pleaseth. This is the last State of the Spirit of Prayer, and is its highest Union with God in this Life. Each of these foregoing States has its Time, its Variety of Workings, its Trials, Temptations, and Purifications, which can only be known by Experience in the Passage through them. The one only and infallible Way to go safely through all the Difficulties, Trials, Temptations, Dryness, or Opposition, of our own evil Tempers, is this: it is to expect nothing from ourselves, to trust to nothing in ourselves, but in every thing expect, and depend upon God for Relief. Keep fast Hold of this Thread, and then let your Way be what it will, Darkness, Temptation, or the Rebellion of Nature, you will be led through all, to an Union with God: For nothing hurts us in any State, but an Expectation of something in it, and from it, which we should only expect from God. We are looking for our own Virtue, our own Piety, our own Goodness, and so live on and on in our own Poverty and Weakness; To-day pleased and comforted with the seeming Strength and Firmness of our own pious Tempers, and fancying ourselves to be somewhat; To-morrow, fallen into our own Mire, we are dejected, but not humbled; we grieve, but it is only the Grief of Pride, at the seeing our Perfection not to be such as we vainly imagined. And thus it will be, till the whole Turn of our Minds is so changed, that we as fully see and know our Inability to have any Goodness of our own, as to have a Life of our own.

[Pryr-2.3-42] For since nothing is, or can be, good in us, but the Life of God manifested in us, how can this be had but from God alone? When we are happily brought to this Conviction, then we have done with all Thought of being our own Builders; the whole Spirit of our Mind is become a mere Faith, and Hope, and Trust in the sole Operation of God's Spirit, looking no more to any other Power, to be formed in Christ new Creatures, than we look to any other Power for the Resurrection of our Bodies at the last Day. Hence may be seen, that the Trials of every State are its greatest Blessings; they do that for us, which we most of all want to have done, they force us to know our own Nothingness, and the All of God.

[Pryr-2.3-43] People who have long dwelt in the Fervours of Devotion, in an high Sensibility of Divine Affections, practicing every Virtue with a kind of Greediness, are frightened, when Coldness seizes upon them, when their Hymns give no Transport, and their Hearts, instead of flaming with the Love of every Virtue, seem ready to be overcome by every Vice. But here, keep fast Hold of the Thread I mentioned before, and all is well. For this Coldness is the Divine Offspring, or genuine Birth, of the former Fervour; it comes from it as a good Fruit, and brings the Soul nearer to God, than the Fervour did. The Fervour was good, and did a good Work in the Soul; it overcame the earthly Nature, and made the Soul delight in God, and spiritual Things; but its Delight was too much an own Delight, a fancied Self-holiness, and occasioned Rest and Satisfaction in Self, which if it had continued uninterrupted, undiscovered, an earthly Self had only been changed into a spiritual Self. Therefore I called this Coldness, or Loss of Fervour, its Divine Offspring, because it brings a Divine Effect, or more fruitful Progress in the Divine Life. For this Coldness overcomes, and delivers us from spiritual Self, as Fervour overcame the earthly Nature. It does the Work that Fervour did, but in an higher Degree, because it gives up more, sacrifices more, and brings forth more Resignation to God, than Fervour did; and therefore it is more in God, and receives more from him. The devout Soul therefore is always safe in every State, if it makes everything an Occasion either of rising up, or falling down into the Hands of God, and exercising Faith, and Trust, and Resignation to him. Fervour is good, and ought to be loved; but Tribulation, Distress, and Coldness, in their Season are better, because they give Means and Power of exercising an higher Faith, a purer Love, and more perfect Resignation to God, which are the best State of the Soul. And therefore the pious Soul that eyes only God, that means nothing but being his alone, can have no Stop put to its Progress; Light and Darkness equally assist him; in the Light he looks up to God; in the Darkness he lays hold on God; and so they both do him the same Good.

[Pryr-2.3-44] This little sketch, Academicus, of the Nature and Progress of the Spirit of Prayer, may show you, that a Manual is not so great a Matter as you imagined.

[Pryr-2.3-45] The best Instruction that I can give you, as helpful, or preparatory to the Spirit of Prayer, is already fully given, where we have set forth the original Perfection, the miserable Fall, and the glorious Redemption of Man. It is the true Knowledge of these great Things that can do all for you, which human Instruction can do. These Things must fill you with a Dislike of your present State, drive all earthly Desires out of your Soul, and create an earnest Longing after your first Perfection. For Prayer cannot be taught you, by giving you a Book of Prayers, but by awakening in you a true Sense and Knowledge of what you are, and what you should be; that so you may see, and know, and feel, what Things you want, and are to pray for. For a Man does not, cannot pray for any thing, because a fine Petition for it is put into his Hands, but because his own Condition is a Reason and Motive for his asking for it. And therefore it is that the Spirit of Prayer, in the First Part, began with a full Discovery and Proof of these high and important Matters, at the Sight of which the World, and all that is in it, shrinks into nothing, and every thing past, present, and to come, awakens in our Hearts a continual Prayer, and longing Desire, after God, Christ, and Eternity.

[Pryr-2.3-46] Acad. I perceive then, Theophilus, that you direct me entirely to my own Prayer in my private Devotions, and not to the Use of any Book. But surely you do not take this to be right in general, that the common People, who are unlearned, and mostly of low Understandings, should kneel down in private, without any borrowed Form of Prayer, saying only what comes then into their own Heads.

[Pryr-2.3-47] Theoph. It would be very wrong, Academicus, to condemn a Manual as such, or to tell any People, learned or unlearned, that they ought not to make any Use of it. This would be quite rash and silly: But it cannot be wrong, or hurtful to any body, to show, that Prayer is the natural Language of the Heart, and, as such, does not want any Form, or borrowed Words. Now all that has been said of Manuals of Prayers, only amounts to thus much; that they are not necessary, nor the most natural and excellent Way of praying. If they happen to be necessary to any Person, or to be his most excellent Way, it is because the natural, real Prayer of his Heart is already engaged, loving, wishing, and longing after, the Things of this Life; which makes him so insensible of his spiritual Wants, so blind and dead as to the Things of God, that he cannot pray for them, but so far as the Words of other People are put into his Mouth. If a Man is blind, and knows it not, he may be told to pray for Sight; if he is sick, and knows nothing of it, he may be told to pray for Health: So if the Soul is in this State, with regard to its spiritual wants, a Manual may be of good Use to it, not so much by helping it to pray, as by showing it, at what a miserable Distance it is from those Tempers which belong to Prayer.

[Pryr-2.3-48] But when a Man has had so much Benefit from the Gospel, as to know his own Misery, his want of a Redeemer, who he is, and how is he to be found; there every thing seems to be done, both to awaken and direct his Prayer, and make it a true Praying in and by the Spirit. For when the Heart really pants and longs after God, its Prayer is a Praying, as moved and animated by the Spirit of God; it is the Breath or Inspiration of God, stirring, moving and opening itself in the Heart. For though the earthly Nature, our old Man, can oblige or accustom himself to take heavenly Words at certain Times into his Mouth, yet this is a certain Truth, that nothing ever did, or can have the least Desire or Tendency to ascend to Heaven, but that which came down from Heaven; and therefore nothing in the Heart can pray, aspire, and long after God, but the Spirit of God moving and stirring in it. Every Breath therefore of the true Spirit of Prayer, can be nothing else but the Breath of the Spirit of God, breathing, inspiring, and moving the Heart, in all its Variety of Motions and Affections, towards God. And therefore every time a good Desire stirs in the Heart, a good Prayer goes out of it, that reaches God as being the Fruit and Work of his Holy Spirit. When any Man, feeling his Corruption, and the Power of Sin in his Soul, looks up to God, with true Earnestness of Faith and Desire to be delivered from it, whether with Words, or without Words, how can he pray better? What need of any Change of Thoughts, or Words, or any Variety of Expressions, when the one Faith and Desire of his Heart made known to God, and continued in, is not only all, but the most perfect Prayer he can make? Again suppose the Soul in another State, feeling with, Joy its offered Redeemer, and opening its Heart for the full Reception of him; if it stands in this State of Wishing and Longing for the Birth of Christ, how can its Prayer be in an higher Degree of Request? Or if it breaks out frequently in these Words, Come, Lord Jesus, come quickly, with all thy holy Nature, Spirit, and Tempers into my Soul, is there any Occasion to enlarge, or alter these Words into another Form of Expression? Can he do better, or pray more, than by continually standing from time to time in this State of wishing to have Christ formed in him? Nay, is it not more likely, that his Heart should be more divided and dissipated by a numerous Change of Expressions, than by keeping united to one Expression that sets forth all that he wants? For it is the Reality, the Steadiness, and Continuity of Desire, that is the Goodness of Prayer, and its Qualification to receive all that it wants. Our Lord said to one that came to him, What wilt thou that I should do unto thee? He answered, Lord, that I may receive my sight: And he received it. Another said, Lord, if thou wilt, thou canst make me clean. And he was cleansed. Tell me what Learning, or fine Parts, are required to make such

Prayers as these? and yet what Wonders of Relief are recorded in Scripture, as given to such short Prayers as these! Or tell me what Blessing of Prayer, or Faith, or Love, may not now be obtained in the same Way, and with as few Words, as then was done? Every Man therefore that has any Feeling of the Weight of his Sin, or any true Desire to be delivered from it by Christ, has Learning and Capacity enough to make his own Prayer. For praying is not speaking forth eloquently, but simply, the true Desire of the Heart; and the Heart, simple and plain in good Desires, is in the truest State of Preparation for all the Gifts and Graces of God. And this I must tell you, that the most simple Souls, that have accustomed themselves to speak their own Desires and Wants to God, in such short, but true Breathings of their Hearts to him, will soon know more of Prayer, and the Mysteries thereof, than any Persons who have only their Knowledge from Learning, and learned Books.

[Pryr-2.3-49] Acad. You seem to me, Theophilus, to have much Truth in what you say, and yet to be in a Way by yourself. I cannot take you to be with those who place all in many and long Forms; and now I take you to be even more against those, who made much Account of what they call a gifted Man, and make that to be the one true Gift of Prayer, when any one is able to pray extempore, or with his own Words, for an Hour or two at a Time.

[Pryr-2.3-50] Theoph. I have shown you, Academicus, that Prayer is purely the Desire of the Heart; that it has not the Nature of praying, but so far as it is the true Language of the Heart. I have shown you the great Benefit that all People must receive from this true Prayer of the Heart. And to remove all Pretence of Want of Ability in the lowest Sort of People to pray from their own Hearts, I have shown, that the most simple, short Petitions, when truly spoken by the Heart, have all the Perfection that Prayer can have.

[Pryr-2.3-51] But mark, Sir, why or when I ascribe this Perfection to it. It is when the Heart stands continually in this State of wishing to have that, which is expressed in so few Words. It is then, that I said, there was no Occasion to enlarge, or alter the Words into another or longer Form, because the Reality, the Steadiness, and the Continuity of the Desire, is the Goodness and Perfection of the Prayer. Now, Sir, let us suppose two Men; the one is frequently an Hour, or two, or a whole Night, on his Knees, in silent Prayer, in high acts of Love, and Faith, and Resignation to God, not outwardly spoken by his Mouth; the other is as long a Time pouring forth the Devotion of his Heart in a Variety of fervent Expressions. May not both these Men justly appeal to me, not only as not condemning, but as asserting, the Goodness of their Length and Manner of Prayer, since I make a short simple Petition to be only then a good Prayer, when it proceeds from a steady, continued Desire of the Heart? It is not therefore Silence, or a simple Petition, or a great Variety of outward Expressions, that alters the Nature of Prayer, or makes it to be good, or better, but only and solely the Reality, Steadiness, and Continuity of the Desire; and therefore whether a Man offers this Desire to God in the silent Longing of the Heart, or in simple short Petitions, or in a great Variety of Words, is of no Consequence; but all of them are equally good, when the true and right State of the Heart is with them.

[Pryr-2.3-52] Thus you see, Academicus, that I am so far from being, as you said, in a Way by myself, that I am with every Man in every Way, whose Heart stands right towards God. But if you would know what I would call a true and great Gift of Prayer, and what I most of all wish for to myself, it is a good Heart, that stands continually inclined towards God.

[Pryr-2.3-53] Acad. I am not sorry, Theophilus, that I have made so unreasonable an Observation upon what you said, since it has occasioned you to give so good and just an Answer to it. But yet this silent Prayer you speak of, is what I never read nor heard anything of before; and it seems to me but like ceasing to pray; and yet you seem to like it in its Turn, as well as any other Way of praying.

[Pryr-2.3-54] Theoph. All that I have said of Prayer, Academicus, has been only to this End, to show you its true and real Nature, whence it is to arise, where it is to be found, and how you are to begin, and become a true Proficient in it. If, therefore, you were at present to look no farther, than how to put yourself in a State of beginning to practise a Prayer proceeding from your own Heart, and continuing in it, leaving all that you are farther to know of Prayer, to be known in its own Time by Experience, which alone can open any true Knowledge in you, this would be much better for you, than to be asking beforehand about such things, as are not your immediate Concern.

[Pryr-2.3-55] Begin to be a Man of Prayer, in this easy, simple, and natural Manner, that has been set before you; and when you are faithful to this Method, you will then need no other Instructor in the Art of Prayer. Your own Heart thus turned to God, will want no one to tell it, when it should be simple in its Petitions, or various in its Expressions, or prostrate itself in Silence before God. But this Hastiness of knowing Things, before they become our Concern, or belong to us, is very common. Thus a Man that has but just entered upon the Reformation of his Life, shall want to read or hear a Discourse upon Perfection, whether it be absolutely attainable or not; and shall be more eager after what he can hear of this Matter, though at such a Distance from himself, than of such Things as concern the next Step that he is to take in his own proper State.

[Pryr-2.3-56] You, my Friend, have already rightly taken the first Step in the spiritual Life; you have devoted yourself absolutely to God, to live wholly to his Will, under the Light and Guidance of his Holy Spirit, intending, seeking nothing in this World, but such a Passage through it, as may tend to the Glory of God, and the Recovery of your own fallen Soul. Your next Step is this, it is a looking to the Continuance of this first Resolution, and Donation of yourself to God, to see that it be kept alive, that every thing you do may be animated and directed by it, and all the Occurrences of every Day, from Morning to Night, be received by you, as becomes a Spirit that is devoted to God. Now this second Step cannot be taken, but purely by Prayer; nothing else has the least Power here but Prayer: I do not mean you must frequently read or say a Number of Prayers (though this in its Turn may be good and useful to you) but the Prayer I mean and which you must practise, if you would take this second Step in the spiritual Life, is Prayer of the Heart, or a Prayer of your own, proceeding from the State of your Heart, and its own Tendency to God. Of all things therefore look to this Prayer of the Heart; consider it as your infallible Guide to Heaven; turn from every thing that is an Hindrance of it, that quenches or abates its Fervour; love and like nothing but that which is suitable to it; and let every Day begin, go on, and end, in the Spirit of it. Consider yourself as always wrong, as having gone aside, and lost your right Path, when any Delight, Desire, or Trouble, is suffered to live in you, that cannot be made a Part of this Prayer of the Heart to God. For nothing so infallibly shows us the true State of our Heart, as that which gives us either Delight or Trouble; for as our Delight and Trouble is, so is the State of our Heart: If therefore you are carried away with any Trouble or Delight, that has not an immediate Relation to your Progress in the Divine Life, you may be assured your Heart is not in its right State of Prayer to God. Look at a Man who is devoted to some one Thing, or has some one great worldly Matter at Heart, he stands turned from every thing that has not some Relation to it; he has no Joy or Trouble but what arises from it; he has no Eyes nor Ears, but to see or hear something about it. All else is a Trifle, but that which some Way or other concerns this great Matter. You need not tell him of any Rules or Methods to keep it in his Thoughts; it goes with him into all Places and Companies; it has his first Thoughts in the

Morning; and every Day is good or bad, as this great Matter seems to succeed or not. This may show you how easily, how naturally, how constantly, our Heart will carry on its own State of Prayer, as soon as God is its great Object, or it is wholly given up to him, as its one great Good. This may also show you, that the Heart cannot enter into a State of the Spirit of Prayer to God, till that which I called the first Step in the spiritual Life is taken, which is the taking God for its All, or the giving itself up wholly to God. But when this Foundation is laid, the Seed of Prayer is sown, and the Heart is in a continual State of Tendency to God; having no other Delight or Trouble in Things of any kind, but as they help or hinder its Union with God. Therefore, Academicus, the Way to be a Man of Prayer, and be governed by its Spirit, is not to get a Book full of Prayers; but the best Help you can have from a Book, is to read one full of such Truths, Instructions, and awakening Informations, as force you to see and know who, and what, and where, you are; that God is your All; and that all is Misery, but a Heart and Life devoted to him. This is the best outward Prayer-Book you can have, as it will turn you to an inward Book, and Spirit of Prayer in your Heart, which is a continual longing Desire of the Heart after God, his Divine Life, and Holy Spirit. When, for the Sake of this inward Prayer, you retire at any time of the Day, never begin till you know and feel, why and wherefore you are going to pray; and let this why and wherefore, form and direct every thing that comes from you, whether it be in Thought or in Word. As you cannot but know your own State, so it must be the easiest Thing in the World to look up to God, with such Desires as suit the State you are in; and praying in this Manner, whether it be in one, or more, or no Words, your Prayer will always be sincere, and good, and highly beneficial to you.—Thus praying, you can never pray in vain; but one Month in the Practice of it, will do you more Good, make a greater Change in your Soul, than twenty Years of Prayer only by Books, and Forms of other Peoples making.

[Pryr-2.3-57] No Vice can harbour in you, no Infirmity take any Root, no good Desire can languish, when once your Heart is in this Method of Prayer; never beginning to pray, till you first see how Matters stand with you; asking your Heart what it wants, and having nothing in your Prayers, but what the known State of your Heart puts you upon demanding, saying, or offering, unto God. A Quarter of an Hour of this Prayer, brings you out of your Closet a new Man; your Heart feels the Good of it; and every Return of such a Prayer, gives new Life and Growth to all your Virtues, with more Certainty, than the Dew refreshes the Herbs of the Field: Whereas, overlooking this true Prayer of your own Heart, and only at certain Times taking a Prayer that you find in a Book, you have nothing to wonder at, if you are every Day praying, and yet every Day sinking farther and farther under all your Infirmities. For your Heart is your Life, and your Life can only be altered by that which is the real Working of your Heart. And if your Prayer is only a Form of Words, made by the Skill of other People, such a Prayer can no more change you into a good Man, than an Actor upon the Stage, who speaks kingly Language, is thereby made to be a King: Whereas one Thought, or Word, or Look, towards God, proceeding from your own Heart, can never be without its proper Fruit, or fail of doing a real Good to your Soul. Again, another great and infallible Benefit of this kind of Prayer is this; it is the only Way to be delivered from the Deceitfulness of your own Hearts.

[Pryr-2.3-58] Our Hearts deceive us, because we leave them to themselves, are absent from them, taken up in outward Things, in outward Rules and Forms of Living and Praying. But this kind of Praying, which takes all its Thoughts and Words only from the State of our Hearts, makes it impossible for us to be Strangers to ourselves. The Strength of every Sin, the Power of every evil Temper, the most secret Workings of our Hearts, the Weakness of any or all our Virtues, is with a Noonday Clearness forced to be seen, as soon as the Heart is made our Prayer-

Book, and we pray nothing, but according to what we read, and find there.

[Pryr-2.3-59] Acad. O Theophilus, you have shown me, that it is almost as easy and natural a Thing to pray, as to breathe; and that the best Prayer in the World, is that which the Heart can thus easily send forth from itself, untaught by any thing, but its own Sense of God and itself. And yet I am almost afraid of loving this kind of Prayer too much. I am not free from suspicions about it: I apprehend it to be that very praying by the Spirit, or as moved by the Spirit, or from a Light within, which is condemned as Quakerism.

[Pryr-2.3-60] Theoph. There is but one good Prayer that you can possibly make, and that is a Prayer in and from, or as the Spirit of God moves you in it, or to it. This, this alone, is a Divine Prayer; no other Prayer has, or can possibly have any Communion with God. Take the Matter thus: Man is a threefold Being; he has three Natures; he partakes of the divine, the elementary, and the diabolical Nature. Had he not these three Natures in a certain Degree in him, he could have no Communion with God, he could not enjoy the Elements, nor could the evil Spirits have the least Power of Access to him.

[Pryr-2.3-61] Now the astral, elementary Nature of Man, in this World, cannot have a Longing after the pure Deity; it cannot hunger, and thirst after the Divine Image, nor desire to be perfect as God is perfect; this is as impossible, as for the Beasts of the Field to long to be Angels. Therefore Flesh and Blood in us, can no more make a Divine Prayer, than in any other Animal of this World.

[Pryr-2.3-62] The diabolical Nature which is in us, can do nothing but that which the Devils do: it can only rise up in its own Pride, Envy, and Self-Exaltation, and only hate all the Goodness that is either in Heaven, or on Earth. And therefore it is a Truth of the greatest Certainty, that no Man ever did, or can send up a Divine and heavenly Prayer to God, or such a Prayer as can reach God, but in and by the Spirit of God in him. Our astral, elementary Man, and our proud, subtle, serpentine Nature, can read, or say a Prayer full of good Words and Wishes, as easily as Satan could use Scripture-Language in the Temptation of Christ; but nothing can wish to be like God, or to unite with his Goodness and Holiness, but that Spirit in us, which partakes of his Divine Nature. Therefore to ridicule praying by the Spirit, or as moved by the Spirit, is ridiculing the one only Prayer that is Divine, or can do us any Divine Good; and to reject and oppose it, as a vain Conceit, is to quench, and suppress all that is holy, heavenly, and Divine, within us. For if this Holy Spirit does not live, and move in us, and bring forth all the praying Affections of our Souls, we may as well think of reaching Heaven with our Hands, as with our Prayers.

[Pryr-2.3-63] Acad. I know not, Theophilus, how to deny anything that you have here said: Yet this Account seems to make no Distinction between our own good Spirit, and the Holy Spirit of God, I took the Inspirations, and Graces of the Holy Spirit to be something, that came into us from without, and to be as distinct from our own Good Spirit, as God is distinct from the Creature.

[Pryr-2.3-64] Theoph. The Holy Spirit of God is as necessary to our Divine Life, or the Life of Grace, as the Air of this World is necessary to our animal Life; and is as distinct from us, and as much without us, as the Air of this World is distinct from, and without, the Creatures that live in it. And yet our own good Spirit is the very Spirit of God, moving and stirring in us. No Animal can unite with, or breathe the Air of this World, till it has first the Air of this World brought forth, as the true Birth of its own Life in itself; this is its only Capacity to live in the Spirit of this World; and the Breath or Spirit that thus arises in its own Life, is the very same Breath, that is in outward Nature, in which it lives. It is strictly thus, with the Spirit of God in our Souls; it must first have a Birth within us, arising from the Life of our Souls, and as such, is our only Capacity to have Life, and live in the Spirit of God himself, and is the very Breath of the Spirit of God, who is yet as distinct from us, as the Breath of our animal Life, that arises from our own Fire, is distinct from the Air of the World in which it lives. And thus, Academicus, our own good Spirit is the very Spirit of the Deity, and yet not God, but the Spirit of God, breathed or kindled into a creaturely Form; and this good Spirit, Divine in its Origin, and Divine in its Nature, is that alone in us, that can reach God, unite with him, cooperate with him, be moved, and blessed by him, as our earthly Spirit is, by the outward Spirit of this elementary World.

[Pryr-2.3-65] Acad. Indeed, Theophilus, you have, in few Words, so gone to the Bottom of this Matter, that nothing is left either for any further Doubt, or Inquiry about it. My own good Spirit is the Breath of God in me, and so related to God, as the Breath of my animal Life is related to the Air, or Spirit of this outward World. It is from God, has the Nature, the Eternity, the Spirituality of God, as the Breath of my Flesh and Blood, has the Grossness, the earthly, transitory Nature of the Spirit of this World. And as all my Communication with this World arises from the Breath of this World, kindled in my own Life, so all my possibility of Communication with God, arises solely from the Breath of his Holy Spirit brought forth in the Life of my Soul; and I can only live in God, by his Spirit having a Birth in me, as I can only live in this World, by having its Spirit born in me. This plain Truth sets all the Scripture-Doctrine, concerning the Necessity, Power, and Operation of the Holy Spirit, in the greatest and most edifying Degree of Clearness. Thus, what can be a more plain, sober, and palpable Truth, than when the Apostle saith, They only are the Sons of God, who are led by the Spirit of God? It is only like saying, that those Creatures only belong to this World, who live in, and by its Spirit. I shall here, Sir, only add, that my Gospel-Faith stands now upon a most solid, and comfortable Foundation; my Heart is all delight, and Devotion to God, when I consider, First, That Christ my Redeemer is the first Seed of the Woman, or Power of Salvation inspoken into fallen Adam; the Immanuel; the God within every Man; the Light that lighteth every Man that cometh into the World. Secondly, That the Holy Spirit of God, the Breath of Eternity, hath also its Seed of life in my Soul; for where the Word, or Son of God is, there is the Spirit of God in the same State; if one is only a Seed of Life, a Spark of Heaven, the other is so also; and these two, thus considered, are the glorious Pearl of Eternity, hidden in every Man's Soul, and so often spoken of before. And thus we understand, how the Whole of our Redemption (according to the plain language of Scripture) is inwardly and outwardly solely the Work of the Light and Spirit of God, a Kingdom of God both within and without us, and to which we do not, cannot live, but so far as we are inspired, moved, and led, by the Spirit of God. Earnestly, therefore, to pray, humbly to hope, and faithfully to expect, to be continually inspired, and animated by the Holy Spirit of God has no more of Vanity, Fanaticism, or enthusiastic Wildness in it, than to hope and pray, to act in every thing from and by a good Spirit. For as sure as the Lip of Truth hath told us, that there is but One that is good, so sure is it, that not a Spark of Goodness, nor a Breath of Piety, can be in any Creature, either in Heaven, or on Earth, but by that Divine Spirit, which is the Breath of God, breathed from himself into the Creature. The Matter is not about Appearances of Goodness, Forms of Virtue, Rules of Religion, or a prudential Piety, suited to Time, and Place, and Character; all these are Degrees of Goodness, that our old Man can as easily trade in, as in any other Matters of this World. But so much as we have of an heavenly and Divine Goodness, or of a Goodness that belongs to Heaven, and has the Nature of Heaven in it, so much we must have of a Divine Inspiration in us. For as nothing can fall to the Earth, but because it has the Nature of the Earth in it; so it is a Truth of the utmost Certainty, that nothing can ascend towards Heaven, or have the least Power to unite with it, but that very Spirit which came down from Heaven, and has the Nature of Heaven in it. This Truth, therefore, that the Kingdom of God is within us, that its light is solely the Lamb of God, its Spirit solely the Spirit of God, stands upon a Rock, against which all Attempts are in vain. All that I now further desire to know, is only this; how I may keep free from all Delusions in this Matter, and not take my own natural Abilities, Tempers, and Passions, or the Suggestions of evil Spirits, to be the Working of the Spirit of God in me. Pray, Sir, tell me how I shall safely know when, and how far, I am led and governed by the Spirit of God?

[Pryr-2.3-66] Theoph. You may know this, Academicus, just as you know, when you are governed by the Spirit of Wrath, Envy, Guile, Craft, or Covetousness. Every Man knows this of himself, as easily, and as certainly as he knows when he is hungry, pleased, or displeased. Now it is the same Thing with regard to the Spirit of God; the Knowledge of it is as perceptible in yourself, and liable to no more delusion. For the Spirit of God is more distinguishable from all other Spirits and Tempers, than any of your natural Affections or Tempers are, from one another; as I will here plainly show you.

[Pryr-2.3-67] "God is unwearied Patience, a Meekness that cannot be provoked; he is an ever-enduring Mercifulness; he is unmixed Goodness, impartial, universal Love; his Delight is in the Communication of himself, his own Happiness, to every thing, according to its Capacity. He does every thing that is good, righteous and lovely, for its own sake, because it is good, righteous, and lovely. He is the Good from which nothing but Good cometh, and resisteth all Evil, only with Goodness." This, Sir, is the Nature and Spirit of God, and here you have your infallible Proof, whether you are moved, and led by the Spirit of God. Here is a Proof that never can fail you; is always at hand; and is liable to no Mistake or Delusion. If it be the earnest Desire, and Longing of your Heart, to be merciful as he is merciful; to be full of his unwearied Patience, to dwell in his unalterable Meekness; if you long to be like him in universal, impartial Love; if you desire to communicate every Good, to every Creature that you are able; if you love and practise every thing that is good, righteous, and lovely, for its own sake, because it is good, righteous, and lovely; and resist no Evil, but with Goodness; then you have the utmost Certainty, that the Spirit of God liveth, dwelleth, and governeth in you. Now all these Tempers are as knowable to every Man, as his own Love and Hatred; and therefore no Man can be deceived as to the Possession of them, but he that chooses to deceive himself. Now if you want any of these Tempers, if the whole Bent of your Heart and Mind is not set upon them, all Pretenses to an immediate Inspiration, and continual Operation of the Spirit of God in your Soul, are vain and groundless. For the Spirit of God is that which I have here described; and where his Spirit dwells and governs, there all these Tempers are brought forth, or springing up, as the certain Fruits of it. What room therefore, Academicus, for so much uncertainty, or Fear of Delusion, in this Matter? Keep but within the Bounds here set you; call nothing a Proof of the Spirit or Work of God in your Soul, but these Tempers, and the Works which they produce; and then, but not till then, you may safely and infallibly say, with St. John, Hereby we know that he abideth in us by the Spirit which he hath given us.

[Pryr-2.3-68] Acad. Indeed, Theophilus, you have given me a short, but very full and satisfactory Answer to my Question. I now perceive, that, as a spiritual Man, or one devoted to the Spirit of God, I am not to look after any Extraordinaries, any new Openings, Illuminations, Visions, or Voices, inward or outward, from God, as Proofs of the Spirit of God dwelling and working in me; but that all my Proof and Security of being governed by the Spirit of God, is to be grounded on other Matters: That the boundless Humility and Resignation of the Holy Jesus; the unwearied Patience, the unalterable Meekness, the impartial, universal Love of God, manifested in my Soul;

are its only Proofs, that God is in me of a Truth. Thus far all is right and good.

[Pryr-2.3-69] But yet, Sir, surely it must be said with Truth, that the Spirit of God often discovers itself, and operates in good Souls in very extraordinary Ways, in uncommon Illuminations, and Openings of Divine Light and Knowledge, in the Revelation of Mysteries, in strong Impulses and Sallies of a wonderful Zeal, full of highest Gifts and Graces of God: and that these have frequently been God's gracious Methods of awakening a sinful World.

[Pryr-2.3-70] Theoph. What you say, Academicus, is very true; and almost every Age of the Church is a sufficient Proof of it. By the Goodness of God, the Church has always had its extraordinary Persons, highly gifted from above, made burning, and shining Lights, and carried into as uncommon Ways of Life, by the same Spirit, and for the same Ends, as John the Baptist was; and as different from common Christians, as he was from the common Jews. But, my Friend, these extraordinary Operations of God's Holy Spirit, and the Wonders of his Gifts and Graces showing themselves at certain Times, and upon certain Persons, through all the Ages of the Church, are not Matters of common Instruction; they belong not to our Subject; it would be Ignorance and Vanity in me, to pretend to let you into the Secret of them; it would be the same Thing in you, to think yourself ready for it.

[Pryr-2.3-71] Would you know the Sublime, the Exalted, the Angelic, in the Christian Life, see what the Son of God saith: Thou shalt love the Lord thy God with all thy Heart, with all thy Soul, with all thy Mind, and with all thy Strength; and thy Neighbour as thyself. On these two, saith he, hang all the Law and the Prophets. And without these two Things, no good Light ever can arise, or enter into your Soul. Take all the Sciences, shine in all the Accomplishments of the lettered World, they will only lead you from one vain Passion to another; every thing you send out from within you is selfish, vain, and bad; every thing you see or perceive from without, will be received with a bad Spirit; till these two heavenly Tempers have overcome the natural Perverseness of fallen Nature. Till then, nothing pure can proceed from within, nor any thing be received in Purity from without.

[Pryr-2.3-72] Think yourself therefore unfit, incapable of judging rightly, or acting virtuously, till these two Tempers have the Government of your Heart. Then every Truth will meet you; no hurtful Error can get Entrance into your Heart; you will neither deceive, nor be deceived; but will have a better Knowledge of all Divine Matters, than all the human Learning in the World can help you to.

[Pryr-2.3-73] Would you know what it is to love God with all your Heart and Soul, &c., you need only look back to that, which has been said of the Nature and Spirit of God {2.3-67}. For when with all your Heart and Soul you love, and long to have, that Nature and Spirit, to be wholly united to it, possessed and governed by it, then you love God with all your Heart and Soul, &c. And then you are first capable of loving yourself and your Neighbour rightly. For so much as you have of the Divine Nature and Spirit in you, just so much Power have you of loving yourself and your Neighbour aright; that is, of loving only and equally, that in yourself and your Neighbour, which the Deity only and equally loves, both in you, and him. But it is time to part, when we have only told our silent Friend, Humanus, that if we live to meet again, we shall, with all our Hearts, receive him as a Speaker amongst us.— And so, Gentlemen, once more, Adieu.

THE SPIRIT OF LOVE
BY

William Law

The Spirit of Love

Part One

In a letter to a friend

My Dear Friend,

[Love-1-1] YOU had no Occasion to make any Apology for the Manner of your Letter to me, for though you very well know that I have as utter an aversion to waste my Time and Thoughts in Matters of theological Debate as in any Contentions merely of a worldly Nature, as knowing that the Former are generally as much, if not more, hurtful to the Heart of Man than the Latter; yet as your Objections rather tend to stir up the Powers of Love than the wrangle of a rational Debate, so I consider them only as Motives and Occasions of edifying both you and myself with the Truth, the Power and Divine Blessedness of the Spirit of Love.

[Love-1-2] You say 'There is nothing in all my Writings that has more affected you than that Spirit of Love that breathes in them, and that you wish for nothing so much as to have a living Sensibility of the Power, Life, and Religion of Love. But you have these two Objections often rising in your Mind: First, that this Doctrine of pure and universal Love may be too refined and imaginary, because you find that however you like it, yet you cannot attain to it, or overcome all That in your Nature which is contrary to it, do what you can; and so are only able to be an Admirer of that Love which you cannot lay hold of. Secondly, Because you find so much said in Scripture of a Righteousness and Justice, a Wrath and Vengeance of God that must be atoned and satisfied, &c., that though you are in Love with that Description of the Deity which I have given, as a Being that is all Love, yet you have some Doubt whether the Scripture will allow of it.'

[Love-1-3] Thus stand your Objections, which will fall into nothing as soon as you look at them from a right Point of View, Which will then be, as soon as you have found the true Ground of the Nature, Power, and Necessity of the blessed Spirit of Love.

[Love-1-4] Now the Spirit of Love has this Original. God, as considered in himself in his Holy Being, before any thing is brought forth by him or out of him, is only an eternal Will to all Goodness. This is the one eternal immutable God, that from Eternity to Eternity changeth not, that can be neither more nor less nor any thing else but an eternal Will to all the Goodness that is in himself, and can come from him. The Creation of ever so many Worlds or Systems of Creatures adds nothing to, nor takes any thing from this immutable God. He always was and always will be the same immutable Will to all Goodness. So that as certainly as he is the Creator, so certainly is he the Blesser of every created Thing, and can give nothing but Blessing, Goodness, and Happiness from himself because he has in himself nothing else to give. It is much more possible for the Sun to give forth Darkness, than for God to do, or be, or give forth anything but Blessing and Goodness. Now this is the Ground and Original of the Spirit of Love in the Creature; it is and must be a Will to all Goodness, and you have not the Spirit of Love till you have this Will to all Goodness at all Times and on all Occasions. You may indeed do many Works of Love and delight in them, especially at such Times as they are not inconvenient to you, or contradictory to your State or Temper or Occurrences in Life. But the Spirit of Love is not in you till it is the Spirit of your Life, till you live freely, willingly, and universally according to it. For every Spirit acts with Freedom and Universality according to what it is. It needs no command to live its own Life, or be what it is, no more than you need bid Wrath be wrathful. And therefore when Love is the Spirit of your Life, it will have the Freedom and Universality of a Spirit; it will always live and work in Love, not because of This or That, Here or There, but because the Spirit of Love can only love, wherever it is or goes or whatever is done to it. As the Sparks know no Motion but that of flying upwards, whether it be in the Darkness of the Night or in the Light of the Day, so the Spirit of Love is always in the same Course; it knows no Difference of Time, Place, or Persons, but whether it gives or forgives, bears or forbears, it is equally doing its own delightful Work, equally blessed from itself. For the Spirit of Love, wherever it is, is its own Blessing and Happiness because it is the Truth and Reality of God in the Soul, and therefore is in the same Joy of Life and is the same Good to itself, everywhere and on every Occasion.

[Love-1-5] Oh Sir! Would you know the Blessing of all Blessings? It is this God of Love dwelling in your Soul and killing every Root of Bitterness which is the Pain and Torment of every earthly, selfish Love. For all Wants are satisfied, all Disorders of Nature are removed, no Life is any longer a Burden, every Day is a Day of Peace, every thing you meet becomes a Help to you because every thing you see or do is all done in the sweet, gentle Element of Love. For as Love has no By-Ends, wills nothing but its own Increase, so every thing is as Oil to its Flame. It must have that which it wills and cannot be disappointed, because every thing naturally helps it to live in its own Way and to bring forth its own Work. The Spirit of Love does not want to be rewarded, honoured, or esteemed. Its only Desire is to propagate itself and become the Blessing and Happiness of every thing that wants it. And therefore it meets Wrath and Evil and Hatred and Opposition with the same one Will as the Light meets the Darkness, only to overcome it with all its Blessings. Did you want to avoid the Wrath and Ill-will or to gain the Favour of any Persons, you might easily miss of your Ends; but if you have no Will but to all Goodness, everything you meet, be it what it Will, must be forced to be assistant to you. For the Wrath of an Enemy, the Treachery of a Friend, and every other Evil only helps the Spirit of Love to be more triumphant, to live its own Life and find all its own Blessings in a higher Degree. Whether therefore you consider Perfection or Happiness, it is all included in the Spirit of Love and must be so for this Reason, because the infinitely perfect and happy God is mere Love, an unchangeable Will to all Goodness; and therefore every Creature must be corrupt and unhappy, so far as it is led by any other Will than the one Will to all Goodness. Thus you see the Ground, the Nature, and Perfection of the Spirit of Love. Let me now in a Word or two show you the Necessity of it. Now the Necessity is absolute and unchangeable. No Creature can be a Child of

God but because the Goodness of God is in it; nor can it have any Union or Communion with the Goodness of the Deity till its Life is a Spirit of Love. This is the one only Band of Union betwixt God and the Creature. All besides this, or that is not this, call it by what Name you Will, is only so much Error, Fiction, Impurity, and Corruption got into the Creature, and must of all Necessity be entirely separated from it before it can have that Purity and Holiness which alone can see God or find the Divine Life. For as God is an immutable Will to all Goodness, so the Divine Will can unite or Work with no creaturely Will but that which willeth with him only that which is good. Here the Necessity is absolute; nothing will do instead of this Will; all Contrivances of Holiness, all Forms of religious Piety, signify nothing without this Will to all Goodness. For as the Will to all Goodness is the whole Nature of God, so it must be the whole Nature of every Service or Religion that can be acceptable to him. For nothing serves God or worships and adores him but that which wills and worketh with him. For God can Delight in nothing but his own Will and his own Spirit, because all Goodness is included in it and can be nowhere else. And therefore every thing that followeth an own Will or an own Spirit forsaketh the one Will to all Goodness, and whilst it doth so, hath no Capacity for the Light and Spirit of God. The Necessity therefore of the Spirit of Love is what God himself cannot dispense with in the Creature, no more than he can deny himself or act contrary to his own holy Being. But as it was his Will to all Goodness that brought forth Angels and the Spirits of Men, so he can Will nothing in their Existence but that they should live and work and manifest that same Spirit of Love and Goodness which brought them into Being. Every thing therefore but the Will and Life of Goodness is an Apostasy in the Creature and is Rebellion against the whole Nature of God.

[Love-1-6] There is no Peace, nor ever can be for the Soul of Man but in the Purity and Perfection of its first created Nature; nor can it have its Purity and Perfection in any other Way than in and by the Spirit of Love. For as Love is the God that created all Things, so Love is the Purity, the Perfection, and Blessing of all created Things; and nothing can live in God but as it lives in Love. Look at every Vice, Pain, and Disorder in human Nature; it is in itself nothing else but the Spirit of the Creature turned from the Universality of Love to some self-seeking or own Will in created Things. So that Love alone is, and only can be, the Cure of every Evil, and he that lives in the Purity of Love is risen out of the Power of Evil into the Freedom of the one Spirit of Heaven. The Schools have given us very accurate Definitions of every Vice, whether it be Covetousness, Pride, Wrath, Envy, &c., and shown us how to conceive them as notionally distinguished from one another. But the Christian has a much shorter Way of knowing their Nature and Power and what they all are and do in and to himself. For call them by what Names you will, or distinguish them with ever so much Exactness, they are all, separately and jointly, just that same one Thing, and all do that same one Work as the Scribes, the Pharisees, Hypocrites, and Rabble of the Jews who crucified Christ were all but one and the same Thing and all did one and the same Work, however different they were in outward Names. If you would therefore have a true Sense of the Nature and Power of Pride, Wrath, Covetousness, Envy, &c., they are in their whole Nature nothing else but the Murderers and Crucifiers of the true Christ of God; not as the High-Priests did many hundred Years ago, nailing his outward Humanity to an outward Cross, but crucifying afresh the Son of God, the holy Immanuel, who is the Christ that every Man crucifies as often as he gives way to Wrath, Pride, Envy, or Covetousness, &c. For every Temper or Passion that is contrary to the new Birth of Christ and keeps the holy Immanuel from coming to Life in the Soul is, in the strictest Truth of the Words, a Murderer and Killer of the Lord of Life. And where Pride and Envy and Hatred, &c., are suffered to live, there the same Thing is done as when Christ was killed and Barrabas was saved alive. The Christ of God was not then first crucified when the Jews brought him to the Cross but Adam and Eve were his first real Murderers; for the Death which happened to them in the Day that they did eat of the earthly Tree was the Death of the Christ of God or the Divine Life in their Souls. For Christ had never come into the World as a second Adam to redeem it had he not been originally the Life and Perfection and Glory of the First Adam. And he is our Atonement and Reconciliation with God, because by and through him brought to Life in us, we are set again in that first State of Holiness, and have Christ again in us as our first Father had at his Creation. For had not Christ been in our first Father as a Birth of Life in him, Adam had been created a mere Child of Wrath, in the same Impurity of Nature, in the same Enmity with God, and in the same Want of an atoning Saviour as we are at this Day.— For God can have no Delight or Union with any Creature but because his well-beloved Son, the express Image of his Person, is found in it.— This is as true of all unfallen as of all fallen Creatures; the one are redeemed and the other want no Redemption, only through the Life of Christ dwelling in them. For as the Word, or Son of God, is the Creator of all Things, and by him every Thing is made that was made, so every Thing that is good and holy in unfallen Angels is as much through his living and dwelling in them as every Thing that is good and holy in redeemed Man is through him. And he is just as much the preserver, the Strength, and Glory, and Life of all the Thrones and Principalities of Heaven as he is the Righteousness, the Peace, and Redemption of fallen Man.

[Love-1-7] This Christ of God hath many Names in Scripture, but they all mean only this, that he is, and alone can be, the Light and Life and Holiness of every Creature that is holy, whether in Heaven or on Earth. Wherever Christ is not, there is the Wrath of Nature or Nature left to itself and its own tormenting Strength of Life, to feel nothing in itself but the vain, restless Contrariety of its own working Properties. This is the one only Origin of Hell, and every kind of Curse and Misery in the Creature. It is Nature without the Christ of God or the Spirit of Love ruling over it. And here you may observe that Wrath has in itself the Nature of Hell, and that it can have no Beginning or Power in any Creature but so far as it has lost the Christ of God. And when Christ is everywhere, Wrath and Hatred Will be nowhere. Whenever therefore you willingly indulge Wrath or let your Mind work in Hatred, you not only work without Christ, but you resist him and withstand his redeeming Power over you. You do in Reality what those Jews did when they said, "We will not have this Man to reign over us." For Christ never was, nor can be, in any Creature but purely as a Spirit of Love.

[Love-1-8] In all the Universe of Nature nothing but Heaven and heavenly Creatures ever had, or could have, been known, had every created Will continued in that State in which it came forth out of and from God. For God can will nothing in the Life of the Creature but a creaturely

Manifestation of his own Goodness, Happiness and Perfection. And therefore, where this is wanted, the Fact is certain that the Creature hath changed and lost its first State that it had from God. Every Thing therefore which is the Vanity, the Wrath, the Torment and Evil of Man or any intelligent Creature is solely the Effect of his Will turned from God and can come from nothing else. Misery and Wickedness can have no other Ground or Root, for whatever wills and works with God must of all Necessity partake of the Happiness and Perfection of God.

[Love-1-9] This therefore is a certain Truth, that Hell and Death, Curse and Misery, can never cease or be removed from the Creation till the Will of the Creature is again as it came from God and is only a Spirit of Love that willeth nothing but Goodness. All the whole fallen Creation, stand it never so long, must groan and travail in Pain; this must be its Purgatory till every Contrariety to the Divine Will is entirely taken from every Creature.

[Love-1-10] Which is only saying that all the Powers and Properties of Nature are a Misery to themselves, can only Work in Disquiet and Wrath till the Birth of the Son of God brings them under the Dominion and Power of the Spirit of Love.

[Love-1-11] Thus Sir, you have seen the Original, immutable Ground and Necessity of the Spirit of Love. It is no imaginary Refinement or speculative Curiosity, but is of the highest Reality and most absolute Necessity. It stands in the Immutability and Perfection of God, and not only every intelligent Creature, be it what and where it will, but every inanimate Thing must work in Vanity and Disquiet till it has its State in and works under, the Spirit of Love. For as Love brought forth all Things, and all Things were what they were and had their Place and State under the working Power of Love, so every Thing that has lost its first-created State must be in restless Strife and Disquiet till it finds it again. There is no sort of Strife, Wrath, or Storm in outward Nature, no Fermentation, Vegetation, or Corruption in any Elementary Things but what is a full Proof and real Effect of this Truth, viz., That Nature can have no Rest but must be in the Strife of Fermentation, Vegetation, and Corruption, constantly doing and undoing, building and destroying, till the Spirit of Love has rectified all outward Nature and brought it back again into that glassy Sea of Unity and Purity in which St. John beheld the Throne of God in the Midst of it. For this glassy Sea, which the beloved Apostle was blessed with the Sight of, is the transparent, heavenly Element in which all the Properties and Powers of Nature move and work in the Unity and Purity of the one Will of God, only known as so many endless Forms of triumphing Light and Love. For the Strife of Properties, of Thick against Thin, Hard against Soft, Hot against Cold, &c., had no Existence till Angels fell, that is till they turned from God to Work with Nature. This is the Original of all the Strife, Division, and Materiality, in the fallen World.

[Love-1-12] No Fluid in this World ferments but because there is some Thickness and Contrariety in it which it would not have. And it ferments only for this Reason, to have a Unity and Clearness in itself which its Nature wants to have. Now when you see this in any Fluid, you see the Work of all fallen Nature and the same, that every Thing else is doing, as well as it can, in its own Way; it is in a restless Working and Strife after a Unity and Purity which it can neither have nor forbear to seek. And the Reason why all Things are doing thus is this, because all the Elements of this World, before they were brought down into their present State, had their Birth and Existence in the Unity and Purity of the heavenly glassy Sea, and therefore must be always in some Sort of Strife and Tendency after their first State, and doomed to Disquiet till it is found. [Love-1-13] This is the Desire of all fallen Nature in this World. It cannot be separated from it but every Part must work in Fermentation, Vegetation, and Corruption, till it is restored to its first Unity and Purity under the Spirit of Love.

[Love-1-14] Every Son of fallen Adam is under this same Necessity of working and striving after something that he neither is nor hath, and for the same Reason, because the Life of Man has lost its first Unity and Purity and therefore must be in a working Strife till all Contrariety and Impurity is separated from it and it finds its first State in God. All evil as well as good Men, all the Wisdom and Folly of this Life, are equally Proof of this. For the Vanity of wicked Men in their various Ways, and the Labours of good Men in Faith and Hope, &c., proceed from the same Cause, viz., from a Want and Desire of having and being something that they neither are nor have. The Evil seek Wrong and the Good seek Right, but they both are Seekers, and for the same Reason, because their present State has not That which it wants to have. And this must be the State of human Life and of every Creature that has fallen from its first State or has something in it that it should not have. It must do as the polluted Fluid does; it must ferment and work, either right or wrong, to mend its State. The muddled Wine always works right to the utmost of its Power because it works according to Nature, but if it had an intelligent free Will it might work as vainly as Man does; it might continually thicken itself, be always stirring up its own Dregs, and then it would seek for its Purity, just as well as the Soul of Man seeks its Happiness, in the Lusts of the Flesh, the Lust of the Eyes, and the Pride of Life. All which must of the same Necessity fall away from the Heart of Man before it can find its Happiness in God, as the Dregs must separate from the Wine before it can have its Perfection and Clearness.

[Love-1-15] Purification therefore is the one Thing necessary, and nothing will do in the stead of it. But Man is not purified till every earthly, wrathful, sensual, selfish, partial, self-willing Temper, is taken from him. He is not dying to himself, till he is dying to these Tempers; and he is not alive in God, till he is dead to them. For he wants Purification only because he has these Tempers, and therefore he has not the Purification which he wants till they are all separated from him. It is the Purity and Perfection of the Divine Nature that must be brought again into him; because in that Purity and Perfection he came forth from God, and could have no less, as he was a Child of God, that was to be blessed by a Life in him, and from him. For nothing impure or imperfect in its Will and Working, can have any Union with God. Nor are you to think that these Words, the Purity and Perfection of God, are too high to be used on this Occasion; for they only mean, that the Will of the Creature, as an Offspring of the Divine Will, must will and work with the Will of God, for then it stands and lives truly and really in the Purity and Perfection of God; and whatever does not thus, is at Enmity with God, and cannot have any Union of Life and Happiness with him, and in him.

[Love-1-16] Now, nothing wills and works with God but the Spirit of Love, because nothing else Works in God himself. The Almighty brought forth all Nature for this only End, that boundless Love might have its Infinity of Height and Depth to dwell and work in, and all the striving and working Properties of Nature are only to give Essence and Substance, Life and Strength, to the invisible hidden Spirit of Love, that it may come forth into outward Activity and manifest its blessed Powers, that Creatures born in the Strength, and out of the Powers of Nature, might communicate the Spirit of Love and Goodness, give and receive mutual Delight and Joy to and from one another. All below this State of Love is a Fall from the one Life of God, and the only Life in which the God of Love can dwell. Partiality, Self, Mine, Thine, &c., are Tempers that can only belong to Creatures that have lost the Power, Presence, and Spirit of the universal Good. They can have no Place in Heaven, nor can be anywhere but because Heaven is lost. Think not, therefore, that the Spirit of pure, universal Love, which is the one Purity and Perfection of Heaven, and all heavenly Natures, has been, or can be carried too high, or its absolute Necessity too much asserted. For it admits of no Degrees of higher or lower, and is not in Being till it is absolutely pure and unmixed, no more than a Line can be straight till it is absolutely free from all Crookedness.

[Love-1-17] All the design of Christian Redemption is, to remove every Thing that is unheavenly, gross, dark, wrathful, and disordered, from every Part of this fallen World. And when you see Earth and Stones, Storms and Tempests, and every kind of Evil, Misery, and Wickedness, you see that which Christ came into the World to remove, and not only to give a new Birth to fallen Man, but also to deliver all outward Nature from its present Vanity and Evil and set it again in its first heavenly State. Now, if you ask, How came all Things into this Evil and Vanity? It is because they have lost the blessed Spirit of Love, which alone makes the Happiness and Perfection of every Power of Nature. Look at Grossness, Coldness, Hardness, and Darkness; they never could have had any Existence, but because the Properties of Nature must appear in this manner when the Light of God is no longer dwelling in them.

[Love-1-18] Nature is at first only spiritual; it has in itself nothing but the spiritual Properties of the Desire, which is the very Being and Ground of Nature. But when these spiritual Properties are not filled and blessed, and all held in one Will by the Light and Love of God ruling in them, then something is found in Nature which never should have been found; viz., the Properties of Nature, in a State of visible, palpable Division and Contrariety to each other. And this new State of the Properties of Nature is the first Beginning and Birth, and Possibility of all that Contrariety that is to be found betwixt Hot and Cold, Hard and Soft, Thick and Thin, &c., all which could have had no Existence, till the Properties of Nature lost their first Unity, and Purity under the Light and Love of God, manifested and working in them. And this is the one true Origin of all the Materiality of this earthly System, and of every Struggle and Contrariety, found in material Things. Had the Properties of Nature been kept by the Creature, in their first State, blessed and overcome with the Light and Love of Heaven dwelling and working in them, no Wrath or Contrariety could ever have been known by any Creature; and had not Wrath and Contrariety entered into the Properties of Nature, nothing Thick or Hard or Dark, &c., could ever have been found or known in any Place. Now every Thing that you see and know of the Things of this World, shows you, that Matter began only in and from the Change of the spiritual Properties of Nature; and that Matter is changed and altered, just as the Light and Purity of Heaven is more or less in it. How comes the Flint to be in such a State of hard, dark Compaction? It is because the Meekness and Fluidity of the Light, and Air, and Water of this World have little or no Existence in it. And therefore, as soon as the Fire has unlocked its hard Compaction and opened in it the Light, and Air, and Water of this World, it becomes transparent Glass, and is brought so much nearer to that first glassy Sea in which it once existed. For the Light, and Air, and Water, of this World, though all of them in a material State, yet have the most of the first heavenly Nature in them; and as these are more, or less, in all material Things, so are they nearer, or farther from, their first heavenly State. And as Fire is the first Deliverer of the Flint from its hard Compaction, so the last universal Fire must begin the Deliverance of this material System and fit every Thing to receive that Spirit of Light and Love, which will bring all Things back again to their first glassy Sea, in which the Deity dwelleth, as in his Throne. And thus, as the earthly Fire turns Flint into Glass, so Earth will become Heaven, and the Contrariety of four divided Elements Will become one transparent Brightness of Glory, as soon as the last Fire shall have melted every Grossness into its first undivided Fluidity, for the Light and Love, and Majesty, of God to be all in all in it. How easy and natural is it to suppose all that is Earth, and Stones, to be dissolved in Water, the Water to be changed into Air, the Air into Aether, and the Aether rarefied into Light? Is there any Thing here impossible to be supposed? And how near a Step is the next, to suppose all this changed or exalted into that glassy Sea, which was everywhere, before the Angels fell? What now is become of hard, heavy, dead, divisible, corruptible Matter? Is it annihilated? No; And yet nothing of it is left; all that you know of it is gone, and nothing but its shadowy Idea will be known in Eternity. Now as this shows you, how Matter can lose all its material Properties, and go back to its first spiritual State, so it makes it very intelligible to you, how the Sin of Angels, which was their sinful Working in and with the Properties of Nature, could bring them out of their first Spirituality into that Darkness, Grossness, and Chaos out of which God raised this material System. See now, Sir, how unreasonably you once told me, that our Doctrine must suppose the Eternity of Matter; for throughout the Whole you might easily have seen, that it neither does nor can suppose it, but demonstrates the Impossibility of it; shows the true Origin of Matter, that it is no older than Sin; could have no Possibility of beginning to be, but from Sin, and therefore must entirely vanish when Sin is entirely done away.

[Love-1-19] If Matter, said you, be not made out of nothing then it must be eternal. Just as well concluded, as if you had said, If Snow and Hail and Ice are not made out of nothing, then they must be eternal. And if your Senses did not force you to know, how these things are created out of something, and are in themselves only the Properties of Light, and Air, and Water, brought out of their first State into such a Compaction and Creation, as is called Snow, Hail, and Ice, your rational Philosophy would stand to its noble Conclusion, that they must be made out of Nothing. Now every time you see Snow or Hail or Ice, you see in Truth and Reality the Creation of Matter, or how this World came to be of such a material Nature as it is. For Earth and Stones, and every other Materiality of this World, came from some antecedent Properties of Nature by that same creating Power or Fiat of God as turns the Properties of Light, and Air, and Water, into the different Materialities of Snow, Hail, and Ice.

[Love-1-20] The first Property of Nature, which is in itself a constringing, attracting, compressing, and coagulating Power, is that working Power from whence comes all Thickness, Darkness, Coldness, and Hardness; and this is the Creator of Snow and Hail and Ice out of something that before was only the Fluidity of Light, Air, and Moisture. Now this same Property of Nature, directed by the Will of God, was the Fiat and creating Power which, on the first Day of this World, compacted, coagulated, or created the wrathful Properties of fallen Nature in the Angelic Kingdom into such a new State as to become Earth and Stones and Water and a visible Heaven. And the new State of the created Heaven and Earth and Stones and Water, &c., came forth by the Fiat of God, or the Working of the first Property of Nature, from the Properties of fallen Nature; just as Snow and Ice and Hail, come forth by the same Fiat from the Properties of Light, Air, and Water. And the created Materiality of Heaven, Earth, Stones, and Water, have no more Eternity in them, than there is in Snow or Hail or Ice, but are only held for a time in their compacted or created State, by the same first astringing Property of Nature, which for a time holds Snow and Hail and Ice in their compacted State.

[Love-1-21] Now here you see with the utmost Certainty that all the Matter or Materiality of this World is the Effect of Sin, and could have its Beginning from nothing else. For as Thickness, Hardness, and Darkness (which is the Essence of Matter) is the Effect of the wrathful predominant Power of the first Property of Nature, and as no Property of Nature can be predominant, or known as it is in itself, till Nature is fallen from its harmonious Unity under the Light and Love of God dwelling in it, so you have the utmost Certainty, that where Matter, or which is the same Thing, where Thickness, Darkness, Hardness, &c., are found, there the Will of the Creature has turned from God and opened a disorderly Working of Nature without God.

[Love-1-22] Therefore as sure as the Materiality of this World standeth in the predominant Power of the first attracting, astringing Property of Nature, or in other Words, is a Thickness, Darkness, Hardness, &c., so sure is it that all the Matter of this World has its Beginning from Sin and must have its End as soon as the Properties of Nature are again restored to their first Unity and blessed Harmony under the Light and Spirit of God.

[Love-1-23] It is no Objection to all this, that Almighty God must be owned to be the true Creator of the Materiality of this World. For God only brought or created it into this Materiality out of the fallen sinful Properties of Nature, and in order to stop their sinful Working, and to put them into a State of Recovery. He created the confused Chaos of the darkened, divided, contrary Properties of spiritual Nature into a further, darker, harder Coagulation and Division, that so the fallen Angels might thereby lose all Power over them, and that this new Materiality might become a Theatre of Redemption and stand its Time under the Dominion of the Lamb of God till all the Wrath and Grossness and Darkness, born of the Sin of the Angels, was fitted to return to its first heavenly Purity.

[Love-1-24] And thus, though God is the Creator of the Materiality of this World, yet seeing he created it out of that Wrath, Division, and Darkness which Sin had opened in Nature, this Truth stands firm, that Sin alone is the Father, first Cause, and Beginner of all the Materiality of this World; and that when Sin is removed from Nature all its Materiality must vanish with it. For when the Properties of Nature are again in the Unity of the one Will of Light and Love, then Hot and Cold, Thick and Thin, Dark and Hard, with every Property of Matter, must give up all their Distinction, and all the divided Elements of this World lose all their Materiality and Division in that first heavenly Spirituality of a glassy Sea from whence they fell.

[Love-1-25] Now as all the whole Nature of Matter, its Grossness, Darkness, and Hardness, is owing to the unequal, predominant Working of the first Property of Nature which is an attracting, astringing, and compressing Desire; so every spiritual Evil, every wicked Working and disorderly State of any intelligent Being is all owing to the same disorderly, predominant Power of the first Property of Nature, doing all that inwardly in the Spirit of the Creature, which it does in an outward Grossness, Darkness, and Hardness. Thus, when the Desire (the first Property of Nature) in any intelligent Creature, leaves the Unity and Universality of the Spirit of Love and contracts or shuts up itself in an own Will, own Love, and Self-seeking, then it does all that inwardly and spiritually in the Soul, which it does in outward Grossness, Hardness, and Darkness. And had not own Will, own Love, and Self-seeking come into the Spirit of the Creature, it never could have found or felt any outward Contrariety, Darkness or Hardness: For no Creature can have any other outward Nature but that which is in the same State with its inward Spirit, and belongs to it as its own natural Growth.

[Love-1-26] Modern Metaphysics has no Knowledge of the Ground and Nature either of Spirit or Body, but supposes them not only without any natural Relation, but essentially contrary to one another, and only held together in a forced Conjunction by the arbitrary Will of God. Nay, if you were to say that God first creates a Soul out of nothing, and when that is done, then takes an understanding Faculty and puts it into it, after that adds a Will and then a Memory, all is independently made, as when a Tailor first makes the Body of a Coat and then adds Sleeves or Pockets to it, were you to say This, the Schools of Descartes, Malebranche, or Locke could have nothing to say against it. And the Thing is unavoidable, for all these Philosophers were so far from knowing the Ground of Nature, how it is a Birth from God, and all Creatures a Birth from Nature, through the working Will of God in and by the Powers of Nature, as they were so far from knowing this, as to hold a Creation out of nothing, so they were necessarily excluded from every fundamental Truth concerning the Origin either of Body or Spirit and their true Relation to one another. For a Creation out of nothing leaves no room for accounting why any Thing is as it is.— Now every wise Man is supposed to have Respect to Nature in every Thing that he would have joined together; he cannot suppose his Work to succeed unless this be done. But to suppose God to create Man with a Body and Soul, not only not naturally related but naturally impossible to be united by any Powers in either of them, is to suppose God acting and creating Man into an unnatural State, which yet he could not do, unless there was such a Thing as Nature antecedent to the Creation of Man. And how can Nature be, or have any Thing but what it is and has from God? Therefore to suppose God to bring any Creature into an unnatural State is to suppose him acting contrary to himself and to that Nature which is from him.

[Love-1-27] Yet all the Metaphysics of the Schools does this. It supposes God to bring a Soul and a Body together which have the utmost natural Contrariety to each other and can only affect or act upon one another by an arbitrary Will of God, willing that Body and Soul, held together by Force, should seem to do that to one another which they have no natural or possible Power to do. But the true Philosophy of this Matter, known only to the Soul, that by a new Birth from above has found its first State in and from God is this: Namely, that Nature is a Birth or Manifestation of the triune invisible Deity. And as it could only come into Existence as a Birth from God, so every Creature or beginning Thing can only come forth as a Birth from and out of Nature by the Will of God, willing it to come forth in such a Birth. And no Creature can have, or be, any Thing, but by and according to the working Powers of Nature; and therefore, strictly speaking, no Creature can be, or be put into an unnatural State. It may indeed lose or fall from its natural Perfection by the wrong Use or Working of its Will; but then its fallen State is the natural Effect of the wrong Use of its Will, and so it only has that which is natural to it. The Truth of the Matter is this: There neither is, nor can be, any Thing, nor any Effect in the whole Universe of Things but by the Way of Birth. For as the working Will is the first Cause or Beginner of every Thing, so nothing can proceed further than as it is driven by the Will and is a Birth of it. And therefore nothing can be in any Thing but what is natural to its own working Will and the true Effect of it. Every Thing that is outward in any Being is only a Birth of its own Spirit, and therefore all Body, whether it be heavenly or earthly or hellish, has its whole Nature and Condition from its own inward Spirit, and no Spirit can have a Body of any other Properties but such as are natural to it as being its own true outward State. For Body and Spirit are not two separate, independent Things, but are necessary to each other, and are only the inward and outward conditions of one and the same Being.

[Love-1-28] Every creaturely Spirit must have its own Body and cannot be without it, for its Body is that which makes it manifest to itself. It cannot be said to exist as a Creature till in a Body, because it can have no Sensibility of itself, nor feel nor find either that it is, or what it is, but in and by its own Body. Its Body is its first Knowledge of its Something and Somewhere.

[Love-1-29] And now, Sir, if you ask why I have gone into this Detail of the Origin and Nature of Body and Spirit, when my Subject was only concerning the Spirit of Love, it is to show you, that Grossness, Darkness, Contrariety, Disquiet, and Fermentation must be the State of the Body and Spirit till they are both made pure and luminous by the Light and Love of Heaven manifested in them. All Darkness, Grossness, and Contrariety must be removed from the Body before it can belong to Heaven, or be united with it; but these Qualities must be in the Body till the Soul is totally dead to Self, Partiality, and Contrariety, and breathes only the Spirit of universal Love, because the State of the Body has nothing of its own, or from itself, but is solely the outward Manifestation of nothing else but that which is inwardly in the Soul. Every Animal of this World has nothing in its outward Form or Shape, every Spirit, whether heavenly or hellish, has nothing in the Nature and State of its Body, but that which is the Form and Growth of its own inward Spirit. As no Number can be any Thing else but that which the Unities contained in it make it to be, so no Body of any Creature can be any Thing else but the Coagulation, or Sum total, of those Properties of Nature that are coagulated in it. And when the Properties of Nature are formed into the band of a creaturely Union, then is its Body brought forth, whether the Spirit of the Creature be earthly, heavenly, or hellish.

[Love-1-30] Nature, or the first Properties of Life, are in a State of the highest Contrariety, and the highest Want of something which they have not. This is their whole Nature and they have nothing else in them. And this is their true Ground and Fitness to become a Life of triumphing Joy and Happiness, viz., when united in the Possession of that which they seek for in their Contrariety. And if Life, in its first Root, was not this Depth of Strife, this Strength of Hunger, and Sensibility of Want, the Fullness of heavenly Joy could not be manifested in it.

[Love-1-31] You are not a Stranger to the Mystery of the Seven Properties of Nature which we have often spoken of; and therefore I shall shorten the Matter, and only say so much of them as may be of Service to our present Subject.

[Love-1-32] Nature, whether eternal or temporal, is That which comes not into Being for its own Self or to be That which it is in itself, but for the Sake of Something that it is not, and has not. And this is the Reason why Nature is only a Desire; it is because it is for the Sake of something else; and is also the Reason why Nature in itself is only a Torment, because it is only a strong Desire, and cannot help itself to that which it wants, but is always working against itself.

[Love-1-33] Now a Desire that cannot be stopped, nor get That which it would have, has a threefold Contrariety, or Working in it, which you may thus conceive as follows: The first and peculiar Property, or the one only Will of the Desire, as such, is to have That which it has not; and all it can do toward having it is to act as if it were seizing it; and this is it which makes the Desire to be a magic Compressing, Inclosing, or Astringing, because that is all that it can do toward Seizing of that which it would have. But the Desire cannot thus magically astringe, compress, or strive to inclose, without Drawing and Attracting: But Drawing is Motion, which is the highest Contrariety and Resistance to compressing or holding together. And thus the Desire, in its magical Working, sets out with two contrary Properties, inseparable from one another and equal in Strength; for the Motion has no Strength but as it is the Drawing of the Desire; and the Desire only draws in the same Degree as it wills to compress and astringe; and therefore the Desire, as astringing, always begets a Resistance equal to itself. Now from this great and equally strong Contrariety of the two first Properties of the Desire, magically pulling, as I may say, two contrary Ways, there arises as a necessary Birth from both of them, a third Property, which is emphatically called a Wheel or whirling Anguish of Life. For a Thing that can go neither inward nor outward, and yet must be and move under the equal Power of both of them, must whirl or turn round; it has no Possibility of doing any Thing else or of ceasing to do that. And that this whirling Contrariety of these inseparable Properties is the great Anguish of Life and may properly be called the Hell of Nature; and every lesser Torment which any Man finds in this mixed World, has all its Existence and Power from the Working of these three Properties: For Life can find no troublesome Motions, or Sensibility of Distress, but so far as it comes under their Power, and enters into their whirling Wheel.

[Love-1-34] Now here you may observe, that as this whirling Anguish of Life is a third State, necessarily arising from the Contrariety of the two first Properties of the Desire, so in this material System, every whirling or orbicular Motion of any Body is solely the Effect or Product of the Contrariety of these two first Properties. For no material Thing can whirl or move round, till it is under the Power of these two Properties; that is, till it can neither go inwards nor outwards, and yet is obliged to move, just as the whirling Anguish of the Desire then begins when it can neither go inwards nor outwards and yet must be in Motion.

[Love-1-35] And this may be again another strict Demonstration to you, that all the Matter of this World is from spiritual Properties, since all its Workings and Effects are according to them: For if Matter does nothing but according to them, it can be nothing but what it is, and has from them.

[Love-1-36] Here also, that is, in these three Properties of the Desire, you see the Ground and Reason of the three great Laws of Matter and Motion, lately discovered, and so much celebrated, and need no more to be told, that the illustrious Sir Isaac plowed with Behmen's Heifer, when he brought forth the Discovery of them. In the mathematical System of this great Philosopher these three Properties, Attraction, equal Resistance, and the orbicular Motion of the Planets as the effect of them, &c., are only treated of as Facts and Appearances, whose Ground is not pretended to be known. But in our Behmen, the illuminated Instrument of God, their Birth and Power in Eternity are opened; their eternal Beginning is shown, and how and why all Worlds, and every Life of every Creature, whether it be heavenly, earthly, or hellish, must be in them, and from them, and can have no Nature either spiritual or material, no kind of Happiness or Misery, but according to the working Power and State of these Properties.

[Love-1-37] All outward Nature, all inward Life, is what it is, and works as it works, from this unceasing, powerful Attraction, Resistance, and Whirling.

[Love-1-38] Every Madness and Folly of Life is their immediate Work and every good Spirit of Wisdom and Love has all its Strength and Activity from them. They equally support Darkness and Light: The one could have no Powers of Thickness and Coldness, the other no Powers of Warmth, Brightness, and Activity but by and through these three Properties acting in a different State. Not a Particle of Matter stirs, rises, or falls, separates from or unites with any other, but under their Power. Not a Thought of the Mind, either of Love or Hatred, of Joy or Trouble, of Envy or Wrath, of Pride and Covetousness, can rise in the Spirit of any Creature, but as these Properties act and stir in it.

[Love-1-39] The next and following Properties, viz., the fourth, called Fire; the fifth, called the Form of Light and Love, and the sixth, Sound, or Understanding, only declare the gradual Effects of the Entrance of the Deity into the three first Properties of Nature, changing, or bringing their strong wrathful Attraction, Resistance, and Whirling, into a Life and State of triumphing Joy, and Fullness of Satisfaction; which State of Peace and Joy in one another is called the Seventh Property, or State of Nature. And this is what Behmen means by his Ternarius Sanctus, which he so often speaks of as the only Place from whence he received all that he said and wrote: He means by it the holy Manifestation of the Triune God in the seven Properties of Nature, or Kingdom of Heaven. And from this Manifestation of God in the seven Properties of Nature, or Kingdom of Heaven, he most wonderfully opens, and accounts for all that was done in the six first working Days of the Creation, showing how every one of the six active Properties had its peculiar Day's Work, till the whole ended or rested in the sanctified, paradisiacal Sabbath of the seventh Day, just as Nature doth in its seventh Property.

[Love-1-40] And now, Sir, you may see in the greatest Clearness how every Thing in this World, every Thing in the Soul and Body of Man, absolutely requires the one Redemption of the Gospel. There is but one Nature in all created Things, whether spiritual or material; they all stand and work upon the same Ground, viz., the three first Properties of Nature. That only which can illuminate the Soul, that alone can give Brightness and Purity to the Body. For there is no Grossness, Darkness, and Contrariety in the Body, but what strictly proceeds from the same Cause that makes Selfishness, Wrath, Envy, and Torment in the Soul; it is but one and the same State and Working of the same three first Properties of Nature. All Evil, whether natural or moral, whether of Body or Spirit, is the sole Effect of the Wrath and Disorder of the Spirits of Nature working in and by themselves. And all the Good, Perfection, and Purity of every Thing, whether spiritual or material, whether it be the Body or Spirit of Man or Angel, is solely from the Power and Presence of the supernatural Deity dwelling and working in the Properties of Nature. For the Properties of Nature are in themselves nothing else but a mere Hunger, Want, Strife, and Contrariety, till the Fullness and Riches of the Deity entering into them unites them all in one Will and one Possession of Light and harmonious Love; which is the one Redemption of the Gospel, and the one Reason why nothing else but the Heart, or Son, or Light of God, can purify Nature and Creature from all the Evil they are fallen into.

[Love-1-41] For nothing can possibly deliver the Soul from its selfish Nature and earthly Passions but that one Power that can deliver Matter from its present material Properties and turn Earth into Heaven: And that for this plain Reason, because Soul and Body, outward Nature and inward Life, have but one and the same Evil in them, and from one and the same Cause.

[Love-1-42] The Deist, therefore, who looks for Life and Salvation through the Use of his Reason, acts contrary to the whole Nature of every Thing that he sees and knows of himself and of the Nature and State of this World. For from one End of it to the other, all its material State, all its gross divided Elements, declare that they are what they are, because the Light and Love of Heaven is not working and manifest in them, and that nothing can take Darkness, Materiality, Rage, Storms, and Tempests from them, but that same heavenly Light and Love which was made Flesh to redeem the fallen Humanity first, and after that the whole material System.

[Love-1-43] Can the Deist with his Reason bring the Light of this World into the Eyes of his Body? If not, how comes it to be less absurd, or more possible, for Reason to bring heavenly Light into the Soul? Can Reason hinder the Body from being heavy, or remove Thickness and Darkness from Flesh and Blood? Yet nothing less than such a Power can possibly help the Soul out of its fallen and earthly State. For the Grossness of Flesh and Blood is the natural State of the fallen Soul; and therefore nothing can purify the Soul, or raise it out of its earthly, corrupt State, but that which hath all Power over all that, that is earthy and material in Nature.

[Love-1-44] To pretend, therefore, that Reason may have sufficient Power to remove all hellish Depravity and earthly Lusts from the Soul, whilst it has not the least Power over Sweet or Sour in any one Particle of Matter in the Body, is as highly absurd, as if a Man should pretend that he has a full Power to alter the inward, invisible, vegetable Life of a Plant, but none at all over its outward State, Colour, Leaves, or Fruit. The Deist therefore, and not the Christian, stands in need of continual Miracles to make good his Doctrine. For Reason can have no Pretence to amend or alter the Life of the Soul, but so far as it can show that it has Power to amend and alter the Nature and State of the Body.

[Love-1-45] The unbelieving Jews said of our Lord, "How can this Man forgive Sins?" Christ showed them how by appealing to that Power which they saw he had over the Body: "Whether," says he, "is it easier to say, Thy Sins are forgiven thee, or to say, Arise, take up thy Bed, and walk?" But the Delusion of the unbelieving Deist is greater than that of the Jew. For the Deist sees, that his Reason has no Power over his Body, can remove no Disease, Blindness, Deafness, or Lameness, from it, and yet will pretend to have Power enough from his Reason to help the Soul out of all its Evil; not knowing that Body and Soul go hand in hand, and are nothing else but the inward and outward State of one and the same Life; and that therefore he only, who can say to the dead Body of Lazarus, "Come forth," can say to the Soul, "Be thou clean." The Deist therefore, if he pleases, may style himself a natural or a moral Philosopher, but with no more Truth than he can call himself a Healer of all the Maladies of the Body. And for a Man to think himself a moral Philosopher, because he has made a choice Collection of Syllogisms, in order to quicken and revive a Divine Goodness in the Soul, or that no Redeemer need come from Heaven, because human Reason, when truly left to itself, has great Skill in chopping of Logic; may justly be deemed such an Ignorance of the Nature of Things as is seldom found in the Transactions of illiterate and vulgar Life. But this by the by.

[Love-1-46] To return to our chief subject: The Sum of all that has been said is this: All Evil, be it what it will, all Misery of every kind, is in its Birth, Working and Extent, nothing else but Nature left to itself, and under the divided Workings of its own Hunger, Wrath, and Contrariety; and therefore no Possibility for the natural, earthly Man to escape eternal Hunger, Wrath, and Contrariety, but solely in the Way as the Gospel teacheth, by denying and dying to Self. On the other hand, all the Goodness and Perfection, all the Happiness, Glory, and Joy that any intelligent, Divine Creature can be possessed of, is, and can be, from nothing else, but the invisible uncreated Light and Spirit of God manifesting itself in the Properties of the creaturely Life, filling, blessing, and uniting them all in one Love and Joy of Life. And thus again: no Possibility of Man's attaining to any heavenly Perfection and Happiness, but only in the Way of the Gospel, by the Union of the Divine and human Nature, by Man's being born again from above of the Word and Spirit of God. There is no Possibility of any other Way, because there is nothing that can possibly change the first Properties of Life into an heavenly State, but the Presence, and working Power, of the Deity united with, and working in them. And therefore the "Word was made Flesh," and must of all Necessity be made Flesh, if Man is to have a heavenly Nature. Now as all Evil, Sin, and Misery, have no Beginning, nor Power of Working, but in the Manifestation of Nature in its divided, contrary Properties; so it is certain that Man has nothing to turn to, seek or aspire after, but the lost Spirit of Love. And therefore it is, that God only can be his Redeemer, because God only is Love; and Love can be nowhere else but in God, and where God dwelleth and worketh.

[Love-1-47] Now the Difficulty which you find in attaining to this Purity, and Universality of the Spirit of Love is because you seek for it, as I once told you, in the Way of reasoning: You would be possessed of it only from a rational Conviction of the Fitness and Amiableness of it. And as this clear Idea does not put you immediately into the real Possession of it, your Reason begins to waver, and suggests to you, that it may be only a fine Notion that has no Ground but in the Power of the Imagination. But this, Sir, is all your own Error, and as contrary to Nature, as if you would have your Eyes do That which only your Hands or Feet can do for you. The Spirit of Love is a Spirit of Nature and Life; and all the Operations of Nature and Life are according to the working Powers of Nature; and every Growth and Degree of Life can only arise in its own Time and Place from its proper Cause, and as the genuine Effect of it. Nature and Life do nothing by Chance or accidentally, but every Thing in one uniform Way. Fire, Air, and Light, do not proceed sometimes from one Thing, and sometimes from another; but wherever they are, they are always born in the same Manner, and from the same Working in the Properties of Nature. So in like Manner, Love is an immutable Birth, always proceeding from the same Cause, and cannot be in Existence till its own true Parents have brought it forth.

[Love-1-48] How unreasonable would it be to begin to doubt whether Strength and Health of Body were real Things, or possible to be had, because you could not by the Power of your Reason take Possession of them? Yet this is as well as to suspect the Purity and Perfection of Love to be only a Notion, because your Reason cannot bring forth its Birth in your Soul. For Reason has no more Power of altering the Life and Properties of the Soul, than of altering the Life and Properties of the Body. That, and That only, can cast Devils and evil Spirits out of the Soul, that can say to the Storm, Be still, and to the Leper, Be thou clean.

[Love-1-49] The Birth of Love is a Form or State of Life, and has its fixed Place in the fifth Form of Nature. The three first Properties or Forms of Nature are the Ground or Band of Life, that is in itself only an extreme Hunger, Want, Strife, and Contrariety. And they are in this State, that they may become a proper Fuel for the fourth Form of Nature, viz., the Fire, to be kindled in them. You will perhaps say, "What is this Fire? What is its Nature? And how is it kindled? And how is it that the Hunger and anguishing State of the Properties, are a Fitness to be a Fuel of this Fire?" It may be answered, This Hunger and Anguish of Nature, in its first Forms, is its Fitness to be changed into a Life of Light, Joy, and Happiness: And that for this Reason, because it is in this Hunger and Anguish only because God is not in it. For as Nature comes from God, and for this only End, that the Deity may manifest Heaven in it, it must stand in an Hunger and anguishing State till the Deity is manifested in it. And therefore its Hunger and Anguish are its true Fitness to be changed into a better State, and this is its Fitness for the Birth of the Fire: For the Fire means nothing, and is nothing else, but That which changes them into a better State. Not as if Fire was a fourth, distinct Thing that comes into them from without, but is only a fourth State, or Condition into which the same Properties are brought.

[Love-1-50] The Fire then is that which changes the Properties into a new and heavenly State: Therefore the Fire does two things; it alters the State of Nature and brings Heaven into it, and

therefore it must Work from a two-fold Power; the Deity and Nature must both be in it. It must have some Strength from Nature, or it could not work in Nature. It must have some Strength from the Deity or it could not overcome and change Nature into a Divine Life. Now all this is only to show you, that the Fire can only be kindled by the Entrance of the Deity, or supernatural God, into a Conjunction or Union with Nature. And this Conjunction of the Deity and Nature maketh, or bringeth forth, that State or Form of Life, which is called and truly is, Fire: First, Because it does that in the spiritual Properties of Nature, which Fire doth in the Properties of material Nature; and Secondly, Because it is that alone, from which every Fire in this World, whether in the Life of animal or vegetable or inanimate Matter, has its Source and Power and Possibility of Burning. The Fire of this World overcomes its Fuel, breaks its Nature, alters its State and changes it into Flame and Light. But why does it do this? Whence has it this Nature and Power? It is because it is a true Outbirth of the eternal Fire, which overcomes the Darkness, Wrath, and Contrariety of Nature, and changes all its Properties into a Life of Light, Joy, and Glory. Not a Spark of Fire could be kindled in this World, nor a Ray of Light come from any material Fire, but because material Nature is, in itself, nothing else but the very Properties of eternal Nature, standing for a Time in a material State or Condition; and therefore they must work in Time as they do in Eternity; and consequently there must be Fire in this World, it must have the same Birth and do the same Work in its material Way, which the eternal Fire hath, and doth in spiritual Nature. And this is the true Ground and Reason why every Thing in this World is delivered as far as it can be from its earthly Impurity, and brought into its highest State of Existence, only by Fire; it is because the eternal Fire is the Purifier of eternal Nature and the Opener of every Perfection, Light, and Glory in it. And if you ask why the eternal Fire is the Purifier of eternal Nature, the Reason is plain; it is because the eternal Fire has its Birth and Nature and Power from the Entrance of the pure, supernatural Deity into the Properties of Nature, which Properties must change their State, and be what they were not before, as soon as the Deity entereth into them. Their Darkness, Wrath, and Contrariety, is driven out of them, and they work and give forth only a Life and Strength of Light, and Joy, and Glory. And this two-fold Operation, viz., on one hand taking from Nature its wrathful Workings, and on the other hand opening a glorious Manifestation of the Deity in them, is the whole Nature and Form of the Fire, and is the Reason why from Eternity to Eternity it is and must be the Purifier of eternal Nature; namely, as from Eternity to Eternity changing Nature into a Kingdom of Heaven. Now every Fire in this World does, and must do, the same Thing in its low Way, to the utmost of its Power, and can do nothing else. Kindle Fire where, or in what you will, it acts only as from and by the Power of this eternal purifying Fire; and therefore it breaks and consumes the Grossness of every Thing, and makes all that is pure and spirituous to come forth out of it; and therefore Purification is its one only Work through all material Nature, because it is a real Out-birth of that eternal Fire which purifies eternal Nature, and changes it into a mere Heaven of Glory.
[Love-1-51] The eternal Fire is called a fourth Form, or State of Nature; because it cannot exist but from the first Three and hath its Work in the fourth Place in the Midst of the seven Forms, changing the three first into the three last Forms of Nature, that is, changing them from their

natural into a heavenly State. So that, strictly speaking, there are but three Forms of Nature in answerableness to the threefold Working of the Triune Deity. For the three last are not three new or different Properties, but are only the three first brought into a new State by the Entrance of the Triune Deity into Conjunction with them. Which Entrance of the supernatural Deity into them is the consuming of all that is bad in them, and turning all their Strength into a working Life of Light, Joy, and heavenly Glory; and therefore has the justest Title to be called Fire, as having no other Nature and Operation in it but the known Nature of Fire, and also as being That from which every Fire in this World has all its Nature and Power of doing as it doth.

[Love-1-52] You once, as I remember, objected to my speaking so much in the Appeal, &c., of the Fire of Life, as thinking it too gross an Expression to be taken in its literal Meaning, when mention is made of the eternal Fire, or the Fire in animal Life. But, Sir, Fire has but one Nature through the whole Universe of Things, and material Fire has not more or less of the Nature of Fire in it, than that which is in eternal Nature; because it has nothing, works nothing, but what it has, and works from thence. How easy was it for you to have seen, that the Fire of the Soul and the Fire of the Body had but one Nature? How else could they unite in their Heat? How easy also to have seen that the Fire of animal Life was the same Fire that burns in the Kitchen? How else could the Kitchen Fire be serviceable to animal Life? What Good could it do you to come to a Fire of Wood where you wanted to have the Heat of your own Life increased? In animal Life the Fire is kindled and preserved in such a Degree, and in such Circumstances, as to be Life, and the Preservation of Life; and this is its Difference from Fires kindled in Wood and burning it to Ashes. It is the same Fire, only in a different State, that keeps up Life and consumes Wood; and has no other Nature in the Wood than in the Animal. Just as in Water that has only so much Fire in it as to make it warm, and Water that is by Fire made boiling hot, the same Nature and Power of Fire is in both, but only in a different State. Now will you say, that Fire is not to be literally understood, when it only makes Water to be warm, because it is not red and flaming as you see it in a burning Coal? Yet this would be as well as to say, that Fire is not literally to be understood in the animal Life, because it is so different from that Fire which you see burning in a Piece of Wood. And thus, Sir, there is no Foundation for any Objection to all that has been said of Fire in the Appeal, &c. It is one and the same great Power of God in the spiritual and material World; it is the Cause of every Life and the Opener of every Power of Nature; and its one great Work through all Nature and Creature, animate and inanimate, is Purification and Exaltation; it can do nothing else, and that for this plain Reason, because its Birth is from the Entrance of the pure Deity into Nature, and therefore must in its various State and Degrees be only doing that which the Entrance of the Deity into Nature does. It must bring every natural Thing into its highest State. But to go back now to the Spirit of Love and show you the Time and Place of its Birth before which it can have no Existence in your Soul, do what you will to have it.

[Love-1-53] The Fire, you see, is the first Overcomer of the hungry, wrathful, self-tormenting State of the Properties of Nature; and it only overcomes them, because it is the Entrance of the pure Deity into them; and therefore That which overcomes them is the Light of the Deity. And this is the true Ground and Reason why every right-kindled Fire must give forth Light, and cannot do otherwise. It is because the eternal Fire is only the Effect or Operation of the supernatural Light of the Deity entering into Nature; and therefore Fire must give forth Light, because it is itself only a Power of the Light, and Light can be nowhere in Nature but as a fifth Form or State of Nature, brought forth by the Fire. And as Light thus brought forth is the first State that is lovely and delightful in Nature, so the Spirit of Love has only its Birth in the Light of Life, and can be nowhere else. For the Properties of Life have no common Good, nothing to rejoice in, till the Light is found; and therefore no possible Beginning of the Spirit of Love till then.

[Love-1-54] The Shock that is given to the three first Properties of Nature by the amazing Light of the Deity breaking in upon them, is the Operation of the Fire, that consumes, or takes away, the wrathful Strength and Contrariety of the Properties, and forces each of them to shrink, as it were, away from itself, and come under the Power of this new-risen Light. Here all Strife of Enmity and wrathful Contrariety in the Properties must cease, because all are united in the Love of the Light, and all equally helping one another to a higher Enjoyment and Delight in it. They are all one Triune Will, all doing the same Thing, viz., all rejoicing in the one Love of the Light. And here it is, in this delightful Unity of Operation, that the Spirit of Love is born, in the fifth Property or Light of Life; and cannot possibly rise up in any Creature till the Properties of its Life are brought into this fifth State, thus changed and exalted into a new Sensibility of Life. Let me give you this Similitude of the Matter: Fancy to yourself a Man shut up in a deep Cave underground, without ever having seen a Ray of the Light, his Body all over tortured with Pain, his Mind distracted with Rage, himself whirling and working with the utmost Fury and Madness, he knows not what; and then you have an Image of the first Properties of Life as they are in themselves before the Fire had done its Work in them.

[Love-1-55] Fancy this Man suddenly struck, or all surrounded, with such a Glare of Light as in the Twinkling of an Eye stopped or struck dead, every Working of every Pain and Rage, both in his Body and Mind; and then you have an Image of the Operation of the Fire, and what it does to the first Properties of Nature. Now as soon as the first Terror of the Light has had its fiery Operation, and struck nothing dead but every working Sensibility of Distress, fancy this Man, as you now well may, in the sweetest Peace of Mind and bodily Sensations, blessed in a new Region of Light, giving Joy to his Mind, and Gratification to every Sense; and then the Transports, the Overflowings of Love and Delight in this new State may give you an Image how the Spirit of Love is, and must be born, when Fire and Light have overcome and changed the State of the first Properties of Nature; and never till then, can have any Existence in any Creature, nor proceed from any other Cause. Thus, Sir, you may sufficiently see, how vainly you attempt to possess yourself of the Spirit of Love by the Power of your Reason; and also what a Vanity of all Vanities there is in the Religion of the Deists, who will have no other Perfection, or Divine Life, but what they can have from their Reason: as great a Contradiction to Nature, as if they would have no Life or Strength of Body, but that which can be had from their Faculty of Reasoning. For Reason can no more alter or exalt any one Property of Life in the Soul, and bring it into its perfect State, than it can add one Cubit to the Stature of the Body. The Perfection of every Life is no way possibly to be had, but as every Flower comes to its Perfection, viz., from its own Seed and Root and the various Degrees of Transmutation which must be gone through before the Flower is found: It is strictly thus with the Perfection of the Soul: All its Properties of Life must have their true natural Birth and Growth from one another. The first, as its Seed and Root, must have their natural change into an higher State; must, like the Seed of the Flower, pass through Death into Life and be blessed with the Fire and Light and Spirit of Heaven, in their Passage to it; just as the Seed passes through Death into Life, blessed by the Fire, and Light, and Air of this World, till it reaches its last Perfection, and becomes a beautiful sweet-smelling Flower. And to think that the Soul can attain its Perfection any other Way, than by the Change and Exaltation of its first Properties of Life, just as the Seed has its first Properties changed and exalted till it comes to have its Flower, is a total Ignorance of the Nature of Things. For as whatever dies cannot have a Death particular to itself, but the same Death in the same Way, and for the same Reasons, that any other Creature, whether Animal or vegetable, ever did or can die; so every Life and Degree of Life, must come into its State and Condition of Life in the same Way, and for the same Reasons as Life, and the Perfection of Life, comes into every other living Creature, whether in Heaven or on Earth. Therefore the Deists' Religion or Reason, which is to raise the Soul to its true Perfection, is so far from being the Religion of Nature, that it is quite unnatural and declared to be so by every Working in Nature. For since Reason can neither give Life nor Death to any one Thing in Nature, but every Thing lives, or dies, according to the Working of its own Properties, every Thing, dead and alive, gives forth a Demonstration, that Nature asks no Counsel of Reason, nor stays to be directed by it. Hold it therefore for a certain Truth, that you can have no Good come into your Soul, but only by the one Way of a Birth from above, from the Entrance of the Deity into the Properties of your own soulish Life. Nature must be set right, its Properties must enter into the Process of a new Birth, it must work to the Production of Light, before the Spirit of Love can have a Birth in it. For Love is Delight, and Delight cannot arise in any Creature till its Nature is in a delightful State, or is possessed of that in which it must rejoice. And this is the Reason why God must become Man; it is because a Birth of the Deity must be found in the Soul, giving to Nature all that it wants, or the Soul can never find itself in a delightful State and only Working with the Spirit of Love. For whilst the Soul has only its natural Life, it can only be in such a State, as Nature, without God, is in, viz., a mere Hunger, Want, Contrariety, and Strife for it knows not what. Hence is all that Variety of blind, restless, contrary Passions, which govern and torment the Life of fallen Man. It is because all the Properties of Nature must Work in Blindness, and be doing they know not what, till the Light of God is found in them. Hence also it is, that That which is called the Wisdom, the Honour, the Honesty, and the Religion of the natural Man, often does as much Hurt to himself, and others, as his Pride, Ambition, Self-Love, Envy, or Revenge, and are subject to the same Humour and Caprice; it is because Nature is no better in one Motion than in another, nor can be so, till something supernatural is come into it. We often charge Men, both in Church and State, with changing their Principles; but the Charge is too hasty; for no Man ever did, or can change his Principles, but by a Birth from above. The natural, called in Scripture, the old Man, is steadily the same in Heart and Spirit in every Thing he does, whatever Variety of Names may be given to his Actions. For Self can have no Motion but what is selfish, which Way soever it goes, or whatever it does, either in Church or State. And be assured of this, that Nature in every Man, whether he be learned or unlearned, is this very Self, and can be nothing else, till a Birth of the Deity is brought forth in it. There is therefore no Possibility of having the Spirit of Love, or any Divine Goodness, from any Power of Nature or Working of Reason. It can only be had in its own Time and Place; and its Time and Place is nowhere, but where Nature is overcome by a Birth of the Life of God in the Properties of the Soul. And thus you see the infallible Truth, and absolute Necessity, of Christian Redemption; it is the most demonstrable Thing in all Nature.— The Deity must become Man, take a Birth in the fallen Nature, be united to it, become the Life of it, or the natural Man must of all Necessity be forever and ever in the Hell of his own Hunger, Anguish, Contrariety, and Self-Torment; and all for this plain Reason, because Nature is, and can be, nothing else, but this Variety of Self-Torment, till the Deity is manifested and dwelling in it. [Love-1-56] And now, Sir, you see also the absolute Necessity of the Gospel-Doctrine of the Cross, viz., of dying to Self, as the one only Way to Life in God. This Cross, or Dying to Self, is the one Morality that does Man any Good. Fancy as many Rules as you will of modeling the moral Behaviour of Man, they all do nothing, because they leave Nature still alive, and therefore can only help a Man to a feigned, hypocritical Art of concealing his own inward Evil, and seeming to be not under its Power. And the Reason why it must be so is plain; it is because Nature is not possible to be reformed; it is immutable in its Workings and must be always as it is, and never any better or worse, than its own untaught Workings are. It can no more change from Evil to Good, than Darkness can Work itself into Light. The one Work therefore of Morality is the one Doctrine of the Cross, viz., to resist and deny Nature, that a supernatural Power or Divine Goodness, may take Possession of it, and bring a new Light into it.

[Love-1-57] In a Word, there are, in all the Possibility of Things, but two States, or Forms of Life; the one is Nature, and the other is God manifested in Nature; and as God and Nature are both within you, so you have it in your Power to live and work with which you will; but are under a Necessity of doing either the one or the other. There is no standing still, Life goes on, and is always bringing forth its Realities, which Way soever it goeth. You have seen, that the Properties of Nature are, and can be, nothing else in their own Life, but a restless Hunger, Disquiet, and blind Strife for they know not what, till the Property of Light and Love has got Possession of them. Now when you see this, you see the true State of every natural Man, whether he be Caesar or Cato, whether he gloriously murders others or only stabs himself; blind Nature does all the Work, and must be the Doer of it, till the Christ of God is born in him. For the Life of Man can be nothing else but a Hunger of Covetousness, a Rising up of Pride, Envy, and Wrath, a medley of contrary Passions, doing and undoing it knows not what because these Workings are essential to the Properties of Nature; they must be always hungering, and working one against another, striving to be above one another, and all this in Blindness, till the Light of God has helped them to one common Good, in which they all willingly unite, rest, and rejoice. In a Word, Goodness is only a Sound and Virtue a mere Strife of natural Passions, till the Spirit of

Love is the Breath of every Thing that lives and moves in the Heart. For Love is the one only Blessing and Goodness, and God of Nature; and you have no true Religion, are no Worshiper of the one true God, but in and by that Spirit of Love, which is God himself living and working in you.

[Love-1-58] But here I take off my Pen and shall leave the remaining Part of your Objection to another Opportunity.

King's Cliff, June 16, 1752

Part Two

The First Dialogue Between Theogenes, Eusebius, and Theophilus

[Love-2.1-1] THEOGENES.   Dear Theophilus, this Gentleman is Eusebius, a very valuable and worthy Curate in my Neighbourhood; he would not let me wait any longer for your second Letter of the Spirit of Love, nor be content till I consented to our making you this Visit. And indeed, we are both on the same Errand and in equal Impatience to have your full Answer to that Part of my Objection, which you reserved for a second Letter.

[Love-2.1-2] Theophilus. My Heart embraces you both with the greatest Affection, and I am much pleased at the Occasion of your Coming which calls me to the most delightful Subject in the World, to help both you and myself to rejoice in that adorable Deity whose infinite Being is an Infinity of mere Love, an unbeginning, never-ceasing, and forever overflowing Ocean of Meekness, Sweetness, Delight, Blessing, Goodness, Patience, and Mercy, and all this as so many blessed Streams breaking out of the Abyss of universal Love, Father, Son, and Holy Ghost, a Triune Infinity of Love and Goodness, for ever and ever giving forth nothing but the same Gifts of Light and Love, of Blessing and Joy, whether before or after the Fall, either of Angels or Men.

[Love-2.1-3] Look at all Nature, through all its Height and Depth, in all its Variety of working Powers; it is what it is for this only End, that the hidden Riches, the invisible Powers, Blessings, Glory, and Love of the unsearchable God, may become visible, sensible, and manifest in and by it.

[Love-2.1-4] Look at all the Variety of Creatures; they are what they are for this only End, that in their infinite Variety, Degrees, and Capacities, they may be as so many speaking Figures, living Forms of the manifold Riches and Powers of Nature, as so many Sounds and Voices, Preachers, and Trumpets, giving Glory and Praise and Thanksgiving to that Deity of Love which gives Life to all Nature and Creature.

[Love-2.1-5] For every Creature of unfallen Nature, call it by what name you Will, has its Form, and Power, and State, and Place in Nature, for no other End, but to open and enjoy, to manifest and rejoice in some Share of the Love, and Happiness, and Goodness of the Deity, as springing forth in the boundless Height and Depth of Nature.

[Love-2.1-6] Now this is the one Will and Work of God in and through all Nature and Creature.

From Eternity to Eternity he can will and intend nothing toward them, in them, or by them, but the Communication of various Degrees of his own Love, Goodness, and Happiness to them, according to their State, and Place, and Capacity in Nature. This is God's unchangeable Disposition toward the Creature; He can be nothing else but all Goodness toward it, because he can be nothing toward the Creature but that which he is, and was, and ever shall be in Himself. [Love-2.1-7] God can no more begin to have any Wrath, Rage, or Anger in Himself, after Nature and Creature are in a fallen State, than He could have been infinite Wrath and boundless Rage everywhere, and from all Eternity. For nothing can begin to be in God, or to be in a new State in Him; every Thing that is in Him is essential to Him, as inseparable from Him, as unalterable in Him as the triune Nature of his Deity.

[Love-2.1-8] Theogenes. Pray, Theophilus, let me ask you, does not Patience and Pity and Mercy begin to be in God, and only then begin, when the Creature has brought itself into Misery? They could have no Existence in the Deity before. Why then may not a Wrath and Anger begin to be in God, when the Creature has rebelled against him, though it neither had nor could have any Existence in God before?

[Love-2.1-9] Theophilus. 'Tis true, Theogenes, that God can only then begin to make known his Mercy and Patience, when the Creature has lost its Rectitude and Happiness, yet nothing then begins to be in God or to be found in him, but that which was always in him in the same infinite State, viz., a Will to all Goodness, and which can will nothing else. And his Patience and Mercy, which could not show forth themselves till Nature and Creature had brought forth Misery, were not new Tempers, or the Beginning of some new Disposition that was not in God before, but only new and occasional Manifestations of that boundless eternal Will to all Goodness, which always was in God in the same Height and Depth. The Will to all Goodness, which is God himself, began to display itself in a new Way when it first gave Birth to Creatures. The same Will to all Goodness began to manifest itself in another new Way, when it became Patience and Compassion toward fallen Creatures. But neither of these Ways are the Beginning of any new Tempers or Qualities in God, but only new and occasional Manifestations of that true eternal Will to all Goodness, which always was, and always will be, in the same Fullness of Infinity in God.

[Love-2.1-10] But to suppose that when the Creature has abused its Power, lost its Happiness and plunged itself into a Misery, out of which it cannot deliver itself, to suppose that then there begins to be something in the holy Deity of Father, Son, and Holy Ghost, that is not of the Nature and Essence of God, and which was not there before, viz., a Wrath, and Fury, and vindictive Vengeance, breaking out in Storms of Rage and Resentment because the poor Creature has brought Misery upon itself, is an Impiety and Absurdity that cannot be enough abhorred. For nothing can be in God, but that which He is and has from Himself, and therefore no Wrath can be in the Deity itself, unless God was in Himself, before all Nature, and from all Eternity, an Infinity of Wrath.

[Love-2.1-11] Why are Love, Knowledge, Wisdom, and Goodness said to be infinite and eternal in God, capable of no Increase or Decrease, but always in the same highest State of Existence?

Why is his Power eternal and omnipotent, his Presence not here, or there, but everywhere the same? No Reason can be assigned, but because nothing that is temporary, limited, or bounded, can be in God. It is his Nature to be that which He is, and all that He is, in an infinite, unchangeable Degree, admitting neither higher, nor lower, neither here nor there, but always, and everywhere, in the same unalterable State of Infinity. If therefore Wrath, Rage, and Resentment could be in the Deity itself, it must be an unbeginning, boundless, never-ceasing Wrath, capable of no more, or less, no up or down, but always existing, always working, and breaking forth in the same Strength, and everywhere equally burning in the Height and Depth of the abyssal Deity. There is no medium here; there must be either all or none, either no Possibility of Wrath, or no Possibility of its having any Bounds. And therefore, if you would not say, that every Thing that has proceeded, or can, or ever shall proceed from God, are and can be only so many Effects of his eternal and omnipotent Wrath, which can never cease, or be less than infinite; if you will not hold this monstrous Blasphemy, you must stick close to the absolute Impossibility of Wrath having any Existence in God. For nothing can have any Existence in God, but in the Way and Manner as his Eternity, Infinity, and Omnipotence have their Existence in him. Have you any Thing to object to this?

[Love-2.1-12] Theogenes. Indeed, Theophilus, both Eusebius and myself have been from the first fully satisfied with what has been said of this Matter in the Book of Regeneration, the Appeal, and the Spirit of Prayer, &c. We find it impossible to think of God as subject to Wrath, or capable of being inflamed by the Weakness, and Folly, and Irregularity of the Creature. We find ourselves incapable of thinking any otherwise of God, than as the one only Good, or, as you express it, an eternal immutable Will to all Goodness, which can will Nothing else to all Eternity, but to communicate Good, and Blessing, and Happiness, and Perfection to every Life, according to its Capacity to receive it.

[Love-2.1-13] Had I an hundred Lives, I could with more Ease part with them, all by suffering an hundred Deaths, than give up this lovely idea of God. Nor could I have any Desire of Eternity for myself, if I had not Hopes, that, by partaking of the Divine Nature, I should be eternally delivered from the Burden and Power of my own Wrath, and changed into the blessed Freedom of a Spirit, that is all Love, and a mere Will to Nothing but Goodness. An Eternity without this, is but an Eternity of Trouble. For I know of no Hell, either here or hereafter, but the Power and Working of Wrath, nor any Heaven, but where the God of Love is all in all, and the working Life of all. And therefore, that the holy Deity is all Love, and Blessing, and Goodness, willing and working only Love and Goodness to every Thing, as far as it can receive it, is a Truth as deeply grounded in me as the feeling of my own Existence. I ask you for no Proof of this; my only Difficulty is how to reconcile this Idea of God to the Letter of Scripture. First, Because the Scripture speaks so much and so often of the Wrath, and Fury, and vindictive Vengeance of God. Secondly, Because the whole Nature of our Redemption is so plainly grounded on such a supposed Degree of Wrath and Vengeance in God, as could not be satisfied, appeased and atoned by any Thing less than the Death and Sacrifice of the only begotten Son of God.

[Love-2.1-14] Theophilus. I will do more for you, Theogenes, in this Matter than you seem to expect. I will not only reconcile the Letter of Scripture with the foregoing Description of God, but will show you, that every Thing that is said of the Necessity of Christ's being the only possible Satisfaction and Atonement of the vindictive Wrath of God is a full and absolute Proof that the Wrath of God spoken of never was, nor is, or possibly can be in God.

[Love-2.1-15] Eusebius. Oh! Theophilus, you have forced me now to speak, and I cannot contain the Joy that I feel in this Expectation which you have raised in me. If you can make the Scriptures do all that which you have promised to Theogenes, I shall be in Paradise before I die. For to know that Love alone was the Beginning of Nature and Creature, that nothing but Love encompasses the whole Universe of Things, that the governing Hand that overrules all, the watchful Eye that sees through all, is nothing but omnipotent and omniscient Love, using an Infinity of Wisdom, to raise all that is fallen in Nature, to save every misguided Creature from the miserable Works of its own Hands, and make Happiness and Glory the perpetual Inheritance of all the Creation is a Reflection that must be quite ravishing to every intelligent Creature that is sensible of it. Thus to think of God, of Providence, and Eternity, whilst we are in this Valley and Shadow of Death, is to have a real Foretaste of the Blessings of the World to come. Pray, therefore, let us hear how the Letter of Scripture is a Proof of this God of Love.

[Love-2.1-16] Theophilus. Before I do this, Eusebius, I think it requisite to show you, in a Word or two, the true Ground and Nature of Wrath in all its Kinds, what it is in itself, whence it has its Birth, Life, and Manner of Existence. And then you will see with your own Eyes why, and how, and where Wrath or Rage can, or cannot be. And until you see this fundamentally in the Nature of things, you cannot be at all qualified to judge of the Matter in Question, but must only think and speak at random, merely as your Imagination is led by the Sound of Words. For until we know, in the Nature of the Thing, what Wrath is in itself, and why, and how it comes into Existence, wherever it is, we cannot say, where it can enter or where it cannot. Nor can we possibly know what is meant by the Satisfaction, Appeasement, or Atonement of Wrath in any Being but by knowing how, and why, and for what Reason Wrath can rise and Work in any Being; and then only can we know how any Wrath, wherever raised, can be atoned or made to cease.

[Love-2.1-17] Now there are two Things, both of them visible to your outward Senses, which entirely open the true Ground and Nature of Wrath, and undeniably show what it is in itself, from whence it arises, and wherein its Life, and Strength, and Being consist. And these two Things are, a Tempest in the Elements of this World, and a raging Sore in the Body of Man, or any other Animal. Now that a Tempest in the Elements is Wrath in the Elements, and a Sore in the Body of an Animal a Wrath in the State of the Juices of the Body, is a Matter, I think, that needs no Proof or Explication. Consider, then, how or why a Tempest arises in the Elements, or an inflamed Sore in the Body, and then you have the true Ground and Nature of Wrath. Now a Tempest does not, cannot arise in the Elements whilst they are in their right State, in their just Mixture or Union with one another. A Sore does not, cannot break forth in the Body, whilst the Body is altogether in its true State and Temperature of its Juices. Hence you plainly see, that Wrath has its whole Nature, and only Ground of its Existence, in and by the Disorder or bad State of the

Thing in which it exists and works. It can have no Place of Existence, no Power of breaking forth, but where the Thing has lost its proper Perfection, and is not as it ought to be. And therefore no good Being, that is in its proper State of Goodness, can, whilst it is in such a State, have any Wrath or Rage in it. And therefore, as a Tempest of any kind in the Elements, is a sure Proof that the Elements are not in their right State, but under Disorder, as a raging Sore in the Body is a certain Indication that the Body is impure and corrupt, and not as it should be; so in whatever Mind, or intelligent Being, Wrath or Rage works and breaks forth, there, there is Proof enough, that the Mind is in that same impure, corrupt, and disordered State, as those Elements that raise a Tempest, and that Body which gives forth an inflamed Sore. And now, Gentlemen, what think you of a supposed Wrath, or Rage in God? Will you have such Things to be in the Deity itself as cannot have Place or Existence even in any Creature, until it is become disordered and impure and has lost its proper State of Goodness?

[Love-2.1-18] Eusebius. But pray, Theophilus, let me observe, that it does not yet appear to me, that there is but one Wrath possible to be in Nature and Creature. I grant there is such a Likeness in the Things you have appealed to, as is sufficient to justify Poets, Orators, or popular Speakers, in calling a Tempest Wrath, and Wrath a Tempest. But this will not do in our present Matter; for all that you have said depends upon this, whether, in a philosophic Strictness in the Nature of the Thing, there can be only one Wrath, wherever it is, proceeding strictly from the same Ground, and having everywhere the same Nature. Now if you can prove this Identity or Sameness of Wrath, be it where it Will, either in an intelligent Mind, the Elements of this World, or the Body of an Animal, then your Point is absolutely gained, and there can be no Possibility for Wrath to have any Existence in the Deity. But as Body and Spirit are generally held to be quite contrary to each other in their most essential Qualities, I do not know how you can sufficiently prove, that they can only have one Kind of Wrath, or that Wrath must have one and the same Ground and Nature, whether it be in Body or Spirit.

[Love-2.1-19] Theophilus. Wrath can have no better or other Ground and Nature in Body, than it has in Spirit, for this Reason, because it can have no Existence or Manner of working in the Body, but what it has directly from Spirit. And therefore, in every Wrath that is visible in any Body whatever, you have a true Manifestation of the Ground and Nature of Wrath, in whatever Spirit it is. And therefore, as there is but one Ground and Nature of Wrath in all outward Things, whether they be animate or inanimate, so you have Proof enough, that so it is with all Wrath in the Spirit or Mind. Because Wrath in any Body or outward Thing, is nothing else but the inward working of that Spirit, which manifests itself by an outward Wrath in the Body.

[Love-2.1-20] And what we call Wrath in the Body, is truly and strictly speaking, the Wrath of the Spirit in the Body.

[Love-2.1-21] For you are to observe, that Body begins not from itself, nor is any Thing of itself, but is all that it is, whether pure or impure, has all that it has, whether of Light or Darkness, and works all that it works, whether of Good or Evil, merely from Spirit. For nothing, my Friend, acts in the whole Universe of Things but Spirit alone. And the State, Condition, and Degree of every Spirit, is only and solely opened by the State, Form, Condition, and Qualities of the Body that belongs to it. For the Body can have no Nature, Form, Condition, or Quality but that which the Spirit that brings it forth, gives to it.

[Love-2.1-22] Was there no eternal, universal Spirit, there could be no eternal or universal Nature; that is, was not the Spirit of God everywhere, the Kingdom of Heaven, or the visible Glory of God, in an outward Majesty of Heaven, could not be everywhere. Now the Kingdom of Heaven is that to the Deity, which every Body is to the Spirit, which liveth, worketh, and manifesteth itself in it. But the Kingdom of Heaven is not God, yet all that it is, and has, and does, is only an outward Manifestation of the Nature, Power, and Working of the Spirit of God.

[Love-2.1-23] It is thus with every creaturely Spirit and its Body, which is the Habitation or Seat of its Power; and as the Spirit is in its Nature, Kind and Degree, whether heavenly, earthly, or hellish, so is its Body. Were there not creaturely Spirits, there could be no creaturely Bodies. And the Reason why there are creaturely Bodies of such various Forms, Shapes, and Powers, is because Spirits come forth from God in various Kinds and Degrees of Life, each manifesting its own Nature, Power, and Condition, by that Body which proceeds from it as its own Birth, or the Manifestation of its own Powers.

[Love-2.1-24] Now the Spirit is not Body, nor is the Body Spirit; they are so essentially distinct, that they cannot possibly lose their Difference, or be changed into one another; and yet all that is in the Body is from the Nature, Will, and Working of its Spirit. There is therefore no possible Room for a Supposition of two Kinds of Wrath, or that Wrath may have two Natures, the one as it is in Spirit, and the other as it is in Body; first, because nothing can be wrathful but Spirit, and secondly, because no Spirit can exert, or manifest Wrath but in and by its Body. The kindling its own Body is the Spirit's only Wrath. And therefore, through the whole Universe of Things, there is and can be but one possible Ground and Nature of Wrath, whether it be in the Sore of an animal Body, in a Tempest of the Elements, in the Mind of a Man, in an Angel, or in Hell.

[Love-2.1-25] Eusebius. Enough, enough, Theophilus. You have made it sufficiently plain, that Wrath can be no more in God Himself than Hell can be Heaven. And therefore we ask no more of you, but only to reconcile this with the Language and Doctrine of the holy Scriptures.

[Love-2.1-26] Theogenes. You are in too much Haste, Eusebius; it would be better to let Theophilus proceed further in this Matter. He has told us what Wrath is in itself, be it where it will; I should be glad to know its one true Original, or how, and where, and why it could possibly begin to be.

[Love-2.1-27] Theophilus. To inquire or search into the Origin of Wrath, is the same Thing as to search into the Origin of Evil and Sin: For Wrath and Evil are but two Words for one and the same Thing. There is no Evil in any Thing, but the Working of the Spirit of Wrath. And when Wrath is entirely suppressed, there can be no more Evil, or Misery, or Sin in all Nature and Creature. This therefore is a firm Truth, that nothing can be capable of Wrath, or be the Beginning of Wrath, but the Creature, because nothing but the Creature can be the Beginner of Evil and Sin.

[Love-2.1-28] Again, the Creature can have no Beginning, or Sensibility of Wrath in itself, but by losing the living Power, the living Presence, and governing Operation of the Spirit of God within it; or in other Words, by its losing that heavenly State of Existence in God, and Influence from Him which it had at its Creation.

[Love-2.1-29] Now no intelligent Creature, whether Angel or Man, can be good and happy but by partaking of, or having in itself, a two-fold Life. Hence so much is said in the Scripture of an inward and outward, an old and a new Man.— For there could be no Foundation for this Distinction, but because every intelligent Creature, created to be good and happy, must of all Necessity have a two-fold Life in it, or it cannot possibly be capable of Goodness and Happiness, nor can it possibly lose its Goodness and Happiness, or feel the least Want of them, but by its breaking the Union of this two-fold Life in itself. Hence so much is said in the Scripture of the quickening, raising, and reviving the inward, new Man, of the new Birth from above, of Christ being formed in us, as the one only Redemption and Salvation of the Soul. Hence also the Fall of Adam was said to be a Death, that he died the Day of his Sin, though he lived so many hundred Years after it: it was because his Sin broke the Union of his two-fold Life and put an End to the heavenly Part of it, and left only one Life, the Life of this bestial, earthly World in him.

[Love-2.1-30] Now there is, in the Nature of the Thing, an absolute Necessity of this two-fold Life in every Creature that is to be good and happy; and the two-fold Life is this, it must have the Life of Nature, and the Life of God in it. It cannot be a Creature, and intelligent, but by having the Life and Properties of Nature; that is, by finding itself to be a Life of various Sensibilities, that hath a Power of Understanding, Willing, and Desiring: This is its creaturely Life, which, by the creating Power of God, it hath in and from Nature.

[Love-2.1-31] Now this is all the Life that is, or can be creaturely, or be a Creature's natural, own Life; and all this creaturely natural Life, with all its various Powers and Sensibilities, is only a Life of various Appetites, Hungers, and Wants, and cannot possibly be any Thing else. God Himself cannot make a Creature to be in itself, or as to its own Nature, any Thing else but a State of Emptiness, of Want, of Appetite, &c. He cannot make it to be good and happy, in and from its natural State: This is as impossible as for God to cease to be the one only Good. The highest Life, therefore, that is natural and creaturely, can go no higher than this; it can only be a bare Capacity for Goodness and Happiness, and cannot possibly be a good and happy Life, but by the Life of God dwelling in, and in Union with it. And this is the two-fold Life, that of all Necessity must be united in every good and perfect and happy Creature.

[Love-2.1-32] See here the greatest of all Demonstrations of the absolute Necessity of the Gospel Redemption and Salvation, and all proved from the Nature of the Thing. There can be no Goodness and Happiness for any intelligent Creature, but in and by this two-fold Life; and therefore the Union of the Divine and human Life, or the Son of God incarnate in Man, to make Man again a Partaker of the Divine Nature, is the one only possible Salvation for all the Sons of fallen Adam, that is, of Adam dead to, or fallen from his first Union with the Divine Life.

[Love-2.1-33] Deism, therefore, or a Religion of Nature, pretending to make Man good and happy without Christ, or the Son of God entering into Union with the human Nature, is the greatest of all Absurdities. It is as contrary to the Nature and Possibilities of Things as for mere Emptiness to be its own Fullness, mere Hunger to be its own Food, and mere Want to be its

Possession of all Things. For Nature and Creature, without the Christ of God or the Divine Life in Union with it, is and can be nothing else but this mere Emptiness, Hunger, and Want of all that which can alone make it good and happy. For God himself, as I said, cannot make any Creature to be good and happy by any Thing that is in its own created Nature; and however high and noble any Creature is supposed to be created, its Height and Nobility can consist in nothing, but its higher Capacity and Fitness to receive a higher Union with the Divine Life, and also a higher and more wretched Misery, when left to itself, as is manifest by the hellish State of the fallen Angels. Their high and exalted Nature was only an enlarged Capacity for the Divine Life; and therefore, when this Life was lost, their whole created Nature was nothing else but the Height of Rage, and hellish Distraction.

[Love-2.1-34] A plain Demonstration, that there can be no Happiness, Blessing, and Goodness for any Creature in Heaven, or on Earth, but by having, as the Gospel saith, Jesus Christ made unto it, Wisdom, Righteousness, Sanctification, and Peace with God.

[Love-2.1-35] And the Reason is this; it is because Goodness and Happiness are absolutely inseparable from God, and can be nowhere but in God. And on the other Hand, Emptiness, Want, Insufficiency, &c., are absolutely inseparable from the Creature, as such; its whole Nature cannot possibly be any Thing else, be it what or where it will, an Angel in Heaven, or a Man on Earth; it is and must be, in its whole creaturely Nature and Capacity, a mere Hunger and Emptiness, &c. And therefore all that we know of God, and all that we know of the Creature, fully proves, that the Life of God in Union with the creaturely Life (which is the Gospel Salvation) is the one only Possibility of Goodness and Happiness in any Creature, whether in Heaven or on Earth.

[Love-2.1-36] Hence also it is enough certain, that this two-fold Life must have been the original State of every intelligent Creature, at its first coming forth from God. It could not be brought forth by God, to have only a creaturely Life of Nature, and be left to that; for that would be creating it under a Necessity of being in Misery, in Want, in Wrath, and all painful Sensibilities. A Thing more unworthy of God, and more impossible for Him to do, than to create numberless earthly Animals under a Necessity of being perpetually pained with Hunger and Thirst, without any Possibility of finding any Thing to eat or to drink.

[Love-2.1-37] For no creaturely Life can in itself be any higher, or better, than a State of Want, or a seeking for something that cannot be found in itself; and therefore, as sure as God is good, as sure as He would have intelligent Beings live a Life of Goodness and Happiness, so sure it is, that such Beings must of all Necessity, in their first Existence, have been blessed with a two-fold Life, viz., the Life of God dwelling in, and united with, the Life of Nature or created Life.

[Love-2.1-38] Eusebius. What an important Matter have you here proved, in the Necessity and Certainty of this two-fold Life in every intelligent Being that is to be good and happy: For this great Truth opens and asserts the certain and substantial Ground of the spiritual Life, and shows, that all Salvation is, and can be nothing else, but the Manifestation of the Life of God in the Soul. How clearly does this give the solid Distinction between inward Holiness, and all outward, creaturely Practices. All that God has done for Man by any particular Dispensations, whether by the Law, or the Prophets, by the Scriptures, or Ordinances of the Church, are only as Helps to a

Holiness which they cannot give, but are only suited to the Death and Darkness of the earthly, creaturely Life, to turn it from itself, from its own Workings, and awaken in it a Faith and Hope, a Hunger and Thirst after that first Union with the Life of the Deity, which was lost in the Fall of the first Father of Mankind.

[Love-2.1-39] How unreasonable is it, to call perpetual Inspiration Fanaticism and Enthusiasm, when there cannot be the least Degree of Goodness or Happiness in any intelligent Being, but what is in its whole Nature, merely and truly the Breathing, the Life, and the Operation of God in the Life of the Creature? For if Goodness can only be in God, if it cannot exist separate from Him, if He can only bless and sanctify, not by a creaturely gift, but by Himself becoming the Blessing and Sanctification of the Creature, then it is the highest Degree of Blindness, to look for any Goodness and Happiness from any Thing, but the immediate Indwelling Union, and Operation of the Deity in the Life of the Creature. Perpetual Inspiration, therefore, is in the Nature of the Thing as necessary to a Life of Goodness, Holiness, and Happiness, as the perpetual Respiration of the Air is necessary to Animal Life.

[Love-2.1-40] For the Life of the Creature, whilst only creaturely, and possessing nothing but itself, is Hell; that is, it is all Pain and Want and Distress. Now nothing, in the Nature of the Thing, can make the least Alteration in this creaturely Life, nothing can help it to be in Light and Love, in Peace and Goodness, but the Union of God with it, and the Life of God working in it, because nothing but God is Light, and Love, and heavenly Goodness. And, therefore, where the Life of God is not become the Life and Goodness of the Creature, there the Creature cannot have the least Degree of Goodness in it.

[Love-2.1-41] What a mistake is it, therefore, to confine Inspiration to particular Times and Occasions, to Prophets and Apostles, and extraordinary Messengers of God, and to call it Enthusiasm, when the common Christian looks, and trusts to be continually led and inspired by the Spirit of God! For though all are not called to be Prophets or Apostles, yet all are called to be holy, as He who has called them is holy, to be perfect as their heavenly Father is perfect, to be like-minded with Christ, to will only as God wills, to do all to his Honour and Glory, to renounce the Spirit of this World, to have their Conversation in Heaven, to set their Affections on Things above, to love God with all their Heart, Soul, and Spirit, and their Neighbour as themselves.

[Love-2.1-42] Behold a Work as great, as Divine and supernatural, as that of a Prophet and an Apostle. But to suppose that we ought, and may always be in this Spirit of Holiness, and yet are not, and ought not to be always moved and led by the Breath and Spirit of God within us, is to suppose that there is a Holiness and Goodness which comes not from God; which is no better than supposing that there may be true Prophets and Apostles who have not their Truth from God.

[Love-2.1-43] Now the Holiness of the common Christian is not an occasional Thing, that begins and ends, or is only for such a Time, or Place, or Action, but is the Holiness of that, which is always alive and stirring in us, namely, of our Thoughts, Wills, Desires, and Affections. If therefore these are always alive in us, always driving or governing our Lives, if we can have no Holiness or Goodness, but as this Life of Thought, Will, and Affection works in us, if we are all called to this inward Holiness and Goodness, then a perpetual, always-existing Operation of the

Spirit of God within us, is absolutely necessary. For we cannot be inwardly led and governed by a Spirit of Goodness, but by being governed by the Spirit of God himself. For the Spirit of God and the Spirit of Goodness are not two Spirits, nor can we be said to have any more of the one, than we have of the other.

[Love-2.1-44] Now if our Thoughts, Wills, and Affections, need only be now and then holy and good, then, indeed, the moving and breathing Spirit of God need only now and then govern us. But if our Thoughts and Affections are to be always holy and good, then the holy and good Spirit of God is to be always operating, as a Principle of Life within us.

[Love-2.1-45] The Scripture saith, "We are not sufficient of ourselves to think a good Thought." If so, then we cannot be chargeable with not thinking, and willing that which is good, but upon this Supposition, that there is always a supernatural Power within us, ready and able to help us to the Good which we cannot have from ourselves.

[Love-2.1-46] The Difference then of a good and a bad Man does not lie in this, that the one wills that which is good, and the other does not, but solely in this, that the one concurs with the living inspiring Spirit of God within him and the other resists it, and is and can be only chargeable with Evil, because he resists it.

[Love-2.1-47] Therefore whether you consider that which is good or bad in a Man, they equally prove the perpetual Indwelling and Operation of the Spirit of God within us, since we can only be bad by resisting, as we are good by yielding to the Spirit of God; both which equally suppose a perpetual Operation of the Spirit of God within us.

[Love-2.1-48] How firmly our established Church adheres to this Doctrine of the Necessity of the perpetual Operation of the Holy Spirit, as the one only Source and Possibility of any Degree of Divine Light, Wisdom, Virtue, and Goodness in the Soul of Man, how earnestly she wills and requires all her Members to live in the most open Profession of it, and in the highest Conformity to it, may be seen by many such Prayers as these, in her common, ordinary, public Service.

[Love-2.1-49] "O God, forasmuch as without Thee we are not able to please Thee, grant that thy Holy Spirit may in all Things direct and rule our Hearts." Again, "We pray Thee, that thy Grace may ALWAYS prevent and follow us, and make us CONTINUALLY to be given to all good Works." Again, "Grant to us, Lord, we beseech Thee, the Spirit to think and do ALWAYS such things as be rightful, that we, who cannot do anything that is good without Thee, may by Thee be enabled to live according to thy Will." Again, "Because the Frailty of Man, without Thee cannot but Fall, keep us ever, by thy Help from all Things hurtful, and lead us to all Things profitable to our Salvation," &c. Again, "O God, from whom all good Things do come, grant to us thy humble Servants, that by thy holy inspiration we may think those Things that be good, and by thy merciful guiding may perform the same."— But now the true Ground of all this Doctrine of the Necessity of the perpetual Guidance and Operation of the Holy Spirit, lies in what has been said above, of the Necessity of a two-fold Life in every intelligent Creature that is to be good and happy. For if the creaturely Life, whilst alone, or left to itself, can only be Want, Misery, and Distress, if it cannot possibly have any Goodness or Happiness in it, till the Life of God is in Union with it, as one Life, then every Thing that you read in the Scripture of the Spirit of God, as the only Principle of Goodness, opens itself to you as a most certain and blessed Truth, about which you can have no doubt.

[Love-2.1-50] Theophilus. Let me only add, Eusebius, to what you have said, that from this absolute Necessity of a two-fold Life, in every Creature, that is, to be good and happy, we may, in a still greater Clearness see the Certainty of that which we have so often spoken of at other Times, namely, that the inspoken Word in Paradise, the Bruiser of the Serpent, the Seed of the Woman, the Immanuel, the holy Jesus (for they all mean the same Thing) is, and was the only possible Ground of Salvation for fallen Man. For if the two-fold Life is necessary, and Man could not be restored to Goodness and Happiness but by the restored Union of this two-fold Life into its first State, then there was an absolute Necessity in the Nature of the Thing, that every Son of Adam should have such a Seed of Heaven in the Birth of his Life, as could, by the Mediation of Christ, be raised into a Birth and Growth of the first perfect Man. This is the one Original Power of Salvation, without which, no external Dispensation could have done any Thing towards raising the fallen State of Man. For nothing could be raised, but what there was to be raised, nor Life be given to any Thing but to that which was capable of Life. Unless, therefore, there had been a Seed of Life, or a smothered Spark of Heaven in the Soul of Man, which wanted to come to the Birth, there had been no Possibility for any Dispensation of God, to bring forth a Birth of Heaven in fallen Man.

[Love-2.1-51] The Faith of the first Patriarchs could not have been in Being; Moses and the Prophets had come in vain, had not the Christ of God lain in a State of Hiddenness in every Son of Man. For Faith, which is a Will and Hunger after God, could not have begun to be, or have any Life in Man, but because there was something of the Divine Nature existing and hid in Man. For nothing can have any longing Desire but after its own Likeness, nor could any Thing be made to Desire God, but that which came from Him, and had the Nature of Him.

[Love-2.1-52] The whole mediatorial Office of Christ, from his Birth to his sitting down in Power at the right Hand of God, was only for this End, to help Man to a Life that was fallen into Death and Insensibility in him. And therefore his mediatorial Power was to manifest itself by Way of a new Birth. In the Nature of the Thing nothing else was to be done, and Christ had no other Way to proceed, and that for this plain Reason, because Life was the Thing that was lost, and Life, wherever it is, must be raised by a Birth, and every Birth must, and can only come from its own Seed.

[Love-2.1-53] But if Christ was to raise a new Life like his own in every Man, then every Man must have had originally, in the inmost Spirit of his Life, a Seed of Christ, or Christ as a Seed of Heaven, lying there as in a State of Insensibility or Death, out of which it could not arise but by the mediatorial Power of Christ, who, as a second Adam, was to regenerate that Birth of his own Life, which was lost in all the natural Sons of Adam the first.

[Love-2.1-54] But unless there was this Seed of Christ, or Spark of Heaven hidden in the Soul, not the least Beginning of Man's Salvation, or of Christ's mediatorial Office could be made. For what could begin to deny Self, if there was not something in Man different from Self? What could begin to have Hope and Faith and Desire of an heavenly Life, if there was not something of Heaven hidden in his Soul, and lying therein, as in a State of Inactivity and Death, till raised by the Mediation of Christ into its first Perfection of Life, and set again in its true Dominion over Flesh and Blood?

[Love-2.1-55] Eusebius. You have, Theophilus, sufficiently proved the Certainty and Necessity of this Matter. But I should be glad if you knew how to help me to some more distinct Idea and Conception of it.

[Love-2.1-56] Theophilus. An Idea is not the Thing to be here sought for; it would rather hinder, than help your true Knowledge of it. But perhaps the following Similitude may be of some Use to you.

[Love-2.1-57] The Ten Commandments, when written by God on Tables of Stone, and given to Man, did not then first begin to belong to Man; they had their Existence in Man, were born with him, they lay as a Seed and Power of Goodness, hidden in the Form and Make of his Soul, and altogether inseparable from it, before they were shown to Man on Tables of Stone. And when they were shown to Man on Tables of Stone, they were only an outward Imitation of that which was inwardly in Man, though not legible because of that Impurity of Flesh and Blood, in which they were drowned and swallowed up. For the earthly Nature, having overcome the Divinity that was in Man, it gave Commandments of its own to Man, and required Obedience to all the Lusts of the Flesh, the Lust of the Eyes, and the Pride of Life.

[Love-2.1-58] Hence it became necessary, that God should give an outward Knowledge of such Commandments as were become inwardly unknown, unfelt, and, as it were, shut up in Death in the Soul.

[Love-2.1-59] But now, had not all that is in these Commandments been really and antecedently in the Soul, as its own Birth and Nature, had they not still lain therein, and, although totally suppressed, yet in such a Seed or Remains, as could be called forth into their first living State, in vain had the Tables of Stone been given to Man; and all outward Writing, or Teaching of the Commandments, had been as useless, as so many Instructions given to Beasts or Stones. If therefore you can conceive, how all that is good and holy in the Commandments, lay hid as an unfelt, unactive Power or Seed of Goodness, till called into Sensibility and stirring by Laws written on Tables of Stone, this may help your Manner of conceiving, and believing, how Christ as a Seed of Life or Power of Salvation, lies in the Soul as its unknown, hidden Treasure, till awakened and called forth into Life by the mediatorial Office and Process of the holy Jesus.

[Love-2.1-60] Again, "Thou shalt love the Lord thy God with all thy Heart, with all thy Soul, and with all thy Strength, and thy Neighbour as thyself." Now these two Precepts, given by the written Word of God, are an absolute Demonstration of the first original Perfection of Man, and also a full and invincible Proof, that the same original Perfection is not quite annihilated, but lies in him as a hidden, suppressed Seed of Goodness, capable of being raised up to its first Perfection. For had not this Divine Unity, Purity, and Perfection of Love toward God and Man, been Man's first natural State of Life, it could have nothing to do with his present State. For had any other Nature, or Measure, or kind of Love begun in the first Birth of his Life, he could only have been called to that. For no Creature has, or can have a Call to be above, or act above its own

Nature. Therefore, as sure as Man is called to this Unity, Purity, and Perfection of Love, so sure is it, that it was, at first, his natural, heavenly State, and still has its Seed, or Remains within him, as his only Power and Possibility of rising up to it again. And therefore, all that Man is called to, every Degree of a new and perfect Life, every future Exaltation and Glory he is to have from the Mediation of Christ, is a full Proof, that the same Perfection was originally his natural State, and is still in him in such a Seed or Remains of Existence, as to admit of a perfect Renewal.

[Love-2.1-61] And thus it is, that you are to conceive of the holy Jesus, or the Word of God, as the hidden Treasure of every human Soul, born as a Seed of the Word in the Birth of the Soul, immured under Flesh and Blood, till as a Day-Star, it arises in our Hearts, and changes the Son of an earthly Adam into a Son of God.

[Love-2.1-62] And was not the Word and Spirit of God in us all, antecedent to any Dispensation or written Word of God, as a real Seed of Life in the Birth of our own Life, we could have no more Fitness for the Gospel-Redemption, than the Animals of this World, which have nothing of Heaven in them. And to call us to Love God with all our Hearts, to put on Christ, to walk according to the Spirit, if these Things had not their real Nature and Root within us, would be as vain and useless, as to make Rules and Orders how our Eyes should smell and taste, or our Ears should see.

[Love-2.1-63] Now this Mystery of an inward Life hidden in Man, as his most precious Treasure, as the Ground of all that can be great or good in him, and hidden only since his Fall, and which only can be opened and brought forth in its first Glory by Him to whom all Power in Heaven and on Earth is given, is a Truth to which almost every Thing in Nature bears full Witness. Look where you will, nothing appears, or works outwardly in any Creature, or in any Effect of Nature, but what is all done from its own inward invisible Spirit, not a Spirit brought into it, but its own inward Spirit, which is an inward invisible Mystery, till made known, or brought forth by outward Appearances.

[Love-2.1-64] The Sea neither is, nor can be moved and tossed by any other Wind, than that which hath its Birth, and Life, and Strength, in and from the Sea itself, as its own Wind. The Sun in the Firmament gives Growth to every Thing that grows in the Earth, and Life to every Thing that lives upon it, not by giving or imparting a Life from without, but only by stirring up in every Thing its own Growth, and its own Life, which lay as in a Seed or State of Death, till helped to come out of it by the Sun, which, as an Emblem of the Redeemer of the spiritual World, helps every earthly Thing out of its own Death into its own highest State of Life.

[Love-2.1-65] That which we call our Sensations, as seeing, hearing, feeling, tasting, and smelling, are not Things brought into us from without, or given unto us by any external Causes, but are only so many inborn, secret States of the Soul, which lie in their State of Hiddenness till they are occasionally awakened, and brought forth into Sensibility by outward Occurrences. And were they not antecedently in the Soul, as States and Forms of its own Life, no outward Objects could bring the Soul into a Sensibility of them. For nothing can have, or be in any State of Sensation, but that which it is, and hath from itself, as its own Birth. This is as certain as that a Circle hath only its own Roundness.

[Love-2.1-66] The stinking Gum gives nothing to the Soul, nor brings any Thing into Sensibility but that which was before in the Soul; it has only a Fitness to awaken, and stir up that State of the Soul, which lay dormant before, and which when brought into Sensibility, is called the Sensation of bad Smelling. And the odoriferous Gum hath likewise but the same Power, viz., a Fitness to stir up that State of Sensation in the Soul, which is called its delightful Smelling. But both these Sensations are only internal States of the Soul, which appear, or disappear, are found, or not found, just as Occasions bring them into Sensibility.

[Love-2.1-67] Again, the greatest Artist in Music can add no Sound to his Instrument, nor make it give forth any other Melody, but that which lieth silently hidden in it, as its own inward State.

[Love-2.1-68] Look now at what you will, whether it be animate, or inanimate: All that it is, or has, or can be, it is and has in and from itself, as its own inward State; and all outward Things can do no more to it, than the Hand does to the Instrument, make it show forth its own inward State, either of Harmony or Discord.

[Love-2.1-69] It is strictly thus with ourselves. Not a Spark of Joy, of Wrath, of Envy, of Love or Grief, can possibly enter into us from without, or be caused to be in us by any outward Thing. This is as impossible, as for the Sound of Metals to be put into a Lump of Clay. And as no Metal can possibly give forth any other, or higher Sound, than that which is enclosed within it, so we, however struck, can give forth no other or higher Sound either of Love, Hatred, Wrath, &c., than that very Degree which lay before shut up within us.

[Love-2.1-70] The natural State of our Tempers has Variety of Covers, under which they lie concealed at Times, both from ourselves and others; but when this or that Accident happens to displace such or such a Cover, then that which lay hid under it breaks forth. And then we vainly think, that this or that outward Occasion has not shown us how we are within, but has only infused or put into us a Wrath, or Grief, or Envy, which is not our natural State or of our own Growth, or has all that it has from our own inward State.

[Love-2.1-71] But this is mere Blindness and Self-Deceit, for it is as impossible for the Mind to have any Grief, or Wrath, or Joy, but what it has all from its own inward State, as for the Instrument to give forth any other Harmony, or Discord, but that which is within and from itself.

[Love-2.1-72] Persons, Things, and outward Occurrences may strike our Instrument improperly, and variously, but as we are in ourselves, such is our outward Sound, whatever strikes us.

[Love-2.1-73] If our inward State is the renewed Life of Christ within us, then every Thing and Occasion, let it be what it will, only makes the same Life to sound forth, and show itself; then if one Cheek is smitten, we meekly turn the other also. But if Nature is alive and only under a religious Cover, then every outward Accident that shakes or disturbs this Cover, gives Leave to that bad State, whether of Grief, or Wrath, or Joy that lay hid within us, to show forth itself.

[Love-2.1-74] But nothing at any Time makes the least Show, or Sound outwardly, but only that which lay ready within us, for an outward Birth, as Occasion should offer.

[Love-2.1-75] What a miserable Mistake is it therefore, to place religious Goodness in outward Observances, in Notions, and Opinions, which good and bad Men can equally receive and practise, and to treat the ready real Power and Operation of an inward Life of God in the Birth of our Souls as Fanaticism and Enthusiasm, when not only the whole Letter and Spirit of Scripture, but every Operation in Nature and Creature demonstrates that the Kingdom of Heaven must be all within us, or it never can possibly belong to us. Goodness, Piety, and Holiness, can only be ours, as thinking, willing, and desiring are ours, by being in us, as a Power of Heaven in the Birth and Growth of our own Life.

[Love-2.1-76] And now, Eusebius, how is the great controversy about Religion and Salvation shortened.

[Love-2.1-77] For since the one only Work of Christ as your Redeemer is only this, to take from the earthly Life of Flesh and Blood its usurped Power, and to raise the smothered Spark of Heaven out of its State of Death, into a powerful governing Life of the whole Man, your one only Work also under your Redeemer is fully known. And you have the utmost Certainty, what you are to do, where you are to seek, and in what you are to find your Salvation. All that you have to do, or can do, is to oppose, resist, and, as far as you can, to renounce the evil Tempers, and Workings of your own earthly Nature. You are under the Power of no other Enemy, are held in no other Captivity, and want no other Deliverance, but from the Power of your own earthly Self. This is the one Murderer of the Divine Life within you. It is your own Cain that murders your own Abel. Now every Thing that your earthly Nature does, is under the Influence of Self-will, Self-love, and Self-seeking, whether it carries you to laudable or blamable Practices, all is done in the Nature and Spirit of Cain and only helps you to such Goodness, as when Cain slew his Brother. For every Action and Motion of Self has the Spirit of Anti-christ and murders the Divine Life within you.

[Love-2.1-78] Judge not therefore of your Self, by considering how many of those Things you do, which Divines and Moralists call Virtue and Goodness, nor how much you abstain from those Things, which they call Sin and Vice.

[Love-2.1-79] But daily and hourly, in every Step that you take, see to the Spirit that is within you, whether it be Heaven, or Earth that guides you. And judge every Thing to be Sin and Satan, in which your earthly Nature, own Love, or Self-seeking has any Share of Life in you; nor think that any Goodness is brought to Life in you, but so far as it is an actual Death to the Pride, the Vanity, the Wrath, and selfish Tempers of your fallen, earthly Life.

[Love-2.1-80] Again, here you see, where and how you are to seek your Salvation, not in taking up your traveling Staff, or crossing the Seas to find out a new Luther or a new Calvin, to clothe yourself with their Opinions. No. The Oracle is at Home, that always and only speaks the Truth to you, because nothing is your Truth, but that Good and that Evil which is yours within you. For Salvation or Damnation is no outward Thing, that is brought into you from without, but is only That which springs up within you, as the Birth and State of your own Life. What you are in yourself, what is doing in yourself, is all that can be either your Salvation or Damnation.

[Love-2.1-81] For all that is our Good and all that is our Evil, has no Place nor Power but within us. Again, nothing that we do is bad, but for this Reason, because it resists the Power and working of God within us; and nothing that we do can be good but because it conforms to the Spirit of God within us. And therefore, as all that can be Good, and all that can be Evil in us, necessarily supposes a God working within us, you have the utmost Certainty that God, Salvation, and the Kingdom of Heaven, are nowhere to be sought, or found, but within you, and that all outward Religion from the Fall of Man to this Day, is not for itself, but merely for the Sake of an inward and Divine Life, which was lost when Adam died his first Death in Paradise. And therefore it may well be said, that Circumcision is nothing, and Uncircumcision is nothing, because nothing is wanted, and therefore nothing can be available, but the new Creature called out of its Captivity under the Death and Darkness of Flesh and Blood, into the Light, Life, and Perfection of its first Creation.

[Love-2.1-82] And thus also, you have the fullest Proof in what your Salvation precisely consists. Not in any historic Faith, or Knowledge of any Thing absent or distant from you, not in any Variety of Restraints, Rules, and Methods of practising Virtues, not in any Formality of Opinion about Faith and Works, Repentance, Forgiveness of Sins, or Justification and Sanctification, not in any Truth or Righteousness, that you can have from yourself, from the best of Men or Books, but wholly and solely in the Life of God, or Christ of God quickened and born again in you, or in other Words, in the Restoration and perfect Union of the first two-fold Life in the Humanity.

[Love-2.1-83] Theogenes. Though all that has passed betwixt you and Eusebius, concerns Matters of the greatest Moment, yet I must call it a Digression, and quite useless to me. For I have not the least Doubt about any of these Things you have been asserting. It is visible enough, that there can be no Medium in this Matter; either Religion must be all spiritual or all carnal; that is, we must either take up with the Grossness of the Sadducees, who say there is neither Angel nor Spirit, or with such Purification as the Pharisees had from their washing of Pots and Vessels, and tithing their Mint and Rue; we must, I say, either acquiesce in all this Carnality, or we must profess a Religion that is all Spirit and Life, and merely for the sake of raising up an inward spiritual Life of Heaven that fell into Death in our first Father.

[Love-2.1-84] I consent also to every Thing that you have said of the Nature and Origin of Wrath. That it can have no Place, nor Possibility of Beginning, but solely in the creaturely Nature, nor even any Possibility of Beginning there, till the Creature has died to, or lost its proper State of Existence in God; that is, till it has lost that Life, and Blessing, and Happiness, which it had in and from God at its first Creation.

[Love-2.1-85] But I still ask, what must I do with all those Scriptures, which not only make God capable of being provoked to Wrath and Resentment, but frequently inflamed with the highest Degrees of Rage, Fury, and Vengeance, that can be expressed by Words?

[Love-2.1-86] Theophilus. I promised, you know, to remove this Difficulty, and will be as good as my Word. But I must first tell you, that you are in much more Distress about it than you need to be. For in the little Book of Regeneration, in the Appeal, in the Spirit of Prayer, &c., which you have read with such entire Approbation, the whole Matter is cleared up from its true Ground, how Wrath in the Scriptures is ascribed to God, and yet cannot belong to the Nature of the Deity.

[Love-2.1-87] Thus you are told in the Appeal, After these two Falls of two orders of Creatures (that is, of Angels and Man), the Deity itself came to have new and strange Names, new and unheard of Tempers and Inclinations of Wrath, Fury, and Vengeance ascribed to it. I call them new, because they began at the Fall; I call them strange because they were foreign to the Deity, and could not belong to God in Himself. Thus, God is said to be a consuming Fire. But to whom? To the fallen Angels and lost Souls. But why, and how, is He so to them? It is because those Creatures have lost all that they had from God but the Fire of their Nature, and therefore God can only be found and manifested in them as a consuming Fire. Now, is it not justly said, that God, who is nothing but infinite Love, is yet in such Creatures only a consuming Fire? And though God be nothing but Love, yet they are under the Wrath and Vengeance of God because they have only that Fire in them which is broken off from the Light and Love of God and so can know or feel nothing of God but his Fire of Nature in them. As Creatures, they can have no Life but what they have in and from God; and therefore that wrathful Life which they have, is truly said to be a Wrath or Fire of God upon them. And yet it is still strictly true that there is no Wrath in God Himself, that He is not changed in his Temper toward the Creatures, that he does not cease to be one and the same infinite Fountain of Goodness, infinitely flowing forth in the Riches of his Love upon all and every Life. (Now, Sir, mind what follows, as the true Ground, how Wrath can and cannot be ascribed to God.) God is not changed from Love to Wrath, but the Creatures have changed their own State in Nature, and so the God of Nature can only be manifested in them, according to their own State in Nature. And, N.B., this is the true Ground of rightly understanding all that is said of the Wrath and Vengeance of God in and upon the Creatures. It is only in such a Sense, as the Curse of God may be said to be upon them, not because any Thing cursed can be in or come from God, but because they have made that Life, which they must have in God, to be a mere Curse to themselves. For every Creature that lives must have its Life in and from God, and therefore God must be in every Creature. This is as true of Devils, as of holy Angels. But how is God in them? N.B. Why, only as He is manifested in Nature. Holy Angels have the Triune Life of God, as manifested in Nature, so manifested also in them, and therefore God is in them all Love, Goodness, Majesty, and Glory, and theirs is the Kingdom of Heaven.

[Love-2.1-88] Devils have nothing of this Triune Life left in them, but the Fire, or Wrath of eternal Nature, broken off from all Light and Love; and therefore the Life that they can have in and from God is only and solely a Life of Wrath, Rage, and Darkness, and theirs is the Kingdom of Hell.

[Love-2.1-89] And because this Life, (though all Rage and Darkness), is a Strength and Power of Life, which they must have in and from God, and which they cannot take out of his Hands, therefore is their cursed, miserable, wrathful Life, truly and justly said to be the Curse and Misery, and Wrath, and Vengeance of God upon them, though God Himself can no more have Curse, Misery, Wrath, and Vengeance than He can have Mischief, Malice, or any fearful Tremblings in his holy Triune Deity.

[Love-2.1-90] See now, Theogenes, what little Occasion you had for your present Difficulty. For here, in the above cited Words, which you have been several Years acquainted with, the true Ground and Reason is plainly shown you, how and why all the Wrath, Rage, and Curse that is anywhere stirring in Nature, or breaking forth in any Creature, is and must be in all Truth called by the Scriptures the Wrath, and Rage, and Vengeance of God, though it be the greatest of all Impossibilities for Rage and Wrath to be in the Holy Deity itself.

[Love-2.1-91] The Scriptures therefore are literally true in all that they affirm of the Wrath, &c., of God. For is it not as literally true of God, that Hell and Devils are his, as that Heaven and holy Angels are his? Must not therefore all the Wrath and Rage of the one, be as truly his Wrath and Rage burning in them, as the Light and Joy and Glory of the other, is only his Goodness opened and manifested in them, according to their State in Nature?

[Love-2.1-92] Take notice of this fundamental Truth.

[Love-2.1-93] Every Thing that works in Nature and Creature, except Sin, is the working of God in Nature and Creature. The Creature has nothing else in its Power but the free Use of its Will; and its free Will hath no other Power, but that of concurring with, or resisting the Working of God in Nature. The Creature with its free Will can bring nothing into Being, nor make any Alteration in the working of Nature, it can only change its own State or Place in the working of Nature, and so feel and find something in its State, that it did not feel or find before.

[Love-2.1-94] Thus God, in the Manifestation of himself in and by Nature, sets before every Man Fire and Water, Life and Death; and Man has no other Power, but that of entering into and uniting with either of these States, but not the least Power of adding to, or taking any Thing from them, or of making them to be otherwise than he finds them.

[Love-2.1-95] For this Fire and Water, this Life and Death, are Nature, and have their unchangeable State in the uniform Working of God in Nature. And therefore, whatever is done by this Fire and Water, this Life and Death in any Creature, may, nay, must, in the strictest Truth, be affirmed of God as done by Him. And consequently, every breathing forth of Fire, or Death, or Rage, or Curse, wherever it is, or in whatever Creature, must be said, in the Language of Scripture, to be a provoked Wrath, or fiery Vengeance of God, poured forth upon the Creature. And yet, every Thing that has been said in Proof of the Wrath of God shows, and proves to you at the same Time, that it is not a Wrath in the Holy Deity itself.

[Love-2.1-96] For you see, as was said above, that God sets before Man Fire and Water, Life and Death; now these Things are not God, nor existent in the Deity itself; but they are that which is, and is called Nature, and as they are the only Things set before Man, so Man can go no further, reach no further, nor find, nor feel, nor be sensible of any Thing else, but that which is to be felt or found in this Nature, or Fire and Water, Life and Death, which are set before him. And therefore all that Man can find or feel of the Wrath and Vengeance of God, can only be in this Fire and this Death, and not in the Deity itself.

[Love-2.1-97] Theogenes. Oh Theophilus, you have given me the utmost Satisfaction on this Point, and in a much better Way than I imagined. I expected to have seen you glossing and criticizing away the literal Expression of Scriptures that affirm the Wrath of God, in order to make good your Point, that the Deity is mere Love.

[Love-2.1-98] But you have done the utmost Justice to the Letter of Scripture, you have established it upon a firm and solid Foundation, and shown that the Truth of Things require it to be so, and that there can be no Wrath anywhere, but what is and must be called the Wrath and

Vengeance of God, and yet is only in Nature.

[Love-2.1-99] What you have here said, seems as if it would clear up many Passages of Scripture that have raised much Perplexity. Methinks I begin to see how the Hardness of Pharaoh's Heart, how Eyes that see not, and Ears that hear not, may, in the strictest Truth, be said to be of or from God, though the Deity, in itself, stands in the utmost Contrariety to all these Things, and in the utmost Impossibility of willing or causing them to be.

[Love-2.1-100] But I must not draw you from our present Matter. You have shown, from the Letter of Scripture, that nothing else is set before Man but Fire and Water, Life and Death; and therefore, no Possibility of Wrath or Love, Joy or Sorrow, Curse or Happiness to be found by Man, but in this State of Nature set before him, or into which at his Creation he is introduced as into a Region of various Sensibilities, where all that he finds or feels, is truly God's, but not God himself, who has his supernatural Residence above, and distinct from every Thing that is Nature, Fire or Water, Life or Death.

[Love-2.1-101] But give me Leave to mention one Word of a Difficulty that I yet have. You have proved that Wrath, Rage, Vengeance, &c., can only exist, or be found in Nature, and not in God; and yet you say, that Nature is nothing else but a Manifestation of the hidden, invisible Powers of God. But if so, must not that which is in Nature be also in God? How else could Nature be a Manifestation of God?

[Love-2.1-102] Theophilus. Nature is a true Manifestation of the hidden, invisible God. But you are to observe, that Nature, as it is in itself, in its own State, cannot have the least possible Spark, or Stirring of Wrath, or Curse, or Vengeance in it: But, on the contrary, is from Eternity to Eternity, a mere Infinity of heavenly Light, Love, Joy, and Glory; and thus it is a true Manifestation of the hidden Deity, and the greatest of Proofs that the Deity itself can have no Wrath in it, since Wrath only then begins to be in Nature, when Nature has lost its first State.

[Love-2.1-103] Theogenes. This is Answer enough. But now another Thing starts up in my Mind. For if the Deity in itself, in its supernatural State, is mere Love, and only a Will to all Goodness, and if Nature in itself is only a Manifestation of this Deity of Love in heavenly Light and Glory, if neither God nor Nature have, or can give forth Wrath, how then can Fire and Water, Life and Death be set before Man? What can they come from, or where can they exist, since God in himself is all Love; and Nature, which is the Kingdom of Heaven, is an Infinity of Joy, Blessing, and Happiness?

[Love-2.1-104] Theophilus. I will open to you all this Matter to the Bottom in as few Words as I can.

[Love-2.1-105] Before God began any Creation, or gave Birth to any Creature, He was only manifested, or known to himself in his own Glory and Majesty; there was nothing but Himself beholding Himself in his own Kingdom of Heaven, which was, and is, and ever will be, as unlimited as Himself.

[Love-2.1-106] Nature, as well as God, is and must be antecedent to all Creature. For as no seeing Eye could be created, unless there was antecedently to it, a natural Visibility of Things, so no Creature could come into a Sensibility of any natural Life, unless such a State of Nature was antecedent to it. For no Creature can begin to be in any World or State of Nature, but by being created out of that World, or State of Nature, into which it is brought to have its Life. For to live in any World, is the same Thing as for a Creature to have all that it is, and has, in and from that World. And, therefore, no Creature can come into any other Kind of Existence and Life, but such as can be had out of that World in which it is to live. Neither can there possibly be any other Difference between created Beings, whether animate or inanimate, but what arises from that out of which they were created. Seeing then, that before the Existence of the first Creatures, there was nothing but God and his Kingdom of Heaven, the first Creatures could receive no other Life but that which was in God, because there was nothing living but God, nor any other Life but his, nor could they exist in any other Place or outward State, but the Kingdom of Heaven, because there was none else in Existence; and therefore, the first Creatures must, of all Necessity, be Divine and heavenly, both in their inward Life and outward State.

[Love-2.1-107] Theogenes. Here then, Theophilus, comes my Question. Where is that Fire and Water, that Life and Death, that is set before the Creature? For as to these first Creatures, nothing is set before them, nothing is within them, or without them, but God and the Kingdom of Heaven.

[Love-2.1-108] Theophilus. You should not have said, There is nothing within them, but God and the Kingdom of Heaven. For that which is their own creaturely Nature within them, is not God, nor the Kingdom of Heaven.

[Love-2.1-109] It has been already proved to your Satisfaction, that no Creature can be Divine, good, and happy, but by having a two-fold Life united in it. And in this two-fold Life of the Creature, is Fire and Water, Life and Death unavoidably set before it. For as its Will worketh with either of these Lives, so will it find either Fire or Water, Life or Death. If its Will turneth from the Life of God, into the creaturely Life, then it enters into a Sensibility of that which is meant by Death and Fire, viz., a wrathful Misery. But if the Will keeps steadily given up to the Deity, then it lives in Possession of that Life and Water, which was its first, and will be its everlasting heavenly Joy and Happiness.

[Love-2.1-110] But to explain this Matter something deeper to you, according to the Mystery of all Things opened by God in his chosen Instrument, Jacob Behmen.

[Love-2.1-111] You know we have often spoken of eternal Nature, that so sure as there is an eternal God, so sure is it, that there is an eternal Nature, as universal, as unlimited as God Himself, and everywhere working where God is, and therefore, everywhere equally existent, as being his Kingdom of Heaven, or outward Manifestation of the invisible Riches, Powers, and Glories of the Deity.

[Love-2.1-112] Before, or without Nature, the Deity is an entire hidden, shut up, unknown, and unknowable Abyss. For Nature is the only Ground, or Beginning of something; there is neither this nor that, no Ground for Conception, no Possibility of Distinction or Difference; there cannot be a Creature to think, nor any Thing to be thought upon, till Nature is in Existence. For all the Properties of Sensibility and sensible Life, every Mode and Manner of Existence, all Seeing, Hearing, Tasting, Smelling, Feeling, all Inclinations, Passions, and Sensations of Joy, Sorrow,

Pain, Pleasure, &c., are not in God, but in Nature. And therefore, God is not knowable, not a Thought can begin about Him, till He manifests himself in, and through, and by the Existence of Nature; that is, till there is something that can be seen, understood, distinguished, felt, &c.

[Love-2.1-113] And this eternal Nature, or the Out-Birth of the Deity, called the Kingdom of Heaven, viz., an Infinity, or boundless Opening of the Properties, Powers, Wonders, and Glories of the hidden Deity, and this not once done, but ever doing, ever standing in the same Birth, for ever and ever breaking forth and springing up in new Forms and Openings of the abyssal Deity, in the Powers of Nature. And out of this Ocean of manifested Powers of Nature, the Will of the Deity, created Hosts of heavenly Beings, full of the heavenly Wonders introduced into a Participation of the Infinity of God, to live in an eternal Succession of heavenly Sensations, to see and feel, to taste and find new Forms of Delight in an inexhaustible Source of ever-changing and never-ceasing Wonders of the Divine Glory.

[Love-2.1-114] Oh Theogenes! What an Eternity is this, out of which, and for which thy eternal Soul was created? What little, crawling Things are all that an earthly Ambition can set before Thee? Bear with Patience for a while the Rags of thy earthly Nature, the Veil and Darkness of Flesh and Blood, as the Lot of thy Inheritance from Father Adam, but think nothing worth a Thought, but that which will bring thee back to thy first Glory, and land thee safe in the Region of Eternity.

[Love-2.1-115] But to return. Nothing is before this eternal Nature, but the holy, supernatural Deity; and every Thing that is after it, is Creature, and has all its creaturely Life and State in it, and from it, either mediately or immediately.

[Love-2.1-116] This eternal Nature hath seven chief or fountain Properties, that are the Doers, or Workers of every Thing that is done in it, and can have neither more nor less, because it is a Birth from, or a Manifestation of the Deity in Nature. For the Perfection of Nature (as was before said of every Divine and happy Creature) is an Union of two Things, or is a two-fold State. It is Nature, and it is God manifested in Nature. Now God is Triune, and Nature is Triune, and hence there arises the Ground of Properties, three and three; and that which brings those three and three into Union, or manifests the Triune God in the Triune Nature, is another Property; so that the glorious Manifestation of the Deity in Nature can have neither more nor less than seven chief or fountain Properties from which every Thing that is known, found, and felt, in all the Universe of Nature, in all the Variety of Creatures either in Heaven or on Earth, hath its only Rise, or Cause, either mediately or immediately.

[Love-2.1-117] Theogenes. You say, Theophilus, that the Triune Deity is united or manifested in Triune Nature, and that thence comes the glorious Manifestation of God in seven heavenly Properties called the Kingdom of Heaven. But how does it appear that this Nature, antecedently to the Entrance of the Deity into it, is Triune? Or what is this Triune Nature, before God is supposed to be in Union with it?

[Love-2.1-118] Theophilus. It is barely a Desire. It neither is, nor has, nor can be any Thing else but a Desire. For Desire is the only Thing in which the Deity can work and manifest itself; for God can only come into That which wants and desires him.

[Love-2.1-119] The Deity is an infinite Plenitude, or Fullness of Riches and Powers, in and from itself; and it is only want and Desire, that is excluded from It, and can have no Existence in it. And here lies the true, immutable Distinction between God and Nature, and shows why neither can ever be changed into the other; it is because God is a universal all; and Nature or Desire is a universal want, viz., to be filled with God.

[Love-2.1-120] Now as Nature can be nothing but a Desire, so nothing is in, or done in any natural Way, but as Desire does it, because Desire is the All of Nature. And, therefore, there is no Strength or Substance, no Power or Motion, no Cause or Effect in Nature, but what is in itself a Desire, or the Working and Effect of it.

[Love-2.1-121] This is the true Origin of Attraction, and all its Powers, in this material World. It gives Essence and Substance to all that is Matter and the Properties of Matter; it holds every Element in its created State; and not only Earth and Stones, but Light and Air and Motion are under its Dominion. From the Centre to the Circumference of this material System, every Motion, Separation, Union, Vegetation, or Corruption begins no sooner, goes on no further, than as Attraction Works.

[Love-2.1-122] Take away Attraction from this material System, and then it has all the Annihilation it can ever possibly have.

[Love-2.1-123] Whence now has Attraction this Nature?

[Love-2.1-124] It is solely from hence; because all Nature from its Eternity, hath been, is, and for ever can be only a Desire, and hath nothing in it but the Properties of Desire.

[Love-2.1-125] Now the essential, inseparable Properties of Desire are the three, and can be neither more nor less; and in this you have that Tri-Unity of Nature which you asked after, and in which the Triune Deity manifesteth itself. I shall not now prove these three Properties of the Desire, because I have done it at large, and plainly enough elsewhere. { Way to Divine Knowledge; Spirit of Love, Part I }

[Love-2.1-126] But to go back now to your Question, Where, or how this Fire and Water, &c., can be found, since God is all Love and Goodness, and his Manifestation in Nature is a mere Kingdom of Heaven. They are to be found in the two-fold State of Heaven, and the two-fold State of every heavenly Creature.

[Love-2.1-127] For seeing that the Perfection of Nature, and the Perfection of the intelligent Creature, consists in one and the same two-fold State, you have here the plainest Ground and Reason why and how every good and happy and new created Being, must of all Necessity, have Fire and Water, Life and Death set before it, or put into its Choice.

[Love-2.1-128] Because it has it in its Power to turn and give up its Will to either of these Lives, it can turn either to God, or Nature, and therefore must have Life and Death, Fire or Water in its Choice.

[Love-2.1-129] Now this two-fold Life, which makes the Perfection of Nature and Creature, is, in other Words, signified by the seven heavenly Properties of Nature; for when God is manifested in Nature, all its seven Properties are in a heavenly State.

[Love-2.1-130] But in these seven Properties, though all heavenly, lieth the Ground of Fire and

Water, &c., because a Division or Separation can be made in them by the Will of the Creature. For the three first Properties are as distinct from the four following ones, as God is distinct from That which wants God. And these three first Properties are the Essence or whole Being of that Desire, which is, and is called Nature, or that which wants God.

[Love-2.1-131] When, therefore, the Will of the Creature turns from God into Nature, it breaks, or looses the Union of the seven heavenly Properties; because Nature, as distinct from God, has only the three first Properties in it. And such a Creature, having broken or lost the Union of the seven Properties, is fallen into the three first, which is meant by Fire and Death. For when the first three Properties have lost God, or their Union with the four following ones, then they are mere Nature, which, in its whole Being, is nothing else but the Strength and Rage of Hunger, an Excess of Want, of Self-Torment, and Self-Vexation. Surely now, my friend, this Matter is enough explained.

[Love-2.1-132] Theogenes. Indeed, Theophilus, I am quite satisfied; for by this Account which you have given of the Ground of Nature, and its true and full Distinction from God, you have struck a most amazing Light into my Mind.

[Love-2.1-133] For if Nature is mere Want, and has nothing in it but a Strength of Want, generated from the three self-tormenting Properties of a Desire, if God is all Love, Joy, and Happiness, an infinite Plenitude of all Blessings, then the Limits and Bounds of Good and Evil, of Happiness and Misery, are made as visibly distinct and as certainly to be known, as the Difference between a Circle and a straight Line.

[Love-2.1-134] To live to Desire, that is, to Nature, is unavoidably entering into the Region of all Evil and Misery; because Nature has nothing else in it. But on the other Hand, to die to Desire, that is, to turn from Nature to God, is to be united with the infinite Source of all that is good, and blessed, and happy.

[Love-2.1-135] All that I wanted to know, is now cleared up in the greatest Plainness. And I have no Difficulty about those passages of Scripture, which speak of the Wrath, and Fury, and Vengeance of God. Wrath is his, just as all Nature is his, and yet God is mere Love, that only rules and governs Wrath, as He governs the foaming Waves of the Sea, and the Madness of Storms and Tempests.

[Love-2.1-136] The following Propositions are as evidently true, as that two and two are four.

[Love-2.1-137] First, That God in his holy Deity is as absolutely free from Wrath and Rage, and as utterly incapable of them as He is of Thickness, Hardness, and Darkness; because Wrath and Rage belong to nothing else, can exist in nothing else, have Life in nothing else, but in Thickness, Hardness, and Darkness.

[Love-2.1-138] Secondly, That all Wrath is Disorder, and can be nowhere but in Nature and Creature, because nothing else is capable of changing from Right to Wrong.

[Love-2.1-139] Thirdly, That Wrath can have no Existence even in Nature and Creature, till they have lost their first Perfection which they had from God, and are become that which they should not have been.

[Love-2.1-140] Fourthly, That all the Wrath, and Fury, and Vengeance, that ever did, or can break forth in Nature and Creature is, according to the strictest Truth, to be called and looked upon as the Wrath and Vengeance of God, just as the Darkness, as well as the Light is, and is to be called his.

[Love-2.1-141] Oh! Theophilus, what a Key have you given me to the right understanding of Scripture!

[Love-2.1-142] For when Nature and Creature are known to be the only Theater of Evil and Disorder, and the holy Deity as that governing Love, which wills nothing but the Removal of all Evil from every Thing, as fast as infinite Wisdom can find Ways of doing it, then whether you read of the raining of Fire and Brimstone, or only Showers of heavenly Manna falling upon the Earth, it is only one and the same Love, working in such different Ways and Diversity of Instruments, as Time, and Place, and Occasion, had made wise, and good, and beneficial.

[Love-2.1-143] Pharaoh with his hardened Heart, and St Paul with his Voice from Heaven, though so contrary to one another, were both of them the chosen Vessels of the same God of Love, because both miraculously taken out of their own State, and made to do all the Good to a blind and wicked World, which they were capable of doing.

[Love-2.1-144] And thus, Sir, are all the Treasures of the Wisdom and Goodness of God, hidden in the Letter of Scripture, made the Comfort and Delight of my Soul, and every Thing I read turns itself into a Motive, of loving and adoring the wonderful Working of the Love of God over all the various Changings of Nature and Creature, till all Evil shall be extinguished, and all Disorder go back again to its first harmonious State of Perfection.

[Love-2.1-145] Depart from this Idea of God, as an Infinity of mere Love, Wisdom, and Goodness, and then every Thing in the System of Scripture, and the System of Nature, only helps the reasoning Mind to be miserably perplexed, as well with the Mercies, as with the Judgments of God.

[Love-2.1-146] But when God is known to be omnipotent Love, that can do nothing but Works of Love, and that all Nature and Creature are only under the Operation of Love, as a distempered Person under the Care of a kind and skillful Physician, who seeks nothing but the perfect Recovery of his Patient, then whatever is done, whether a severe Caustic, or a pleasant Cordial is ordered, that is, whether because of its Difference, it may have the different Name of Mercy or Judgment, yet all is equally well done, because Love is the only Doer of both, and does both, from the same Principle, and for the same End.

[Love-2.1-147] Theophilus. Oh Theogenes, Now you are according to your Name, you are born of God. For when Love is the Triune God that you serve, worship, and adore, the only God, in whom you desire to live and move and have your Being, then of a Truth God dwelleth in you, and you in God.

[Love-2.1-148] I shall now only add this one Word more, to strengthen and confirm your right understanding of all that is said of the Wrath, or Rage of God in the Scriptures.

[Love-2.1-149] The Psalmist, you know, saith thus of God, "He giveth forth his Ice like Morsels, and who is able to abide his Frosts?" Now, Sir, if you know how to explain this Scripture, and can show how Ice and Frost can truly be ascribed to God, as His, though absolutely impossible to have any Existence in Him, then you have an easy and unerring Key, how the Wrath, and Fury, and Vengeance, that anywhere falls upon any Creature is, and may be truly ascribed to God, as his, though Fury and Vengeance are as inconsistent with, and as impossible to have any Existence in the Deity, as lumps of Ice, or the Hardness of intolerable Frosts.

[Love-2.1-150] Now in this Text, setting forth the Horror of God's Ice and Frost, you have the whole Nature of Divine Wrath set before you. Search all the Scriptures, and you will nowhere find any Wrath of God, but what is bounded in Nature, and is so described, as to be itself a Proof, that it has no Existence in the holy supernatural Deity.

[Love-2.1-151] Thus says the Psalmist again, "The Earth trembled and quaked, the very Foundations also of the Hills shook, and were removed, because he was wroth." No Wrath here but in the Elements.

[Love-2.1-152] Again, "There went a Smoke out in his Presence, and a consuming Fire out of his Mouth, so that Coals were kindled at it. The Springs of Water were seen, and the Foundations of the round World were discovered at thy chiding, O Lord, at the blasting of the Breath of thy Displeasure."

[Love-2.1-153] Now every Working of the Wrath of God, described in Scripture, is strictly of a Piece with this, it relates to a Wrath solely confined to the Powers and working Properties of Nature, that lives and moves only in the Elements of the fallen World, and no more reaches the Deity, than Ice or Frost do.

[Love-2.1-154] The Apostle saith, "Avenge not yourselves, for it is written, Vengeance is mine, I Will repay, saith the Lord."

[Love-2.1-155] This is another full Proof, that Wrath or Vengeance is not in the holy Deity itself, as a Quality of the Divine Mind; for if it was, then Vengeance would belong to every Child of God, that was truly born of Him, or he could not have the Spirit of his Father, or be perfect as his Father in Heaven is perfect.

[Love-2.1-156] But if Vengeance only belongs to God, and can only be so affirmed of Him, as Ice and Frost are His, and belong to Him, if it has no other Manner of Working, than as when it is said, "He sent out his Arrows and scattered them, He cast forth Lightnings and destroyed them"; then it is certain, that the Divine Vengeance is only in fallen Nature, and its disordered Properties, and is no more in the Deity itself, than Hailstones and Coals of Fire.

[Love-2.1-157] And here you have the true Reason, why Revenge or Vengeance is not allowed to Man; it is because Vengeance can only work in the evil, or disordered Properties of fallen Nature. But Man being Himself a Part of fallen Nature, and subject to its disordered Properties, is not allowed to work with them, because it would be stirring up Evil in himself, and that is his Sin of Wrath, or Revenge.

[Love-2.1-158] God therefore reserves all Vengeance to Himself, not because wrathful Revenge is a Temper or Quality that can have any Place in the Holy Deity, but because the holy supernatural Deity, being free from all the Properties of Nature, whence partial Love and Hatred spring, and being in Himself nothing but an Infinity of Love, Wisdom, and Goodness, He alone knows how to over-rule the Disorders of Nature, and so to repay Evil with Evil, that the highest good may be promoted by it.

[Love-2.1-159] To say, therefore, that Vengeance is to be reserved to God, is only saying in other Words, that all the Evils in Nature are to be reserved and turned over to the Love of God, to be healed by his Goodness. And every Act of what is called Divine Vengeance, recorded in Scripture, may, and ought, with the greatest strictness of Truth, be called an Act of the Divine Love.

[Love-2.1-160] If Sodom flames and smokes with stinking Brimstone, it is the Love of God that kindled it, only to extinguish a more horrible Fire. It was one and the same infinite Love, when it preserved Noah in the Ark, when it turned Sodom into a burning Lake, and overwhelmed Pharaoh in the Red Sea. And if God commanded the Waters to destroy the old World, it was as high an Act of the same infinite Love toward that Chaos, as when it said to the first Darkness upon the Face of the Deep, "Let there be Light, and there was Light."

[Love-2.1-161] Not a Word in all Scripture concerning the Wrath or Vengeance of God but directly teaches you these two infallible truths. First, that all the Wrath spoken of worketh nowhere but in the wrathful, disordered Elements and Properties of fallen Nature. Secondly, that all the Power that God exercises over them, all that he doth at any Time or on any Occasion with or by them is only and solely the one Work of his unchangeable Love toward Man.

[Love-2.1-162] Just as the good Physician acts from only one and the same good Will toward his Patient, when he orders bitter and sour, as when he gives the pleasant Draughts.

[Love-2.1-163] Now, suppose the good Physician to have such intense Love for you, as to disregard your Aversion toward them, and to force such Medicines down your Throat, as can alone save your Life; suppose he should therefore call himself your severe Physician, and declare himself so rigid toward you, that he would not spare you, nor suffer you, go where you would, to escape his bitter Draughts, till all Means of your Recovery were tried, then you would have a true and just, though low Representation of those bitter Cups, which God in his Wrath forceth fallen Man to drink.

[Love-2.1-164] Now as the bitter, sour, hot, &c., in the Physician's Draughts, are not Declarations of any the like Bitterness, Heat, or Sourness in the Spirit of the Physician that uses them, but are Things quite distinct from the State and Spirit of his Mind, and only manifest his Care and Skill in the right Use of such Materials toward the Health of his Patient; so in like Manner, all the Elements of fallen Nature are only so many outward Materials in the Hands of God, formed and mixed into Heat and Cold, into fruitful and pestilential Effects, into Serenity of Seasons, and blasting Tempests, into Means of Health and Sickness, of Plenty and Poverty, just as the Wisdom and Goodness of Providence sees to be the fittest to deliver Man from the miserable Malady of his earthly Nature and help him to become heavenly-minded.

[Love-2.1-165] If, therefore, it would be great Folly to suppose Bitterness, or Heat, &c., to be in the Spirit of the Physician, when he gives a hot or bitter Medicine, much greater Folly surely must it be, to suppose that Wrath, Vengeance, or any pestilential Quality, is in the Spirit of the holy Deity, when a Wrath, a Vengeance, or Pestilence is stirred up in the fallen Elements by the Providence of God, as a proper Remedy for the Evil of this, or that Time or Occasion.

[Love-2.1-166] Hear these decisive words of Scripture, viz., "Whom the Lord loveth, he chasteneth." What a Grossness therefore of Mistake is it to conclude, that Wrath must be in the Deity, because He chastens and threatens Chastisement, when you have God's own Word for it, that nothing but his Love chasteneth? Again, Thus saith the Lord, "I have smitten you with Blasting and Mildew. Your Vineyards, and your Fig Trees, and your Olive Yards, did the Palmer-Worm devour," and then the Love that did this makes this Complaint, "Yet ye have not returned to me." Again, "Pestilence have I sent amongst you; I have made the Stink of your Tents come up even into your Nostrils," &c. And then the same Love that did this, that made this Use of the disordered Elements, makes the same Complaint again, "Yet have ye not returned to me" (Amos 4:9-10).

[Love-2.1-167] Now, Sir, How is it possible for Words to give stronger Proof, that God is mere Love, that he has no Will toward fallen Man but to bless him with Works of Love, and this as certainly, when he turns the Air into a Pestilence, as when he makes the same Air rain down Manna upon the Earth, since neither the one nor the other are done, but as Time, and Place, and Occasion, render them the fittest Means to make Man return and adhere to God, that is, to come out of all the Evil and Misery of his fallen State? What can infinite Love do more, or what can it do to give greater Proof, that all that it does proceeds from Love? And here you are to observe, that this is not said from human Conjecture, or any imaginary Idea of God, but is openly asserted, constantly affirmed, and repeated in the plainest Letter of Scripture. But this Conversation has been long enough. And I hope we shall meet again To-morrow.

The Second Dialogue between Theogenes, Eusebius, and Theophilus

[Love-2.2-1] EUSEBIUS.   There is no Occasion to resume any Thing of our Yesterday's Discourse. The following Propositions are sufficiently proved.

[Love-2.2-2] First, That God is an abyssal Infinity of Love, Wisdom, and Goodness; that He ever was, and ever will be one and the same unchangeable Will to all Goodness and Works of Love, as incapable of any Sensibility of Wrath, or acting under it, as of falling into Pain or Darkness, and acting under their Direction.

[Love-2.2-3] Secondly, That all Wrath, Strife, Discord, Hatred, Envy, or Pride, &c., all Heat and Cold, all Enmity in the Elements, all Thickness, Grossness, and Darkness are Things that have no Existence but in and from the Sphere of fallen Nature.

[Love-2.2-4] Thirdly, That all the Evils of Contrariety and Disorder in fallen Nature are only as so many Materials in the Hands of infinite Love and Wisdom, all made to work in their different Ways, as far as is possible, to one and the same End, viz., to turn temporal Evil into eternal Good.

[Love-2.2-5] So that whether you look at Light or Darkness, at Night or Day, at Fire or Water, at Heaven or Earth, at Life or Death, at Prosperity or Adversity, at blasting Winds or heavenly Dews, at Sickness or Health, you see nothing but such a State of Things, in and through which, the supernatural Deity wills and seeks the Restoration of fallen Nature and Creature to their first Perfection.

[Love-2.2-6] It now only remains, that the Doctrine of Scripture concerning the Atonement, necessary to be made by the Life, Sufferings, and Death of Christ be explained, or in other Words, the true Meaning of that Righteousness or Justice of God, that must have Satisfaction done to it, before Man can be reconciled to God.

[Love-2.2-7] For this Doctrine is thought by some to favour the Opinion of a Wrath and Resentment in the Deity itself.

[Love-2.2-8] Theophilus. This Doctrine, Eusebius, of the Atonement made by Christ, and the absolute Necessity and real Efficacy of it, to satisfy the Righteousness, or Justice of God, is the very Ground and Foundation of Christian Redemption, and the Life and Strength of every Part of it. But then, this very Doctrine is so far from favouring the Opinion of a Wrath in the Deity itself, that it is an absolute full Denial of it, and the strongest of Demonstrations, that the Wrath, or Resentment, that is to be pacified or atoned, cannot possibly be in the Deity itself.

[Love-2.2-9] For this Wrath that is to be atoned and pacified is, in its whole Nature, nothing else but Sin, or Disorder in the Creature. And when Sin is extinguished in the Creature, all the Wrath that is between God and the Creature is fully atoned. Search all the Bible, from one End to the other, and you will find, that the Atonement of that which is called the Divine Wrath or Justice, and the extinguishing of Sin in the Creature, are only different Expressions for one and the same individual Thing. And therefore, unless you will place Sin in God, that Wrath, that is to be atoned or pacified, cannot be placed in Him.

[Love-2.2-10] The whole Nature of our Redemption has no other End, but to remove or extinguish the Wrath that is between God and Man. When this is removed, Man is reconciled to God. Therefore, where the Wrath is, or where that is which wants to be atoned, there is that which is the blamable Cause of the Separation between God and Man; there is that which Christ came into the World to extinguish, to quench, or atone. If, therefore, this Wrath, which is the blamable Cause of the Separation between God and Man, is in God Himself, if Christ died to atone, or extinguish a Wrath that was got into the holy Deity itself, then it must be said, that Christ made an Atonement for God, and not for Man; that He died for the Good and Benefit of God, and not of Man; and that which is called our Redemption, ought rather to be called the Redemption of God, as saving and delivering Him, and not Man, from his own Wrath.

[Love-2.2-11] This Blasphemy is unavoidable, if you suppose that Wrath, for which Christ died, to be a Wrath in God Himself.

[Love-2.2-12] Again, The very Nature of Atonement absolutely shows, that that which is to be atoned cannot possibly be in God, nor even in any good Being. For Atonement implies the Alteration, or Removal of something that is not as it ought to be. And therefore, every Creature, so long as it is good, and has its proper State of Goodness, neither wants, nor can admit of any Atonement, because it has nothing in it that wants to be altered or taken out of it. And therefore, Atonement cannot possibly have any Place in God, because nothing in God either wants, or can receive Alteration; neither can it have Place in any Creature, but so far as it has lost, or altered that which it had from God, and is fallen into Disorder; and then, that which brings this Creature back to its first State, which alters that which is wrong in it, and takes its Evil out of it, is its true and proper Atonement.

[Love-2.2-13] Water is the proper Atonement of the Rage of Fire; and that which changes a Tempest into a Calm is its true Atonement. And, therefore, as sure as Christ is a Propitiation and Atonement, so sure is it, that that which he does, as a Propitiation and Atonement, can have no Place, but in altering that Evil and Disorder which, in the State and Life of the fallen Creature, wants to be altered.

[Love-2.2-14] Suppose the Creature not fallen, and then there is no Room nor Possibility for Atonement; a plain and full Proof, that the Work of Atonement is nothing else but the altering or quenching that which is Evil in the fallen Creature.

[Love-2.2-15] Hell, Wrath, Darkness, Misery, and eternal Death, mean the same Thing through all Scripture, and these are the only Things from which we want to be redeemed; and where there is nothing of Hell, there, there is nothing of Wrath, nor any Thing that wants, or can admit of the Benefits of the Atonement made by Christ.

[Love-2.2-16] Either, therefore, all Hell is in the Essence of the holy Deity, or nothing that wants to be atoned by the Merits and Death of Christ, can possibly be in the Deity itself.

[Love-2.2-17] The Apostle saith, that "we are by Nature Children of Wrath"; the same Thing as when the Psalmist saith, "I was shapen in Wickedness, and in Sin hath my Mother conceived me." And therefore, that Wrath which wants the Atonement of the Sufferings, Blood, and Death of Christ, is no other than that Sin, or sinful State, in which we are naturally born. But now, if this Wrath could be supposed to be in the Deity itself, then it would follow, that by being by Nature Children of Wrath, we should thereby be the true Children of God; we should not want any Atonement, or new Birth from above, to make us Partakers of the Divine Nature, because that Wrath that was in us would be our dwelling in God and he in us.

[Love-2.2-18] Again, All Scripture teaches us, That God wills and desires the Removal, or Extinction of that Wrath, which is betwixt God and the Creature; and therefore, all Scripture teaches, that the Wrath is not in God; for God cannot will the Removal, or Alteration of any Thing that is in Himself; this is as impossible, as for him to will the Extinction of his own Omnipotence. Nor can there be any Thing in God, contrary to, or against his own Will; and yet, if God wills the Extinction of a Wrath that is in Himself, it must be in Him, contrary to, or against his own Will.

[Love-2.2-19] This, I presume, is enough to show you, that the Atonement made by Christ is itself the greatest of all Proofs, that it was not to atone or extinguish any Wrath in the Deity itself; nor, indeed, any Way to affect, or alter any Quality, or Temper in the Divine Mind, but purely and solely to overcome and remove all that Death and Hell, and Wrath, and Darkness, that had opened itself in the Nature, Birth, and Life of fallen Man.

[Love-2.2-20] Eusebius. The Truth of all this is not to be denied. And yet it is as true, that all our Systems of Divinity give quite another Account of this most important Matter. The Satisfaction of Christ is represented as a Satisfaction made to a wrathful Deity; and the Merits of the

Sufferings and Death of Christ, as that which could only avail with God, to give up his own Wrath, and think of Mercy toward Man. Nay, what is still worse, if possible, the Ground, and Nature, and Efficacy of this great Transaction between God and Man, is often explained by Debtor and Creditor: Man, as having contracted a Debt with God that he could not pay, and God, as having a Right to insist upon the Payment of it; and therefore, only to be satisfied by receiving the Death and Sacrifice of Christ, as a valuable Consideration, instead of the Debt that was due to Him from Man.

[Love-2.2-21] Theophilus. Hence you may see, Eusebius, how unreasonably Complaint has been sometimes made against the Appeal, the Spirit of Prayer, &c., as introducing a Philosophy into the Doctrines of the Gospel, not enough supported by the Letter of Scripture; though every Thing there asserted has been over and over shown to be well grounded on the Letter of Scripture, and necessarily included in the most fundamental Doctrines of the Gospel.

[Love-2.2-22] Yet they who make this Complaint, blindly swallow a Vanity of Philosophy, in the most important part of Gospel Religion, which not only has less Scripture for it than the Infallibility of the Pope, but is directly contrary to the plain Letter of every single Text of Scripture that relates to this Matter: as I will now show you.

[Love-2.2-23] First, The Apostle saith, "God so loved the World, that he gave his only begotten Son, that all who believe in Him should not perish but have everlasting Life." What becomes now of the Philosophy of Debtor and Creditor, of a Satisfaction made by Christ to a Wrath in God? Is it not the grossest of all Fictions, and in full Contrariety to the plain written Word of God? "God so loved the World"; behold the Degree of it? But when did He so love it? Why, before it was redeemed, before He sent or gave his only Son to be the Redeemer of it. Here you see, that all Wrath in God, antecedent to our Redemption, or the Sacrifice of Christ for us, is utterly excluded; there is no Possibility for the Supposition of it, it is as absolutely denied as Words can do it. And therefore the infinite Love, Mercy, and Compassion of God toward fallen Man, are not purchased, or procured for us by the Death of Christ, but the Incarnation and Sufferings of Christ come from, and are given to us by the infinite antecedent Love of God for us, and are the gracious Effects of his own Love and Goodness toward us.

[Love-2.2-24] It is needless to show you, how constantly this same Doctrine is asserted and repeated by all the Apostles.

[Love-2.2-25] Thus says St. John again, "In this was manifested the Love of God toward us, because he sent his only begotten Son into the World, that we might live through him." Again, "this is the Record, that God hath given unto us eternal Life; and this Life is in his Son." Again, "God," saith St. Paul, "was in Christ, reconciling the World unto Himself, not imputing their Trespasses to them." Which is repeated, and further opened in these Words, "Giving Thanks unto the Father, who hath made us meet to be Partakers of the Inheritance of the Saints in Light, who hath delivered us from the Power of Darkness, and hath translated us into the Kingdom of his dear Son" (Col. 1:12-13). And again, "Blessed be the God and Father of our Lord Jesus Christ, who hath blessed us with all spiritual Blessings in heavenly Places in Christ" (Eph. 1:3).

[Love-2.2-26] How great therefore, Eusebius, is the Error, how total the Disregard of Scripture, and how vain the Philosophy, which talks of a Wrath in God antecedent to our Redemption, or of a Debt which he could not forgive us, till he had received a Valuable Consideration for it, when all Scriptures from Page to Page tells us, that all the Mercy and Blessing and Benefits of Christ, as our Saviour, are the free antecedent Gift of God Himself to us, and bestowed upon us for no other Reason, from no other Motive, but the Infinity of his own Love toward us, agreeable to what the Evangelical Prophet saith of God, "I am He that blotteth out Transgressions for my own sake" (Isa. 43:25), that is, not for any Reason or Motive that can be laid before me but because I am Love itself, and my own Nature is my immutable Reason why nothing but Works of Love, Blessing, and Goodness, can come from me.

[Love-2.2-27] Look we now at the Scripture Account of the Nature of the Atonement and Satisfaction of Christ, and this will further show us, that it is not to atone, or alter any Quality or Temper in the Divine Mind, nor for the Sake of God, but purely and solely to atone, to quench, and overcome that Death, and Wrath, and Hell, under the Power of which Man was fallen.

[Love-2.2-28] "As in Adam all die, so in Christ shall all be made alive." This is the whole Work, the whole Nature, and the sole End of Christ's Sacrifice of Himself; and there is not a Syllable in Scripture, that gives you any other account of it. It all consists, from the Beginning to the End, in carrying on the one Work of Regeneration; and therefore the Apostle saith, "The first Adam was made a living Soul, but the last or Second Adam was made a Quickening Spirit," because sent into the World by God to quicken and revive that Life from above which we lost in Adam. And he is called our Ransom, our Atonement, &c., for no other Reason, but because that which He did and suffered in our fallen Nature, was as truly an efficacious Means of our being born again to a new heavenly Life, of Him, and from Him, as that which Adam did, was the true and natural Cause of our being born in Sin, and the Impurity of bestial Flesh and Blood.

[Love-2.2-29] And as Adam, by what He did, may be truly said to have purchased our Misery and Corruption, to have bought Death for us, and to have sold us into a Slavery under the World, the Flesh, and the Devil, though all that we have from him, or suffer by him, is only the inward working of his own Nature and Life within us, so, according to the plain meaning of the Words, Christ may be said to be our Price, our Ransom, and Atonement; though all that He does for us, as Buying, Ransoming, and Redeeming us, is done wholly and solely by a Birth of his own Nature and Spirit brought to Life in us.

[Love-2.2-30] The apostle saith, "Christ died for our Sins." Thence it is, that He is the great Sacrifice for Sin and its true Atonement. But how and why is he so? The Apostle tells you in these Words, "The Sting of Death is Sin;— but Thanks be to God, who giveth us the Victory through our Lord Jesus Christ"; and therefore Christ is the Atonement of our Sins when, by and from Him, living in us, we have Victory over our sinful Nature.

[Love-2.2-31] The Scriptures frequently say, Christ gave himself for us. But what is the full Meaning, Effect, and Benefit, of his thus giving Himself for us? The Apostle puts this out of all Doubt, when he says, "Jesus Christ, who gave Himself for us, that He might redeem us from all Iniquity, and purify to Himself a peculiar People;—that He might deliver us from this present World,—from the Curse of the Law,—from the Power of Satan,— from the Wrath to come"; or as the Apostle saith in other Words, "that He might be made unto us, Wisdom, Righteousness, and Sanctification."

[Love-2.2-32] The whole Truth therefore of the Matter is plainly this. Christ given for us, is neither more nor less, than Christ given into us. And he is in no other Sense, our full, perfect, and sufficient Atonement, than as his Nature and Spirit are born, and formed in us, which so purgeth us from our Sins, that we are thereby in Him, and by Him dwelling in us, become new Creatures, having our Conversation in Heaven.

[Love-2.2-33] As Adam is truly our Defilement and Impurity, by his Birth in us, so Christ is our Atonement and Purification, by our being born again of Him, and having thereby quickened and revived in us that first Divine Life, which was extinguished in Adam. And therefore, as Adam purchased Death for us, just so in the same Manner, in the same Degree, and in the same Sense, Christ purchases Life for us. And each of them only, and solely by their own inward Life within us.

[Love-2.2-34] This is the one Scripture Account of the whole Nature, the sole End, and full Efficacy of all that Christ did, and suffered for us. It is all comprehended in these two Texts of Scripture: (1) "That Christ was manifested to destroy the Works of the Devil; (2) That as in Adam all die, so in Christ shall all be made alive." From the Beginning to the End of Christ's atoning Work, no other Power is ascribed to it, nothing else is intended by it, as an Appeaser of Wrath, but the destroying of all that in Man which comes from the Devil; no other Merits, or Value, or infinite Worth, than that of its infinite Ability, and Sufficiency to quicken again in all human Nature, that Heavenly Life that died in Adam.

[Love-2.2-35] Eusebius. Though all that is here said seems to have both the Letter and the Spirit of Scripture on its Side, yet I am afraid it will be thought not enough to assert the infinite Value and Merits of our Saviour's Sufferings. For it is the common Opinion of Doctors that the Righteousness or Justice of God must have Satisfaction done to it; And that nothing could avail with God, as a Satisfaction, but the infinite Worth and Value of the Sufferings of Christ.

[Love-2.2-36] Theophilus. It is true, Eusebius, that this is often, and almost always thus asserted in human Writers, but it is neither the Language nor the Doctrine of Scripture.

[Love-2.2-37] Not a Word is there said of a Righteousness or Justice as an Attribute in God, that must be satisfied; or that the Sacrifice of Christ, is that which satisfies the Righteousness that is in God Himself.

[Love-2.2-38] It has been sufficiently proved to you, that God wanted not to be reconciled to fallen Man; that He never was anything else toward him but Love; and that his Love brought forth the whole Scheme of his Redemption. Thence it is, that the Scriptures do not say that Christ came into the World to procure us the Divine Favour and good Will, in order to put a Stop to antecedent righteous Wrath in God toward us. No, the Reverse of all this is the Truth, viz., that Christ and his whole mediatorial Office came purely and solely from God, already so reconciled to us, as to bestow an Infinity of Love upon us. "The God of all Grace," saith the Apostle, "who hath called us to his eternal Glory by Jesus Christ" (1 Pet. 5:10). Here you see, Christ is not the Cause or Motive of God's Mercy toward fallen Man, but God's own Love for us, his own Desire of our eternal Glory and Happiness hath for that End given us Christ, that we may be made Partakers of it. The same as when it is again said, "God was in Christ reconciling the World to Himself," that is, calling, and raising it out of its ungodly and miserable State.

[Love-2.2-39] Thus all the Mystery of our Redemption proclaims nothing but a God of Love toward fallen Man. It was the Love of God, that could not behold the Misery of fallen Man, without demanding and calling for his Salvation. It was Love alone, that wanted to have full Satisfaction done to it, and such a Love as could not be satisfied, till all that Glory and Happiness that was lost by the Death of Adam, was fully restored and regained again by the Death of Christ.

[Love-2.2-40] Eusebius. But is there not some good Sense, in which Righteousness or Justice may be said to be satisfied by the Atonement and Sacrifice of Christ?

[Love-2.2-41] Theophilus. Yes, most certainly there is. But then it is only that Righteousness or Justice that belongs to Man, and ought to be in him. Now Righteousness, wherever it is to be, has no Mercy in itself; it makes no Condescensions; it is inflexibly rigid; its Demands are inexorable; Prayers, Offerings, and Entreaties have no Effect upon it; it will have nothing but itself, nor will it ever cease its Demands, or take any Thing in lieu of them, as a Satisfaction instead of itself. Thus, "Without Holiness," saith the Apostle, "no Man shall see the Lord." And again, "Nothing that is defiled, or impure, can enter into the Kingdom of Heaven." And this is meant by Righteousness being rigid and having no Mercy; it cannot spare, or have Pity, or hear Entreaty, because all its Demands are righteous, and good, and therefore must be satisfied, or fulfilled.

[Love-2.2-42] Now Righteousness has its absolute Demands upon Man, because Man was created righteous, and has lost that original Righteousness, which he ought to have kept in its first Purity. And this is the one, only Righteousness, or Justice, which Christ came into the World to satisfy, not by giving some highly valuable Thing as a Satisfaction to it, but by bringing back, or raising up again in all human Nature, that Holiness or Righteousness, which originally belonged to it. For to satisfy Righteousness, means neither more nor less than to fulfill it. Nor can Righteousness want to have Satisfaction in any Being, but in that Being, which has fallen from it; nor can it be satisfied, but in restoring or fulfilling Righteousness in that Being, which had departed from it. And therefore the Apostle saith, that "we are created again unto Righteousness in Christ Jesus." And this is the one and only Way of Christ's expiating, or taking away the Sins of the World, namely, by restoring to Man his lost Righteousness. For this End, saith the Scripture, "Christ gave Himself for the Church, that He might sanctify and cleanse it, that he might present it to Himself a glorious Church, not having Spot, or Wrinkle, or any such Thing, but that it should be holy and without Blemish" (Eph. 5:25-27).

[Love-2.2-43] This is the one Righteousness, which Christ came into the World to satisfy, by fulfilling it himself, and enabling Man by a new Birth from him to fulfill it. And when all Unrighteousness is removed by Christ from the whole human Nature, then all that Righteousness is satisfied, for the doing of which, Christ poured out his most precious, availing, and meritorious Blood.

[Love-2.2-44] Eusebius. Oh Theophilus, the Ground on which you stand must certainly be true. It so easily, so fully solves all Difficulties and Objections, and enables you to give so plain and solid an Account of every Part of our Redemption. This great Point is so fully cleared up to me, that I do not desire another Word about it.

[Love-2.2-45] Theophilus. However, Eusebius, I will add a Word or two more upon it, that there may be no Room left, either for misunderstanding, or denying what has been just now said of the Nature of that Righteousness, which must have full Satisfaction done to it by the Atoning and Redeeming Work of Christ. And then you will be fully possessed of these two great Truths. First, That there is no righteous Wrath in the Deity itself, and therefore none to be atoned there. Secondly, That though God is in Himself a mere Infinity of Love, from whom nothing else but Works of Love and Blessing and Goodness can proceed, yet sinful Men are hereby not at all delivered from That which the Apostle calls the Terrors of the Lord, but that all the Threatenings of Woe, Misery, and Punishment, denounced in Scripture against Sin and Sinners, both in this World, and that which is to come, stand all of them in their full Force, and are not in the least Degree weakened, or less to be dreaded because God is all Love.

[Love-2.2-46] Every Thing that God hath created, is right and just and good in its Kind, and hath its own Righteousness within itself. The Rectitude of its Nature is its only Law; and it hath no other Righteousness, but that of continuing in its first State. No Creature is subject to any Pain, or Punishment, or Guilt of Sin, but because it has departed from its first right State, and only does, and can feel the painful Loss of its own first Perfection. And every intelligent Creature, that departs from the State of its Creation, is unrighteous, evil, and full of its own Misery. And there is no Possibility for any disordered, fallen Creature to be free from its own Misery and Pain, till it is again in its first State of Perfection. This is the certain and infallible Ground of the absolute Necessity, either of a perfect Holiness in this Life, or of a further Purification after Death, before Man can enter into the Kingdom of Heaven.

[Love-2.2-47] Now this Pain and Misery, which is inseparable from the Creature that is not in that State in which it ought to be, and in which it was created, is nothing else but the painful State of the Creature for Want of its own proper Righteousness, as Sickness is the painful State of the Creature for Want of its own proper Health.

[Love-2.2-48] No other Righteousness, or other Justice, no other severe Vengeance, demands Satisfaction, or torments the Sinner, but that very Righteousness, which once was in him, which still belongs to him, and therefore will not suffer him to have any Rest or Peace, till it is again in him as it was at the first. All, therefore, that Christ does as an Atonement for Sin, or as a Satisfaction to Righteousness, is all done in, and to, and for Man, and has no other Operation but that of renewing the fallen Nature of Man, and raising it up into its first State of original Righteousness. And if this Righteousness, which belongs solely to Man, and wants no Satisfaction, but that of being restored and fulfilled in the human Nature, is sometimes called the Righteousness of God, it is only so called, because it is a Righteousness which Man had originally from God, in and by his Creation; and, therefore, as it comes from God, has its whole Nature and Power of Working as it does from God, it may very justly be called God's Righteousness.

[Love-2.2-49] Agreeably to this Way of ascribing that to God, which is only in the State and

Condition of Man, the Psalmist saith of God, "Thine Arrows stick fast in me, and thy Hand presseth me sore." And yet nothing else, or more is meant by it, than when he saith, "My Sins have taken such Hold of me that I am not able to look up—My Iniquities are gone over my Head, and are like a sore Burden too heavy for me to bear."

[Love-2.2-50] Now, whether you call this State of Man the Burden of his Sins and Wickednesses, or the Arrows of the Almighty, and the Weight of God's Hand, they mean but one and the same Thing, which can only be called by these different Names, for no other Reason but this, because Man's own original Righteousness, which he had from God, makes his sinful State a Pain and Torment to him, and lies heavy upon him in every Commission of Sin. And when the Psalmist again saith, "Take thy Plague away from me, I am even consumed by means of thy heavy Hand," it is only praying to be delivered from his own Plague, and praying for the same Thing as when he saith, in other Words, "Make me a clean Heart, O God, and renew a right Spirit within me."

[Love-2.2-51] Now this Language of Scripture, which teaches us to call the Pains and Torments of our Sins, the Arrows, Darts, and Strokes of God's Hand upon us, which calls us to own the Power, Presence, and Operation of God, in all that we feel and find in our own inward State, is the Language of the most exalted Piety, and highly suitable to that Scripture which tells us, "That in God we live, and move, and have our Being". For by teaching us to find, and own the Power and Operation of God in every Thing that passes within us, it keeps us continually turned to God for all that we want, and by all that we feel within ourselves, and brings us to this best of all Confessions, that Pain, as well as Peace of Mind, is the Effect and Manifestation of God's infinite Love and Goodness toward us.

[Love-2.2-52] For we could not have this Pain and Sensibility of the Burden of Sin, but because the Love and Goodness of God made us originally righteous and happy; and therefore, all the Pains and Torments of Sin come from God's first Goodness toward us, and are in themselves merely and truly the Arrows of his Love, and his blessed Means of drawing us back to that first righteous State in and for which his first and never ceasing Love created us.

[Love-2.2-53] Eusebius. The Matter, therefore, plainly stands thus. There is no righteous Wrath, or vindictive Justice In the Deity itself, which, as a Quality or Attribute of Resentment in the Divine Mind, wants to be contented, atoned, or satisfied; but Man's Original Righteousness, which was once his Peace, and Happiness, and Rest in God, is by the Fall of Adam become his Tormentor, his Plague, that continually exercises its good Vengeance upon him, till it truly regains its first State in him.

[Love-2.2-54] Secondly, Man must be under this Pain, Punishment, and Vengeance to all Eternity; there is no Possibility, in the Nature of the Thing, for it to be otherwise, though God be all Love, unless Man's lost Righteousness be fully again possessed by him. And, therefore, the Doctrine of God's being all Love, of having no Wrath in Himself, has nothing in it to abate the Force of those Scriptures which threaten Punishment to Sinners, or to make them less fearful of living and dying in their Sins.

[Love-2.2-55] Theophilus. What you say, Eusebius, is very true; but then it is but half the Truth of this Matter. You should have added, that this Doctrine is the one Ground, and only Reason, why the Scriptures abound with so many Declarations of Woe, Misery, and Judgments, sometimes executed, and sometimes only threatened by God, and why all Sinners to the End of the World must know and feel "that the Wrath of God is revealed from Heaven against all Ungodliness and Unrighteousness, and that Indignation and Wrath, Tribulation and Anguish, must be upon every Soul of Man that doth Evil" (Rom. 1:18, 2:8-9).

[Love-2.2-56] For all these Things, which the Apostle elsewhere calls "the Terrors of the Lord", have no Ground, nothing that calls for them, nothing that vindicates the Fitness and Justice of them, either with Regard to God or Man, but this one Truth, viz., That God is in Himself a mere Infinity of Love, from whom nothing but outflowings of Love and Goodness can come forth from Eternity to Eternity. For if God is all Love, if he wills nothing toward fallen Man but his full Deliverance from the blind Slavery and Captivity of his earthly, bestial Nature, then every kind of Punishment, Distress, and Affliction, that can extinguish the Lusts of the Flesh, the Lust of the Eyes, and the Pride of this Life, may and ought to be expected from God, merely because he is all Love and good Will toward fallen Man.

[Love-2.2-57] To say, therefore, as some have said, If God is all Love toward fallen Man, how can he threaten or chastise Sinners? This is no better than saying, If God is all Goodness in Himself, and towards Man, how can He do that in and to Man, which is for his Good? As absurd as to say, If the able Physician is all Love, Goodness, and good Will toward his Patients, how can he blister, purge, or scarify them, how can he order one to be trepanned, and another to have a Limb cut off? Nay, so absurd is this Reasoning, that if it could be proved, that God had no Chastisement for Sinners, the very Want of this Chastisement would be the greatest of all Proofs, that God was not all Love and Goodness toward Man.

[Love-2.2-58] The meek, merciful, and compassionate Jesus, who had no Errand in this World but to bless and save Mankind, said, "If thy right Eye or thy right Hand offend thee, pluck out the one, cut off the other, and cast them from thee." And that He said all this from mere Love, he adds, It is better for thee to do this, than that thy whole Body should be cast into Hell". Therefore, if the Holy Jesus had been wanting in this Severity, he had been wanting in true Love toward Man.

[Love-2.2-59] And therefore, the pure, mere Love of God, is that alone from which Sinners are justly to expect from God, that no Sin will pass unpunished, but that his Love will visit them with every Calamity and Distress, that can help to break and purify the bestial Heart of Man, and awaken in him true Repentance and Conversion to God. It is Love alone in the holy Deity, that Will allow no Peace to the wicked, nor ever cease its Judgments, till every Sinner is forced to confess, That it is good for him that he has been in Trouble, and thankfully own, That not the Wrath, but the Love of God, has plucked out that right Eye, cut off that right Hand, which he ought to have done, but would not do, for himself and his own Salvation.

[Love-2.2-60] Again, this Doctrine that allows of no Wrath in the Divine Mind, but places it all in the Evil State of fallen Nature and Creature, has every Thing in it that can prove to Man the dreadful Nature of Sin, and the absolute Necessity of totally departing from it. It leaves no Room for Self-Delusion, but puts an End to every false Hope, or vain seeking for Relief in any Thing else, but the total Extinction of Sin. And this it effectually does, by showing, that Damnation is no foreign, separate, or imposed State, that is brought in upon us, or adjudged to us by the Will of God, but is the inborn, natural, essential State of our own disordered Nature, which is absolutely impossible, in the Nature of the Thing, to be any Thing else but our own Hell, both here and hereafter, unless all Sin be separated from us, and Righteousness be again made our natural State, by a Birth of itself in us. And all this, not because God will have it so, by an arbitrary Act of his sovereign Will, but because he cannot change his own Nature, or make any Thing to be happy and blessed, but only that which has its proper Righteousness, and is of one Will and Spirit with Himself.

[Love-2.2-61] If then every Creature that has lost, or is without the true Rectitude of its Nature, must as such, be of all Necessity, absolutely separated from God, and necessarily under the Pain and Misery of a Life that has lost all its own natural Good; if no Omnipotence or Mercy, or Goodness of God, can make it to be otherwise, or give any Relief to the Sinner, but by a total Extinction of Sin by a Birth of Righteousness in the Soul, then it fully appears, that according to this Doctrine, every Thing in God, and Nature, and Creature, calls the Sinner to an absolute Renunciation of all Sin, as the one only possible Means of Salvation, and leaves no Room for him to deceive himself with the Hopes that any Thing else will do instead of it. Vainly therefore is it said, That if God be all Love, the Sinner is let loose from the dreadful Apprehensions of living and dying in his Sins.

[Love-2.2-62] On the other Hand, deny this Doctrine, and say, with the current of scholastic Divines, That the Sinner must be doomed to eternal Pain and Death, unless a supposed Wrath, in the Mind of the Deity, be first atoned and satisfied; and that Christ's Death was that valuable Gift, or Offering made to God, by which alone he could be moved to lay aside, or extinguish his own Wrath toward fallen Man; say this, and then you open a wide Door for Licentiousness and Infidelity in some, and superstitious Fears in others.

[Love-2.2-63] For if the Evil, the Misery, and sad Effects of Sin, are placed in a Wrath in the Divine Mind, what can this beget in the Minds of the pious, but superstitious Fears about a supposed Wrath in God which they can never know when it is, or is not, atoned? Every Kind of Superstition has its Birth from this Belief, and cannot well be otherwise. And as to the Licentious, who want to stifle all Fears of gratifying all their Passions, this Doctrine has a natural Tendency to do this for them. For if they are taught, that the Hurt and Misery of Sin, is not its own natural State, not owing to its own Wrath and Disorder, but to a Wrath in the Deity, how easy is it for them to believe, either that God may not be so full of Wrath as is given out, or that he may overcome it himself, and not keep the Sinner eternally in a Misery that is not his own, but wholly brought upon him from without, by a Resentment in the Divine Mind.

[Love-2.2-64] Again, this Account which the Schools give of the Sacrifice of Christ, made to atone a Wrath in the Deity by the infinite Value of Christ's Death, is that alone which helps Socinians, Deists, and Infidels of all Kinds, to such Cavils and Objections to the Mystery of our Redemption, as neither have, nor can be silenced by the most able Defenders of that scholastic

Fiction. The Learning of a Grotius or Stillingfleet, when defending such an Account of the Atonement and Satisfaction, rather increases than lessens the Objections to this Mystery: But if you take this Matter as it truly is in itself, viz., That God is in Himself all Love and Goodness, therefore can be nothing else but all Love and Goodness toward fallen Man, and that fallen Man is subject to no Pain or Misery, either present or to come, but what is the natural, unavoidable, essential Effect of his own evil and disordered Nature, impossible to be altered by himself, and that the infinite, never ceasing Love of God, has given Jesus Christ in all his Process, as the highest, and only possible Means, that Heaven and Earth can afford, to save Man from himself, from his own Evil, Misery, and Death, and restore to him his original Divine Life. When you look at this Matter in this true Light, then a God, all Love, and an Atonement for Sin by Christ, not made to pacify a Wrath in God, but to bring forth, fulfill, and restore Righteousness in the Creature that had lost it, has every Thing in it that can make the Providence of God adorable, and the State of Man comfortable.

[Love-2.2-65] Here all Superstition and superstitious Fears are at once totally cut off, and every Work of Piety is turned into a Work of Love. Here every false Hope of every Kind is taken from the Licentious; they have no Ground left to stand upon: Nothing to trust to, as a Deliverance from Misery, but the one total Abolition of Sin.

[Love-2.2-66] The Socinian and the Infidel are here also robbed of all their Philosophy against this Mystery; for as it is not founded upon, does not teach an infinite Resentment, that could only be satisfied by an infinite Atonement, as it stands not upon the Ground of Debtor and Creditor, all their Arguments which suppose it to be such, are quite beside the Matter and touch nothing of the Truth of this blessed Mystery. For it is the very Reverse of all this, it declares a God that is all Love; and the Atonement of Christ to be nothing else in itself, but the highest, most natural, and efficacious Means through all the Possibility of Things, that the infinite Love and Wisdom of God could use, to put an End to Sin, and Death, and Hell, and restore to Man his first Divine State or Life. I say, the most natural, efficacious Means through all the Possibilities of Nature; for there is nothing that is supernatural, however mysterious, in the whole System of our Redemption; every Part of it has its Ground in the Workings and Powers of Nature, and all our Redemption is only Nature set right, or made to be that which it ought to be.

[Love-2.2-67] There is nothing that is supernatural, but God alone; every Thing besides Him is from and subject to the State of Nature. It can never rise out of it, or have anything contrary to it. No Creature can have either Health or Sickness, Good or Evil, or any State either from God, or itself, but strictly according to the Capacities, Powers, and Workings of Nature.

[Love-2.2-68] The Mystery of our Redemption, though it comes from the supernatural God, has nothing in it but what is done, and to be done, within the Sphere, and according to the Powers of Nature. There is nothing supernatural in it, or belonging to it, but that supernatural Love and Wisdom which brought it forth, presides over it, and will direct it till Christ, as a second Adam, has removed and extinguished all that Evil, which the first Adam brought into the human Nature.

[Love-2.2-69] And the whole Process of Jesus Christ, from his being the inspoken Word or Bruiser of the Serpent given to Adam, to his Birth, Death, Resurrection, and Ascension into

Heaven, has all its Ground and Reason in this, because nothing else in all the Possibilities of Nature, either in Heaven or on Earth, could begin, carry on, and totally effect Man's Deliverance from the Evil of his own fallen Nature.

[Love-2.2-70] Thus is Christ the one, full, sufficient Atonement for the Sin of the whole World, because He is the one only natural Remedy, and possible Cure of all the Evil that is broken forth in Nature, the one only natural Life, and Resurrection of all that Holiness and Happiness that died in Adam. And seeing all this Process of Christ is given to the World, from the supernatural, antecedent, infinite Love of God, therefore it is, that the Apostle saith, "God was in Christ reconciling the World to Himself." And Christ in God, is nothing else in his whole Nature, but that same, certain, and natural Parent of a Redemption to the whole human Nature, as fallen Adam was the certain and natural Parent of a miserable Life to every Man that is descended from him: With this only Difference, that from fallen Adam we are born in Sin, whether we will or no, but we cannot have the new Birth which Christ has all Power to bring forth in us, unless the Will of our Heart closes with it.

[Love-2.2-71] But as nothing came to us from Adam, but according to the Powers of Nature, and because he was that which he was with Relation to us; so it is with Christ and our Redemption by Him: All the Work is grounded in, and proceeds according to the Powers of Nature, or in a Way of natural Efficacy or Fitness to produce its Effects; and every Thing that is found in the Person, Character, and Condition of Christ, is only there as his true and natural Qualification to do all that He came to do, in us, and for us. That is to say, Christ was made to be that which He was; He was a Seed of Life in our first fallen Father; He lived as a Blessing of Promise in the Patriarchs, Prophets, and Israel of God; He was born as a Man of a pure Virgin; He did all that He did, whether as suffering, dying, conquering, rising, and ascending into Heaven, only as so many Things, which as naturally and as truly, according to the Nature of Things, qualified Him to be the Producer, or Quickener of a Divine Life in us, as the State and Condition of Adam qualified him to make us the slavish Children of earthly, bestial Flesh and Blood.

[Love-2.2-72] This is the comfortable Doctrine of our Redemption; nothing in God but an Infinity of Love and Goodness toward our fallen Condition; nothing in Christ, but that which had its Necessity in the Nature of Things, to make Him able to give, and us to receive, our full Salvation from Him.

[Love-2.2-73] I will now only add, That from the Beginning of Deism, and from the Time of Socinus, to this Day, not a Socinian or Deist has ever seen or opposed this Mystery in its true State, as is undeniably plain from all their Writings.

[Love-2.2-74] A late Writer, who has as much Knowledge, and Zeal, and Wit in the Cause of Deism, as any of his Predecessors, is forced to attack our Redemption by giving this false Account of it.

[Love-2.2-75] "That a perfectly innocent Being, of the highest Order among intelligent Natures, should personate the Offender, and suffer in his Place and Stead, in order to take down the Wrath and Resentment of the Deity against the Criminal, and dispose God to show Mercy to him,—the Deist conceives to be both unnatural, and improper, and therefore not to be ascribed to God without Blasphemy."

[Love-2.2-76] And again, "The common Notion of Redemption among Christians seems to represent the Deity in a disagreeable Light, as implacable and revengeful," &c.

[Love-2.2-77] What an Arrow is here, I will not say, shot beside the Mark, but shot at nothing! Because nothing of that, which he accuses is to be found in our Redemption. The God of Christians is so far from being, as he says, implacable and revengeful, that you have seen it proved from Text to Text, that the whole Form and Manner of our Redemption comes wholly from the free, antecedent, infinite Love and Goodness of God towards fallen Man. That the innocent Christ did not suffer, to quiet an angry Deity, but merely as co-operating, assisting, and uniting with that Love of God, which desired our Salvation. That He did not suffer in our Place or Stead, but only on our Account, which is a quite different Matter. And to say, that He suffered in our Place or Stead, is as absurd, as contrary to Scripture, as to say, that He rose from the Dead, and Ascended into Heaven in our Place and Stead, that we might be excused from it. For his Sufferings, Death, Resurrection, and Ascension are all of them equally on our Account, for our Sake, for our Good and Benefit, but none of them possible to be in our Stead.

[Love-2.2-78] And as Scripture and Truth affirm, that He ascended into Heaven for us, though neither Scripture nor Truth will allow it to be in our Place and Stead, so for the same Reasons, it is strictly true, that He suffered, and died for us, though no more in our Place or Stead, nor any more desirable to be so, than his Ascension into Heaven for us should be in our Place and Stead.

[Love-2.2-79] I have quoted the above Passage, only to show you, that a Defender of Deism, however acute and ingenious, has not one Objection to the Doctrine of our Redemption, but what is founded on the grossest Ignorance, and total Mistake of the whole Nature of it. But when I lay this gross Ignorance to the Deists' Charge, I do not mean any natural Dullness, Want of Parts, or Incapacity in them to judge aright, but only that something or other, either Men or Books, or their own Way of Life, has hindered their seeing the true Ground and real Nature of Christianity, as it is in itself.

[Love-2.2-80] Eusebius. I would fain Hope, Theophilus, that from all that has been said in the Demonstration of the Fundamental Errors of the Plain Account, the Appeal to all that doubt, &c., and the rest that follow, to these Dialogues; in all which, Christianity and Deism, with their several Merits, are so plainly, and with so much good Will and Affection toward all Unbelievers, represented to them, all that are serious and well-minded amongst the Deists will be prevailed upon to reconsider the Matter. For though some People have been hasty enough to charge those Writings with Fanaticism, or Enthusiasm, as disclaiming the Use of our Reason in Religious Matters, yet this Charge can be made by none, but those who, having not read them, take up with hearsay Censures.

[Love-2.2-81] For in those Books, from the Beginning to the End, nothing is appealed to but the natural Light of the Mind, and the plain, known Nature of Things; no one is led, or desired to go one Step further. The Use of Reason is not only allowed, but asserted, and proved to be of the same Service to us in Things of Religion, as in Things that relate to our Senses in this World {Demonstration of Errors of the Plain Account}.

[Love-2.2-82] The true Ground, Nature, and Power of Faith is opened, by fully proving, that this Saying of Christ, "According to thy Faith, so be it done unto Thee," takes in every Individual of human Nature; and that all Men, whether Christians, Deists, Idolaters, or Atheists, are all of them equally Men of Faith, all equally, and absolutely governed by it, and therefore must have all that they have, Salvation or Damnation, strictly and solely according to their Faith {Way to Divine Knowledge}. All this is so evidently proved, that I can't help thinking, but that every considerate Reader must be forced to own it.

[Love-2.2-83] Theogenes. All this is well said. But let us now return to the finishing of our main Point, which was to show, that the Doctrine of a God all Love, does not only not destroy the Necessity of Christ's Death and the infinite Value and Merits of it, but is itself the fullest Proof and strongest Confirmation of both.

[Love-2.2-84] Theophilus. How it could enter into anyone's Head, to charge this Doctrine with destroying the Necessity and Merits of Christ's Death, is exceeding strange.

[Love-2.2-85] For look where you will, no other Cause, or Reason of the Death of Christ, can be found but in the Love of God toward fallen Man. Nor could the Love of God will or accept of the Death of Christ, but because of its absolute Necessity, and availing Efficacy to do all that for fallen Man, which the Love of God would have to be done for him.

[Love-2.2-86] God did not, could not, love or like or desire the Sufferings and Death of Christ, for what they were in themselves, or as Sufferings of the highest Kind. No, the higher and greater such Sufferings had been, were they only considered in themselves, the less pleasing they had been to a God, that wills nothing but Blessing and Happiness to every Thing capable of it.

[Love-2.2-87] But all that Christ was and did and suffered was infinitely prized, and highly acceptable to the Love of God, because all that Christ was, and did, and suffered in his own Person, was That which gave him full Power, to be a common Father of Life to all that died in Adam.

[Love-2.2-88] Had Christ wanted anything that he was, or did, or suffered in his own Person, he could not have stood in that Relation to all Mankind as Adam had done. Had he not been given to the first fallen Man, as a Seed of the Woman, as a Light of Life, enlightening every Man that comes into the World, He could not have had his Seed in every Man, as Adam had, nor been as universal a Father of Life, as Adam was of Death. Had he not in the Fitness, or Fullness of Time, become a Man, born of a pure Virgin, the first Seed of Life in every Man, must have lain only as a Seed, and could not have come to the Fullness of the Birth of a new Man in Christ Jesus. For the Children can have no other State of Life, but that which their Father first had. And therefore Christ, as the Father of a regenerated human Race, must first stand in the Fullness of that human State, which was to be derived from him into all his Children.

[Love-2.2-89] This is the absolute Necessity of Christ's being all that he was, before he became Man; a Necessity arising from the Nature of the Thing. Because he could not possibly have had the Relation of a Father to all Mankind, nor any Power to be a Quickener of a Life of Heaven in them, but because He was both God in himself, and a Seed of God in all of them.

[Love-2.2-90] Now all that Christ was, and did, and suffered, after He became Man, is from the same Necessity founded in the Nature of the Thing. He suffered on no other Account, but because that which he came to do in, and for the human Nature, was and could be nothing else in itself, but a Work of Sufferings and Death.

[Love-2.2-91] A crooked Line cannot become straight, but by having all its Crookedness given up, or taken from it. And there is but one Way possible in Nature for a crooked Line to lose its Crookedness.

[Love-2.2-92] Now the Sufferings and Death of Christ stand in this kind of Necessity. He was made Man for our Salvation, that is, He took upon Him our fallen Nature, to bring it out of its evil crooked State, and set it again in that Rectitude in which it was created.

[Love-2.2-93] Now there was no more two Ways of doing this, than there are two Ways of making a crooked Line to become straight.

[Love-2.2-94] If the Life of fallen Nature, which Christ had taken upon Him, was to be overcome by Him, then every Kind of suffering and dying, that was a giving up, or departing from the Life of fallen Nature, was just as necessary, in the Nature of the Thing, as that the Line to be made straight must give up, and Part with every Kind and Degree of its own Crookedness.

[Love-2.2-95] And therefore the Sufferings and Death of Christ were, in the Nature of the Thing, the only possible Way of his acting contrary to, and overcoming all the Evil that was in the fallen State of Man.

[Love-2.2-96] The Apostle saith, "The Captain of our Salvation was to be made perfect through Sufferings." This was the Ground and Reason of his Sufferings. Had he been without them, He could not have been perfect in Himself, as a Son of Man, nor the Restorer of Perfection in all Mankind. But why so? Because his Perfection, as a Son of Man, or the Captain of human Salvation, could only consist in his acting in, and with a Spirit suitable to the first created State of perfect Man; that is, He must in his Spirit be as much above all the Good and Evil of this fallen World, as the first Man was.

[Love-2.2-97] But now, He could not show that He was of this Spirit, that He was under no Power of fallen Nature, but lived in the Perfection of the first created Man; He could not do this, but by showing, that all the Good of the earthly Life was renounced by Him, and that all the Evil which the World, the Malice of Men and Devils, could bring upon Him, could not hinder his living wholly and solely to God, and doing his Will on Earth with the same Fullness, as Angels do it in Heaven.

[Love-2.2-98] But had there been any Evil in all fallen Nature, whether in Life, Death, or Hell, that had not attacked Him, with all its Force, He could not have been said to have overcome it. And therefore so sure as Christ, the Son of Man, was to overcome the World, Death, Hell, and Satan, so sure is it, that all the Evils which they could possibly bring upon Him, were to be felt and suffered by Him, as absolutely necessary in the Nature of the Thing, to declare his Perfection, and prove his Superiority over them. Surely, my Friend, it is now enough proved to you, how a God all Love toward fallen Man, must love, like, desire, and delight in all the Sufferings of Christ, which alone could enable Him, as a Son of Man, to undo, and reverse all that Evil, which the first Man had done to all his Posterity.

[Love-2.2-99] Eusebius. Oh, Sir, in what an adorable Light is this Mystery now placed. And yet in no other Light than that in which in the plain Letter of all Scripture sets it. No Wrath in God, no fictitious Atonement, no Folly of Debtor and Creditor, no suffering in Christ for Sufferings' sake, but a Christ suffering and dying, as his same Victory over Death and Hell, as when He rose from the Dead and ascended into Heaven.

[Love-2.2-100] Theophilus. Sure now, Eusebius, you plainly enough see wherein the infinite Merits, or the availing Efficacy, and glorious Power of the Sufferings and Death of Christ consist; since they were that, in and through which Christ himself came out of the State of fallen Nature, and got Power to give the same Victory to all his Brethren of the human Race.

[Love-2.2-101] Wonder not, therefore, that the Scriptures so frequently ascribe all our Salvation to the Sufferings and Death of Christ, that we are continually referred to them, as the Wounds and Stripes by which we are healed, as the Blood by which we are washed from our Sins, as the Price (much above Gold and precious Stones) by which we are bought.

[Love-2.2-102] Wonder not also that in the Old Testament, its Service Sacrifices, and Ceremonies were instituted to typify, and point at the great Sacrifice of Christ, and to keep up a continual Hope, strong Expectation, and Belief of it. And that in the New Testament, the Reality, the Benefits, and glorious Effects of Christ our Passover being actually sacrificed for us, are so joyfully repeated by every Apostle.

[Love-2.2-103] It is because Christ, as suffering and dying, was nothing else but Christ conquering and overcoming all the false Good, and the hellish Evil, of the fallen State of Man.

[Love-2.2-104] His Resurrection from the Grave, and Ascension into Heaven, though great in themselves, and necessary Parts of our Deliverance, were yet but the Consequences and genuine Effects of his Sufferings and Death. These were in themselves the Reality of his Conquest; all his great Work was done and effected in them and by them, and his Resurrection and Ascension were only his entering into the Possession of that, which his Sufferings and Death had gained for him.

[Love-2.2-105] Wonder not then, that all the true Followers of Christ, the Saints of every Age, have so gloried in the Cross of Christ, have imputed such great Things to it, have desired nothing so much, as to be Partakers of it, to live in constant Union with it. It is because his Sufferings, his Death, and Cross, were the Fullness of his Victory over all the Works of the Devil. Not an Evil in Flesh and Blood, not a Misery of Life, not a Chain of Death, not a Power of Hell and Darkness, but were all baffled, broken, and overcome by the Process of a suffering, and dying Christ. Well therefore may the Cross of Christ be the Glory of Christians.

[Love-2.2-106] Eusebius. This Matter is so solidly and fully cleared up, that I am almost ashamed to ask you any Thing further about it. Yet explain a little more, if you please, how it is, that the Sufferings and Death of Christ, gave Him Power to become a common Father of Life to all that died in Adam. Or how it is, that we, by Virtue of them, have Victory over all the Evil of our fallen State.

[Love-2.2-107] Theophilus. You are to know, Eusebius, that the Christian Religion is no arbitrary System of Divine worship, but is the one true, real, and only Religion of Nature; that is, it is wholly founded in the Nature of Things, has nothing in it supernatural or contrary to the Powers and Demands of Nature; but all that it does, is only in, and by, and according to the Workings and Possibilities of Nature.

[Love-2.2-108] A Religion that is not founded in Nature, is all Fiction and Falsity, and as mere a nothing as an Idol. For as no Creature can be, or have any Thing, but what it is and has from the Nature of Things, nor have any Thing done to it, Good or Harm, but according to the unalterable Workings of Nature, so no Religion can be of any Service, but that which works with and according to the Demands of Nature. Nor can any fallen Creature be raised out of its fallen State, even by the Omnipotence of God, but according to the Nature of Things, or the unchangeable Powers of Nature; for Nature is the Opening and Manifestation of the Divine Omnipotence; it is God's Power-world; and therefore all that God doth, is and must be done in and by the Powers of Nature. God, though omnipotent, can give no Existence to any Creature, but it must have that Existence in Space and Time.— Time cometh out of the Eternity, and Space cometh out of the Infinity of God—God hath an omnipotent Power over them, in them, and with them, to make both of them set forth and manifest the Wonders of his supernatural Deity. Yet Time can only be subservient to the Omnipotence of God, according to the Nature of Time; and Space can only obey his Will, according to the Nature of Space; but neither of them can, by any Power, be made to be in a supernatural State, or be any Thing but what they are in their own Nature.

[Love-2.2-109] Now Right and Wrong, Good and Evil, True and False, Happiness and Misery, are as unchangeable in Nature, as Time, and Space. And every State and Quality that is creaturely, or that can belong to any Creature, has its own Nature, as unchangeably as Time and Space have theirs.

[Love-2.2-110] Nothing therefore can be done to any Creature supernaturally, or in a Way that is without, or contrary to the Powers of Nature; but every Thing or Creature that is to be helped, that is to have any Good done to it, or any Evil taken out of it, can only have it done so far, as the Powers of Nature are able and rightly directed to effect it.

[Love-2.2-111] And this is the true Ground of all Divine Revelation, or that Help which the supernatural Deity vouchsafes to the fallen State of Man. It is not to appoint an arbitrary System of religious Homage to God, but solely to point out, and provide for Man, blinded by his fallen State, that one only Religion, that, according to the Nature of Things, can possibly restore to him his lost Perfection. This is the Truth, the Goodness, and the Necessity of the Christian Religion; it is true, and good, and necessary, because it is as much the one only natural and possible Way of overcoming all the Evil of fallen Man, as Light is the one only natural, possible Thing that can expel Darkness.

[Love-2.2-112] And therefore it is, that all the Mysteries of the Gospel, however high, are yet true and necessary Parts of the one Religion of Nature; because they are no higher, nor otherwise, than the natural State of fallen Man absolutely stands in Need of. His Nature cannot be helped, or raised out of the Evils of its present State, by any Thing less than these Mysteries; and therefore, they are in the same Truth and Justness to be called his natural Religion, as that Remedy which alone has full Power to remove all the Evil of a Disease, may be justly called its natural Remedy.

[Love-2.2-113] For a Religion is not to be deemed natural, because it has nothing to do with Revelation; but then is it the one true Religion of Nature, when it has every Thing in it that our natural State stands in need of; every Thing that can help us out of our present Evil, and raise and exalt us to all the Happiness which our Nature is capable of having. Supposing, therefore, the Christian scheme of Redemption to be all that, and nothing else in itself, but that which the Nature of Things absolutely requires it to be, it must, for that very Reason, have its Mysteries.

[Love-2.2-114] For the fallen, corrupt, mortal State of Man, absolutely requires these two Things as its only Salvation. First, the Divine Life, or the Life of God, must be revived in the Soul of Man. Secondly, there must be a Resurrection of the Body in a better State after Death. Now nothing in the Power of Man, or in the Things of this World, can effect this Salvation. If, therefore, this is to be the Salvation of Man, then some Interposition of the Deity is absolutely necessary, in the Nature of the Thing, or Man can have no Religion that is sufficiently natural; that is to say, no Religion that is sufficient, or equal to the Wants of his Nature.

[Love-2.2-115] Now this necessary Interposition of the Deity, though doing nothing but in a natural Way, or according to the Nature of Things, must be mysterious to Man, because it is doing something more and higher than his Senses or Reason ever saw done, or possible to be done, either by himself, or any of the Powers of this World.

[Love-2.2-116] And this is the true Ground and Nature of the Mysteries of Christian Redemption. They are, in themselves, nothing else but what the Nature of Things requires them to be, as natural, efficacious Means of our Salvation, and all their Power is in a natural Way, or true Fitness of Cause for its Effect; but they are mysterious to Man, because brought into the Scheme of our Redemption by the Interposition of God, to work in a Way and manner above, and superior to all that is seen and done in the Things of the World.

[Love-2.2-117] The Mysteries, therefore, of the Gospel are so far from showing the Gospel not to be the one true Religion of Nature, that they are the greatest Proof of it, since they are that alone which can help Man to all that good which his natural State wants to have done to it.

[Love-2.2-118] For instance, if the Salvation of Man absolutely requires the Revival or Restoration of the Divine Life in the human Nature, then nothing can be the one, sufficient, true Religion of Nature, but that which has a natural Power to do this.

[Love-2.2-119] What a Grossness of Error is it, therefore, to blame that Doctrine which asserts the Incarnation of the Son of God, or the Necessity of the Word being made Flesh, when in the Nature of the Thing, nothing else but this very Mystery can be the natural, efficacious Cause of the Renewal of the Divine Life in the human Nature, or have any natural Efficacy to effect our Salvation?

[Love-2.2-120] Having now, Eusebius, established this Ground, that nothing is, or can be a Part of true, natural Religion, or have any real Efficacy, as a Means of Salvation, but only that which has its Efficacy in and from the Nature of Things, or in the natural Fitness of Cause to produce its Effect, you are brought into the clear View of this Truth, viz., That the Religion of Deism is false, and vain, and visionary, and to be rejected by every Man as the mere enthusiastic, fanatic

Product of pure Imagination; and all for this plain Reason, because it quite disregards the Nature of Things, stands wholly upon a supernatural Ground, and goes as much above and as directly contrary to the Powers of Nature, as that Faith that trusts in, and prays to a wooden God.

[Love-2.2-121] I say not this (as is too commonly done) in the Spirit of Accusation, or to raise an Odium. No, by no Means. I have the utmost Aversion to such a Procedure; I would no more bring a false Charge against the Deist, than I would bear false Witness against an Apostle. And I desire to have no other Temper, Spirit or Behaviour toward them, but such as the loving God with all my Heart, and loving them as I Love myself, requires of me. And in this Spirit of Love, I charge them with visionary Faith, and enthusiastic Religion; and only so far, as I have from Time to Time proved, that they trust to be saved by that, which according to the unchangeable Nature of Things can have no Power of Salvation in it.

[Love-2.2-122] For a Religion, not grounded in the Power and Nature of Things, is unnatural, supernatural, superrational, and is rightly called either Enthusiasm, Vision, Fanaticism, Superstition, or Idolatry, just as you please. For all these are but different Names for one and the same religious Delusion. And every Religion is this Delusion, but that one Religion which is required by, and has its Efficacy in and from the unchangeable Nature of Things.

[Love-2.2-123] And thus stands the Matter betwixt the Deists and myself. If I knew how to do them or the Subject more Justice, I would gladly do it; having no Desire, either for them or myself, but that we may all of us be delivered from every Thing that separates us from God, all equal Sharers of every Blessing that He has for human Nature, all united in that Spirit of Love and Goodness for which he created us, and all blessed with that Faith and Hope to which the God of Love has called us, as the one, only, possible, natural, and full Means of ever finding ourselves saved, and redeemed from all the Evils both of Time and Eternity.

[Love-2.2-124] And now, Eusebius, upon this Ground, viz., (1) That there is but one true Religion, and that it is the Religion of Nature. (2) That a Religion has no Pretense to be considered as the Religion of Nature, because it rejects Divine Revelation, and has only human Reason for its Guide, but wholly and solely because it has every Good in it that the natural State of Man wants, and can receive from Religion. (3) That nothing can be any religious Good, or have any real Efficacy, as a Means of Salvation, but only that which has its Efficacy in and from the natural Power of Things, or the Fitness and Sufficiency of Cause to produce its Effect. (4) That the Religion of the Gospel, in all its Mysteries and Doctrines, is wholly grounded in the natural Powers of Things, and their Fitness to produce their Effects. Upon this Ground I come to answer your Question, viz., How it is that the Sufferings and Death of Christ gave Him full Power to become a common Father of Life to all those that died in Adam? Or how it is that we, by Virtue of them, are delivered out of all the Evils of our fallen State?

[Love-2.2-125] The Sufferings and Death of Christ have no supernatural Effect that is above, or contrary to Nature; because the Thing itself is impossible. For a Thing is only therefore impossible, because the Nature of Things will not allow it.

[Love-2.2-126] The Fall of all Mankind in Adam is no supernatural Event or Effect, but the natural and necessary Consequence of our Relation to him. Could Adam at his Fall into this earthly Life have absolutely overcome every Power of the World, the Flesh, and the Devil, in the same Spirit as Christ did, he had been his own Redeemer, had risen out of his Fall, and ascended into Paradise, and been the Father of a paradisiacal Offspring, just as Christ, when He had overcome them all, rose from the Dead, and ascended into Heaven. But Adam did not do this, because it was as impossible, in the Nature of the Thing, as for a Beast to raise itself into an Angel. If therefore Man is to come out of his fallen State, there must be something found out that, according to the Nature of Things, hath Power to effect it. For it can no more be done supernaturally by any Thing else, than it could by Adam.

[Love-2.2-127] Now the Matter stood thus: The Seed of all Mankind was in the Loins of fallen Adam. This was unalterable in the Nature of the Thing, and therefore all Mankind must come forth in his fallen State.

[Love-2.2-128] Neither can they ever be in any State whatever, whether earthly or heavenly, but by having an earthly Man, or a heavenly Man for their Father. For Mankind, as such, must of all Necessity be born of, and have that Nature which it hath from a Man. And this is the true Ground, and absolute Necessity of the one Mediator, the Man Christ Jesus. For seeing Mankind, as such, must have that Birth and Nature which they have from Man; seeing they never could have had any Relation to Paradise, or any Possibility of partaking of it, but because they had a paradisiacal Man for their Father, nor could have had any Relation to this earthly World, or any Possibility of being born earthly, but because they had an earthly Man for their Father; and seeing all this must be unalterably so forever, it plainly follows, that there was an utter Impossibility for the Seed of Adam ever to come out of its fallen State, or ever have another or better Life, than they had from Adam, unless such a Son of Man could be brought into Existence, as had the same Relation to all Mankind as Adam had, was as much in them all as Adam was, and had as full Power according to the Nature of Things, to give a heavenly Life to all the Seed in Adam's loins, as Adam had to bring them forth in earthly Flesh and Blood.

[Love-2.2-129] And now, Sir, that Christ was this very Son of Man, standing in the same Fullness of Relation to all Mankind as Adam did, having his Seed as really in them all, as Adam had, and as truly and fully qualified, according to the Nature of Things, to be a common and universal Father of Life, as Adam was of Death to all the human Race, shall in a Word or two be made as plain and undeniable, as that two and two are four.

[Love-2.2-130] The Doctrine of our Redemption absolutely asserts, that the Seed of Christ was sown into the first fallen Father of Mankind, called the Seed of the Woman, the Bruiser of the Serpent, the ingrafted Word of Life, called again in the Gospel, that Light which lighteth every Man that cometh into the World. Therefore Christ was in all Men, in that same Fullness of Relation of a Father to all Mankind, as the first Adam was. Secondly, Christ was born of Adam's Flesh and Blood, took the human Nature upon him, and therefore stood as a human Creature in the same Relation to Mankind, as Adam did. Nothing therefore was further wanting in Christ, to make him as truly a natural Father of Life to all Mankind, as Adam was at first, but God's Appointment of him to that End.

[Love-2.2-131] For as Adam could not have been the natural Father of Mankind, but because

God created and appointed him for that End, so Christ could not have been the natural Regenerator, or Redeemer of a heavenly Life that was lost in all Mankind, but because God had appointed and brought him into the World for that End. Now that God did this, that Christ came into the World by Divine Appointment, to be the Saviour, the Resurrection and Life of all Mankind, is a Truth as evident from Scripture, as that Adam was the first Man.

[Love-2.2-132] And thus it appears, in the utmost degree of Plainness and Certainty, that Christ in his single Person was, according to the Nature of Things, as fully qualified to be a common Redeemer, as Adam was, in his single Person, to be a common Father of all Mankind. He had his Seed in all Mankind, as Adam had. He had the human Nature, as Adam had. And He had the same Divine Appointment as Adam had. But Christ, however qualified to be our Redeemer, could not be actually such, till He had gone through, and done all that, by which our Redemption was to be effected.

[Love-2.2-133] Adam, however qualified, yet could not be the Father of a paradisiacal Offspring, till he had stood out his Trial, and fixed Himself victorious over every Thing that could make Trial of Him. In like manner, Christ, however qualified, could not be the Redeemer of all Mankind, till he had also stood out his Trial, had overcome all That by which Adam was overcome, and had fixed Himself triumphantly in that Paradise which Adam had lost.

[Love-2.2-134] Now as Adam's Trial was, Whether he would keep Himself in his paradisiacal State, above and free from all that was Good and Evil in this earthly World? So Christ's trial was, Whether, as a Son of Man, and loaded with the Infirmities of fallen Adam, sacrificed to all that which the Rage and Malice of the World, Hell, and Devils could possibly do to him; whether He in the midst of all these Evils, could live and die with his Spirit as contrary to them, as much above them, as unhurt by them, as Adam should have lived in Paradise?

[Love-2.2-135] And then it was, that every Thing which had overcome Adam, was overcome by Christ; and Christ's Victory did, in the Nature of the Thing, as certainly and fully open an Entrance for Him, and all his Seed into Paradise, as Adam's Fall cast him and all his Seed into the Prison and Captivity of this earthly, bestial World.

[Love-2.2-136] Nothing supernatural came to pass in either Case, but Paradise lost, and Paradise regained, according to the Nature of Things, or the real Efficacy of Cause to produce its Effects.

[Love-2.2-137] Thus is your Question fully answered; viz., How and why the Sufferings and Death of Christ enabled him to be the Author of Life to all that died in Adam? Just as the Fall of Adam into this World, under the Power of Sin, Death, Hell, and the Devil, enabled him to be the common Father of Death, or was the natural, unavoidable Cause of our being born under the same Captivity; just so, that Life, and Sufferings, and Death of Christ, which declared his breaking out from them, and Superiority over them, must in the Nature of the Thing as much enable Him to be the common Author of Life, that is, must as certainly be the full, natural, efficacious Cause of our inheriting Life from Him. Because, by what Christ was in Himself, by what He was in us, by his whole State, Character, and the Divine Appointment, we all had that natural Union with Him, and Dependence upon Him, as our Head in the Way of Redemption, as we had with Adam as our Head in the Way of our natural Birth. So that as it must be said, that because Adam fell, we must of all Necessity be Heirs of his fallen State, so with the same Truth and from the same Necessity of the Thing, it must be said, that because Christ our Head is risen victorious out of our fallen State, we as his Members, and having his Seed within us, must be and are made Heirs of all his Glory. Because in all Respects we are as strictly, as intimately connected with, and related to Him as the one Redeemer, as we are to Adam as the one Father of all Mankind. So that Christ by his Sufferings and Death become in all of us our Wisdom, our Righteousness, our Justification and Redemption, is the same sober and solid Truth, as Adam by his Fall become in all of us our Foolishness, our Impurity, our Corruption, and Death.

[Love-2.2-138] And now, my Friends, look back upon all that has been said, and then tell me, Is it possible more to exalt or magnify the infinite Merits, and availing Efficacy of the Sufferings and Death of Christ, than is done by this doctrine? Or whether every Thing that is said of them in Scripture, is not here proved, from the very Nature of the Thing, to be absolutely true? And again, Whether it is not sufficiently proved to you, that the Sufferings and Death of Christ are not only consistent with the Doctrine of a God all Love, but are the fullest and most absolute Proof of it?

[Love-2.2-139] Eusebius. Indeed, Theophilus, you have so fully done for us all that we wanted to have done, that we are now ready to take Leave of you. As for my Part, I want to return Home to enjoy my Bible, and delight myself with reading it in this comfortable Light, in which you have set the whole Ground and Nature of our Redemption. I am now in full Possession of this glorious Truth, that God is mere Love, the most glorious Truth that can possess and edify the Heart of Man. It drives every Evil out of the Soul, and gives Life to every Spark of Goodness that can possibly be kindled in it. Everything in Religion is made amiable, by being a Service of Love to the God of Love.

[Love-2.2-140] No Sacrifices, Sufferings, and Death, have any Place in Religion, but to satisfy and fulfill that Love of God, which could not be satisfied without our Salvation. If the Son of God is not spared, if He is delivered up to the Rage and Malice of Men, Devils, and Hell, it is because, had we not had such a Captain of our Salvation made perfect through Sufferings, it never could have been sung, "Oh Death, where is thy Sting, Oh Grave, where is thy Victory!" It never could have been true, that "as by one Man Sin entered into the World, and Death by Sin, so by one Man came the Resurrection of the Dead." It never could have been said " that as in Adam all die, so in Christ shall all be made alive."

[Love-2.2-141] Therefore, dear Theophilus, adieu. God is Love, and He that hath learnt to live in the Spirit of Love, hath learnt to live and dwell in God. Love was the Beginner of all the Works of God, and from Eternity to Eternity nothing can come from God, but a Variety of Wonders, and Works of Love, over all Nature and Creature.

[Love-2.2-142] Theophilus. God prosper, Eusebius, this Spark of Heaven in your Soul. May it, like the Seraphim's Coal taken from the Altar, purify your Heart from all its Uncleanness. But before you leave me, I beg one more Conversation to be on the practical Part of the Spirit of Love, that so Doctrine and Practice, hearing and doing, may go Hand in Hand.

The Third Dialogue Between Theogenes, Eusebius, and Theophilus

[Love-2.3-1] EUSEBIUS.   You have shown great Good-will toward us, Theophilus, in desiring another Meeting before we leave you. But yet I seem to myself to have no Need of that which you have proposed by this Day's Conversation. For this Doctrine of the Spirit of Love cannot have more Power over me, or be more deeply rooted in me; than it is already. It has so gained and got Possession of my whole Heart, that every Thing else must be under its Dominion. I can do nothing else but love; it is my whole Nature. I have no Taste for any Thing else. Can this Matter be carried higher in Practice?

[Love-2.3-2] Theophilus. No higher, Eusebius. And was this the true State of your Heart, you would bid fair to leave the World as Elijah did; or like Enoch to have it said of you, that you lived wholly to love, and was not. For was there nothing but this Divine Love alive in you, your fallen Flesh and Blood would be in Danger of being quite burnt up by it. What you have said of yourself, you have spoken in great Sincerity, but in a total Ignorance of yourself, and the true Nature of the Spirit of Divine Love. You are as yet only charmed with the Sight, or rather the Sound of it; its real Birth is as yet unfelt, and unfound in you. Your natural Complexion has a great deal of the animal Meekness and Softness of the Lamb and the Dove, your Blood and Spirit are of this Turn; and therefore a God all Love, and a Religion all Love, quite transport you; and you are so delighted with it, that you fancy you have nothing in you but this God and Religion of Love. But, my Friend, bear with me, if I tell you, that all this is only the good Part of the Spirit of this bestial World in you, and may be in any unregenerate Man, that is of your Complexion. It is so far from being a genuine Fruit of Divine Love, that if it be not well looked to, it may prove a real Hindrance of it, as it oftentimes does, by its appearing to be that which it is not.

[Love-2.3-3] You have quite forgot all that was said in the Letter to you on the Spirit of Love, that it is a Birth in the Soul, that can only come forth in its proper Time and Place, and from its proper Causes. Now nothing that is a Birth can be taken in, or brought into the Soul by any notional Conception, or delightful Apprehension of it. You may love it as much as you please, think it the most charming Thing in the World, fancy everything but Dross and Dung in Comparison of it, and yet have no more of its Birth in you, than the blind Man has of that Light, of which he has got a most charming Notion. His Blindness still continues the same; he is at the same Distance from the Light, because Light can only be had by a Birth of itself in seeing Eyes. It is thus with the Spirit of Love; it is nowhere, but where it rises up as a Birth.

[Love-2.3-4] Eusebius. But if I am got no further than this, what Good have I from giving in so heartily to all that you have said of this Doctrine? And to what End have you taken so much Pains to assert and establish it?

[Love-2.3-5] Theophilus. Your Error lies in this; you confound two Things, which are entirely distinct from each other. You make no Difference betwixt the Doctrine that only sets forth the Nature, Excellence, and Necessity of the Spirit of Love, and the Spirit of Love itself; which yet are two Things so different, that you may be quite full of the former, and at the same Time quite empty of the latter. I have said every Thing that I could , to show you the Truth, Excellence, and

Necessity of the Spirit of Love. It is of infinite Importance to you to be well established in the Belief of this Doctrine. But all that I have said of it, is only to induce and encourage you to buy it, at its own Price and to give all that for it, which alone can purchase it. But if you think (as you plainly do) that you have got it, because you are so highly pleased with that which you have heard of it, you only embrace the Shadow, instead of the Substance, of that which you ought to have.

[Love-2.3-6] Eusebius. What is the Price that I must give for it?

[Love-2.3-7] Theophilus. You must give up all that you are, and all that you have from fallen Adam; for all that you are and have from him is that Life of Flesh and Blood, which cannot enter into the Kingdom of God.

[Love-2.3-8] Adam, after his Fall, had nothing that was good in him, nothing that could inherit an eternal Life in Heaven, but the Bruiser of the Serpent, or the Seed of the Son of God that was reserved, and treasured up in his Soul. Every Thing else in him was devoted to Death, that this incorruptible Seed of the Word might grow up into a new Name in Christ Jesus.

[Love-2.3-9] All the Doctrine of God's Reprobation and Election relates wholly and solely to these two Things, viz., the earthly bestial Nature from Adam, and the incorruptible Seed of the Word, or Immanuel in every Man.

[Love-2.3-10] Nothing is elected, is foreseen, predestinated, or called according to the Purpose of God, but this Seed of the new Man, because the one eternal, unchangeable Purpose of God towards Man is only this, namely, that Man should be a heavenly Image, or Son of God. And therefore nothing can be elected, or called according to the Purpose of God, but this Seed of a heavenly Birth, because nothing else is able to answer, and fulfill the Purpose of God. But every Thing else that is in Man, his whole earthly, bestial Nature, is from Sin and is quite contrary to God's Purpose in the Creation of Man.

[Love-2.3-11] On the other Hand, nothing is reprobated, rejected, or cast out by God, but the earthly Nature which came from the Fall of Adam. This is the only Vessel of Wrath, the Son of Perdition, that can have no Share in the Promises and Blessings of God.

[Love-2.3-12] Here you have the whole unalterable Ground of Divine Election and Reprobation; it relates not to any particular Number of People or Division of Mankind, but solely to the two Natures that are, both of them, without Exception, in every Individual of Mankind. All that is earthly, serpentine, and devilish in every Man, is reprobated and doomed to Destruction; and the heavenly Seed of the new Birth in every Man, is That which is chosen, ordained, and called to eternal Life.

[Love-2.3-13] Election therefore and Reprobation, as respecting Salvation, equally relate to every Man in the World; because every Man, as such, hath That in him which only is elected, and that in him which only is reprobated, namely, the earthly Nature, and the heavenly Seed of the Word of God.

[Love-2.3-14] Now all this is evident, from the very Nature of the Thing. As soon as you but suppose Man at his Fall to have a Power of Redemption, or Deliverance from the Evil of his fallen Nature, engrafted into him, you then have the first unchangeable Ground of Election and

Reprobation; you are infallibly shown what it is that God elects and reprobates, and the absolute Impossibility of any Thing else being reprobated by God, but that fallen, evil Nature from which he is to be redeemed, or of any Thing else being elected by God, but that Seed of a new Birth, which is to bring forth his Redemption.

[Love-2.3-15] Here therefore you have a full Deliverance from all Perplexity upon this Matter, and may rest yourself upon this great, comfortable, and most certain Truth, that no other Election or Reprobation, with regard to Salvation, ever did, or can belong to any one individual Son of Adam, but that very same Election and Reprobation, which both of them happened to, and took Place in Adam's individual Person. For all that which was in Adam, both as fallen and redeemed, must of all Necessity be in every Son of Adam; and no Man can possibly stand in any other Relation to God than Adam did, and therefore cannot have either more or less, or any other Divine Election and Reprobation than Adam had. For from the Moment of Man's Redemption, which began at the Fall, when the incorruptible Seed of the Word was given into Adam, every Son of Adam, to the End of the World, must come into it, under one and the same Election and Reprobation with Regard to God. Because the whole earthly Nature, from which Man was to be redeemed, and the Seed of the Word, by which he was to be redeemed, were both of them in every Man, one as certainly as the other.

[Love-2.3-16] Now this being the inward, essential State of every Man born into the World, having in himself all that is elected and all that is reprobated by God, hence it is that in order to publish the Truth and Certainty of such Election and Reprobation, and the Truth and Certainty of that two-fold Nature in Man, on which it is grounded, hence it is that the Spirit of God in holy Scripture, represents this Matter to us by such outward Figures, as are yet in themselves not figurative, but real Proofs of it.

[Love-2.3-17] This is first of all done under the Figures of Cain and Abel, the two first Births from Adam, where the one is murdered by the other, hereby demonstrating to us, by this Contrariety and Difference of these two first Births, the inward real State of the Father of them, namely, that the same two-fold Nature was in him, that discovered itself in these two first Births from him.

[Love-2.3-18] The same Thing is, age after age set forth in Variety of Figures, more especially Ishmael and Isaac, in Esau and Jacob. And all this, only further to confirm and establish this great Truth, viz., That such Strife and Contrariety as appeared in the Sons of the same Father, were not only outward Representations, but full Proofs of that inward Strife and Contrariety, which not only existed in their Fathers, but universally in every human Creature. For Cain and Abel had not come from Adam, but because both their Natures were antecedently in him, and in the same State of Opposition and Contrariety to each other. And as Cain and Abel were no other than the genuine Effects of the two-fold State, which Adam as fallen and redeemed, was then in, so every Man, descended from Adam, is in himself infallibly all that which Adam was, and has as certainly his own Cain and Abel within himself as Adam had. And from the Beginning to the End of the human Race, all that which came to pass so remarkably in the Births of Cain and Abel, Ishmael and Isaac, Esau and Jacob, all that same, some Way or other, more or less, comes to pass in every Individual of Mankind. In one Man, his own Abel is murdered by his own Cain, and in another, his own Jacob overcomes his own Esau that was born with him.

[Love-2.3-19] And all the Good or the Evil that we bring forth in our Lives, is from nothing else, but from the Strife of these two Natures within us, and their Victory over one another. Which Strife, no Son of Adam could ever have known anything of, had not the free Grace and Mercy of God chosen and called all Mankind to a new Birth of Heaven within them, out of their corrupt and fallen Souls. No possible War, or Strife of Good against Evil, could be in fallen Man, but by his having from God a Seed of Life in him, ordained and predestinated to overcome his earthly Nature. For that which is put into him by God, as the Power of his Redemption, must be contrary to that from which he is to be redeemed.

[Love-2.3-20] And thus a War of Good against Evil, set up within us, by the free Grace and Mercy of God to us, is the greatest of all Demonstrations, that there is but one Election, and but one Reprobation, and that all that God rejects and reprobates, is nothing else but that corrupt Nature which every individual Man, Abel as well as Cain, has in himself from Adam as fallen; and that all that God elects, predestinates, calls, justifies, and glorifies, is nothing else but that heavenly Seed, which every individual Man, Pharaoh as well as Moses, has in himself from Adam, as redeemed.

[Love-2.3-21] And thus you have an unerring Key to all that is said in Scripture of the Election falling upon Abel, Isaac, and Jacob, &c., and of the Reprobation falling upon Cain, Ishmael, and Esau; not because God has Respect to Persons, or that all Men did not stand before him in the same Covenant of Redemption; but the Scriptures speak thus, that the true Nature of God's Election and Reprobation may thereby be made manifest to the World.

[Love-2.3-22] For the earthly Nature, which God only reprobates, having broke forth in Predominance in Cain, Ishmael, and Esau, they became proper Figures of that which God reprobates, and were used by God as such. And the heavenly Seed, which is alone elected to eternal Glory, having broken forth in Predominance in Abel, Isaac, Jacob, &c., they became proper Figures of that which God only elects, and were used by God as such.

[Love-2.3-23] Nothing is here to be understood personally, or according to the Flesh of these Persons on either Side; but all that is said of them is only as they are Figures of the earthly Nature, and heavenly Seed in every Man. For nothing is reprobated in Cain, but that very same which is reprobated in Abel, viz., the earthly Nature; nor is anything elected in Jacob but that very same which is equally elected in Esau, viz., the heavenly Seed.

[Love-2.3-24] And now, Gentlemen, you may easily apprehend, how and why a God, in whose holy Deity no Spark of Wrath or Partiality can possibly arise, but who is from Eternity to Eternity only flowing forth in Love, Goodness, and Blessing to every Thing capable of it, could yet say of the Children, before they were born, or had done either Good or Evil, 'Jacob have I loved, and Esau have I hated. It is because Esau signifies the earthly, bestial Nature, that came from Sin; and Jacob signifies the incorruptible Seed of the Word that is to overcome Esau and change his Mortal into Immortality.

[Love-2.3-25] But now I stop, for you may perhaps think that I have here made a Digression from our proposed Subject.

[Love-2.3-26] Eusebius. A Digression you may call it, if you please, Theophilus, but it is such a Digression, as has entirely prevented my ever having one more anxious Thought about God's Decrees of Election and Reprobation.

[Love-2.3-27] The Matter now stands in open Daylight, notwithstanding that Thickness of learned Darkness, under which it has been hidden, from the Time of St. Austin to this Day. And now, Sir, proceed as you please, to lay open all my Defects, in the Spirit of Love; for I am earnestly desirous of being set right in so important a Matter.

[Love-2.3-28] Theogenes. Let me first observe to Theophilus, that I am afraid the Matter is much worse with me, than it is with you. For though this Doctrine seems to have got all my Heart, as it is a Doctrine, yet I am continually thrown out of it in Practice, and find myself as daily under the Power of my old Tempers and Passions, as I was before I was so full of this Doctrine.

[Love-2.3-29] Theophilus. You are to know, my Friends, that every Kind of Virtue and Goodness may be brought into us by two different Ways. They may be taught us outwardly by Men, by Rules and Precepts; and they may be inwardly born in us, as the genuine Birth of our own renewed Spirit. In the former Way, as we learn them only from Men, by Rules and Documents of Instruction, they at best only change our outward Behaviour and leave our Heart in its natural State, and only put our Passions under a forced Restraint, which will occasionally break forth in spite of the dead Letter of Precept and Doctrine. Now this Way of Learning and attaining Goodness, though thus imperfect, is yet absolutely necessary, in the Nature of the Thing, and must first have its Time, and Place, and Work in us; yet it is only for a Time, as the Law was a Schoolmaster to the Gospel. We must first be Babes in Doctrine, as well as in Strength, before we can be Men. But of all this outward Instruction, whether from good Men, or the Letter of Scripture, it must be said, as the Apostle saith of the Law, "that it maketh nothing perfect;" and yet is highly necessary in order to Perfection.

[Love-2.3-30] The true Perfection and Profitableness of the holy written Word of God is fully set forth by St. Paul to Timothy: "From a Child," saith he, "thou hast known the Scriptures, which are able to make thee wise unto Salvation, which is by Faith in Christ Jesus." Now these Scriptures were the Law and the Prophets, for Timothy had known no other from his Youth. And as they, so all other Scriptures since, have no other Good or Benefit in them, but as they lead and direct us to a Salvation, that is not to be had in themselves, but from Faith in Christ Jesus. Their Teaching is only to teach us, where to seek and to find the Fountain and Source of all Light and Knowledge.

[Love-2.3-31] Of the Law, saith the Apostle, "it was a Schoolmaster to Christ:" Of the Prophets, he saith the same. "Ye have," says he, "a more sure Word of Prophecy, whereunto you do well, that ye take Heed, as unto a Light that shineth in a dark Place, until the Day dawn, and the Day-Star ariseth in your Hearts." The same Thing is to be affirmed of the Letter of the New Testament; it is but our Schoolmaster unto Christ, a Light like that of Prophecy, to which we are to take great Heed, until Christ, as the Dawning of the Day, or the Day-Star, ariseth in our Hearts. Nor can the Thing possibly be otherwise; no Instruction that comes under the Form of

Words can do more for us, than Sounds and Words can do; they can only direct us to something that is better than themselves, that can be the true Light, Life, Spirit, and Power of Holiness in us.

[Love-2.3-32] Eusebius. I cannot deny what you say, and yet it seems to me to derogate from Scripture.

[Love-2.3-33] Theophilus. Would you then have me to say, that the written Word of God is that Word of God which liveth and abideth forever; that Word, which is the Wisdom and Power of God; that Word, which was with God, which was God, by whom all Things were made; that Word of God, which was made Flesh for the Redemption of the World; that Word of God, of which we must be born again; that Word which lighteth every Man, that cometh into the World; that Word, which in Christ Jesus is become Wisdom, and Righteousness, and Sanctification in us; would you have me say, that all this is to be understood of the written Word of God? But if this cannot possibly be, then all that I have said is granted, namely, that Jesus is alone that Word of God, that can be the Light, Life, and Salvation of fallen Man. Or how is it possible more to exalt the Letter of Scripture, than by owning it to be a true, outward, verbal Direction to the one only true Light, and Salvation of Man?

[Love-2.3-34] Suppose you had been a true Disciple of John the Baptist, whose only Office was to prepare the Way to Christ, how could you have more magnified his Office, or declared your Fidelity to him, than by going from his Teaching, to be taught by that Christ to whom he directed you? The Baptist was indeed a burning and a shining Light, and so are the holy Scriptures; "but he was not that Light, but was sent to bear Witness to that Light. That was the true Light, which lighteth every Man, that cometh into the World."

[Love-2.3-35] What a Folly would it be, to say that you had undervalued the Office and Character of John the Baptist, because he was not allowed to be the Light itself, but only a true Witness of it, and Guide to it? Now if you can show, that the written Word in the Bible can have any other, or higher Office, or Power, than such a ministerial one as the Baptist had, I am ready to hear you.

[Love-2.3-36] Eusebius. There is no Possibility of doing that.

[Love-2.3-37] Theophilus. But if that is not possible to be done, then you are come to the full Proof of this Point, viz., that there are two Ways of attaining Knowledge, Goodness, Virtue, &c., the one by the Ministry of outward, verbal Instruction, either by Men or Books, and the other by an inward Birth of Divine Light, Goodness, and Virtue, in our own renewed Spirit: and that the former is only in order to the latter, and of no Benefit to us, but as it carries us further than itself, to be united in Heart and Spirit with the Light, and Word, and Spirit of God. Just as the Baptist had been of no Benefit to his Disciples, unless he had been their Guide from himself to Christ.

[Love-2.3-38] But to come now closer to our Subject in Hand.

[Love-2.3-39] From this two-fold Light, or Teaching, there necessarily arises a two-fold State of Virtue and Goodness. For such as the Teacher, or Teaching is, such is the State and Manner of the Goodness, that can be had from it. Every Effect must be according to the Cause that produces it. If you learn Virtue and Goodness only from outward Means, from Men, or Books, you may be virtuous and good according to Time, and Place, and outward Forms; you may do Works of Humility, Works of Love and Benevolence, use Times and Forms of Prayer; all this Virtue and Goodness is suitable to this Kind of Teaching, and may very well be had from it. But the Spirit of Prayer, the Spirit of Love, and the Spirit of Humility, or of any other Virtue, are only to be attained by the Operation of the Light and Spirit of God, not outwardly teaching, but inwardly bringing forth a new-born Spirit within us.

[Love-2.3-40] And now let me tell you both, that it is much to be feared that you as yet stand only under this outward Teaching; your good Works are only done under Obedience to such Rules, Precepts, and Doctrines, as your Reason assents to, but are not the Fruits of a new-born Spirit within you. But till you are thus renewed in the Spirit of your Minds, your Virtues are only taught Practices, and grafted upon a corrupt Bottom. Every-thing you do will be a mixture of good and bad; your Humility will help you to Pride, your Charity to others will give Nourishment to your own Self-Love; and as your Prayers increase, so will the Opinion of your own Sanctity. Because, till the Heart is purified to the Bottom, and has felt the Axe at the Root of its Evil (which cannot be done by outward Instruction) every Thing that proceeds from it partakes of its Impurity and Corruption.

[Love-2.3-41] Now that Theogenes is only under the Law, or outward Instruction, is too plain from the Complaint that he made of himself. For notwithstanding his Progress in the Doctrine of Love, he finds all the Passions of his corrupt Nature still alive in him, and himself only altered in Doctrine and Opinion.

[Love-2.3-42] The same may well be suspected of you, Eusebius, who are so mistaken in the Spirit of Love, that you fancy yourself to be wholly possessed of it, from no other Ground, but because you embrace it, as it were, with open Arms, and think of nothing but living under the Power of it. Whereas, if the Spirit of Love was really born in you from its own Seed, you would account for its Birth, and Power in you, in quite another Manner than you have here done; you would have known the Price that you had paid for it, and how many Deaths you had suffered, before the Spirit of Love came to Life in you.

[Love-2.3-43] Eusebius. But surely, Sir, imperfect as our Virtues are, we may yet, I hope, be truly said to be in a State of Grace; and if so, we are under something more than mere outward Instruction. Besides, you very well know, that it is a Principle with both of us, to expect all our Goodness from the Spirit of God dwelling and working in us. We live in Faith and Hope of the Divine Operation; and therefore I must needs say, that your Censure upon us seems to be more severe than just.

[Love-2.3-44] Theophilus. Dear Eusebius, I censure neither of you, nor have I said one Word by Way of Accusation. So far from it, that I love and approve the State you are both in. It is good and happy for Theogenes, that he feels and confesses, that his natural Tempers are not yet subdued by Doctrine and Precept. It is good and happy for you also, that you are so highly delighted with the Doctrine of Love, for by this means each of you have your true Preparation for further Advancement. And though your State has this Difference, yet the same Error was common to both of you. You both of you thought, you had as much of the Spirit of Love as you could, or ought to have; and therefore Theogenes wondered he had no more Benefit from it; and you wondered that I should desire to lead you further into it. And therefore, to deliver you from this Error, I have desired this Conference upon the practical Ground of the Spirit of Love, that you may neither of you lose the Benefit of that good State in which you stand.

[Love-2.3-45] Eusebius. Pray therefore proceed as you please. For we have nothing so much at Heart, as to have the Truth and Purity of this Divine Love brought forth in us. For as it is the highest Perfection that I adore in God, so I can neither wish nor desire any Thing for myself, but to be totally governed by it. I could as willingly consent to lose all my Being, as to find the Power of Love lost in my Soul. Neither Doctrine, nor Mystery, nor Precept has any Delight for me, but as it calls forth the Birth, and Growth, and Exercise of that Spirit, which doth all that it doth, toward God and Man, under the one Law of Love. Whatever therefore you can say to me, either to increase the Power, manifest the Defects, or remove the Impediments of Divine Love in my Soul, will be heartily welcome to me.

[Love-2.3-46] Theophilus. I apprehend that you don't yet know what Divine Love is in itself, nor what is its Nature and Power in the Soul of Man. For Divine Love is perfect Peace and Joy, it is a Freedom from all Disquiet, it is all Content and mere Happiness; and makes every Thing to rejoice in itself. Love is the Christ of God; wherever it comes, it comes as the Blessing and Happiness of every natural Life, as the Restorer of every lost Perfection, a Redeemer from all Evil, a Fulfiller of all Righteousness, and a Peace of God which passeth all Understanding. Through all the Universe of Things, nothing is uneasy, unsatisfied, or restless, but because it is not governed by Love, or because its Nature has not reached or attained the full Birth of the Spirit of Love. For when that is done, every Hunger is satisfied, and all complaining, murmuring, accusing, resenting, revenging, and striving are as totally suppressed and overcome as the Coldness, Thickness, and Horror of Darkness are suppressed and overcome by the breaking forth of the Light. If you ask, why the Spirit of Love cannot be displeased, cannot be disappointed, cannot complain, accuse, resent, or murmur? It is because Divine Love desires nothing but itself; it is its own Good, it has all when it has itself, because nothing is good but itself, and its own working; for Love is God, and he that dwelleth in God, dwelleth in Love. Tell me now, Eusebius, are you thus blessed in the Spirit of Love?

[Love-2.3-47] Eusebius. Would you have me tell you that I am an Angel, and without the Infirmities of human Flesh and Blood?

[Love-2.3-48] Theophilus. No, but I would have you judge of your State of Love by these Angelic Tempers, and not by any Fervour or Heat that you find in yourself. For just so much, and so far as you are freed from the Folly of all earthly Affections, from all Disquiet, Trouble, and Complaint about this, or that, just so much, and so far is the Spirit of Love come to Life in you. For Divine Love is a new Life, and new Nature, and introduces you into a new World; it puts an End to all your former Opinions, Notions, and Tempers; it opens new Senses in you, and makes you see high to be low, and low to be high; Wisdom to be Foolishness, and Foolishness Wisdom; it makes Prosperity and Adversity, Praise and Dispraise, to be equally nothing. "When I was a Child," saith the Apostle, "I thought as a Child, I spake as a Child, but when I became a

Man, I put away childish Things." Whilst Man is under the Power of Nature, governed only by worldly Wisdom, his Life (however old he may be) is quite childish; every Thing about him only awakens childish Thoughts, and Pursuits in him; all that he sees and hears, all that he desires or fears, likes or dislikes, that which he gets, and that which he loses, that which he hath, and that which he hath not, serve only to carry him from this Fiction of Evil to that Fiction of Good, from one Vanity of Peace to another Vanity of Trouble. But when Divine Love is born in the Soul, all childish Images of Good and Evil are done away, and all the Sensibility of them is lost, as the Stars lose their Visibility when the Sun is risen.

[Love-2.3-49] Theogenes. That this is the true Power of the Spirit of Divine Love, I am fully convinced from my own Uneasiness at finding, that my natural Tempers are not overcome by it. For whence could I have this Trouble, but because that little Dawning that I have of the Spirit of Love in me, maketh just Demands to be the one Light, Breath, and Power of my Life, and to have all that is within me overcome and governed by it. And therefore I find, I must either silence this small Voice of new-risen Love within me, or have no Rest from Complaints and Self-condemnation, till my whole Nature is brought into Subjection to it.

[Love-2.3-50] Theophilus. Most rightly judged, Theogenes. And now we are fairly brought to the one great practical Point, on which all our Proficiency in the Spirit of Love entirely depends, namely, that all that we are, and all that we have from Adam, as fallen, must be given up, absolutely denied and resisted, if the Birth of Divine Love is to be brought forth in us. For all that we are by Nature is in full Contrariety to this Divine Love, nor can it be otherwise; a Death to itself is its only Cure, and nothing else can make it subservient to Good; just as Darkness cannot be altered, or made better in itself, or transmuted into Light; it can only be subservient to the Light, by being lost in it and swallowed up by it.

[Love-2.3-51] Now this was the first State of Man; all the natural Properties of his creaturely Life, were hid in God, united in God, and glorified by the Life of God manifested in them, just as the Nature and Qualities of Darkness are lost and hid, when enlightened and glorified by the Light. But when Man fell from, or died to the Divine Life, all the natural Properties of his creaturely Life, having lost their Union in and with God, broke forth in their own natural Division, Contrariety, and War against one another, just as the Darkness, when it has lost the Light, must show forth its own Coldness, Horror, and other uncomfortable Qualities. And as Darkness, though in the utmost Contrariety to Light, is yet absolutely necessary to it, and without which no Manifestation or Visibility of Light could possibly be, so it is with the natural Properties of the creaturely Life; they are in themselves all Contrariety to the Divine Life, and yet the Divine Life cannot be communicated but in them and by them.

[Love-2.3-52] Eusebius. I never read, or heard of the Darkness being necessary to Light: It has been generally considered as a negative Thing, that was nothing in itself, and only signified an Absence of Light. But your Doctrine not only supposes Darkness to be something positive, that has a Strength and Substantiality in itself, but also to be antecedent to the Light, because necessary to bring it into Manifestation. I am almost afraid to hear more of this Doctrine. It Sounds harsh to my Ears.

[Love-2.3-53] Theophilus. Don't be frightened, Eusebius. I will lead you into no Doctrine, but what is strictly conformable to the Letter of Scripture, and the most orthodox Piety. The Scripture saith, "God is Light, and in Him is no Darkness at all"; therefore the Scripture affirmeth Light to be superior, absolutely separate from, and eternally antecedent to Darkness; and so do I. In this Scripture you have a noble and true Account of Light, what it is, where it is, and was, and always must be. It can never change its State or Place, be altered in itself, be anywhere, or in another Manner, than as it was, and will be, from and to all Eternity. When God said, "Let there be Light, and there was Light," no Change happened to eternal Light itself, nor did any Light then begin to be; but the Darkness of this World then only began to receive a Power, or Operation of the eternal Light upon it, which it had not before; or Eternity then began to open some Resemblance of its own Glory in the dark Elements, and Shadows of Time, and thus it is, that I assert the Priority and Glory of Light, and put all Darkness under its Feet, as impossible to be any Thing else but its Footstool.

[Love-2.3-54] Eusebius. I am quite delighted with this. But tell me now, how it is that Light can only be manifested in, and by Darkness.

[Love-2.3-55] Theophilus. The Scripture saith that "God dwelleth in the Light, to which no Man can approach": Therefore the Scripture teacheth, that Light in itself is, and must be invisible to Man, that it cannot be approached, or made manifest to him, but in and by something that is not Light. And this is all that I said, and the very same Thing that I said, when I affirmed that Light cannot be manifested, or have any Visibility to created Eyes, but in and through and by Darkness.

[Love-2.3-56] Light, as it is in itself, is only in the Supernatural Deity; and that is the Reason, why no Man or any created Being, can approach to it, or have any Sensibility of it, as it is in itself. And yet no Light can come into this World, but that in which God dwelt before any World was created. No Light can be in Time, but that which was the Light of Eternity. If therefore the Supernatural Light is to manifest something of its incomprehensible Glory, and make itself, in some Degree, sensible and visible to the Creature, this supernatural Light must enter into Nature, it must put on Materiality. Now Darkness is the one only Materiality of Light, in and through which it can become the Object of creaturely Eyes; and till there is Darkness, there is no possible Medium, or Power, through which the Supernatural Light can manifest something of itself, or have any of its Glory visible to created Eyes. And the Reason why Darkness can only be the Materiality of Light, is this, it is because Darkness is the one only Ground of all Nature, and of all Materiality, whether in Heaven or on Earth. And therefore every Thing that is creaturely in Nature, that has any Form, Figure, or Substance, from the highest Angel in Heaven to the lowest Thing upon Earth, hath all that it hath of Figure, Form, or Substantiality only and solely from Darkness. Look at the glittering Glory of the Diamond and then you see the one Medium, through which the Glory of the incomprehensible Light can make some Discovery or Manifestation of itself. It matters not, whether you consider Heaven or Earth, eternal or temporal Nature, nothing in either State can be capable of visible Glory, Brightness, or Illumination, but that which standeth in the State of the Diamond, and has its own Thickness of Darkness. And if the Universe of eternal and temporal Nature is everywhere Light, it is because it has Darkness everywhere for its Dwelling Place. Light, you know, is by variety of modern Experiments declared to be material; the Experiments are not to be disputed. And yet all these Experiments are only so many Proofs, not of the Materiality of Light, but of our Doctrine, viz., that Materiality is always along with visible Light, and also that Light can only open, and display something of itself, in and by Darkness, as its Body of Manifestation and Visibility. But Light cannot possibly be material, because all Materiality, as such, be it what and where it will, is nothing else but so much Darkness. And therefore to suppose Light to be material, is the same Absurdity, as to suppose it to be Darkness; for so much Materiality is so much Darkness, and it is impossible to be otherwise. Again, All Matter has but one Nature; it admits of neither more nor less, but wherever it is, all that is material is equally there. If therefore Light was material, all the Materiality in the World must be Light, and equally so. For no Materiality could be Light, unless Light was essential to Matter, as such, no more than any Materiality could be extended, unless Extension was essential to Matter as such.

[Love-2.3-57] Eusebius. What is it then, that you understand by the Materiality of Light?

[Love-2.3-58] Theophilus. No more than I understand by the Materiality of the Wisdom, Mercy, and Goodness of God, when they are made intelligible and credible to me, by the Materiality of Paper and Ink, &c. For Light is as distinct from, and superior to all that Materiality, in and by which it gives forth some Visibility of itself, as the Wisdom, Mercy, and Goodness of God, are distinct from and superior to all that written Materiality, in and through which they are made in some Degree intelligible, and credible to human Minds.

[Love-2.3-59] The incomprehensible Deity can make no outward Revelation of his Will, Wisdom, and Goodness, but by articulate Sounds, Voices, or Letters written on Tables of Stone, or such-like Materiality. Just so, the invisible, inaccessible, supernatural Light can make no outward Visibility of itself, but through such Darkness of Materiality, as is capable of receiving its Illumination. But as the Divine Will, Wisdom, and Goodness, when making outward Revelation of themselves, by the Materiality of Things, are not therefore material, so neither is the Light material when it outwardly reveals something of its invisible, incomprehensible Splendour and Glory, by and through the Materiality of Darkness.

[Love-2.3-60] All Light then, that is natural, and visible to the Creature, whether in Heaven, or on Earth, is nothing else but so much Darkness illuminated; and that which is called the Materiality of Light, is only the Materiality of Darkness, in which the Light incorporateth itself.

[Love-2.3-61] For Light can be only that same invisible, unapproachable Thing, which it always was in God, from all Eternity. And that which is called the Difference of Light, is only the Difference of that Darkness, through which the Light gives forth different Manifestations of itself. It is the same, whether it illuminates the Air, Water, a Diamond, or any other Materiality of Darkness. It has no more Materiality in itself, when it enlightens the Earth, than when it enlightens the Mind of an Angel, when it gives Colour to Bodies, than when it gives Understanding to Spirits.

[Love-2.3-62] Sight and Visibility is but one Power of Light, but Light is all Power; it is Life and every joyful Sensibility of Life is from it. "In Him," says the Apostle, "was Light, and the Light was the Life of Men." Light is all Things, and Nothing. It is Nothing, because it is supernatural; it is all Things, because every good Power and Perfection of every Thing is from it. No Joy, or Rejoicing in any Creature, but from the Power and Joy of Light. No Meekness, Benevolence, or Goodness, in Angel, Man, or any Creature, but where Light is the Lord of its Life. Life itself begins no sooner, rises no higher, has no other Glory than as the Light begins it and leads it on. Sounds have no Softness, Flowers and Gums have no Sweetness, Plants and Fruits have no Growth, but as the Mystery of Light opens itself in them.

[Love-2.3-63] Whatever is delightful and ravishing, sublime and glorious, in Spirits, Minds or Bodies, either in Heaven, or on Earth, is from the Power of the supernatural Light, opening its endless Wonders in them. Hell has no Misery, Horror, or Distraction, but because it has no Communication with the supernatural Light. And did not the supernatural Light stream forth its Blessings into this World, through the Materiality of the Sun, all outward Nature would be full of the Horror of Hell.

[Love-2.3-64] And hence are all the Mysteries and Wonders of Light, in this material System, so astonishingly great and unsearchable; it is because the natural Light of this World is nothing else but the Power and Mystery of the supernatural Light, breaking forth, and opening itself, according to its Omnipotence, in all the various Forms of elementary Darkness which constitute this temporary World.

[Love-2.3-65] Theogenes. I could willingly hear you, Theophilus, on this Subject till Midnight, though it seems to lead us away from our proposed Subject.

[Love-2.3-66] Theophilus. Not so far out of the Way, Theogenes, as you may imagine; for Darkness and Light are the two Natures that are in every Man, and do all that is done in him.

[Love-2.3-67] The Scriptures, you know, make only this Division: The Works of Darkness are Sin, and they who walk in the Light are the Children of God. Therefore Light and Darkness do every Thing, whether good or evil, that is done in Man.

[Love-2.3-68] Theogenes. What is this Darkness in itself, or where is it?

[Love-2.3-69] Theophilus. It is everywhere, where there is Nature and Creature. For all Nature, and all that is natural in the Creature, is in itself nothing else but Darkness, whether it be in Soul or Body, in Heaven or on Earth. And therefore, when the Angels (though in Heaven) had lost the supernatural Light, they became imprisoned in the Chains of their own natural Darkness. If you ask, Why Nature must be Darkness? It is because Nature is not God, and therefore can have no Light as it is Nature. For God and Light are as inseparable, as God and Unity are inseparable. Every Thing, therefore, that is not God, is and can be nothing else in itself but Darkness, and can do nothing but in, and under, and according to the Nature and Powers of Darkness.

[Love-2.3-70] Theogenes. What are the Powers of Darkness?

[Love-2.3-71] Theophilus. The Powers of Darkness are the Workings of Nature or Self: For Nature, Darkness, and Self are but three different Expressions for one and the same Thing.

[Love-2.3-72] Now every evil, wicked, wrathful, impure, unjust Thought, Temper, Passion, or Imagination, that ever stirred or moved in any Creature; every Misery, Discontent, Distress,

Rage, Horror, and Torment, that ever plagued the Life of fallen Man or Angel are the very Things that you are to understand by the Powers or Workings of Darkness, Nature, or Self. For nothing is evil, wicked, or tormenting, but that which Nature or Self doth.

[Love-2.3-73] Theogenes. But if Nature is thus the Seat and Source of all Evil, if every Thing that is bad is in it and from it, how can such a Nature be brought forth by God who is all Goodness?

[Love-2.3-74] Theophilus. Nature has all Evil, and no Evil in itself. Nature, as it comes forth from God, is Darkness without any Evil of Darkness in it; for it is not Darkness without, or separate from Light, nor could it ever have been known to have any Quality of Darkness in it, had it not lost that State of Light in which it came forth from God, only as a Manifestation of the Goodness, Virtues, and Glories of Light. Again, it is Nature, viz., a Strife and Contrariety of Properties for this only End, that the supernatural Good might thereby come into Sensibility, be known, found and felt, by its taking all the Evil of Strife and Contrariety from them, and becoming the Union, Peace, and Joy of them all. Nor could the Evil of Strife, and Contrariety of Will, ever have had a Name in all the Universe of Nature and Creature, had it all continued in that State in which it came forth from God. Lastly, it is Self, viz., an own Life, that so, through such an own Life, the universal, incomprehensible Goodness, Happiness, and Perfections of the Deity, might be possessed as Properties and Qualities of an own Life in creaturely finite Beings.

[Love-2.3-75] And thus, all that is called Nature, Darkness, or Self, has not only no Evil in it, but is the only true Ground of all possible Good.

[Love-2.3-76] But when the intelligent Creature turns from God to Self or Nature, he acts unnaturally, he turns from all that which makes Nature to be good, he finds Nature only as it is in itself, and without God. And then it is, that Nature, or Self, hath all Evil in it. Nothing is to be had from it, or found in it, but the Work and Working of every Kind of Evil, Baseness, Misery, and Torment, and the utmost Contrariety to God and all Goodness. And thus also you see the Plainness and Certainty of our Assertion, that Nature or Self hath all Evil, and no Evil in it.

[Love-2.3-77] Theogenes. I plainly enough perceive, that Nature or Self, without God manifested in it, is all Evil and Misery. But I would, if I could, more perfectly understand the precise Nature of Self, or what it is that makes it to be so full of Evil and Misery.

[Love-2.3-78] Theophilus. Covetousness, Envy, Pride, and Wrath, are the four Elements of Self, or Nature, or Hell, all of them inseparable from it. And the Reason why it must be thus, and cannot be otherwise, is because the natural Life of the Creature is brought forth for the Participation of some high supernatural Good in the Creator. But it could have no Fitness or possible Capacity to receive such Good, unless it was in itself both an Extremity of Want, and an extremity of Desire of some high Good. When, therefore, this natural Life is deprived of, or fallen from God, it can be nothing else in itself but an Extremity of Want, continually desiring, and an Extremity of Desire, continually wanting. And hence it is, that its whole Life can be nothing else but a Plague and Torment of Covetousness, Envy, Pride, and Wrath, all which is precisely Nature, Self, or Hell.

[Love-2.3-79] Now Covetousness, Pride, and Envy, are not three different Things, but only three different Names, for the restless Workings of one and the same Will or Desire, which, as it differently torments itself, takes different Names; for nothing is in any of them, but the working of a restless Desire, and all this because the natural Life of the Creature can do nothing else but work as a Desire. And therefore, when fallen from God, its three first Births, and which are quite inseparable from it, are Covetousness, Envy, and Pride. It must covet, because it is a Desire proceeding from Want; it must envy, because it is a Desire turned to Self; it must assume and arrogate, because it is a Desire founded on a real Want of Exaltation, or a higher State.

[Love-2.3-80] Now Wrath, which is a fourth Birth from these three, can have no Existence, till some or all of these three are contradicted, or have something done to them that is contrary to their Will; and then it is that Wrath is necessarily born, and not till then.

[Love-2.3-81] And thus you see in the highest Degree of Certainty, what Nature or Self is, as to its essential, constituent Parts. It is the three forementioned, inseparable Properties of a Desire thrown into a fourth of Wrath, that can never cease, because their Will can never be gratified. For these four Properties generate one another, and therefore generate their own Torment. They have no outward Cause, nor any inward Power of altering themselves. And therefore, all Self, or Nature, must be in this State till some supernatural Good comes into it, or gets a Birth in it. And therefore, every Pain or Disorder, in the Mind or Body of any intelligent Creature, is an undeniable Proof that it is in a fallen State, and has lost that supernatural Good for which it was created. So certain a Truth is the fallen State of all Mankind. And here lies the absolute, indispensable Necessity of the one Christian Redemption. Till fallen Man is born again from above, till such a supernatural Birth is brought forth in him, by the eternal Word and Spirit of God, he can have no possible Escape or Deliverance from these four Elements of Self or Hell.

[Love-2.3-82] Whilst Man indeed lives amongst the Vanities of Time, his Covetousness, Envy, Pride, and Wrath, may be in a tolerable State, may help him to a Mixture of Peace and Trouble; they may have at Times their Gratifications, as well as their Torments. But when Death has put an End to the Vanity of all earthly Cheats, the Soul that is not born again of the supernatural Word and Spirit of God, must find itself unavoidably devoured, or shut up in its own, insatiable, unchangeable, self-tormenting Covetousness, Envy, Pride, and Wrath. Oh! Theogenes, that I had Power from God to take those dreadful Scales from the Eyes of every Deist, which hinder him from seeing and feeling the infinite importance of this most certain Truth!

[Love-2.3-83] Theogenes. God give a Blessing, Theophilus, to your good Prayer. And then let me tell you, that you have quite satisfied my Question about the Nature of Self. I shall never forget it, nor can I ever possibly have any Doubt of the Truth of it.

[Love-2.3-84] Theophilus. Let me however go a little deeper in the Matter. All Life, and all Sensibility of Life, is a Desire; and nothing can feel or find itself to exist, but as it finds itself to have and be a Desire; and therefore, all Nature is a Desire; and all that Nature does, or works, is done by the Working of Desire. And this is the Reason why all Nature, and the natural Life of every Creature, is a State of Want, and therefore must be a State of Misery and Self-Torment, so long as it is mere Nature, or left to itself. For every Desire, as such, is and must be made up of Contrariety, as is sufficiently shown elsewhere. { Way to Divine Knowledge; Spirit of Love. }

And its essential Contrariety, which it has in itself, is the one only possible Beginning or Ground of its Sensibility. For nothing can be felt, but because of Contrariety to that which feels. And therefore no creaturely Desire can be brought into Existence, or have any possible Sensibility of itself, but because Desire, as such, is unavoidably made up of that Contrariety, whence comes all Feeling, and the Capacity of being felt.

[Love-2.3-85] Again, All natural Life is nothing else but a mere Desire founded in Want; now Want is contrary to Desire; and, therefore every natural Life, as such, is in a State of Contrariety and Torment to itself. It can do nothing but work in, and feel its own Contrariety, and so be its own unavoidable, incessant Tormentor.

[Love-2.3-86] Hence we may plainly see, that God's bringing a sensible Creature into Existence is his bringing the Power of Desire into a creaturely State; and the Power and Extent of its own working Desire is the Bounds or Limits of its own creaturely Nature. And, therefore every intelligent Creature, of whatever Rank in the Creation, is and can be nothing else, in its creaturely or natural State, but a State of Want; and the higher its natural State is supposed to be, the higher is its Want, and the greater its Torment, if left only in its natural State. And this is the Reason of the excessive Misery and Depravity of the fallen Angels.

[Love-2.3-87] Now the Contrariety that is in Desire, and must be in it, because it is a Desire, and the only Ground of all Sensibility, is plainly shown you by the most undeniable Appearance in outward or material Nature. All that is done in outward Nature is done by the working of Attraction. And all Attraction is nothing else but an inseparable Combination and incessant Working of three contrary Properties, or Laws of Motion. It draws, it resists its own Drawing; and from this Drawing and Resisting, which are necessarily equal to one another, it becomes an orbicular, or whirling Motion, and yet draws and resists, just as it did before.

[Love-2.3-88] Now this threefold Contrariety in the Motions, or Properties of Attraction, by which all the Elements of this material World are held and governed, and made to bring forth all the Wonders in all Kinds of animate and inanimate Things, this Contrariety, being the only possible Ground of all material Nature, is a full Demonstration, (1) That Contrariety is the one only possible Ground of Nature and all natural Life, whether it be eternal or temporal, spiritual or material; (2) That no other Contrariety is, or can be in the Properties or Laws of Attraction in this material Nature, but that one and the same Contrariety, which was from Eternity in spiritual Nature, is inseparable from it, and can be nowhere but in it. For Time can only partake of Eternity, it can have nothing in it but the Working of Eternity, nor be any Thing but what it is by the Working of Eternity in it. It can have nothing that is its own, or peculiar to it, but its transitory State, and Form, and Nature. It is a mere Accident, has only an occasional Existence; and whatever is seen, or done in it, is only so much of the Working of Eternity seen and done in it.

[Love-2.3-89] For Attraction, in the material World, has not only nothing material in it, but is impossible to be communicated to Matter; or rather Matter has no possible Capacity to receive Attraction. It can no more receive or obey the Laws of Attraction, than it can make Laws for Angels. It is as incapable of moving, or stirring itself, as it is of making Syllogisms. For Matter is, in itself, only Death, Darkness, and Inactivity, and is as utterly incapable of moving itself, as it is of illuminating or creating itself; nothing can be done in it, and by it, but that which is done by something that is not material.

[Love-2.3-90] Therefore, that which is called the Attraction of Materiality, is in itself nothing else but the Working of the spiritual Properties of Desire, which has in itself those very three inseparable Contrarieties, which make the three Contrarieties in the Motions of Attraction. Material Nature, being an accidental, temporary, transitory Out-Birth from eternal Nature, and having no Power of existing, but under it and in Dependence upon it, the spiritual Properties of eternal Nature do, as it were, materialize themselves for a Time, in their temporary Out-Birth and force Matter to work as they work, and to have the same contradictory Motions in it, which are essential to eternal Nature.

[Love-2.3-91] And thus the three inseparable, contrary Motions of Matter, are in the same Manner, and for the same Reason, a true Ground of a material Nature in Time, as the three inseparable, contrary, contradictory Workings of Desire, are a true Ground of spiritual Nature in Eternity. And you are to observe, that all that is done in Matter and Time, is done by the same Agents, or spiritual Properties, which do all that is naturally done in Eternity, in Heaven or in Hell. For nothing is the Ground of Happiness and Glory in Heaven, nothing is the Ground of Misery, Woe and Distraction in Hell, but the Working of these same contrary Properties of Desire, which work Contrariety in the Attraction of Matter and bring forth all the Changes of Life and Death in this material System. They are unchangeable in their Nature, and are everywhere the same; they are spiritual in Hell, and on Earth, as they are in Heaven. Considered as in themselves, they are everywhere equally good and equally bad; because they are everywhere equally the Ground and only the Ground for either Happiness or Misery. No possible Happiness, or Sensibility of Joy for any Creature, but where these contrary Properties work, nor any Possibility of Misery but from them.

[Love-2.3-92] Now Attraction, acting according to its three invariable, inseparable Contrarieties of Motion, stands in this material Nature, exactly in the same Place and for the same End, and doing the same Office, as the three first Properties of Desire do in eternal or spiritual Nature. For they can be, or do nothing with Regard to Earth and Time, but that same which they are, and do in Heaven and Eternity.

[Love-2.3-93] In eternal Nature, the three contrary Properties of Desire, answering exactly to the three contrary Motions of material Attraction, are in themselves only Resistance, Rage, and Darkness, and can be nothing else, till the supernatural Deity kindles its Fire of Light and Love in them; and then all their raging Contrarieties are changed into never-ceasing Sensibilities of Unity, Joy, and Happiness.

[Love-2.3-94] Just so, in this material System, suppose there to be nothing in it but the contrary Motions of Attraction, it could be nothing else but Rage against Rage in the Horror of Darkness.

[Love-2.3-95] But when the same supernatural Light, which turns the first fighting Properties of Nature into a Kingdom of Heaven, gives forth something of its Goodness into this World, through the kindled Body of the Sun, then all the fighting, contradictory Motions of Attraction, serve only to bring new Joys into the World, and open every Life, and every Blessing of Life, that can have Birth in a System of transitory Matter.

[Love-2.3-96] Theogenes. Oh Theophilus, you quite surprise me by thus showing me, with so much Certainty, how the Powers of Eternity work in the Things of Time. Nothing is done on Earth, but by the unchangeable Workings of the same spiritual Powers, which work after the same Manner, both in Heaven and in Hell. I now sufficiently see how Man stands in the midst of Heaven and Hell, under an absolute Necessity of belonging wholly to the one, or wholly to the other, as soon as this Cover of Materiality is taken off from him.

[Love-2.3-97] For Matter is his only Wall of Partition between them, he is equally nigh to both of them; and as Light and Love make all the Difference there is between Heaven and Hell, so nothing but a Birth of Light and Love in the Properties of his Soul, can possibly keep Hell out of it, or bring Heaven into it.

[Love-2.3-98] I now also see the full Truth and Certainty of what you said of the Nature and Power of Divine Love, viz., "that it is perfect Peace and Joy, a Freedom from all Disquiet, making every Thing to rejoice in itself; that it is the Christ of God, and wherever it comes, it comes as the Blessing and Happiness of every natural Life; as the Restorer of every lost Perfection; a Redeemer from all Evil; a Fulfiller of all Righteousness; and a Peace of God, which passes all Understanding." So that I am now, a thousand Times more than ever, athirst after the Spirit of Love. I am willing to sell all, and buy it; its Blessing is so great, and the Want of it so dreadful a State, that I am even afraid of lying down in my Bed, till every working Power of my Soul is given up to it, wholly possessed and governed by it.

[Love-2.3-99] Theophilus. You have Reason for all that you say, Theogenes; for were we truly affected with Things, as they are our real Good or real Evil, we should be much more afraid of having the Serpents of Covetousness, Envy, Pride, and Wrath, well nourished and kept alive within us, than of being shut up in a Pest-house, or cast into a Dungeon of venomous Beasts. On the other Hand, we should look upon the lofty Eloquence, and proud Virtue of a Cicero, but as the Blessing of Storm and Tempest, when compared with the heavenly Tranquillity of that meek and lowly Heart, to which our Redeemer has called us.

[Love-2.3-100] I said the Serpents of Covetousness, Envy, Pride, and Wrath, because they are alone the real, dreadful, original Serpents; and all earthly Serpents are but transitory, partial, and weak Out-Births of them. All evil, earthly Beasts, are but short-lived Images, or creaturely Eruptions of that hellish Disorder, that is broken out from the fallen spiritual World; and by their manifold Variety, they show us that Multiplicity of Evil, that lies in the Womb of that Abyss of dark Rage, which (N.B.) has no Maker, but the three first Properties of Nature, fallen from God, and working in their Darkness.

[Love-2.3-101] So that all evil, mischievous, ravenous, venomous Beasts, though they have no Life, but what begins in and from this material World, and totally ends at the Death of their Bodies, yet have they no Malignity in their earthly, temporary Nature, but from those same wrathful Properties of fallen Nature, which live and work in our eternal fallen Souls. And therefore, though they are as different from us, as Time from Eternity, yet wherever we see them, we see so many infallible Proofs of the Fall of Nature, and the Reality of Hell. For was there no Hell broken out in spiritual Nature, not only no evil Beast, but no bestial Life, could ever have come into Existence.

[Love-2.3-102] For the Origin of Matter, and the bestial, earthly Life, stands thus. When the Fall of Angels had made their Dwelling-Place to be a dark Chaos of the first Properties of Nature left to themselves, the infinite Wisdom and Goodness of God created, or compacted this spiritual Chaos into a material Heaven, and a material Earth, and commanded the Light to enter into it. Hence this Chaos became the Ground, or the Materiality of a new and temporary Nature, in which the heavenly Power of Light, and the Properties of Darkness, each of them materialized, could work together, carrying on a War of Heaven against Earth; so that all the evil Workings of fallen spiritual Nature, and all the Good that was to overcome it, might be equally manifested both by the good and bad State of outward Nature, and by that Variety of good and bad living Creatures, that sprung up out of it; to stand in this State, viz., of a spiritual Chaos changed into a Materiality of Light striving against Darkness, till the omnipotent Wisdom and Goodness of God, through the Wonders of a first and second Adam, shall have made this Chaotic Earth to send as many Angels into the highest Heaven, as fell with Lucifer into the hellish Chaos.

[Love-2.3-103] But to return. I have, I hope, sufficiently opened unto you the malignant Nature of that Self, which dwells in, and makes up the working Life of every Creature that has lost its right State in God; viz., that all the Evil that was in the first Chaos of Darkness, or that still is in Hell and Devils, all the Evil that is in material Nature and material Creatures, whether animate, or inanimate, is nothing else, works in, and with nothing else, but those first Properties of Nature, which drive on the Life of fallen Man in Covetousness, Envy, Pride, and Wrath.

[Love-2.3-104] Theogenes. I could almost say, that you have shown me more than enough of this Monster of Self, though I would not be without this Knowledge of it for half the World. But now, Sir, what must I do to be saved from the Mouth of this Lion, for he is the Depth of all Subtlety, the Satan that deceiveth the whole World. He can hide himself under all Forms of Goodness, he can watch and fast, write and instruct, pray much, and preach long, give Alms to the Poor, visit the Sick, and yet often gets more Life and Strength, and a more immovable Abode, in these Forms of Virtue, than he has in Publicans and Sinners.

[Love-2.3-105] Enjoin me therefore whatever you please; all Rules, Methods, and Practices, will be welcome to me, if you judge them to be necessary in this Matter.

[Love-2.3-106] Theophilus. There is no need of a Number of Practices, or Methods in this Matter. For to die to Self, or to come from under its Power, is not, cannot be done by any active Resistance we can make to it by the Powers of Nature. For Nature can no more overcome or suppress itself, than Wrath can heal Wrath. So long as Nature acts, nothing but natural Works are brought forth; and therefore the more Labour of this Kind, the more Nature is fed and strengthened with its own Food.

[Love-2.3-107] But the one true Way of dying to Self is most simple and plain, it wants no Arts or Methods, no Cells, Monasteries, or Pilgrimages, it is equally practicable by every Body, it is always at Hand, it meets you in every Thing, it is free from all Deceit, and is never without

Success.

[Love-2.3-108] If you ask, What is this one true, simple, plain, immediate and unerring Way? It is the Way of Patience, Meekness, Humility, and Resignation to God. This is the Truth and Perfection of dying to Self; it is nowhere else, nor possible to be in any Thing else, but in this State of Heart.

[Love-2.3-109] Theogenes. The Excellence and Perfection of these Virtues I readily acknowledge; but alas, Sir, how will this prove the Way of overcoming Self to be so simple, plain, immediate, and unerring, as you speak of? For is it not the Doctrine of almost all Men, and all Books, and confirmed by our own woeful Experience, that much Length of Time, and Exercise and Variety of Practices and Methods are necessary, and scarce sufficient to the Attainment of any one of these four Virtues?

[Love-2.3-110] Theophilus. When Christ our Saviour was upon Earth, was there any Thing more simple, plain, immediate, unerring, than the Way to Him? Did Scribes, Pharisees, Publicans, and Sinners, want any Length of Time, or Exercise of Rules and Methods, before they could have Admission to him, or have the Benefit of Faith in him?

[Love-2.3-111] Theogenes. I don't understand why you put this Question; nor do I see how it can possibly relate to the Matter before us.

[Love-2.3-112] Theophilus. It not only relates to, but is the very Heart and Truth of the Matter before us: It is not appealed to, by Way of Illustration of our Subject, but is our Subject itself, only set in a truer and stronger Light. For when I refer you to Patience, Meekness, Humility, and Resignation to God, as the one simple, plain, immediate, and unerring Way of dying to Self, or being saved from it, I call it so for no other Reason, but because you can as easily and immediately, without Art or Method, by the mere Turning and Faith of your Mind, have all the Benefit of these Virtues, as Publicans and Sinners, by their turning to Christ, could be helped and saved by him.

[Love-2.3-113] Theogenes. But, good Sir, would you have me then believe, that my turning and giving up myself to these Virtues is as certain and immediate a Way of my being directly possessed and blessed by their good Power, as when Sinners turned to Christ to be helped and saved by him? Surely this is too short a Way, and has too much of Miracle in it, to be now expected.

[Love-2.3-114] Theophilus. I would have you strictly to believe all this, in the fullest Sense of the Words, and also to believe, that the Reasons why you, or any others are for a long Time vainly endeavouring after, and hardly ever attaining these First-rate Virtues, is because you seek them in the Way they are not to be found, in a Multiplicity of human Rules, Methods, and Contrivances, and not in that Simplicity of Faith, in which, those who applied to Christ, immediately obtained that which they asked of Him.

[Love-2.3-115] "Come unto me, all ye that labour and are heavy laden, and I will refresh you." How short and simple and certain a Way to Peace and Comfort, from the Misery and Burden of Sin! What becomes now of your Length of Time and Exercise, your Rules and Methods, and round-about Ways, to be delivered from Self, the Power of Sin, and find the redeeming Power and Virtue of Christ? Will you say, that turning to Christ in Faith was once indeed the Way for Jews and Heathens to enter into Life, and be delivered from the Power of their Sins, but that all this Happiness was at an End, as soon as Pontius Pilate had nailed this good Redeemer to the Cross, and so broken off all immediate Union and Communion between Faith and Christ?

[Love-2.3-116] What a Folly would it be to suppose, that Christ, after his having finished his great Work, overcome Death, ascended into Heaven, with all Power in Heaven and on Earth, was become less a Saviour and gave less certain and immediate Helps to those, that by Faith turn to him now, than when he was clothed with the Infirmity of our Flesh and Blood upon Earth? Has He less Power, after he has conquered, than whilst he was only resisting and fighting our Enemies? Or has He less good Will to assist his Church, his own Body, now he is in Heaven, than he had to assist Publicans, Sinners, and Heathens before he was glorified, as the Redeemer of the World? And yet this must be the Case, if our simply turning to Him in Faith and Hope, is not as sure a Way of obtaining immediate Assistance from him now, as when he was upon Earth.

[Love-2.3-117] Theogenes. You seem, Sir, to me to have stepped aside from the Point in Question, which was not, Whether my turning or giving myself up to Christ, in Faith in him, would not do me as much Good as it did to them, who turned to him when He was upon Earth? But whether my turning in Faith and Desire, to Patience, Meekness, Humility, and Resignation to God, would do all that as fully for me now, as Faith in Christ did for those who became his Disciples?

[Love-2.3-118] Theophilus. I have stuck closely, my Friend, to the Point before us. Let it be supposed, that I had given you a Form of Prayer in these Words. O Lamb of God, that takest away the Sins of the World; Or, O Thou Bread that camest down from Heaven; Or, Thou that art the Resurrection, and the Life, the Light and Peace of all holy Souls, help me to a living Faith in Thee. Would you say, that this was not a Prayer of Faith in and to Christ, because it did not call Him Jesus, or the Son of God? Answer me plainly.

[Love-2.3-119] Theogenes. What can I answer you, but that this is a most true and good Prayer to Jesus, the Son of the living God? For who else but He was the Lamb of God, and the Bread that came down?

[Love-2.3-120] Theophilus. Well answered, my Friend. When therefore I exhort you to give up yourself in Faith and Hope, to Patience, Meekness, Humility, and Resignation to God, what else do I do, but turn you directly to so much Faith and Hope in the true Lamb of God? For if I ask you, what the Lamb of God is, and means, must you not tell me, that it is, and means, the Perfection of Patience, Meekness, Humility, and Resignation to God? Can you say, it is either more or less than this? Must you not therefore say, that a Faith of Hunger and Thirst, and Desire of these Virtues, is in Spirit and Truth, the one very same Thing, as a Faith of Hunger and Thirst, and Desire of Salvation through the Lamb of God? And consequently, that every sincere Wish and Desire, every inward Inclination of your Heart, that presses after these Virtues, and longs to be governed by them, is an immediate direct Application to Christ, is worshipping and falling down before him, is giving up yourself unto him, and the very Perfection of Faith in him?

[Love-2.3-121] If you distrust my Words, hear the Words of Christ himself. "Learn of me," says

He, "for I am meek and lowly of Heart, and ye shall find Rest unto your Souls." Here you have the plain Truth of our two Points fully asserted, First, That to be given up to, or stand in a Desire of, Patience, Meekness, Humility, and Resignation to God, is strictly the same Thing, as to learn of Christ, or to have Faith in Him. Secondly, That this is the one simple, short, and infallible Way to overcome, or be delivered from all the Malignity and Burden of Self expressed in these Words, "and ye shall find Rest unto your Souls."

[Love-2.3-122] And all this, because this simple Tendency, or inward Inclination of your Heart to sink down into Patience, Meekness, Humility, and Resignation to God, is truly giving up all that you are, and all that you have from fallen Adam; it is perfectly leaving all that you have, to follow and be with Christ, it is your highest Act of Faith in him and Love of Him, the most ardent and earnest Declaration of your cleaving to him with all your Heart, and seeking for no Salvation but in him, and from him. And therefore all the Good, and Blessing, Pardon, and Deliverance from Sin that ever happened to anyone from any Kind, or Degree of Faith and Hope, and Application to Christ, is sure to be had from this State of Heart, which stands continually turned to him in a Hunger, and Desire, of being led and governed by his Spirit of Patience, Meekness, Humility, and Resignation to God. Oh Theogenes, could I help you to perceive or feel what a Good there is in this State of Heart; you would Desire it with more Eagerness, than the thirsty Hart desireth the Water-Brooks, you would think of nothing, desire nothing, but constantly to live in it. It is a Security from all Evil, and all Delusion; no Difficulty, or Trial, either of Body or Mind, no Temptation either within you, or without you, but what has its full Remedy in this State of Heart. You have no Questions to ask of any Body, no new Way that you need inquire after; no Oracle that you need to consult; for whilst you shut up yourself in Patience, Meekness, Humility, and Resignation to God, you are in the very Arms of Christ, your whole Heart is his Dwelling-Place, and He lives and works in you, as certainly as he lived in, and governed that Body and Soul, which he took from the Virgin Mary.

[Love-2.3-123] Learn whatever else you will from Men and Books, or even from Christ Himself, besides, or without these Virtues, and you are only a poor Wanderer in a barren Wilderness, where no Water of Life is to be found. For Christ is nowhere, but in these Virtues, and where they are, there is He in his own Kingdom. From Morning to Night, let this be the Christ that you follow, and then you will fully escape all the religious Delusions that are in the World, and what is more, all the Delusions of your own selfish Heart.

[Love-2.3-124] For to seek to be saved by Patience, Meekness, Humility, and Resignation to God, is truly coming to God through Christ; and when these Tempers live and abide in you, as the Spirit and Aim of your Life, then Christ is in you of a Truth, and the Life that you then lead, is not yours, but it is Christ that liveth in you. For this is following Christ with all your Power: You cannot possibly make more Haste after Him, you have no other Way of walking as he walked, no other Way of being like Him, of truly believing in him, of showing your Trust in him, and Dependence upon him, but by wholly giving up yourself to That, which He was, viz., to Patience, Meekness, Humility, and Resignation to God.

[Love-2.3-125] Tell me now, have I enough proved to you, the short, simple, and certain Way of destroying that Body of Self, which lives and works in the four Elements of Covetousness, Envy, Pride, and Wrath?

[Love-2.3-126] Theogenes. Enough of all Reason. But as to Covetousness, I thank God, I cannot charge myself with it, it has no Power over me, nay I naturally abhor it. And I also now clearly see, why I have been so long struggling in vain against other selfish Tempers.

[Love-2.3-127] Theophilus. Permit me, my Friend, to remove your Mistake. Had Covetousness, no Power over you, you could have no other selfish Tempers to struggle against. They are all dead, as soon as Covetousness has done working in you. You take Covetousness to relate only to the Wealth of this World. But this is but one single Branch of it, its Nature is as large as Desire, and wherever selfish Desire is, there is all the evil Nature of Covetousness.

[Love-2.3-128] Now Envy, Pride, Hatred, or Wrath, can have no Possibility of Existence in you, but because there is some selfish Desire alive in you, that is not satisfied, not gratified, but resisted or disappointed. And therefore so long as any selfish Tempers, whether of Envy, Uneasiness, Complaint, Pride, or Wrath, are alive in you, you have the fullest Proof, that all these Tempers are born and bred in and from your own Covetousness, that is, from that same selfish bad Desire, which when it is turned to the Wealth of this World is called Covetousness. For all these four Elements of Self, or fallen Nature, are tied together in one inseparable Band, they mutually generate, and are generated from one another, they have but one common Life, and must all of them live, or all die together. This may show you again the absolute Necessity of our one simple and certain Way of dying to Self, and the absolute Insufficiency of all human Means whatever to effect it.

[Love-2.3-129] For consider only this, that to be angry at our own Anger, to be ashamed of our own Pride, and strongly resolve not to be weak, is the Upshot of all human Endeavours; and yet all this is rather the Life, than the Death of Self. There is no Help, but from a total Despair of all human Help. When a Man is brought to such an inward full Conviction, as to have no more Hope from all human Means, than he hopes to see with his Hands, or hear with his Feet, then it is, that he is truly prepared to die to Self, that is, to give up all Thoughts of having or doing any Thing that is good, in any other Way but that of a meek, humble, patient, total Resignation of himself to God. All that we do before this Conviction, is in great Ignorance of ourselves, and full of Weakness and Impurity. Let our Zeal be ever so wonderful, yet if it begins sooner, or proceeds further, or to any other Matter, or in any other Way, than as it is led and guided by this Conviction, it is full of Delusion. No Repentance, however long or laborious, is Conversion to God, till it falls into this State. For God must do all, or all is nothing; but God cannot do all, till all is expected from Him; and all is not expected from Him, till by a true and good Despair of every human Help, we have no Hope, or Trust, or Longing after any Thing but a patient, meek, humble, total Resignation to God.

[Love-2.3-130] And now, my dear Friends, I have brought you to the very Place for which I desired this Day's Conversation; which was, to set your Feet upon sure Ground, with Regard to the Spirit of Love. For all that Variety of Matters through which we have passed, has been only a Variety of Proofs, that the Spirit of Divine Love can have no Place, or Possibility of Birth in any fallen Creature, till it wills and chooses to be dead to all Self, in a patient, meek, humble Resignation to the good Power and Mercy of God.

[Love-2.3-131] And from this State of Heart also it is, that the Spirit of Prayer is born, which is the Desire of the Soul turned to God. Stand, therefore, steadfastly in this Will, let nothing else enter into your Mind, have no other Contrivance, but everywhere, and in every Thing, to nourish and keep up this State of Heart, and then your House is built upon a Rock; you are safe from all Danger; the Light of Heaven, and the Love of God, will begin their Work in you, will bless and sanctify every Power of your fallen Soul; you will be in a Readiness for every Kind of Virtue and good Work, and will know what it is to be led by the Spirit of God.

[Love-2.3-132] Theogenes. But, dear Theophilus, though I am so delighted with what you say, that I am loath to stop you, yet permit me to mention a Fear that rises up in me. Suppose I should find myself so overcome with my own Darkness and selfish Tempers, as not to be able to sink from them into a Sensibility of this meek, humble, patient, full Resignation to God, what must I then do, or how shall I have the Benefit of what you have taught me?

[Love-2.3-133] Theophilus. You are then at the very Time and Place of receiving the fullest Benefit from it, and practicing it with the greatest Advantage to yourself. For though this patient, meek Resignation is to be exercised with Regard to all outward Things, and Occurrences of Life, yet it chiefly respects our own inward State, the Troubles, Perplexities, Weaknesses, and Disorders of our own fallen Souls. And to stand turned to a patient, meek, humble Resignation to God, when your own Impatience, Wrath, Pride, and Irresignation, attack yourself, is a higher and more beneficial Performance of this Duty, than when you stand turned to Meekness and Patience, when attacked by the Pride, or Wrath, or disorderly Passions of other People. I say, stand turned to this patient, humble Resignation, for this is your true Performance of this Duty at that Time; and though you may have no comfortable Sensibility of your performing it, yet in this State you may always have one full Proof of the Truth and Reality of it, and that is, when you seek for Help no other Way, nor in any Thing else, neither from Men nor Books, but wholly leave and give up yourself to be helped by the Mercy of God. And thus, be your State what it will, you may always have the full Benefit of this short and sure Way of resigning up yourself to God. And the greater the Perplexity of your Distress is, the nearer you are to the greatest and best Relief, provided you have but Patience to expect it all from God. For nothing brings you so near to Divine Relief, as the Extremity of Distress; for the Goodness of God hath no other Name or Nature, but the Helper of all that wants to be helped; and nothing can possibly hinder your finding this Goodness of God, and every other Gift and Grace that you stand in Need of; nothing can hinder or delay it, but your turning from the only Fountain of Life and living Water, to some cracked Cistern of your own Making; to this or that Method, Opinion, Division, or Subdivision amongst Christians, carnally expecting some mighty Things either from Samaria, or Jerusalem, Paul or Apollos, which are only and solely to be had by worshipping the Father in Spirit and in Truth, which is then only done, when your whole Heart and Soul and Spirit trusts wholly and solely to the Operation of that God within you, in whom we live, move, and have our Being. And be assured of this, as a most certain Truth, that we have neither more nor less of the Divine

Operation within us, because of this or that outward Form, or Manner of our Life, but just and strictly in that Degree, as our Faith, and Hope, and Trust, and Dependence upon God, are more or less in us.

[Love-2.3-134] What a Folly then to be so often perplexed about the Way to God? For nothing is the Way to God, but our Heart. God is nowhere else to be found; and the Heart itself cannot find Him, or be helped by any Thing else to find Him, but by its own Love of Him, Faith in Him, Dependence upon Him, Resignation to Him, and Expectation of all from Him.

[Love-2.3-135] These are short, but full Articles of true Religion, which carry Salvation along with them, which make a true and full Offering and Oblation of our whole Nature to the Divine Operation, and also a true and full Confession of the Holy Trinity in Unity. For as they look wholly to the Father, as blessing us with the Operation of his own Word, and Spirit, so they truly confess, and worship the holy Trinity of God. And as they ascribe all to, and expect all from this Deity alone, so they make the truest and best of all Confessions, that there is no God but one.

[Love-2.3-136] Let then Arians, Semi-Arians, and Socinians, who puzzle their laborious Brains to make Paper-Images of a Trinity for themselves, have nothing from you but your Pity and Prayers; your Foundation standeth sure, whilst you look for all your Salvation through the Father, working Life in your Soul by his own Word, and Spirit, which dwell in Him, and are one Life, both in Him and you.

[Love-2.3-137] Theogenes. I can never enough thank you, Theophilus, for this good and comfortable Answer to my scrupulous Fear. It seems now, as if I could always know how to find full Relief in this humble, meek, patient, total Resignation of myself to God. It is, as you said, a Remedy that is always at hand, equally practicable at all Times, and never in greater Reality, than when my own Tempers are making War against it in my own Heart.

[Love-2.3-138] You have quite carried your Point with me. The God of Patience, Meekness, and Love, is the one God of my Heart. It is now the whole Bent and Desire of my Soul, to seek for all my Salvation in and through the Merits and Mediation of the meek, humble, patient, resigned, suffering Lamb of God, who alone hath Power to bring forth the blessed Birth of these heavenly Virtues in my Soul. He is the Bread of God, that came down from Heaven, of which the Soul must eat, or perish and pine in everlasting Hunger. He is the Eternal Love and Meekness, that left the Bosom of his Father, to be Himself the Resurrection of Meekness and Love in all the darkened, wrathful Souls of fallen Men. What a Comfort is it, to think that this Lamb of God, Son of the Father, Light of the World, who is the Glory of Heaven, and Joy of Angels, is as near to us, as truly in the midst of us, as he is in the midst of Heaven; and that not a Thought, Look, and Desire of our Heart, that presses toward Him, longing to catch, as it were, one small Spark of his heavenly Nature, but is in as sure a Way of finding Him, touching Him, and drawing Virtue from Him as the Woman who was healed, by longing but to touch the Border of his Garment.

[Love-2.3-139] This Doctrine also makes me quite weary and ashamed of all my own natural Tempers, as so Many Marks of the Beast upon me; every Whisper of my Soul that stirs up Impatience, Uneasiness, Resentment, Pride, and Wrath within me, shall be rejected with a Get thee behind me, Satan, for it is his, and has its whole Nature from him. To rejoice in a

Resentment gratified, appears now to me to be quite frightful. For what is it, in reality, but rejoicing that my own Serpent of Self has new Life and Strength given to it, and that the precious Lamb of God is denied Entrance into my Soul. For this is the strict Truth of the Matter. To give into Resentment, and go willingly to gratify it, is calling up the Courage of your own Serpent, and truly helping it to be more stout and valiant, and successful in you.— On the other Hand, to give up all Resentment of every Kind, and on every Occasion, however artfully, beautifully, outwardly coloured, and to sink down into the Humility of Meekness under all Contrariety, Contradiction, and Injustice, always turning the other Cheek to the Smiter, however haughty, is the best of all Prayers, the surest of all Means to have nothing but Christ living and working in you, as the Lamb of God, that taketh away every Sin that ever had Power over your Soul.

[Love-2.3-140] What a Blindness was it in me, to think that I had no Covetousness because the Love of Pelf {money or gain}, was not felt by me! For to covet, is to desire. And what can it signify whether I desire This or That? If I desire any Thing but that which God would have me to be and do, I stick in the Mire of Covetousness, and must have all that Evil and Disquiet living and working in me, which robs Misers of their Peace both with God and Man.

[Love-2.3-141] Oh sweet Resignation of myself to God, happy Death of every selfish Desire, blessed Unction of a holy Life, the only Driver of all Evil out of my Soul, be thou my Guide and Governor wherever I go! Nothing but thou can take me from myself, nothing but thou can lead me to God; Hell has no Power where thou art; nor can Heaven hide itself from thee. Oh may I never indulge a Thought, bring forth a Word, or do any Thing for myself or others, but under the Influence of thy blessed Inspiration!

[Love-2.3-142] Forgive, dear Theophilus, this Transport of my Soul; I could not stop it. The Sight, though distant, of this heavenly Canaan, this Sabbath of the Soul, freed from the miserable Labour of Self, to rest in Meekness, Humility, Patience, and Resignation under the Spirit of God, is like the joyful Voice of the Bridegroom to my Soul, and leaves no Wish in me, but to be at the Marriage Feast of the Lamb.

[Love-2.3-143] Theophilus. Thither, Theogenes, you must certainly come, if you keep to the Path of Meekness, Humility, and Patience, under a full Resignation to God. But if you go aside from it, let the Occasion seem ever so glorious, or the Effects ever so wonderful to you, it is only preparing for yourself a harder Death. For die you must to all, and every Thing that you have worked or done under any other Spirit, but that of Meekness, Humility, and true Resignation to God. Every Thing else, be it what it will, hath its Rise from the Fire of Nature, it belongs to nothing else, and must of all Necessity be given up, lost, and taken from you again by Fire, either here or hereafter.

[Love-2.3-144] For these Virtues are the only Wedding Garment; they are the Lamps and Vessels well furnished with Oil.

[Love-2.3-145] There is nothing that will do in the Stead of them; they must have their own full and perfect Work in you, if not before, yet certainly after the Death of the Body, or the Soul can never be delivered from its fallen wrathful State. And all this is no more than is implied in this Scripture Doctrine, viz., that there is no Possibility of Salvation, but in and by a Birth of the meek, humble, patient, resigned Lamb of God in our Souls. And when this Lamb of God has brought forth a real Birth of his own Meekness, Humility, and full Resignation to God in our Souls, then are our Lamps trimmed, and our Virgin-hearts made ready for the Marriage Feast. [Love-2.3-146] This Marriage Feast signifies the Entrance into the highest State of Union, that can be between God and the Soul, in this Life. Or in other Words, it is the Birth-Day of the Spirit of Love in our Souls, which whenever we attain it, will feast our Souls with such Peace and Joy in God, as will blot out the Remembrance of every Thing, that we called Peace or Joy before. [Love-2.3-147] In the Letter on the Spirit of Love, you have been shown, according to the Mystery of all Things opened by the Goodness of God in the blessed Behmen, the Time and Place of its Birth. That it neither does, nor can possibly begin any sooner, than at the Entrance or Manifestation of the Divine Light, in the three first wrathful, self-tormenting Properties of Nature, which are and must be the Ground of every natural Life, and must be Darkness, Rage, and Torment, till the Light of God, breaking in upon them, changes all their painful working into the strongest Sensibilities of Love, Joy, and Triumph, in the Perception and Possession of a new Divine Life.

[Love-2.3-148] Now all that we have said To-day of the Necessity of the fallen Souls dying to Self, by Meekness, Patience, Humility, and full Resignation to God is strictly the same Thing, and asserted from the same Ground as when it was then said, that the three first Properties of Nature must have their wrathful Activity taken from them, by the Light of God breaking in upon them, or manifesting itself in them. Now this was always the State of Nature, it never was a State of Wrath, because it never was without the Light of God in it. But the natural, creaturely Life, having a Possibility of falling, and having actually fallen from God, has found and felt what never ought to have been found and felt, viz., what Nature is in itself, without the Manifestation of the Deity in it.

[Love-2.3-149] Therefore, as sure as the Light of God, or the Entrance of the Deity into the three first Properties of Nature, is absolutely necessary to make Nature to be a heavenly Kingdom of Light and Love, so sure and certain is it, that the creaturely Life, that is fallen from God under the wrathful first Properties of Nature, can have no Deliverance from it, cannot have a Birth of heavenly Light and Love, by any other possible Way, but that of dying to Self, by Meekness, Humility, Patience, and full Resignation to God.

[Love-2.3-150] And the Reason is this. It is because the Will is the Leader of the creaturely Life, and it can have nothing but that to which its Will is turned. And therefore it cannot be saved from, or raised out of the Wrath of Nature, till its Will turns from Nature, and wills to be no longer driven by it. But it cannot turn from Nature, or show a Will to come from under its Power, any other Way, than by turning and giving up itself to that Meekness, Humility, Patience, and Resignation to God, which so far as it goes, is a leaving, rejecting, and dying to all the Guidance of Nature.

[Love-2.3-151] And thus you see, that this one simple Way is, according to the immutable Nature of Things, the one only possible and absolutely necessary Way to God. It is as possible to go two contrary Ways at once, as to go to God any other Way than this. But what is best of all, this Way is absolutely infallible; nothing can defeat it. And all this infallibility is fully grounded in the two-fold Character of our Saviour (1) As he is the Lamb of God, a Principle, and Source of all Meekness, and Humility in the Soul, and (2) As he is the Light of Eternity, that blesses eternal Nature, and turns it into a Kingdom of Heaven.

[Love-2.3-152] For in this two-fold Respect, he has a Power of redeeming us, which nothing can hinder; but sooner or later, he must see all his and our Enemies under his Feet, and all that is fallen in Adam into Death must rise and return to a Unity of an Eternal Life in God.

[Love-2.3-153] For, as the Lamb of God, he has all Power to bring forth in us a Sensibility and a Weariness of our own wrathful State, and a Willingness to fall from it into Meekness, Humility, Patience, and Resignation to that Mercy of God which alone can help us. And when we are thus weary and heavy laden, and willing to get Rest to our Souls, in meek, humble, patient Resignation to God, then it is, that He, as the Light of God and Heaven, joyfully breaks in upon us, turns our Darkness into Light, our Sorrow into Joy, and begins that Kingdom of God and Divine Love within us which will never have an End.

[Love-2.3-154] Need I say more, Theogenes, to show you how to come out of the Wrath of your evil earthly Nature, into the sweet Peace and Joy of the Spirit of Love? Neither Notions, nor Speculations, nor Heat, nor Fervour, nor Rules, nor Methods can bring it forth. It is the Child of Light, and cannot possibly have any Birth in you, but only and solely from the Light of God rising in your own Soul, as it rises in heavenly Beings. But the Light of God cannot arise, or be found in you, by any Art or Contrivance of your own, but only and solely in the Way of that Meekness, Humility, and Patience, which waits, trusts, resigns to, and expects all from the inward, living, life-giving Operation of the Triune God within you, creating, quickening, and reviving in your fallen Soul that Birth and Image, and Likeness of the Holy Trinity, in which the first Father of Mankind was created.

[Love-2.3-155] Theogenes. You need say no more, Theophilus; you have not only removed that Difficulty which brought us hither, but have, by a Variety of Things, fixed and confirmed us in a full Belief of that great truth elsewhere asserted, namely "That there is but one Salvation for all Mankind, and that is the Life of God in the Soul. And also, that there is but one possible Way for Man to attain this Life of God, not one for a Jew, another for a Christian, and a third for a Heathen. No, God is one, and the Way to it is one, and that is, the Desire of the Soul turned to God."

[Love-2.3-156] Therefore, dear Theophilus, adieu. If we see you no more in this Life, you have sufficiently taught us how to seek, and find every kind of Goodness, Blessing, and Happiness, in God alone.

Made in the USA
Monee, IL
12 September 2021